HOW TO HEAR GOD

10 Ways God Speaks

How to Hear God: 10 Ways God Speaks

Copyright © 2020 Sterling Harris

ISBN: 9798623746900

Assistant Project Editors:

Dr. Peter Running | Leah Harris

HOW TO HEAR GOD

10 Ways God Speaks

STERLING HARRIS

Tall Pine

To all the people who want a better relationship with God, desire to know Jesus intimately and hear the voice of the Holy Spirit.

CONTENTS

ACKNOWLEDGEMENTS

This book would not have been possible without my Heavenly Father's love, the precious Blood of Jesus and the power of the Holy Spirit. To my God, my Father and my Eternal Best Friend I am forever grateful to You for blessing me and filling my heart with Your love, Your presence, Your goodness through our intimate love relationship!

To my brilliant and beautiful wife, Leah Harris, you are a Proverbs 31 woman in every sense of what the Bible describes. Thank you for your love, encouragement and continual support of all kinds! To my daughter Gracie Elizabeth Harris, Daddy loves you and may this book mark your generation and many others to come! To my Mom and Dads, Jamie and Peter Running, Charlie Harris, wow, thank you for your wisdom and helping to create an environment for me to thrive and to write so much of this book at the Running Retreat!

To my brother Gerald, thank you for believing in me, being my brothers' keeper and for your faithful financial support of this ministry. To my brother Devonric Johnson, thank you for showing me what perseverance truly looks like and showing me how to lovingly give to others. To my Granny Mary L. Harris, whose legacy of love has marked my life forever!

To all of the Sterling Harris Ministry Partners, thank you for all of the love, prayers, service and financial seed you have sown into our ministry. May God bless you 100 fold of what you have sown into God's Kingdom! To all my other family, friends and loved ones, too numerous to mention, thank you all for the deposits of love, hope, faith, support and blessings you have sown into my heart and life. To all of you, I am eternally grateful and honored by your lives! To God be the Glory!

1

THE JOURNEY AND THE QUEST BEGIN

THE GOAL FOR THIS BOOK IS TO SHARE WITH YOU CLEAR, POWER-ful and practical teachings, testimonies and examples with exercises, which will help you to have a healthy and a more intimate love relationship with Jesus Christ. A relationship where you continually open your heart to receive God's love, then give that love back to Him in loving devotion to Him, then in-turn through this continual love exchange you become God's love and go out and love others around you out of the overflow of your vibrant daily relationship with God. Hearing God's active voice and being able to sense your Heavenly Father's activity in and around your daily life all empowered by His Holy Spirit is vital to have a healthy relationship with God. Hearing God speak, knowing His Word and sensing His activity is the source of all truth in your life. Our heart's desire is to help you fall deeper in love with God and to have a life transformation of becoming more like Jesus! As you read and interact with this book I am praying, believing and declaring over you right now that the Holy Spirit is going to supernaturally increase your spiritual hearing, your spiritual senses and He is going to bring a greater measure of awareness and revelation of the Father's love into your heart so you can experience His goodness at deeper levels than ever before! I pray everything that Jesus died for us to have comes upon you and rests and resides on your life!

I don't have all the answers when it comes to hearing God's voice and sensing His activity. I am still in the process of hungering and desperately seeking to know God at deeper levels everyday of my life! However, by the grace of God He has taught me some things that if you put them into action will help you radically deepen your relationship with God. These are teachings, tactics and truths God wanted me to share and impart to you. When God called me to write this book He woke me up out of my sleep and spoke to me through a series of flowing thoughts and said, "Sterling, I want My people to hear My voice and know Me through a daily love relationship. I want you to write a book about that subject." Then He brought to my remembrance a sermon I had done on the subject entitled "How to Hear God, 10 Ways God Speaks" and so this book was born out of that sermon, my experiences over the years of having an intimate spiritual relationship with Him and what Father God has poured into my heart over the time of writing this book to share with you about the never ending love He has for you! As I wrote this book I continually prayed for everyone who would encounter this book, for the anointing of God's supernatural love and power to transform your heart and mind to know the Father's love at deeper levels than ever before! I know as you read this book my prayers will be answered, that everything in your life is about to shift and increase in amazing ways!

Because people have so many definitions and preconceived notions about the words "relationship", "intimacy" and "love" which can be based on healthy or unhealthy life experiences such as your family upbringing and childhood, I felt the need to define these terms so we are working off of the same base understanding and definition. We are defining "relationship" as the way in which you relate to God through His unconditional love for you, as well as the intimacy you share with Him on a daily basis. It is also the state of being connected to God through fellowship and experience-based knowledge. A healthy relationship provides a loving and safe place where your heart, emotions, feelings and thoughts are accepted, understood, valued and exchanged between you and God on a consistent basis. An earthly example of this would be a loving and healthy friendship; a marriage or family relationship built on trust and most certainly the acceptance and the love of Jesus.

We are defining "intimacy" as a close, familiar, affectionate and loving personal relationship built on trust with God. It is also the lifelong process of experiencing God within the context of a detailed heart knowledge, fellowship, closeness and a deep understanding of His love, nature, character and ways. It involves the sharing and exchanging of your innermost thoughts, feelings, emotions and actions in a relational way with Him on a daily basis. At the very core of our being every person has the basic needs of being loved, accepted, understood, safe and having a purpose. You can only experience these basic needs unconditionally and eternally through a daily spiritual love relationship with God. We are defining "love" as the Greek word that the Bible uses in the New Testament to describe the love of God which is "agape". Defined as unconditional love, love by: choice, decision and by an act of the will. The word denotes undefeatable goodwill towards people, the sacrificial work of Jesus and love which persists regardless of circumstances. This kind of love seeks the highest good. It is not based on, nor does it need chemistry, emotions or feelings. This is a self-giving and sacrificial love by decision it is not based on your actions but on God's determined decision to love you unconditionally as His son or daughter.

Why does God want a relationship with you and for you to be intimately involved with Him on a daily basis? Well, when God created mankind, He created us in the image of Himself. He breathed His Spirit into us, so we could be spiritually connected to Him, because God wanted a family. As you go through this book it is important to remember you are not an orphan in God's eyes, you are a cherished son or daughter of His, God loves you, He wants to speak to you and to have an intimate relationship with you. Believers in Christ are also referred to in the Bible as the "Bride of Christ" so it is a healthy and vibrant marital relationship that God wants with each and every person. God wants a healthy family relationship with you! Because many people have not had healthy, godly family experiences, we often project these experiences on our relationship with God, so it is important to read this book in the context of God's love and longing to have a deep fellowship with you.

God is not a God of rejection. Often the fear of rejection, which opposes our basic needs being met, is at the root cause of a lot of fear, distrust, hurt, shame and pain that we experience throughout our lives. Our Heavenly Father is a God of love. He desires a loving, healthy, intimate, relationship with you daily. If you are feeling rejected by God then it's ok, that is all about to change. As you read and interact with this book you will hear God's voice through the power of the Holy Spirit. Right now, you are just listening to the wrong voices! It's time to focus on and base your life on God's love, grace and compassion for you. The wonderful thing is through the blood of Jesus Christ we have unrestricted free access to all of these needs being met by our Heavenly Father's grace, love and Holy Spirit.

We all hear voices in our mind every day, whether we want to admit it or not. "Self-talk" the inner dialogue of our own conscience is a very powerful force both positively and negatively. Often, negative thoughts will come into our minds with all kinds of fear-based statements, recommendations and ideas. We hear demonic voices with suggestions, telling us to do self-centered and often sinful things. We also have a voice that suggests to us God-centered, positive, faith-filled and loving ideas towards ourselves and others. As we train up in discerning between God's voice, our conscience, our flesh, and the voice of the enemy, we grow in that ability. This allows our spirit to take over more and more, as we yield to God's voice and activity in our lives. The more proficient we become at this, we live more by the Spirit and less by the flesh, if we are paying attention and practicing hearing and submitting to God's voice daily. That is the difference between living your life by self-will and living by God's Will, which is thinking, speaking and acting like Jesus. To do that we need to hear God's active voice, know His Word and sense His activity in our daily lives. So, let's define what we mean when we are talking about "God's active voice". Many people, when you ask them if God speaks to them, will refer to signs and circumstances that they have experienced where they believe God spoke to them through these things or even through other people. This certainly can be acknowledged as God speaking to you, as His activity in your life, as well as it can be God guiding and communicating with you. However, we are defining God's "active voice" as the personal and direct communication between you and God where you experience the Holy Spirit speaking directly to you about your life, other people and circumstances. This book is going to empower you to hear God's active voice with more clarity, heighten your awareness of God's activity, and open your heart to hear God speak to you throughout your daily life.

The active living voice of the Holy Spirit is vital to developing a healthy relationship with God and walking by the Spirit on a daily basis. Walking by the Spirit means allowing the Holy Spirit to guide your thoughts, words, and actions. In other words, allow the Holy Spirit to be the driver of your car and your internal navigation system! The same God that created the Heavens and Earth and spoke them into existence, wants to speak newness into your mind and heart every day; in every area of your life! Hearing God speak and sensing His activity, will transform your mind and heart and thus, your life! Always remember, God wants to speak to you more than you want to hear Him! He loves you so much more than you can ever imagine. He wants a relationship, a fellowship, a friendship, a partnership, and intimacy with you, more than you do! So much so that He sacrificed Himself to get you into Heaven with Him for all eternity and also to get His own Holy Spirit into you right now, today, where you can know Him by experience and by His active voice.

Ask yourself some empowering questions before we start; because when you ask yourself empowering questions, you get empowering answers. It sounds simple, but how many of us play disempowering and self-defeating games daily? Games such as, "Why me?" "Why me God, why did these things happen to me?" "What if?" "What if God does not answer my prayer, what if God does not provide what I need?" and of course the infamous, "I can't!" game. "I can't do it, I am not talented enough, I can't achieve that, no one in my family ever has, and I don't have what it takes, I can't do that I am not strong enough."

Are your life experiences your truth, or is your truth God's Word and

God's active voice within you? Do you live with God's Word and voice being your final authority, or is your authority your circumstances, emotions, and fears? Is your value and your worth based on what you do or what your job is? Is your self-worth tied to what others think or say about you and your experiences with them? Or, is it based on what God says about you? You need to hear God's voice. Information merely creates thinking, the revelation, the revealing of God's active voice, His Word and His activity in your life creates transformation. This process of transformation will remove and change any limiting belief systems. Strongholds that restrict freedom of your mind and heart will be broken. Interacting relationally with God's word and Holy Spirit will empower you to create new ways of thinking, speaking and acting which creates Godly supernatural freedom that transforms your mind, heart, and life. For so many of us, the question is not, "Do you believe in God," but, "What do you believe about God?" We need to have several questions answered. For instance, Does God actually speak? What does God think about me? Does God really like me?; Does He really care about every detail of my life and want to be involved?; and, does God really have a purpose for my life? When you hear from God personally on these matters, His voice, His Word and His presence will awaken in you and answer all of these questions on a personal level for you and more!

You were created and designed to hear and to be a receiver of God's active voice, like a radio receiver receives words from a radio station. God's voice and activity are likened to a radio station, in that you must tune into it in order to benefit from the broadcast. So many of us don't yet know how to tune in to God's frequency. So, we are going to demystify how to hear God's voice and sense His activity in your life! If you are ready, it's time to get tuned in, it is time to stop playing the "I can't game" and start playing the "I AM game" so let's get started! Tune your radio dials to "I am a beloved child of God and God is speaking to me!"

SALVATION AND HEARING GOD

Salvation in Jesus Christ is the most important step in your love relationship with God because it is the first step, or the first date, if you will, with God. People ask all the time: "How do I give my life to Jesus, and what does it mean when I do?"

Well, it starts with a prayer of salvation that allows you to surrender your life over to God, by confessing Jesus Christ as the Lord of your life and that God raised Him from the dead defeating death and sin for you. This is basically saying: "God, I recognize that I want You to be the King, the Leader, and the Lord of my life. I am making an agreement with You and surrendering my life over to You by giving of myself, and my will over to

Your care." You are asking the Lord to come make His home inside of your spirit and for the total forgiveness of your sins through the Blood of Jesus Christ. That means God's Spirit will actually come and live, dwell and inhabit your spirit through the blood agreement you are entering into through the death, burial and resurrection of Jesus Christ. You will become connected with God and become spiritually alive in Him. Jesus paid His very life to get you into Heaven and also to get Heaven, in this case God's Holy Spirit, into you; thus, making your spirit a totally new creation! (2 Corinthians 5:17) Because Jesus Himself tells us we must be born again spiritually through Him.

People often ask me "Sterling why would God send anyone to hell?" The answer is, God does not send anyone to hell. People choose to go to hell by refusing the free gift of salvation through the life and blood of Jesus Christ. The Bible says hell was NOT made for people. Hell was made for the devil and his demons. God gave His very own Son Jesus, who was willingly beaten, spit on, crucified, killed, shedding His holy blood to ensure your eternal salvation in Heaven and so that His Spirit could come and live in you right now! The real questions are: "Why would you not receive a free gift like that? Why would you not want to have all of your sins forgiven? To have God live inside of you here on earth now, actively guiding, directing and loving you through this life and to spend eternity in Heaven with Him?"

At the end of the day salvation in Jesus Christ is all that will really matter in this life and the next. So as a friend, I am not threatening you with hell and neither is God, although some people make it seem like that. The Bible says that He died for us regardless of all of our junk and the sins we have committed and that even when we are faithless, God is always faithful, and He is always love. There is a saying that friends warn, and enemies threaten. What God is doing is warning you and inviting you into a relationship with Him because that's what He does as your friend and your Heavenly Father. God's desire is that no one live or die without a personal relationship with Him and that all people have everlasting life through Him! God has done everything for you to receive this free gift of grace through Jesus Christ. It's your free will choice to receive it. This begs the question, why would you not choose Jesus? You have sin, fear, shame, pride and bondage to lose and everything to gain!

If I was going to give you the free gift of a million dollars in cash, would you take it? Of course you would, because of the value and benefit of the gift. How much more important is accepting and receiving the free gift of eternal life in Heaven and having God's Spirit come and live inside of you to lovingly guide and direct your life into peace, joy and freedom no matter what comes your way! You are so highly valued and worthy of love that

God paid the highest price that He could pay to redeem you from sin, which means to buy you back from sin and totally remove sin from you and justify you; which means to make you righteous. This means God puts you into right standing with Himself and makes it " just as if " you had never sinned before. So, when God sees you, instead of seeing the times you sinned, missed the mark or messed things up, He sees Jesus and what He paid and has done for you. Jesus took your sin upon Himself when He willingly went to the cross and paid the entire cost for your past, present and future sin so God can come live inside of you, and so you could be with Him in Heaven for eternity!

A lot of people ask, "What if I have doubts in my head?" That's a good question. God has an answer for us in Romans 10:9-10. It says, *"If you believe in your heart that God has raised Jesus from the dead, you will be saved."* The key word here is "heart", which in this context is referring to the spirit of a person or their will. Notice the scripture did not say, "believe with your head." It said with your "heart", which in this case is your spirit. It's that gut feeling at the core of your being. You know, that sense in your gut telling you something and when you don't listen to it, you usually end up in some kind of turmoil. We can all probably relate to a time that happened. So you can have doubts going on in your head and belief in your heart in Jesus and still receive the free gift of salvation.

Remember, salvation is the first step, the first date with God that starts your love relationship with Him. As you develop this love relationship with God, like any other healthy relationship, it will get more meaningful and deeper the more attention and effort you give to it! As you come to know God by salvation and as your savior after that first date, you spend the rest of your life getting to know God through experiences, becoming more intimate with Him and personally encountering His love. Like any other healthy relationship, this one too, will take time, attention, effort and trust daily.

PRAYER OF SALVATION

If you do not know Jesus as your Savior and Lord or you're unsure if you have been born again, or if you would just like to reaffirm your salvation through Jesus Christ, simply pray the following prayer in faith from your heart and Jesus will be your Lord!

Dear Heavenly Father, I come to You in the Name of Jesus Christ. Your Word says, **"Whosoever shall call on the name of the Lord, shall be saved," (Acts 2:21).** *I am calling on You, and I come surrendering my life and my will to You. I pray and ask Jesus to come into my heart and be Lord over my life according to Romans 10:9-10:* **"If you confess** *with your mouth the Lord Jesus and believe in your heart that God raised Him from the dead, you will be saved. For with the heart, one believes unto righteousness (right standing with God), and with the mouth, confession is made unto Salvation."*

I do that now. I confess that Jesus is Lord of my life, and I believe in my heart that God raised Him from the dead. I ask You, Holy Spirit, to come make Your home inside of me and live in me. I confess and repent of all of my sins to You, Lord, and ask for forgiveness for them right now, in the Name of Jesus. I receive You Jesus, as My Lord and Savior. By Your Blood Jesus, I receive my complete and total forgiveness of sins. I thank You, God, that I am now born again and a new creation according to Your Word in 2 Corinthians 5:17! I am a Christian, a child of Almighty God, and a child of the One True King! I have salvation and I am saved! I am now in the family of God! Thank You, Jesus!

Congratulations! If you prayed this prayer, then you were born again and now have eternal life in Christ Jesus! All of your sins... past, present and future are now forgiven! The Holy Spirit now lives inside of you! You are in total right standing with God and you have power over all the demonic forces that would try to attack you. The word of God says that everyone in Heaven rejoices at your salvation (Luke 15:7-10). So right now, Heaven is having a party because of your decision! God has a huge smile on His face! Praise God! Go ahead shout out loud "I love You Jesus" and celebrate!

If you prayed this prayer, please email us at info@sterlingharris.org so we can hear your testimony, pray for you, and send you a free gift from our ministry. We want to also encourage you to connect with a local Bible believing Church in your area that welcomes God's love, voice, presence, and the Holy Spirit. As you are visiting and looking for a Church pray, listen and allow God to lead you to a Church family that is right for you. God bless YOU! And remember this always, Jesus loves YOU!

GETTING OUR HEARTS READY TO RECEIVE

While reading these 10 ways God speaks, there will be a lot of practical teachings, examples and exercises. It is very important to take the time to interact with this book and focus on engaging the Holy Spirit in faith while doing the exercises. It is also vital to pay attention to, and see how these examples relate to you because these are common examples of the ways God speaks. You will have a lot of "Aha" moments while interacting with this book. You will hear examples and go "Aha! I have had that happen to me", "I have experienced that"; "Is that what that was? That was God!"

Like I use to do, you probably chalked it up to luck or coincidence which, by the way, do not exist. More on that in the Circumstances chapter of this book. Or perhaps you dismissed it and said, that was crazy or weird. I hear people saying those things all the time, even though they might have been seeking or praying about that very thing! I use to miss God's activity in my daily life all the time because I struggled with knowing if it was Him speaking to me or not. It is the goal of this book to awaken your spiritual ears to hear God's active voice and heighten your awareness of God's activity in your daily life. Thus tuning into God's radio frequency so you can hear Him and know Him in a real, personal and powerful way.

I will be sharing a lot in this book about my personal struggle about releasing false religious mindsets and transitioning into a healthy, daily, spiritual love relationship with Jesus Christ, empowered by the Holy Spirit. As I share my experiences, testimonies and God stories with you always keep in mind God wants to do the same kinds of things in your life and even more because of His great love for you! Testimonies are like big golden windows in which you can see spiritual concepts of faith and God's truth modeled through. So when you hear testimonies, examples and God stories receive them as a personal invitation from God, for you to experience Him in similar ways as well.

I also want to be clear that no matter what denomination a Church is affiliated with if it promotes the love of Jesus and believes in the Gospel message of redemption through the precious Blood of Jesus Christ for all who believe and are receiving His Holy Spirit, then I love and support what they are doing for God's Kingdom. If a Church is about spreading the "Good News" about the Father's love demonstrated through Jesus Christ than I am beyond thankful and joyful for them! It is all about starting and developing a spiritual and loving relationship with Jesus Christ. Our Ministry's whole mission and heart cry is for you to walk in the fullness of the Gospel, the fullness of Jesus, the fullness of the Holy Spirit and the fullness of your Heavenly Father's love for you. My heart's desire for you is to take your love, faith and power in Jesus, to your highest maximized potential. This will give Jesus His desire and His maximum return on what He paid for, which is you becoming just like Him, being fully transformed into His very image and nature! This is about us living to our fullest potential in Christ Jesus by His Spirit in us, because of the Father's great love for us! Where who Jesus is becomes who you are! Where Christlikeness becomes the foundation of your life! This book is not about religious views. It's about you developing a healthy and wholistic intimate daily spiritual love relationship with God through hearing His active voice and sensing His activity in your daily life. Because true success in life is knowing God through an intimate fellowship and loving relationship.

When taking a trip, it is always good to have a road map or a navigation system to help us find the way. Are you the type of person who is all about the destination, the journey, or can you enjoy both? This book is about enjoying both. We are concerned about the destination and ending up where we want to be, in Heaven, with our God for all eternity. However, the journey and how we get there is important as well, and that is what the majority of this book covers is your life long journey in developing a loving and vibrant relationship with God. Learning to hear God's active voice and sensing His activity in our daily lives is our road map, or navigation system, in the journey of living a joyful and victorious life!

It is important to start out our journey with a kind of guideline, attributes and the nature of God when hearing God's voice and sensing His activity in your daily lives, that way you will know what to look for and what His voice and activity will come with.

You will learn the nature of God's voice and sensing His activity in your daily lives. You will know what to look for and what His voice is guiding you to know and experience. I will submit to you that there are four distinctive attributes of God's voice. You will know when you are hearing the inner voice of your own conscious, the voice of your fleshly desires, the voice of the enemy (the devil, evil spirits, satan) or God's voice. When you hear or sense the opposite of these four attributes of God's voice and activity, you will know that you must have taken a detour and gotten off the path of hearing and experiencing God's voice and activity.

HOW TO DISCERN IF YOU ARE HEARING GOD AND SENSING HIS ACTIVITY

1. Does what I sense, see and/or hear line up with the scripture as well as the ways and nature of God, which is love? God's voice and activity will always be in line with His word, character and nature. You must know it is God's desire for you to realize His broadcast is aligned with the love He has promised through His word!
2. Does His inner voice come with a flow to it, a sense of peace, love, hope and wisdom? This inner voice will often sound similar to your inner voice but it will come with a realization and flow to it that will be slightly different from yours.
3. Does it produce the "Fruit of the Spirit" as defined in Galatians 5:22-23? *"But the fruit of the Spirit is love, joy, peace, patience, kindness, goodness, faithfulness, gentleness and self-control. ESV"*
4. Does it have the result of producing freedom and releasing you from bondage i.e. fear, worry, shame, anxiety, insecurity,

depression, doubt, or unworthiness? All divine truth has the ability to set people free and where the Spirit of the Lord is there is freedom (2 Corinthians 3:17).

Always remember there is no transformation and relationship without encountering the Lord. You cannot live off of yesterday's encounters of His love, goodness and presence. Even with God you will still be thirsty and hungry if you are not constantly drinking and eating of a healthy spiritual love relationship with God every day all day! It is the "manna principle" in the Old Testament where the children of Israel were in the wilderness and God provided manna for them to eat. The manna could not be saved overnight except for on the Sabbath day so they could rest and focus solely on God . If they tried to save the manna any other day it would spoil (Exodus 16:13-31). Matthew 6:11 says, in what is referred to as the Lord's Prayer ***"give this day our daily bread."*** The bread is referring to Jesus as the Bread of Life and His word. We have to live in a place of pursuit after God's heart, voice and presence. We can't live off of yesterday's encounter! We need to communicate with Him everyday for our lives to be truly peaceful, powerful and guided by God's Spirit. A fire needs additional wood and oxygen to keep burning! If you want to be and stay on fire for God you have to keep feeding the flame of God within you!

2

GOD'S WORD

THE VERSE IS THE VOICE

GOD REVEALS HIS WILL BY HIS WORD. THE BIBLE IS GOD SPEAKING directly to you, your circumstances, your relationships and everything that pertains to life and godliness. The Bible is a manifestation of God upon this earth. God will never do anything contrary to His word, and as Believers, we are to do our very best to base our thoughts, will, emotions, decisions, and perceptions on the word of God. We are to give the Bible "first place" in our heart, our mind, and our life. Making the decision and commitment to base our thoughts, feelings, words and actions on the Bible, is a key principle to hearing God and following His lead.

Jesus Himself was The Word: ***In the beginning [before all time] was the Word (Christ), and the Word was with God, and the Word was God Himself. John 1:1 AMP*** As Believers we are to become like Jesus so, in essence, we are to become the Word of God by living it out in our daily lives.

The word of God is the language and customs of God, and it is His revealed will for your life. It also provides you with your benefit package as a Believer in Christ and the power you have by being in Christ Jesus. It would be no different than gathering information for you to move to a foreign country. What things are vital for you to know to be successful in that country? You would want to know the language and the customs of that country to better equip yourself to function in that society, and you would read up on these things and learn them. You would also immerse yourself in the culture, customs and language when you got to that country in order to quickly acclimate to your new country. The same level of success is achieved by reading, studying and immersing yourself in the word of God when you move into a relationship with Christ. ***"Every Scripture passage is inspired by God. All of them are useful for teaching, pointing out errors, correcting people, and training them for a life that has God's approval." 2 Timothy 3:16 GWT***

All Scripture is God Breathed, the Bible is from God. Use it as if it was from God Himself because it is! I use to think that the Bible was just a set of rules I needed to follow to be a "good person" and if I didn't do what it said I was a "bad person" and God was looking down and was going to zap me or punish me. I thought if I followed the rules this would cause God to love me, and if I didn't follow them then God loved me less, that He was angry or ashamed of me. In essence I was often working hard to try to be "good enough" for God which is a "slave and orphan mentality" which creates guilt and shame, instead of being in a love relationship with God and knowing Him as my Heavenly Father that loves me unconditionally as His son which is a "sonship mentality". That slavery to my own self effort stopped me from entering into my real identity in life as a beloved child of the One True King! I shifted my thinking when God showed me a simple but profound example. Let's say you have an 8-year-old son or daughter and you tell them; "Don't touch this stove, it is hot and will burn you and cause you pain." If they did touch it and burned themselves or didn't follow the rules would you love them any less? The answer is no! If they followed your directions and did not touch the stove and as a result did not burn themselves and followed the rules would you love them anymore? The answer is again no! You love that child just because they are your son or your daughter. The same is true for God; His love is unconditional and it does not change!

My whole perception of the Bible was incorrect! The Bible is actually God's love letter to me telling me and showing me how to live in an intimate relationship with Him. It is there to guide you away from trouble and pain. God's word is here to help you transform your mind, will, emotions and heart. It's to encourage and strengthen you. Predominantly, it is there to build your faith because ***"Faith comes by hearing and hearing by the Word of God." Romans 10:17*** So that you can come to know God and believe deeply in Him. The entire Bible is about God's relentless and loving pursuit of us as His family, beloved sons and daughters of God. As well as the process of restoring us back into right relationship with God after that relationship was broken in the Garden of Eden by the sin and resulting fall of Adam and Eve. Their sin separated them from God spiritually, in that God's Spirit could no longer live inside of their spirits because God's Spirit cannot live where sin is living, because He is holy. That is one of the main reasons Jesus came and died taking all of our sin upon Himself so God's Spirit could once again live and make His home in us. The fall of man was based on mankind's misuse of freewill by disobeying God and looking to redefine good and evil on our own terms and not God's.

God does not want a relationship with us, or obedience from us, out of fear but out of our love and devotion for Him. I use to get so confused on this because I would read the Bible and it tells us to "fear God" and refers to "the fear of the Lord" but it is not how most of us think of fear, like we should be scared or frightened by God because of some punishment that He might do to us if we don't love and obey Him. When I really made the commitment to live my life by the Word of God this is one of the first questions I had for God. Why did the Bible say over 300 times "do not fear" but then it says to "fear God"? I knew God would not contradict Himself so there had to be an answer. So I did some studying on this question. I did some research on the word "fear" in the original Hebrew and Greek text that the Bible was written in and realized there were a couple of meanings for the word fear. I compared them to when the Bible was saying "do not fear" and then the other use of the word fear, when it came to "fearing God", and God lead me to my answer! I found out the word fear the Bible uses when it refers to "fear God" or "the fear of the Lord" it is actually referring to having a loving, reverent, respect and awe of God based on His love for us and out of our love and devotion for Him (Strong's H3374). It is a sense of being fully submitted to God and wanting to represent Him well because of your dedication, awe and wonderment for Him. So from now on when you see the word "fear" in the Bible when it refers to God you can replace that word with "love and respect God", "the reverent love of the Lord" or "having a loving, respectful reverence and awe of God"! For a practical illustration of the "fear of the Lord" I like to use my grandmother because most of us know of at least one person in our lives who we give this kind of reverence, love and respect to, for me it was my granny. This is a person in our lives who we love and respect so much we want to honor them through the way we live our lives. I know there were times in my life I thought to myself "Oh I cannot do that because my grandmother would not approve of it, if she found out I know she would be hurt by my actions". Or on the positive side, "My grandmother would be so honored and proud of me for doing this because I know she would make the same kind of decision if she were me in this situation". This understanding helped me to envision what a healthy "fear of the Lord" looks like. God wants our love, respect, devotion, reverence, fascination, wonderment and awe for Him to surpass any human relationship we have here on Earth. As we live in the "fear of the Lord" the Bible says we gain wisdom and all types of amazing blessings from our Heavenly Father!

The commandments in the Bible are not just a record of things not to do, like I use to think. They are guidelines for the protection of our body, soul and spirit! The commandments were not meant as a set of "do's" and "dont's". They are meant to guide us away from things that would cause pain to ourselves and others. *"Your Word is a lamp to guide my feet and a light for my path." Psalms 119:105 ESV* God knows that if I lie I will hurt myself and others. If I steal I will hurt myself and others. These choices of sin have negative consequences and hinder me from who God lovingly wants me to be. These sinful decisions of disobedience to God's Word also cause me and others hurt and pain. God wants you to be loving, joyful and peaceful within yourself, with Him and with others. The Bible was meant to cultivate and mold your heart to have an intimate relationship with God that is real, personal, accepting and loving. For instance in relationships where we value and love the other person, such as in a healthy marriage or friendship, we are influenced, guided and compelled to action by the love, loyalty, devotion and respect we have for that person. Because of that love we will often choose to start and stop doing certain things to honor the love we have for the person. For instance in a healthy marriage you stop pursuing any other romantic relationships and you don't look for ways to sin against your spouse, on the contrary the love you have for them compels you to take actions which will bring joy, peace and comfort to their lives. Also within a healthy relationship you will start doing things you have not normally done before because of your love for the other person. This may include doing activities the other person likes, spending quality time with them, listening to and caring about how their day went or taking on chores such as cleaning, mowing the lawn and taking out the trash. This is the same concept in a deepening relationship with God. He wants us to be so in love with Him that we are guided by His Word out of the love, respect and childlike awe we have for Him. Jesus said, *"If you love me, you will keep my commandments." John 14:15 ESV* This loving devotion to God and commitment to His Word through fellowship with the Holy Spirit is what will give us the leverage to change and transform our lives into becoming Christlike which is the purpose of every born again Child of God.

When you are in love with God and totally possessed, driven and guided by His love, everything in your life will constantly increase and shift you towards living God's best for your life. That means more peace for your soul! Joy no matter the circumstances! Freedom for your heart! You will have prosperity in every sense of the word, which means to have an abundant supply of God and all of His goodness. As you live a lifestyle guided by the Word of God because of the love of God, you come to know Him by experience that causes you to come into your true identity, value and purpose as a son and daughter of God and the cost He paid for you to have life in Him. You will replace your old identity based on unhealthy inner vows, judgments, perceptions and lies you believed about God, yourself and others, and replace it with the truth in God's Word about who you truly are. You will come to experience the life of Jesus in you, coming out of you because of the very life Jesus sacrificed for you, His own. You are worth the very life and blood of Jesus Christ! That's your value the highest cost that God could pay, the great exchange Jesus sinless life for your sinful life so you could be made righteous, holy, forgiven and totally free from the slavery of sin! However, if you don't know the real truth and continue in the truth of God's Word merely by default, you will fall for lies and fear-based thinking like unworthiness, guilt, shame, worry and unforgiveness.

"For the Word of God is living and active, sharper than any two-edged sword, piercing to the division of soul and of spirit, of joints and of marrow, and discerning the thoughts and intentions of the heart." Hebrews 4:12 ESV

The Bible is not just a book. It is the voice of God and it has the power of God in it and on it as you hear, read and speak it over yourself and others. It will transform our mind, our will and our emotions; which is the human soul. It also feeds and strengthens our human spirit which allows for a greater connection and clarity with the Holy Spirit within us. Reading and hearing the Word of God also renews our bodies bringing health and healing to it. The Word of God is alive and active! *"Now may the God of peace make you holy in every way, and may your whole spirit and soul and body be kept blameless" 1 Thessalonians 5:23 NLT* The Word of God is a seed which has the power to produce what it says. Just like any seed you plant, the ability and power to produce is in the seed once it is planted into the right conditions, in fertile soil.

When you buy tomato seeds at a store and you look on the package and see these large plants yielding these big juicy tomatoes, you recognize that the ability and power to produce that plant and its fruit is contained within those tiny little seeds. *"Being born again, not of corruptible seed, but of incorruptible, by the Word of God, which liveth and abideth forever." 1 Peter 1:23 KJV*

In the same way, the Word of God is an incorruptible seed that has the ability and power within itself to produce in your life what it says, like God's promises, growing in the fruit of the Spirit, blessings, strengthening your human spirit, wisdom, character, forgiveness, healing for your body and soul. However, a seed will not produce and benefit you unless you sow it into good ground. A tomato seed has to be planted in fertile and soft ground, watered, put into sunlight and if you want maximum growth you will need to pull up the weeds around it that will potentially suck out some of the nutrients in the ground thus affecting the growth of the seed and the production of the plant.

In like manner the Word of God has to be continually sown into the ground of the garden of your heart and mind and it is planted by hearing the Word of God (Romans 10:17). Once it is planted you have to water it consistently referring to interacting with Holy Spirit as you read, hear, study and meditate on the Word of God in your daily life. Then the seed requires sunlight which is a relationship with Jesus who is the light of the world and receiving your Heavenly Father's warm loving presence. Finally if you want maximum yield, results and increase in your life you have to tend the garden of your heart and pull out the weeds of fear, doubt, unforgiveness, shame, worry, unworthiness and offense of any type or kind such as irritation and frustration.

Let's look at how Jesus described it, **"The Kingdom of God is like a farmer who scatters seed on the ground. Night and day, while he's asleep or awake, the seed sprouts and grows, but he does not understand how it happens. The earth produces the crops on its own. First a leaf blade pushes through, then the heads of wheat are formed, and finally the grain ripens. And as soon as the grain is ready, the farmer comes and harvests it with a sickle, for the harvest time has come."** *Mark 4:26-29 NLT* Jesus just promised us if we sow the seed of His Word into our hearts and continually water it than the Word will work even when we are sleeping it is working in us and for us!

When I first began to read the Bible for myself I didn't really understand it and how a book could transform my life and help me grow closer to a God I could not see. When I made the commitment and determined decision to say no matter what I am going to read and study the Bible because if God said it would guide me, speak to me and transform me into being more like Christ then I was going to put God to His Word! The Bible says: **"If any of you lacks wisdom [to guide him through a decision or circumstance], he is to ask of [our benevolent] God, who gives to everyone generously and without rebuke or blame, and it will be given to him."** *JAMES 1:5 AMP*

I began, and still do claim and declare this scripture over my mind and heart, especially when I am reading the Bible, even when I don't feel like I understand it I ask God and thank Him for His Wisdom. At first I felt the same and acted the same. I had negative thoughts like "you don't understand this", "you are never going to understand this", "reading this book is not going to change anything, you're still going to be the same person with the same problems after you read it, so stop wasting your time", "it is just a

GOD'S WORD | 19

book", "men wrote this and changed it up it's not even from God Himself." At the same time, I knew from playing football and working out that it takes time, effort, commitment and attention to develop good technique, skill and positive change. You could not just work out for one week and expect powerful results and massive positive change in the way your body looked; that would be foolish.

In the same manner you would not play an organized sports game like football or basketball without training, practicing and putting in a game plan for that week's game. As an athlete I also realized the importance of practicing the fundamentals, knowing no matter the level of athlete whether it is high school, college or professional, they all practice the fundamental techniques of their particular sport on a daily basis. So too I needed to practice the fundamentals of my faith by reading God's Word, engaging the Holy Spirit and spending time with Jesus. I knew as I did that, positive growth and results have to follow!

When you read the Bible don't be surprised when the enemy tries to tempt you with bizarre thoughts or negative thinking or tries to distract you. He knows how powerful the Word of God can be when you get it into your heart. Sometimes when you read the Bible you just laugh at your negative thoughts and the enemy and just thank God that His Word is true. Sometimes I just laugh, not because I feel like it but to get that heaviness off of me. I will say, "ha, ha, ha, on the devil, I know God loves me, that the Word of God is true and I accept it as truth and I receive it 100 fold in my life". This is a good tactic against the attack of the enemy when he brings lying thoughts such as the Word of God not being true, that it is not really going to change anything in your life or that it can't help you or you will never understand all this.

It may sound strange but laughing by faith is a great tactic because just the act of laughing has been proven to shift your mood, reduce stress, break up negative thoughts and increases endorphins in your brain. Try just laughing for the next minute or so by faith and you will most likely find yourself laughing even more!

Remember this truth, the Bible when received into your heart through reading, hearing and studying the Word and interacting with Holy Spirit, can and will change, renew and transform you. The enemy is trying to create shame and guilt and hinder you from reading God's Word. When that happens realize it's just the enemy trying to come against the transformation that the Word of God causes in your life! Just praise God anyways and laugh at the thoughts and thank God for His Word! I still have to do this from time to time. So realize the enemy uses the same tricks on everyone, don't let him convince you that you're the only one struggling with this.

So I listened to the voice of God in the back of my mind that came with a peace saying, "Keep going and seek first the Kingdom of God and His righteousness" which also kept coming up in daily devotionals, conversations and sermons I was hearing. I knew it was God encouraging me to keep reading the Word and seeking Him in prayer. As I continued to read the Word over the time period of a couple of months I started noticing when I was going to make decisions parts of verses I had read previously would come to my mind and give me guidance on what to do. Oftentimes God would bring to my remembrance a story I had read or a parable Jesus had told would play in my mind like a video.

I listened to those promptings and I began to think differently, speak differently and I began to handle daily adversity, stress and irritation in much more positive and loving ways. I began to realize that the spiritual muscle I had been working out by reading and listening to the Word was beginning to come out of my heart. *"The good man out of the good treasure of his heart brings forth what is good; and the evil man out of the evil treasure brings forth what is evil; for his mouth speaks from that which fills his heart. Luke 6:45 NAS*

I was filling my heart and mind with God's Word and feeding my spirit the spiritual food it needed to grow in muscle and in strength and I was beginning to see the results of it! The seed of God's Word was growing inside of me and now it was bearing fruit I could see, taste and experience! For the first time in my life I saw how powerful God's Word was in helping me live a fuller, richer life that was real and personal to me. I have seen this same truth play out in the lives of all of the people who will make the commitment and decision to read and listen to God's Word on a daily basis and do their best to make it their final authority and decision maker. Jesus said : *"I am the vine; you are the branches. The one who remains in me and I in him, produces much fruit" John 15:5 CSB*

God also opens up His Word for us depending on what we need at that particular time. For instance, when the daily devotional seems to speak to the very circumstances you have been dealing with, that is God speaking. When you are reading the Word, and it seems to be speaking directly to you by answering some questions you had or comforts you on some level, it may even be a passage that you have read before, but today it seems to have taken on a different meaning to it, that is God speaking to you. Sometimes I will just pray asking God to speak to me through His Word. I will open up my Bible and often a passage on the page I open to seems to be highlighted and stands out to me. As I read, it speaks to my heart comfort, encouragement, correction and love. Other times I will just flip through my Bible until something stands out to me or hits my heart in a way that is peaceful and comforting that comes with this inward knowing that God is speaking this to my heart and my current situation. For those of you who mostly use a Bible app on your smartphone, I have had the same type of things happen, just let the Lord lead you in the same way. This kind of interaction with God's Word is when you take the written Word of God referred to as the "logos" Word of God (Strong's G3056) and then when the Holy Spirit brings passages to our attention that apply to and guide us in a personal and current way this is known in the Greek as the "rhema" Word of God. Rhema refers to a word that is spoken. It literally means "utterance" such as when you take God's Word and speak it out verbalizing it (Strong's G4487). The active voice of the Holy Spirit is also the rhema or spoken Word of God.

Jesus said to them, "This is what I told you while I was still with you: Everything must be fulfilled that is written about me in the Law of Moses, the Prophets and the Psalms." Then He opened their minds so they could understand the Scriptures. Luke 24:44-45 NIV

I love when I get revelation knowledge like this, which is when God opens up scripture for us and really breathes a fresh understanding on it that applies to our life in a real, personal and powerful way. Getting a good study Bible is also a very practical way for God to open up His Word. My personal favorite, of which I have many, is "The Spirit Filled Life Study Bible". A good study Bible will have a history of the time period and what was happening in the setting and background of what your reading. It will give you definitions of various words in the Bible that give you a clearer picture of the original Hebrew and Greek languages. These are the two predominant languages that the Bible was originally written in. These definitions are often called "word studies". I would also suggest you get the Strong's Concordance and Blue Letter Bible app for your phone, or you can get the books if you prefer. These resources will enable you to look up various words in the Bible to get a better understanding of them.

It is amazing the revelation you can receive from studying the meaning of just one word! The Hebrew and Greek languages often have rich layers of meaning and word pictures that go along with just one word and when you study those meanings out it will give you a clearer and fuller understanding of the Word of God and how amazing the Bible truly is. A good study Bible will also explain some of the various customs at the time the Bible was written, as well as provide sound teaching about Biblical truths that make the Bible easier for you to understand and how it relates to your life in practical ways.

When reading the Bible to better understand it, you want to look at several things. First, content; what is being said. Second, context; who is speaking, why are they saying what they are saying and what message are they communicating to us? Third, history and culture of the time; this will help you to understand what is going on and why certain things are happening. Fourth, you want to look at the emotional aspect of the text. For example, when Jesus was crucified on the cross for our sins; put yourself in the shoes of Jesus. What kind of sensations, feelings and emotions would you have had or do you think Jesus went through and battled? This type of thinking will help you connect with the text on an emotional human level and in this case appreciate Jesus and His love for you in a deeper way.

You can also ask yourself three questions as you read the Bible that will help you better understand and apply the Scripture to your life.

1. What did the passage I just read mean to the people back in the time it was written?
2. What does the passage I just read mean to us now and how does it apply to our lives today?
3. What does this passage mean to me personally and how can I currently apply this to my life?

Keeping these fundamentals in mind when reading the Bible will help you understand in context what the scriptures are saying to you. You can not only read the Word and understand it but most importantly you can become the Word of God and be transformed by it. All of this combined together opens up your understanding and through it all you want to interact with Holy Spirit through prayer and asking God questions, listening and meditating on what you're reading and how it applies to your life. I often pray "God I thank You that You are opening up the Word for me and showing me how to become this Word."

I use to get so overwhelmed at all the changes I felt I needed to make and all of the teaching that was out there! How would I choose the right one? Then God reminded me that He sent the Holy Spirit to lead me and teach me all truth and to pray for and thank Him for that leading because all teaching is not created equal and not all teaching is going to prosper your life. I have prayed for years "God I thank You that You are leading me and directing me to every video, person, book and teaching I need to encounter. I thank You Lord that You are bringing that into My Path in Jesus Name." I have so many testimonies about how He has done that over the years. I have been thanking Him and praising Him for continually answering that prayer. When that is your heart's desire God will answer you in powerful and profound ways.

An illustration of how this manifested in my life was there was a season in my life that I was trying to understand the power of prayer and how it worked and why God wanted us to pray and what our prayers did in the unseen and seen realms. I was walking to lunch one day and a guy walked up to me and said, "Hey this is going to sound a little strange but God told me to give these to you". They were three mini books from Kenneth E. Hagin on the power of prayer! I felt peace about reading them and my spirit agreed with what I read, even though some of the teaching was quite new to me. God used these books to open my mind and heart to the power of prayer and our authority on this earth that God had given us and how He wants us to use that authority. How God, by His own design, wants and in some cases needs our prayers, cooperation and consent to take action. I began to understand that prayer changes our hearts, moves things supernaturally in the spiritual realm and how that affects the natural seen realm. I have dozens of stories over the years of friends sending me certain books and of the Holy Spirit leading me to certain ministry's YouTube Channels. Because of my heart's position, it allowed God to guide me and direct me in getting revelation knowledge and thus becoming His Word.

When it comes to reading or listening to the Bible; interact with the Holy Spirit. Ask God questions when you don't understand something or you want a deeper understanding of how what you are reading or hearing applies to your life. Then listen to His direction and stay alert for His activity. The Holy Spirit will answer you in various ways such as a flowing thought that comes with wisdom that you sense is from God. He may bring a scripture to your mind. He may have you Google something that leads you to an answer. You may have a conversation with someone where it seems as if God is speaking to you through them. A daily devotional you read may seem to give you direction and encouragement, or a sermon you hear. It may be an impression you sense in your spirit. A good rule to follow is if you read or experience something and you sense God is speaking to you He probably is. I always suggest that you default on the side of righteousness and acknowledge God's activity even if you are not sure, be patient, knowing the Word works and that God will answer you and open up His Word for you because of the great love He has for you! He will always confirm Himself so just keep reading, listening, acknowledging and acting upon His Word.

Even while writing this book most of the scriptures God brought to my mind, such as words, phrases, sermons, Christian songs, Bible verses and parables would come up and seem to rise inward from my spirit and heart to my mind. They would remind me of a particular verse of scripture that applied to what I was writing. A lot of the times I would not even know the chapter and verse, often times it was just a part of a verse I knew was in the Bible but not sure exactly where. Then I would Google it and God would lead me to the right one. God does this often in my daily life as I am talking and listening to Him throughout my day, as well as during my conversations with other people and in my personal quiet time and journaling with Him. He will bring the Word to my heart and mind, which gives me insight into the wisdom God is showing me. It leads to a flow of practical wisdom and insightful thoughts. This brings the Word of God to life in your daily circumstances and in the lives of others thus making the Bible real, personal and practical. You were never meant to just read the Bible you were made to become the Word of God manifested on this earth. The Apostle Paul calls us walking, talking letters of recommendation for others to read and experience. *"You yourselves are our letter, written on our hearts, known and read by everyone. You show that you are a letter from Christ, the result of our ministry, written not with ink but with the Spirit of the living God, not on tablets of stone but on tablets of human hearts." 2 Corinthians 3:2-3 NIV*

I want to encourage you to do your "own research" like when you started being romantically interested in someone you pursued them, you checked them out and wanted to get to know them on a personal level; their likes, dislikes, personality, and how they think. If we are being honest you probably even stalked some of their social media accounts when you first met them to get a feel for them. You also spent time listening to them, conversing, and spending quality alone time with them. God wants us to pursue a relationship with Him in much the same way! When you liked a car, wanted a job, followed your favorite music group, you did your own research in all kinds of areas of your life. Except now, so often, in our spiritual life, which is the most important and vital area of our life, we just believe in something that someone else tells us instead of reading the Word for ourselves. Ask the Holy Spirit to teach you about the scriptures and make a commitment to do your own personal research in God's Word! *"Study and be eager and do your utmost to present yourself to God, approved (tested by trial), a workman who has no cause to be ashamed, correctly analyzing and accurately dividing [rightly handling and skillfully teaching] the Word of Truth." 2 Timothy 2:15 AMPC*

The Word of God has to be first place in your life: that means you make the choice, commitment and daily decision that your thoughts, feelings, perceptions, emotions, will, words and your actions are all based off of God's Word, God's nature and God's love for you, your love for God and God's love for others expressing itself through you! You allow the Holy Spirit to guide and direct your mind, will, emotions, intellect and you train your soul on a daily basis to be under the control of the Holy Spirit. This is done by an act of your will through teaming up and partnering with God on a daily basis and allowing His Presence and Word to cultivate and mold your heart and life. When you put the Word of God first place in your life you make the decision to not allow your life circumstances to speak louder than God's truth. You refuse to allow challenges, trials, injustices, hardships and the storms of life to have a greater influence on you than the truth of what God says in His Word and through His Holy Spirit. This concept sounds simple and it is, however we all have and will experience challenging situations in our lives which speak very loudly and at times they seem to consume our minds and lives. Even in those times we have to make the daily decision to allow the Word of God and the Holy Spirit to be the filter and regulator of our thoughts, emotions and actions. They will act as an umpire or referee like in a sports game, they keep us safely in line with the guidelines of the will of God for our lives while allowing us to still play and live our lives freely. As I have made the daily decision to put the Word of God first place in my life I have developed a mindset that says anything outside of Jesus, His Word and His Spirit I don't need, nor do I want that in my life. I can assure you that it takes time to develop this mindset and it will be tested, but it is such a free, happy, loving, joyful and peaceful way to live! I invite you to make the choice to live a life based off of God's Word, promises and love.

It's important to understand that your daily choices and acts of faith will trigger, activate and cause God's favor, blessings and breakthrough in your life; as you put your faith into action through obedience, walking in love and being a doer of the Word of God. Putting your faith into action means to act on what you believe in, to have corresponding actions that are linked to your faith and belief in the Word of God as well as what God says to you personally. Often times you have to step out on your faith and put it into action which will in turn release God to act on the faith you released in the form of your faith-based actions. ***"For those of us who believe, faith activates the promise and we experience the realm of confident rest!" Hebrews 4:3 TPT*** You have examples of this throughout the Bible: when God called Abraham, God said "Go to a land that I will show you" he went by faith and then God showed him the promised land (Genesis 12:1). The Jordan River parted when the priests stepped into the river by faith in what God had spoken to Joshua (Joshua 3:15-17). In the New Testament the 10 lepers were cleansed as they went to the temple as Jesus had instructed them to (Luke 17:14). When you are unsure about God's will for you in a specific matter it is important to be patient and continue to stay in a close daily relationship with God, living by His Word and continuing to do the last thing you sensed God told you to do. Continuing in your daily relationship with God and acting on the Word of God by faith will trigger wisdom, blessings and breakthroughs to happen and God's path for you will eventually become clear.

Putting your faith in God into action is the answer to all of life's questions and challenges, even when you can't see a way out of your circumstances and situations. Your trust and faith in God will set you above any challenges, struggles or forces that are trying to bring you down! I have seen submission and obedience to God's active voice and His Word always come with a blessing meaning when you live out the Word of God by faith the blessings of God supernaturally chase you down and overtake you! *"All these blessings will come upon you and overtake you if you pay attention to the voice of the Lord your God." Deuteronomy 28:2*

The writer of Hebrews describes putting your faith into action plainly and clearly:

The fundamental fact of existence is that this trust in God, this faith, is the firm foundation under everything that makes life worth living. It's our handle on what we can't see. The act of faith is what distinguished our ancestors, set them above the crowd. By faith, we see the world called into existence by God's Word, what we see, created by what we don't see. Hebrews 11:1-3 MSG

So, let's get a working understanding of faith and define faith practically. Faith is believing in and acting on God's Word as if it is true and having a righteous expectation of God being trustworthy and good to His Word and promises. The Bible says, *"Now faith is the substance of things hoped for, the evidence of things not seen." Hebrews 11:1 NKJV* I like to use an illustration of comparing a large jet airplane to a small single engine one propeller plane. For me I have a greater "substance" of hope in the largeness and soundness of a large jet airplane to get me where I need to go safely. I have more righteous expectation in a large jet airplane because it has a lot more substance to it compared to a smaller single engine one propeller airplane; because to me there is not a lot of substance there. My evidence of things not yet seen is the reading I have done in regard to the safety of large jetliners coupled with my experiential knowledge of being safe on many of the large jetliners I have flown in over the years. Even though in the future I will most likely not fly on the same jetliners as I have in times past, the substance of the airplane and the evidence of my experience with large jet airplanes causes me to have faith that the airplane I am flying on next, is going to get me where I need to be quickly and safely. My corresponding actions based on my faith and what I believe are, I walk onto the plane feeling relaxed and secure, ready to enjoy my flight. In the same way the substance of my faith is based on the righteous expectation of God being trustworthy and good to His Word and the evidence of my faith is all the experiential knowledge I have of God being trustworthy and good to His Word through reading, listening and studying the Bible and within my own personal relationship with God. Faith is not an I wish so, faith is an I know so, based on God's Word, Spirit and our personal experiential knowledge of God!

It is important to understand as you step out on your faith on a daily basis there will naturally be some sort of tension between what you are believing and acting on by faith and the doubt within your carnal mind. This is often the unseen tension between us stepping out on faith in God's Word into the supernatural versus, the natural seen realm of reality in which our minds are trying to process how unseen spiritual realities are going to affect a physical world. Even with this understood we must still choose to step out and act on our faith in God's Word and promises. Because everything we do in regard to God takes faith. Hearing God's active voice, sensing His activity and understanding how God is speaking to us all takes engaging our faith. Everything you will read in this book takes faith to believe, receive and operate in. ***"And without faith it is impossible to please God, because anyone who comes to Him must believe that He exists and that He rewards those who earnestly seek Him." Hebrews 11:6 NIV*** The wonderful thing is, God gives us all by His grace a "measure of faith" as well as His Word, in order to help us to develop our faith (Romans 12:3). The accountability we have is to choose to act on our faith in God's Word no matter the circumstances we face. So it becomes not a matter of having enough faith, but using and developing the faith God has already given us! This is what I believe the Bible is referring to when it speaks of "fight the good fight of faith" acting on your faith and putting the Word of God first place in your life regardless of your life experiences or circumstances (1 Timothy 6:12).

Following God, putting your faith into action in loving submission to God's voice, Word, and Spirit, will allow you to access and benefit from treasures and provision in heavenly places. Which will cause the blessings and promises of God to be fulfilled and become a reality in your life. These types of manifestations and breakthroughs is what we are all longing and contending for to happen within our personal lives. Walking in the light of God's Word, means being a doer of the Word of God, becoming the Word of God here on earth, for people to see and experience the love of God through. This kind of daily life lived in God results in breakthroughs and answered prayer. It sets you in a place of true blessings and prosperity which means having an abundant supply of love, peace, joy, freedom, a sound mind, bodily healing and the power of God in and upon your life. Jesus paid the highest price Heaven had to offer for you to live in these freedoms. It's time to apply the Word to our lives so Jesus can get what He paid for.

7 PRACTICAL TIPS TO GETTING GOD'S WORD INTO YOUR MIND AND HEART ARE:

1) IF YOU ARE JUST STARTING OUT READING THE BIBLE I SUGGEST STARTING WITH THE BOOK OF MARK IN THE NEW TESTAMENT.

It's a short book and will allow you to start becoming familiar with the life, teachings and ministry of Jesus. Then I suggest you keep reading and finish the New Testament and then read the New Testament again, starting with the Book of Matthew. Then, after you have read most of the New Testament twice, if you want to read the Old Testament and start at the beginning in Genesis you can do this. I suggest this because as you read the Old Testament it is important to read it through the filter and lens of the New Testament and the understanding of the finished works of Jesus Christ.

This will help you understand questions like why God had the people set up a sacrificial system and other things in the Old Testament that were really physical examples and representations of Jesus and the New Covenant we have with God today, because of what Jesus did for us on the Cross. The Bible explains to us that things in the Old Testament were shadows, types and prophetic pictures of things to come meaning they were often physical representations of what God would later do spiritually in the New Testament through Jesus. For example in the Old Testament God's Presence dwelled in a Temple, now we as Believers in Jesus we are the Temple of God and the presence of God's Holy Spirit now lives in us instead of dwelling in a Temple.

2) DOWNLOAD THE YOUVERSION BIBLE APP, THE BLUE LETTER BIBLE APP ON YOUR PHONE FOR FREE OR OTHER BIBLE APPS LIKE IT.

These apps will give you a lot of different translations to choose from. I personally like the English Standard Version ESV, the Amplified Bible (AMP), the New International Version NIV and the Message Bible. All of these translations put the original Hebrew and Greek language of the Bible into today's terms making it easier for us to understand. A lot of these translations have an icon of a speaker by them, meaning it has an audio option which will read you the Bible! So those of you who don't like to read all the time or you are in a place where you can't read, you can listen to the Word and feed your spirit person that lives inside you, which is what the Bible refers to as the new man the spiritual food it needs (Ephesians 4:24). So when I get up in the morning I will listen to a couple of books in the Bible while I get ready and start my day with the Word of God. You can also watch the Bible on video which is something I enjoy doing. On the YouVersion Bible app, in the video section, you can listen and watch video reenactments of the Bible which allows for a different experience of hearing and seeing the Bible. Ministries like the Bible Project offer animated reenactments and overviews of the Bible as well as various Word studies that are very informative and easy to understand. There is also a non-animated option offered by the LUMO Project and the Jesus Film Project which is offered on the YouVersion Bible app video section as well. You can also find and subscribe to these resources on YouTube. I have really enjoyed these resources and pick them depending on what I am in the mood for. They give you a really great sense of the context of what is happening within the chapter and verses being read.

When reading or listening to the Word I often start off by praying *"God let me become Your Word, I thank You Jesus for intimate knowledge of You, please open the eyes of my heart Lord I thank You for the Spirit of Revelation and the Spirit of Wisdom in the knowledge of Your Word, of Your love, by Your Holy Spirit. Amen."* (Ephesians 1:17-18) My prayer is that God changes me from the inside out and speaks to me and causes His Word to come alive to me! When this is your heart's desire as you read the Word of God, the favor and wisdom of Heaven will come upon you and you will see radical breakthroughs and results in your life! You will begin to walk in the light of the Word of God; meaning the promises and blessings of God like peace, wisdom, freedom and joy will become a daily reality in your life.

Getting tuned into God's frequency on a constant basis is key to having a rich relationship with Him. I also take the time to listen to my Bible app on my way to work in the car or while I am working out instead of listening to music or talk radio I will listen to God's Word. If you still want to listen to those things try splitting the time in half and take half the time to listen to God's Word and the other half to music or talk radio. Be intentional at the same time be practical about it, you know your downtime better than anyone make the choice to fill that time with God's Word in your ears!

I want to encourage you to look at potential times you have that you can use to get in the Word for example in your commute to work and from work, working out, down time at home instead of watching mindless TV (which most of us do) watch half of the time in sermons from various anointed preachers and teachers who are Biblically based and Holy Spirit lead, turn on a sermon or your Bible app on when you go to bed at night.

Your spirit never sleeps and you want to constantly be feeding your spirit person. It is not that I stopped doing the things of this world that were not adding value to my life like watching a whole bunch of mindless TV programs or listening to music that did not glorify God in order to decompress, escape reality or in the name of "entertainment".

I just don't have time for those types of things in my life anymore because Jesus, His Word, and what God does for my mind and heart became more important to me. I am consumed with my relationship with Him and that makes everything else in my life richer and fuller. I have tasted and seen how good a healthy and intimate relationship with God is and so now I do everything I can to cultivate and grow deeper in that relationship. God is wanting the same kind of relationship with you and the amazing thing is, God will actually give you the desire and passion to pursue Him if you will just begin to ask Him for it in prayer. Let this be your prayer and the intent of your heart, *"God please place a deep desire into my heart for Your voice, presence, Word and Spirit. Thank You God for the burning passion and desire to pursue You Lord, in Jesus Name I pray! Amen."*

3) SET A READING PLAN UP THAT IS MEASURABLE, ATTAINABLE AND TIME SENSITIVE.

For instance I am going to commit to read the Bible 15 minutes a day, 5 days a week. This is measurable meaning you know if you achieved the goal you set or not, and it's also attainable; with that said make sure you set something that is doable for you. It may stretch you, but it's something you can make a daily habit of. Lastly this example is time sensitive; please make sure you set a time block where you can give the Word attention and allow the Holy Spirit to speak to you and ask God questions about what you are reading. For instance, when I don't understand something I read, I will get still and say, "Holy Spirit" and present my question then I will listen for His active voice which often for me comes in a flowing thought or a video type answer that plays in my mind that relates to the question I asked. Then I reread the area of scripture that I have questions about and oftentimes God will give me Wisdom on it that I did not have before. If you don't sense anything don't get frustrated, keep reading and seeking God's Word and be on the lookout for His answer. There have been times two weeks after I have asked Him a question, I will be reading the Word or a daily devotional and it's like the answer jumps off the page at me. I know that's God speaking to me. I also utilize online commentaries, the Strong's Concordance and the Vines Bible Dictionary which will give you Hebrew and Greek meanings of words in the Bible as well as Biblical history, cultural practices which will give you greater insight and understanding of the Bible. There are a lot of resources you can use to get answers and enlightenment to the scriptures. I always encourage people to allow the Holy Spirit to lead you in reading things on the internet. Make sure you have a peace about what you are reading. You can even ask a trustworthy person in your local Church for guidance.

4) INTERACT WITH THE WORD OF GOD THROUGH THE HOLY SPIRIT.

As you are reading, underline things that stand out to you, highlight passages that seem to speak to your heart and then write notes throughout your Bible on what you sense God is saying to you and showing you. My Bible is all marked up, written in, highlighted with notes everywhere. The best way you can honor God's Word is to get it into your heart and interact with it. Also, asking the Holy Spirit to explain things to you and give you examples of how this applies to your life is a great thing to practice. Listening to what you sense God is telling you is key. In any relationship listening to what the other person has to say is vital in developing a strong relationship with that person, the same is true with God. Ask God questions about what you are reading for example: What is this passage saying to me? What does it say about God? Is this a promise of God? Is this a statement by God? How does this apply to my life? As you ask God's Spirit that lives in you these questions give Him time to open your mind up to the answers. The answers to these types of questions usually will come to you in flowing thoughts of peace and wisdom, videos that play in your mind about past events that may apply to this scripture or maybe God plays the scene out within your imagination of what you are reading. I often get flowing thoughts from the Holy Spirit that will open up the scriptures for me in a way I can understand them. Remember the Word of God is a seed. The seed, just like in nature, has all the power within it to produce a plant and fruit if it is planted, watered, and gets sunlight. We all know plants take time to grow. So does the Word of God! The more you get it into your heart, the more questions you ask, the more it will grow in your heart and the more wisdom, guidance and fruit you will gain from it. Some people say they don't understand the Bible. However, like anything else it takes: time, attention, commitment and action to develop and cultivate a mind that is guided by the Word of God. It's like learning a new song. At first, we don't know the words but after singing it several times we learn the song by heart. The same concept is applied to learning our multiplication tables or our ABC's. We learn them by heart through repetition and a decision to learn them and apply them to our lives. For example when you're reading and studying for a test you generally have to read and study the material over and over again.

Have you ever been reading something for your job or studying for a test, or something like that, and you have no idea what you just read? We all have had that type of experience at some point in our lives if we are being honest. So what do you do? Well you go back and read it again and study it for your test until you understand it. The same is true with the Word of God. Sometimes you have read a passage several times, or maybe even looked up some additional information about the passage on the internet. The point is in the natural we will reread and research what we need to learn for a test or a job but when it comes to spiritual things and the Word of God we often times don't think to do that. Personally I just kind of threw my hands up and said I don't understand this stuff. I thought I was just suppose to get it because I believed in Jesus. I now know that I am not alone in that thinking. Now I recognize that this is not an effective way of thinking when it comes to growing in the Word of God and in my relationship with Jesus. So now, because I know better, I do better! I pray, now that I have shared this with you, you will do better also! The Word of God is in some ways the same as the examples used above except for God's Spirit will actually guide you, help you and empower you to understand the Word of God and to apply it to your daily life!

When reading the scripture, as we shared above, pause and listen and ask "God how does this apply to my life, is there anything I need to confess to You, repent of or receive from You". I often pray and listen as I read the Word and I pause and allow God to speak to me. As I read and listen, if I sense God is saying "you have an issue in this area" I will go through confession, repentance and receiving His forgiveness, thus allowing the Word of God to clean my heart and transform my mind (we have included a step by step process of confession of sin and repentance in Chapter 2). It's important to interact with the Holy Spirit while reading the Bible. As you make it interactive you allow God's Spirit to teach you and guide you. Your interaction with God, while listening to and reading the Word, will vary depending on what you're doing at the time and your circumstances. Just keep an open mind about interacting with God. The most important thing is that you are reading and listening to God's Word. He loves that and He will bless your time and effort abundantly even when you don't feel it. Also don't get caught up in performance or perfection. I use to think I could only read God's Word at certain times, like when I felt I could give it my undivided attention, or that I have to read my Bible because I have been sinning. This kind of thinking causes guilt and shame, which will limit your relationship with God. It's a bunch of lies from the devil anyways.

While you do want to have devoted quiet time where you can read the Word and interact with God, the Bible says to keep His Word before us all the time. There are days that I read or listen to 5 to 10 chapters or even several books in the Bible. At other times I get so caught up in what God is showing me and saying to me in a particular passage that I don't get past the first paragraph of the first chapter that I am reading. The most important thing is keep giving the Word of God time and attention on a daily basis in your life. Just like your smartphone needs new updates that make the phone run smoother and fixes problems within the software of your phone, you need a new download and updated software from the Holy Spirit by renewing your mind with the Word of God daily.

5) CONFESSION OF GOD'S WORD OVER YOUR LIFE ON A DAILY BASIS IS A KEY TO MAKING IT A PART OF YOUR MINDSET, PERCEPTIONS, BELIEFS, THOUGHTS, WORDS AND ACTIONS.

This causes continual growth, transformation and breakthroughs in your life! The word "confession" in this context meaning declaring, proclaiming and speaking by making verbal faith statements based on what the Bible says about who you are (your identity and value in Christ), what you have (God's Promises to you) and what you can do (your access, authority and power in God).

Jesus, when teaching His disciples about how to pray effectively with authority, taught the power of faith filled confessions. Previously, in the scripture below, Jesus had spoken to a fig tree for being unfruitful and commanded that "no one shall eat from it again". Afterwards it withered up from the roots and died. His disciples seeing this phenomenon asked Him how His verbally spoken words could affect the physical and material world. So Jesus answered and said to them, **"Have faith in God. For assuredly, I say to you, whoever says to this mountain, 'Be removed and be cast into the sea,' and does not doubt in his heart, but believes that those things he says will be done, he will have whatever he says. Therefore I say to you, whatever things you ask when you pray, believe that you receive them, and you will have them. Mark 11:22-24 NKJV**

Notice Jesus said for us to do the speaking and confessing. So by faith we are to speak to the mountains in our lives; meaning the areas within our lives where we need change, transformation, blessings and breakthrough. Then by continually believing in faith within our hearts, which in this case is referring to the human spirit and saying what God says about our "mountains", we will have whatever we continually say and believe by faith in God's Word. Notice it said to "not doubt in your heart". The Bible did not say "in your head", so you can have doubts come into your mind but have belief in your heart by confessing what God says

about yourself, another person or situation and still experience breakthrough. So we see how powerful faith filled confessions can be. True
"Bible humility" means to put yourself under the Word of God and being
God reliant instead of self-dependent. Meaning, you are whoever the
Word says you are, you can do whatever the Word says you can do, and
you have whatever the Word says you have, no matter what or how you
feel at the time, what your behavior has been good or bad, what the
natural looks like or what varying religious beliefs say. When you put
yourself totally under and subjected to the Word of God that is true Bible
humility by definition. For example the Bible says you are in Christ and
you have been made His righteousness, holiness, and you have His power
residing in you that's who you are, you are a joint heir with Jesus Christ, a
son and daughter of God the Father (2 Corinthians 5:21, Romans 8:17).
That means if you are a Believer in Jesus Christ you are righteous,
meaning you are in right standing with God whether you feel like your
behavior or conduct has warranted it or not! The Word says you will lay
your hands on the sick and they will recover so through God you have the
authority and power to heal others through the mighty name of Jesus
Christ no matter what you feel or see; you are to believe and be a doer of
the Word (Mark 16:17). That means the healing power of God comes
when you lay your hands on the sick no matter what you experience in the
natural. The Bible says you have the total and complete forgiveness and
removal of sin by the precious blood of Jesus and that His blood cleanses
you of all sin, no matter whether you feel forgiven or not, that is what you
have in Christ (1 John 1:7,9).

Basing your thoughts, words, value, identity and actions on the Word of
God no matter what it looks like in the seen or natural realm is true humility, as defined in the Bible and thus in the sight of God. For years I suffered
with this false sense of humility thinking I will never be good enough or
righteous before God because all of the sin I had committed. Because I
heard all these preachers say, to a bunch of born again Believers in Jesus,
that we are all "sinners" and then they would even quote the same scripture
"No one is righteous, no not one, we have all fallen short of God's
glory"(Romans 3:10) and then I saw you needed to be righteous to benefit
from God's wisdom, blessings and favor. So I always thought to myself if I
can just be a good enough person maybe one day I will be righteous and
have it all figured out like these people in the Bible. All the while if I had
just read the Bible for myself that statement above in Romans 3:10 is in the
Bible, but if you keep reading in the Book of Romans it qualifies us to be
made the righteousness of God in Christ Jesus!

"The righteousness of God which comes by believing with

personal trust and confident reliance on Jesus Christ (the Messiah). [And it is meant] for all who believe.

For there is no distinction, since all have sinned and are falling short of the honor and glory which God bestows and receives. [All] are justified and made upright and in right standing with God, freely and gratuitously by His grace (His unmerited favor and mercy), through the redemption which is [provided] in Christ Jesus, through faith.

This was to show God's righteousness, it was to demonstrate and prove at the present time (in the now season) that He Himself is righteous and that He justifies and accepts as righteous him who has [true] faith in Jesus." Romans 3:22-26 AMPC

So all the time I was made Jesus's righteousness, holiness and wisdom and did not even know it! So today I can stand in true Bible humility and say I am the righteousness of God in Christ Jesus. I have the same right standing with God as Jesus does because I have been made His righteousness! Now I live with a righteousness consciousness, instead of a sin consciousness, meaning I live with a mindset and awareness of being made righteous through the blood of Jesus Christ and I live from a place knowing that my righteousness, holiness and relationship with God is irrevocable and not based on what I did or do but what Jesus did for me. I am no longer a "sinner saved by grace", I am no longer a "sinner" at all now that is not my identity, I am a born-again son and saint of God! The Bible says I am no longer a "sinner" I am a "saint", the Bible over and over refers to "the Church" which is you and all the Believers in Jesus worldwide as well as the local Church assemblies as "saints". That does not mean I no longer sin but when I do sin I repent, I thank God for His forgiveness and worship Him for making me the righteousness of God in Christ. No longer being a sinner means my identity in Christ has changed when I gave my life to Jesus the old nature in me died and God made me into a whole new creation, He gave me His Nature through the Holy Spirit and made me into His Righteousness. So now since I have given my life to Jesus I am a saint of God, I am a son of God and my value, identity, worthiness and forgiveness is in Christ. For the Bible says in 1 Corinthians 15:34 to awaken to your righteousness consciousness and sin not. So I moved from righteousness not being something I do, but righteousness being who I am. It is my identity in Christ. So therefore as a by-product of my identity being the righteousness and holiness of Jesus, since I am righteous and holy, then I produce the fruit of righteousness in my life. It is a totally different mindset, instead of trying to be something I am not, I have become who God says I am through believing the Word of God about my identity and developing an intimate relationship with God. So therefore, what I do is no longer who I am, but it is who I am in Christ that causes me to do and take action on my identity and value in Christ as a beloved son of God. So a son of God is who I am and preaching is what I do. My value is no longer in what I do for a living or what others say about me but in who the Bible says I am in Christ. I pray my personal journey of finding out who I am in Christ supernaturally shifts your perspective to one of righteousness consciousness and you begin to believe and confess, "I am the righteousness of God in Christ Jesus" based on God's loving Word!

Faith Filled confessions will produce the positive self-image of God inside of your being, and will transform your soul and your life. As your soul goes so will your life! Your life will go in the direction of your predominant thinking and the words you speak. Therefore, your life will most often only rise as high as the level of the verbal confessions you make about yourself and others. Everything in the universe started with God speaking words. The Bible tells us God used words to create the entire world and everything in it except for humans. God chose to breathe His Spirit into Adam, in order to create mankind in the image of Himself and unlike all the creatures on Earth God gave humans the power of words. We still live in a world today that is shaped and dominated by the words people speak. Words create images inside of you for example if I said the words "royal blue baseball cap" in your mind that created an image of what I said. In the same way, if a child is told they are worthless, it creates an image of worthlessness inside of them which leads to all kinds of issues. However, if a child has faith filled positive words of value, positive identity and worthiness based on the love of Jesus spoken over them growing up, they will have a similar image of the worthiness and value only found in Jesus inside of them based on the words they had spoken over them. Words have creative power! The Bible tells us that "life and death" are in the power of the words that we speak and those who love to speak those words will eat the fruit of their words either for life and blessings or for death and curses. (Proverbs 18:21)

Ask yourself this question. How did you come to believe the negative things you believe about yourself and your life? I submit to you that it was through the words spoken over you by your parents, family, classmates, spouse, coworkers, others in your life, yourself and the demonic enemy. So how do you change your life and increase your self-worth and self-esteem? This is accomplished by hearing, thinking, speaking and acting on the faith filled loving and powerful Words of God. Think about every negative, fearful, condescending and non constructive word that has been spoken over your life by the enemy, others around you and by yourself and how they have affected your life and self-esteem. Now imagine your life if none of those words were ever spoken and instead they were replaced with faith filled loving words and affirmations. How different would your life be? Would you feel differently about yourself, others and even God? If we are being honest with ourselves words have had a great impact on our lives. So how important and vital does that make confessing the Word of God over our lives and the lives of others in our life's path especially those closest to us? Vitally important. Because our identity is based on the narrative or the story we tell ourselves about ourselves. Thus what we tell ourselves is what we truly end up believing and acting upon. That is why it is so important to know and confess the truth of what God says about you! A practical way to do this is to create and write out your own personal "I am" page and read it over yourself a couple of times a week. You can do this by writing down all the positive things God says about you in His Word, write down everything good about you that you can think of and every positive attribute, gift, talent and ability you believe you have. If you are having trouble finding positive things about you in God's Word there are plenty of resources on the internet. When I was doing this I Googled "Who I am in Christ scriptures" and found a whole list of resources. I also asked the people who are the closest to me what positive things they saw in me and I wrote that down on the list as well. The page starts with the statement "I am" and then you begin to declare each faith filled positive thing over yourself making the overall statement that this is who you are and your real identity in Christ. I did this several times a week for months when I was working on believing, receiving and establishing my identity of who I truly am in Christ and who God has made me to be. I still go back to this list from time to time to read it over myself and it is always refreshing to my heart.

Confessing the Word of God over your life will cause the image of Jesus, which is our true identity, value, worthiness and righteousness in Christ to be formed inside of us. Thus we become the Word of God physically in this world for all to see and experience God through His love, grace and Holy Spirit within us. As we confess God's Word on healing, prosperity, peace, love, value, righteousness; those words create images which begin to form on the inside of us. Then we begin to see ourselves as being whole, healed, delivered, prosperous, righteous and valuable; therefore we start to take action on what we believe and see. At the same time God is moving on your behalf in the spiritual realm to bring His Word to pass in your life! ***"Let us seize and hold tightly the confession of our Faith without wavering, for He who promised is reliable and trustworthy and faithful [to His Word]." Hebrews 10:23 AMP***

How I use confession throughout the day is when I run into situations that I might have a tendency to get worried, fearful, irritated or doubtful I will stop scattered and racing thoughts by confessing God's Word when it comes to the situation. So for example if I begin to think about something that is going on in the future with my finances that can often create worry I begin to pray over and confess the Word of God over my finances in that particular situation "Lord I thank You that You said in Philippians 4:19 that You will meet all of my needs according to Your riches in glory by Christ Jesus and that in Psalms 23 that The Lord is my shepherd I shall not want for anything! I thank You Lord that Your blessings and favor cover my finances, in Jesus name." I might make that same type of confession 5 to 10 times depending on how many fearful thoughts I get about that particular situation. I have developed these confessions based on God's Word. They are tools in my spiritual toolbox and weapons of warfare in my fight to continually stay in faith. There are specific confessions I use for specific situations and I would encourage you to sit down with God and come up with some of your own regarding things such as blessing your body, mind, life, understanding and wisdom, finances, family, marriage, school and work.

I often have people say to me, "This hearing Jesus, understanding the Word and the Bible confession stuff just does not work for me. Just because I hear, say and read some words my life is supposed to change, I don't believe it. I got real problems." That too is a confession of faith in the negative sense, not a good one but a confession nonetheless which has the power to keep you bound up and thus hindering your relationship with God, as well as your life, purpose and destiny. There is a difference in knowing about the Bible and knowing about Jesus versus knowing Him intimately and being in love with Jesus, tuning into God's frequency, seeking out and following His voice and applying the Word of God to your life through the power of the Holy Spirit. You see growing up attending Church I knew about Jesus and the Bible for many years of my life, I was even saved and baptized at 12 years old. However, little in my life actually changed, I still felt far off from God and somewhat empty inside. But when I came to know Jesus, His Word and His Spirit and applied this intimate knowledge of Him to my life and heart everything in my life began to change and increase. To the point where the emptiness was gone and the void I had always sensed in my heart was finally filled! God, just like the loving Father He is, warns us what you don't know can hurt you and effect your life in a negative way. **"My people are destroyed from lack of knowledge. Because they have rejected knowledge." Hosea 4:6 NIV** These passages are referring to having a working heart level knowledge of God's Word, intimately knowing God for yourself and acting by faith upon that knowledge. **"Therefore my people go into captivity for lack of knowledge." Isaiah 5:14 New Heart English Bible** For many years as a

Christian my lack of intimate working knowledge of God and His Word caused destruction, bondage and captivity within my life through various self-defeating and limited mindsets but not anymore! Because now I know God's Love, Word and Spirit intimately and I choose to personally apply my experiential working knowledge of God to my life on a daily basis! Now reading, hearing and confessing the Word is about coming to know Him more intimately.

Let me give you an analogy I think we can all see and relate to very easily when it comes to applying Jesus, His Word, Spirit, Blood and Name to your life because this book and God are all about practical application. Let me start out with a simple question. Can you walk past soap and your hands get cleaned? Can you look at soap and your hands get clean? Can you read all about the soap and its chemical makeup and your hands get clean? Can you work in or go to a soap factory and your hands get clean? The answer to all of these questions is of course "no". You have to grab the soap, turn on the water, apply the soap to your hands and thoroughly rub your hands together, then rinse them off and dry them to get them clean. You have to apply the soap, you have to have an encounter, and interaction with it, and then comes the transformation from dirty hands to clean hands. Likewise owning a Bible, looking at your Bible, knowing about God, going to Church or even working in ministry are all great things to do however, they are not the foundation of an intimate and healthy relationship with God. You have to apply Jesus, His Word, Spirit, Blood and Name to your life, you have to have encounters, interactions and intimate fellowship with God and through that relational process comes the life transformation! The Bible says for the Word of God to always be coming out of your mouth by faith in order for your life to be truly prosperous and successful (Joshua 1:8)! So let's look at some more application.

If I get irritated with someone I will say "Lord I thank you that I am a forgiver and Your Word says love even your enemies and pray for them (Matthew 5:43) so Lord I forgive this person who has irritated me and I pray blessings over them and their family and I cast and release this irritation over to You in Jesus Name" (1 Peter 5:7).

I have struggled with self-image and self-worth issues throughout my life. So, I will often confess God's Word concerning my value and identity in Christ, whenever I get negative thoughts about my worthiness and/or my body. For example, I will say, *"Lord, I thank You that my value is in You, that You love me so much You gave Your life just for me (John 3:16). Lord, I thank You that I am fearfully and wonderfully made by You, and I am Your treasured possession, and You did not give me a spirit of fear but a Spirit of power, love, and a sound mind. Lord, I thank You that I love myself, and I am worthy of Your love!"* The Bible says in Proverbs 18:21 that ***"the tongue***

has the power of life and death, and those who love it will eat its fruit." The reality is what we are speaking to ourselves and others, is actually bringing those things into being.

Notice in these confessions I used what I call "affirmative thankful prayer;" that means I am speaking to God and to myself about who I am, and what I have in Christ, and I am thanking God that is who and what I am. When the will of God is known you can always use affirmative thankful prayer. Most of the confessions that I pray are based off of God's Word. Therefore, you can actually thank God for His Word and what it says you have in Him. You also can pause and listen to God after the confessions and ask Him, "God, what are You saying about this confession and also what are You saying about the lies I am hearing? Give me some truth, Lord." Then these flowing thoughts will often come to your mind about God's truth in regard to the situation you are dealing with or maybe you will experience a sense of peace come over you. This will often lead you to confessing more of God's Word and goodness over your thoughts, feelings, and circumstances. It also allows you to have some interaction with God that grows faith, trust, and intimacy; just like in any other relationship with healthy communication.

6) MEDITATION ON THE WORD AND THINKING ABOUT IT THROUGHOUT THE DAY.

Meditation involves the same energy as worrying but with one exception that makes all the difference. With meditation, you turn your focus to the POSITIVE FAITH FILLED POWER of God and His Word. Worry holds you captive with fearful and defeating thoughts. If you're anxiously thinking about something over and over again, you know how to worry, and that means that you also know how to meditate. Now is the time you TAKE CONTROL and meditate on God, as you talk to Him about anything and everything in your daily life, and then you listen to what you sense He is saying to you. God is always speaking. We just have to get on His frequency; which is what this book is designed to do. Meditation on and in God's Word brings revelation a revealing of God's nature, ways, character, will and Word in real, personal and powerful ways and revelation brings manifestation. The word manifestation means to show fourth and to make known, it is where Bible truths become a reality in your life (Strong's 5321). Thus bringing the unseen spiritual realm into the seen physical realm where you can personally experience the Word of God and spiritual realities coming to life in your life!

The Bible actually says meditation on the Word of God which in this following verse is referred to as the "Book of the Law" is a key part of living out God's success plan for your life! **"Keep this Book of the Law always on your lips; meditate on it day and night, so that you may be careful to do everything written in it. Then you will be prosperous and successful." Joshua 1:8 NIV** I will often get one scripture and just say it over and over again throughout the day, and I'll ask God questions about the scripture. "God, what are you saying to me personally in this scripture? How does this apply to my life? What do You want me to do in response to this scripture? Am I currently living this scripture out in my life effectively? Lord, how can I incorporate this scripture into my daily life more effectively?" I will carry on this back and forth conversation with God. Sometimes, I write down what I sense He is telling me. As I think on the scripture(s) over and over again, it becomes part of my perceptions, rules, values and thus, my daily thinking and decision-making. Throughout the day I practice meditation, visualization and daydreaming about Bible stories, scriptures and the parables and sayings of Jesus. For example, meditating on 2 Corinthians 5:21 AMP literally, changed the way I view my value and worth as a son of God. **"He made Christ who knew no sin to [judicially] be sin on our behalf, so that in Him we would become the righteousness of God [that is, we would be made acceptable to Him and placed in a right relationship with Him by His gracious lovingkindness]."**

So, as I meditated on this scripture, God began to open it up for me, and I still use this scripture to boost my self-esteem and self-worth in God; whenever I don't feel worthy, righteous, and good enough. Being righteous, means to be in right standing with God morally, legally, and relationship wise. It means God does not count your trespasses and sin against you. He put it all on Jesus so when God sees you, He in essence, sees the goodness of Jesus within you! That's GOOD! I remind myself that it does not matter how I feel, God says I am valuable, I am righteous, I am worthy, I am His son, and my value and my worth is not in what I do or don't do, how much I serve, or who I help, but it is in my identity in Christ, as a righteous son of The King!

I sometimes struggle with performance-based Christianity. Trying to work harder, be better, serve more, do more, and give more. In the right context, these can be good things. However, when you begin to base your value, worthiness, and identity on how good of a person you are, how much better you are than some other people you know, or how much "worse" someone else is than you that you perceive is getting blessed, you have now left grace and entered into the "law of works". The Bible says, that trying to live by the law of works, you have fallen from grace and Christ is of no effect to you in your life (Galatians 5:4). This means you block and hinder the blessings of God's grace that He wants to do within your life. I use to suffer from the trap of comparison all the time! I would say things in my mind like, "Lord, You should bless me because I am a good person and I do more than so many of the people I know and I see You are blessing them!" I would say things like, "Lord, I am not 'as bad as' that person and I do more 'good' than this person and it seems to me like You are blessing them, Lord!" You see I was basing my value on the social norms or what I perceived as being "good" or "not as bad" and I unintentionally and unknowingly took myself out of the position of God's grace to effectively operate in my life as a son. I was basing God blessing me and loving me on my own works, self-effort and my limited self-perception instead of God's grace and His righteousness that He gave to me through my faith in Jesus out of the Father's love for me as His son. Comparing yourself to other people, being critical of others and basing your worthiness of God's love and grace on your perceived performance will steal your joy, rob you of your peace and hinder blessings and breakthroughs in your life. This type of thinking also creates frustration and bitterness in your heart.

Even now, sometimes I will feel like I have not helped enough people today; I need to give more; I didn't do enough for God; I did not see anyone healed today; I had some really negative thoughts today; I don't feel like a son of God; I don't feel righteous; and I don't feel forgiven. At those times, God brings this scripture, as well as some others, to my mind in order to remind me, I am not what I do and I am not even what Christ does through me. I am a righteous son of God, and my value and identity are in Christ alone. He paid for me on the cross; which is the most expensive thing God had to give, His only begotten Son's life, in essence God's own life! You see, the cross is not just about the forgiveness of my sin. It's also about the revealing of my value as a son of God and what He was willing to sacrifice and pay to get me into Heaven and also to get Heaven, His Holy Spirit, into me.

Through meditating on and in God's Word I came to realize Christianity is not a religion. It is a life-giving, transformative, creative inhabitation of Jesus Christ abiding in you through the indwelling of the Holy Spirit. The value of something such as a product, commodity or service is based on what someone is willing to pay for it. God owns everything in the universe, He made it. There have been studies done by various scientists and space exploration companies that estimate that the asteroids floating around space have hundreds of billions of dollars in natural resources in them and that's God garbage, the stuff that He didn't use to make into planets or stars! So how much are you worth? God gave His very own blood and surrendered His life just for you! That is how much He loves you and that is how much He knows your worth! You are worth the blood of Jesus! You are worth the most valuable thing that Heaven had to give and the streets in Heaven are made of pure gold! Come on! It is time to wake up to your worthiness in Christ! You are worthy because God bought you back and freed you from the slavery of sin with His very own blood through Jesus Christ and He put His Spirit in you as a Believer! It is time to realize that you are worthy, valuable, loved and cared for because God says so! He backed up His Words with the blood and life of His only begotten Son! You are worth the very blood and life of Jesus Christ, God's one and only begotten Son, who was fully God and fully man and God humbled Himself and took the form of flesh just to have an intimate relationship with you because you are worth it! You are worthy because Jesus said so and He demonstrated it on the cross, as well as by giving you the Holy Spirit as a seal of your worth! So next time you have thoughts of unworthiness, shame, doubt or fear, realize your value and identity in Christ and that He says you are worthy and worth His very life!

When I meditate on that truth in the scripture it reminds me of my value as a righteous son of God. I want to encourage you to meditate on the scriptures to build your faith, love, identity and value in Christ!

7) MAKE A PRACTICE OF READING THE SCRIPTURE IN THE FIRST PERSON.

I began to practice this with John 3:16 and Psalms 91, I would often confess the Psalms personalizing them putting my name in the Bible where it reads as a personal love letter to us, which it is. This exercise was foundational in building my faith, hearing God's voice, and being rooted and grounded in my identity and value as a son of God. Psalms 51 and Deuteronomy 28:1-14 are two of my favorite scriptures to practice this with. Here is an example of what I am talking about: *"For God so loved Sterling, that He gave His only Son, so that since Sterling believes in Him I should not perish but have eternal life. For God did not send His Son into the world to condemn me, but in order that I might be saved through Him." John 3:16-17* (Personalized for Sterling Harris).

3

PRAYER

A TWO-WAY DIALOG WITH GOD

PRAYER IS ANY TIME YOU INTENTIONALLY TURN YOUR HEART TO communicate with God. There is no special formula you need in order to pray and communicate with Him. God simply wants to hear from your heart. He knows how you feel and what you are thinking already! He is looking for you to talk with Him about your daily life and involve Him in every area of your life. This is a KEY to living a victorious life in Jesus Christ. God created us to worship Him through a relationship with Him and placed a void in our hearts that only He can fill with His Presence. Prayer is about a personal relationship with your Heavenly Father. It is about having your focus on Jesus Christ and it is about a two-way communication and intimacy with the Holy Spirit. Prayer is not about a list or a one-way monologue. It's about a Love Relationship with God. Prayer is any communication with God and can take on many forms. You can pray out loud by yourself; you can talk to God within your mind; you can pray "breath prayers" where you can talk with God under your normal voice tone. Any time you open your heart to God in any way He is always there. Here is a simple but profound truth. God wants to speak to you more than you want to hear from Him! God is just waiting for you to open your heart and listen to and receive His love and communication.

This relationship is like any other. It is built on communication and knowing each other intimately through personal experiences. When you pray, you speak and then you listen as prayer is a two-way communication that entails talking to God about anything and everything in your life on a daily, moment by moment basis. Just like any other relationship, at various points in your conversation, stopping to listen to what is being said to you by God is vital. It is even more important to exercise this practice of listening to what He is saying to you in prayer because this is where you will get your sense of relationship from and ultimately your guidance. In my personal experience, listening to what God is communicating to me is where I feel the most fulfilled and it is the part of my relationship with God that I was missing for so many years. Who really wants to be in a relationship where the communication is one-way? The answer is no one truly wants a relationship like that including God! This is a Biblical truth, God wants to be intimately involved in every aspect and every area of your life, and it does not matter big, small, and everything in between because it is all important to Him. Receiving this truth alone and acting on it can change your life forever! ***"Draw near to God and He will draw near to you." James 4:8 (ESV)***

So who is the person you talk to the most? Yourself, of course. We all talk to ourselves all throughout the day. This internal communication with ourselves can easily be directed to God in the form of prayer and worship. If you can talk to yourself all day long, why can't you talk to God? You can! It is simple. When you open your heart to Him, He sees your honest effort, and He hears you! People often think they cannot find time to pray. The reality is prayer is communication and you are doing that internally all day long with yourself. As you realize throughout the day that you are talking to yourself, you need only to turn your conversation towards God. Instead, talk to Him about all things as you ask for His direction, guidance, will, love, peace, and joy to come into your mind and heart. This is a form of practicing God's Presence which is you being intentional about keeping your focus and inner dialogue with yourself 'God centered' and engaging God throughout your day. Instead of just talking to yourself, engage the Holy Spirit within you in conversation and be mindful of God in you and around you. Most of my daily communications with God are conversations based on our friendship, companionship and loving relationship. When you think about it in those terms, talking to the Creator of the Universe makes more sense than talking to yourself. The power and beauty of it all is that we have unlimited access to Him that was bought and paid for by the blood of Jesus! Whenever you pray and communicate with God I would invite you to approach it through this filter, lens and mindset.

WHEN IN PRAYER THERE ARE 5 KEYS THAT YOU WANT TO KEEP IN MIND AS A FILTER TO VIEW PRAYER THROUGH:

1) Pray in complete transparency with God, real conversations, in complete love and intimacy with God. Don't hold anything back be open,

honest, vulnerable and real. Because God already knows the situation. What He wants is a healthy relationship and daily two way conversations with you as His son or daughter. Be completely open and transparent before Him.

2) Pray like God is near you, lives inside of you and is always with you, pray as if God is not far from you because all of those statements are true for every Believer in Jesus. For Scripture is very clear, *"God has said, "Never will I leave you; never will I forsake you." Hebrews 13:5 NIV* Some people will say, "yes the Bible says that Sterling but what about when Jesus said on the cross; *'My God, My God why have You forsaken Me'? Matthew 27:46 ESV* Didn't God leave Jesus at that time because Jesus became sin for us?" I have even heard some preachers preach that the Holy Spirit left Jesus on the cross. The short answer to both of those last two sentences is emphatically, no. God the Father did not leave Jesus on the cross and no the Holy Spirit did not leave Jesus on the cross. This always bothered me when I would read it because the Bible seemed to contradict itself but I never bothered to do my own research. So when I began walking closer with God and came upon this verse again I started studying the context of what Jesus was saying and after doing my own research I found out Jesus was actually quoting Psalms 22 and alluding to Him being crucified on the cross as the fulfillment of that Scripture. *"My God, my God, why have you forsaken me? Why are You so far from saving me, so far from my cries of anguish?" Psalms 22:1 NIV* After reading this Psalm myself, I came to realize it foretold of Jesus Christ's sufferings, especially while He was on the cross, in detail over 1,000 years before Jesus came physically to the Earth and died on the cross for our sins and so that the Holy Spirit could come and live inside of us! I would invite you to read Psalm 22 for yourself, it is totally amazing! This Psalm talks about the piercing of Jesus' hands and feet, the Romans soldiers casting lots to divide His garments and many more mind-blowing details! Therefore, you can be assured God will forever be with you and within you as a Believer and Follower of Jesus! So always stay God inside minded as you talk and listen to God's voice and being watchful for His activity in your daily life. God is always speaking to you everyday the real question is are you tuned into His frequency and aware of His love language with you?

3) Pray out of *bold desperation*; meaning you want and need His Presence, you want His love, and you want all of Him. Boldly realizing that He loves you and wants to talk to you more than you want to hear! Realizing that without Him you don't truly have anything. God loves a person that is *boldly desperate* to know His love, presence and ways. This does not mean begging God to love you and to talk to you. He already loves you and He is

already speaking to you and longs in His heart to have a deeper relationship with you based on healthy communication and love.

4) Pray as if you are in a two-way conversation with God because you are! Remember to pause and listen for the Holy Spirit to speak to you. Try and listen just as much as you talk, if you keep this mindset you will stay mindful of listening to God. Listening is an essential part of prayer, it is where the intimacy in your relationship with God is built through the two way interaction between you and God.

5) Pray from a place of thanksgiving and praise. Praising and thanking God for who He is, how much He loves you, who you are in Him as His son or daughter, and for His promises in His Holy Word to become a reality in your life. This is positive affirmative thankful praying. This is where you pray the solution and the promises of God *over* and *to* your situation. For example "Lord I thank You for Your love and Your goodness, I thank You for Your Favor over my life, I praise You Lord for adopting me as Your son, Lord I am praising You that all of Your promises over my life are done and fulfilled in Jesus Name!" One of the seven Hebrew Words used for the praise and worship of God in the Bible is the Word *"Towdah"* (to-daw') which means to extend or raise your hands in thanksgiving for something that hasn't yet occurred or that you haven't yet received (Strong's #8426).

I believe praise and thanksgiving are the highest forms of faith when you thank God by faith for things you have not yet received that are based on the righteous expectation of God being good to His Word, nature and character which is really what Biblical hope is (Strong's G1680). Biblical hope is something that is certain but you have not yet taken full possession of it in the natural realm however, in the spiritual realm it is already yours. A modern day example of Biblical hope is when I received a full scholarship to play college football at Southern Methodist University (SMU). I signed a contract with them which was a letter of intent to play football for SMU in February but I did not start college till the fall semester. So when people asked me where I was going to attend college, my "Biblical hope" was to start SMU in the fall semester based on the letter of intent I signed which was legally binding for SMU.

So I was basing my "hope" on SMU being good to their word and the contract I signed with them, even though I had not physically taken possession of what had been promised. The same goes with God I am basing my hope on the righteous expectation of God being good to His Word, even though I have not yet taken possession of it in the natural realm. So now when I read the word "hope" in the Bible I apply this meaning to the context of what I am reading and not the "wishing" connotation most people think of when they hear the word hope. ***"Let us hold fast the*** *confession of our hope without wavering, for He who promised is faithful." Hebrews 10:23 ESV*

When Jesus was telling us how to have faith in God and how to move mountains in our lives; meaning praying and getting results He said: *"Therefore I tell you, all the things you pray and ask for — believe that you have received them, and you will have them. And whenever you stand praying, if you have anything against anyone, forgive him." Mark 11:24-25 HCSB*

Notice He said, *believe you have already received the things you're asking for by faith.* How do you do that? By affirmative thankful praying. For instance if I tell my 6-year-old godson that I am taking him to a water park on Friday and it is Monday, he is going to praise and thank me all week long for taking him to the water park. He is also going to tell anyone who will listen, with excitement, that his Uncle Sterling is taking him to the water park on Friday. He might even throw in a comment about what an awesome Uncle I am. What is he doing? He is believing, or having faith, in my word to him and he has received in his little heart that he will be going to the water park on Friday. God wants us to have childlike faith just like that in the things He promises us in His Word and through what His Spirit tells us.

When I pray I often speak God's Word over my life while praising and thanking Him that it is coming to pass; meaning the promises I am thanking Him for based on the Bible are becoming reality in my life. It is important to understand the Biblical truth that God in His goodness has given mankind free will, dominion and authority on the Earth, which is the delegated power to act on His behalf as managers of this world. God set up these spiritual laws which even He chooses to operate within. So in essence God, by His own design, wants and in some cases needs, your prayers, cooperation and consent to take action within the Earth, your life and in the lives of others! This is one of the great truths to understanding the power of your prayers! As you keep these 5 keys in mind as a filter and lens to view prayer through; you will see your prayer life grow, flourish and expand. That will cause your prayers to become more effective and powerful! Let's be honest we all want our prayer life to be more effective and powerful. If we didn't you wouldn't be reading this book!

God is not limited in the ways He speaks to you this is a Spirit to spirit exchange. God can choose to communicate with you in a variety of ways and combinations some of which we will cover throughout this book. However, God's active voice generally fits into 3 main categories which also can be in a variety of ways and combinations.

1. Visual, this can be an image, series of images, video, vision, text

or words that you see within your mind. These inner visual experiences can range from being extremely vivid to very faint. They can also be visual in the sense of experiencing an outward projection of your mind and imagination upon the physical world around you kind of like you seeing a faint hologram. This is often referred to as "seeing in the spirit" meaning God is utilizing your mind and imagination to project these hologram like images on to the physical world around you to show you spiritual realities through His divine perspective and insight. These internal visualizations can be interpreted literally, figuratively or metaphorically depending on what God is trying to communicate to you. This is an aspect of what the Bible refers to as having *eyes to see*, it is talking about your spiritual eyesight and perception.

2. Inner auditory, which often come as flowing thoughts in your mind that are usually accompanied by a sense of peace, hope and wisdom. The series of words, impressions and thoughts from God is also known as the *still small voice and the delicate whispering voice*. This is an aspect of what the Bible refers to when it talks about having *ears to hear*, it is talking about your spiritual hearing and perception.

3. Kinetic, which comes through senses of peace, joy, comfort, goose bumps, tingling, warm sensations, eyes watering and other types of physical senses that come through spiritual experiences and encounters with God's presence. These senses can also come with an inward knowing or an impression you get about what you are feeling and sensing.

Why do we focus on these 3 main categories when it comes to God's active voice? Think about this, if Jesus came to model for us how to live our lives by having an intimate relationship with our Heavenly Father and Jesus Himself stated He only said what He hears the Father saying and Jesus only did what He saw the Father doing and the Bible says Jesus sensed things within His Spirit from God then you too as Believers in Jesus are supposed to be able hear the Father's active voice, see what the Father is showing you and sense what God is communicating to you. (John 5:19,12:49 Mark 2:8).Therefore, it is only right that as followers of Jesus you are able to spiritually hear, see and sense what God is saying to you through the Holy Spirit just like Jesus did as our model and Savior!

You want to keep a sense of expectancy in receiving answers from God, and don't stop listening and looking for God's activity until you sense God is speaking to you. Just like in any human relationship, the more you develop this dialogue, the easier it will become to hear God and sense what He is communicating to you. It is important to remember that God speaks to us all differently so no two relationships with God are the same! Our mission here is to shed some light on various things we have experienced so that it might help you identify and develop your own two-way communication and love language with God. I also want to caution you to not try to box God into communicating with you in the ways you normally hear Him. Don't expect Him to speak in just one way. He speaks in various ways, so take into account God's active voice, His activity around you, as well as confirmations of what you sense He has been saying to you and showing you. It's God's love language with you. God speaking to you can be as simple as an inward knowing and the sense God is within you, listening to you and guiding you as you talk to and connect with Him. God will speak through all kinds of activity, details and confirmations with His purpose always being to draw you into a deeper intimate love relationship with Him and cultivating your heart to be more in line with His! It is important to be fluent in God's language; His Word, because some of the ways He communicates in prayer is by bringing a Scripture to your mind or a spiritual principle that will seem to be an answer and a response to your dialogue with Him.

Visually God wants you to see things from His unique perspective, often times differently than you may have previously experienced. He may accomplish this by visually showing you a situation in your mind in image and video form. This enlightenment will come with a sense of peace, almost a knowing, that will make things more clear for you and answer some things you were talking to Him about. The images, scenes and videos that you see within your mind's eye can be literal, figurative and metaphorical word pictures of what God is communicating to your heart. Some literal examples can be that you see a scripture or a phrase within your imagination or a memory or a scene from your past within your mind that gives you a direct answer to what your praying about. For instance you ask God what He thinks about you and then you see the words "You're Mine. I love you" in big golden letters and the background of the screen in your mind is bright white. In this case even the colors you see in your mind have meaning to them. Biblically gold stands for value, royalty and sonship and white stands for purity, holiness and God's presence.

Years ago after I began to hear God's active voice, but before I made the commitment to full time preaching and ministry, I asked God what my purpose in life was. At that time I was still thinking about continuing my career solely in the business and sales field. Then I saw a vision of me preaching on a platform to 1,000's of people and then I got a memory from my childhood of dreams I use to have of speaking to large groups of people and I thought as a child that meant I wanted to be the President of the United States because that is the person I associated with speaking to large groups of people. As God brought these images of me preaching and snapshots of scenes from my life to my mind I realized God had been calling me to preach His Word since I was a small child but I always felt disqualified and inadequate to be a preacher. I had a false perception that I was not "good enough" to preach God's Word and that you had to be "perfect" to represent God on that level. Those were all lies from the enemy and my own self doubt that almost derailed my whole life and purpose. It was in that moment of hearing from God in such a powerful way that all of the shame, guilt and feelings of disqualification about preaching seemed to melt away in His presence and be removed from my heart. That is what hearing God's active voice and encountering His presence for yourself can do! It is powerful and life transforming!

Figuratively God loves to use word associations, word pictures, puns and object lessons to create colorful imagery in speaking to us visually. I was working with a woman who was really struggling with giving her life to Jesus and the truth of Him being the only way to have an intimate relationship with God. I shared the gift of salvation through Jesus Christ with her but she told me she was still unsure. I smiled and told her "it's ok, Jesus is going to show Himself to you because of the Father's love for you!" As I said that, God put it on my heart to walk her through a couple of activations in hearing Him for herself. In this case God "put it on my heart" by me seeing myself visually in my mind taking her through some exercises in hearing God. She went through Exercise #1 of this book and as she did she saw in her mind a picture of a large stone and then a pathway to a high mountain with a beautiful stream of water running out of the side of the mountain. At first she had no idea what it all meant but for me I had a sense of what God was saying to her. Because I had experienced Him using these kinds of images before, as well as knowing what the Bible has to say about these images, and as she was telling me what she saw God began using His active voice coupled with some of that prior knowledge to download to me what He was saying to her. I explained to her that God uses word associations, word pictures and figurative language which are object lessons for what He is trying to communicate to us.

As she was sharing what she saw there were several scriptures that God brought to my mind to give me an interpretation of what He was saying. It was like putting together a wonderful God inspired love puzzle! The large stones stood for Jesus as the great cornerstone and I saw the word "Peter" in my mind and I knew God wanted me to show her the verses referring to Jesus as the "cornerstone" in the Book of Peter in the Bible. As this happened I got goose bumps on my arms and from the top of my head down my back which God uses as a spiritual confirmation of His Presence which is like Him kinetically saying, "Yes, what your spiritually hearing, seeing and sensing is correct and from Me". When I flipped open the Bible to the Book of Peter, she and I got more than we bargained for! God was answering a lot of the questions in her heart about giving her life to Jesus, Him being the only way and in two verses she realized God is real, He listens, He loves her and that He wanted a personal relationship with her through Jesus Christ!

"As you come to Him, the living Stone—rejected by humans but chosen by God and precious to Him you also, like living stones, are being built into a spiritual house to be a holy priesthood, offering spiritual sacrifices acceptable to God through Jesus Christ.

For in Scripture it says: "See, I lay a Stone in Zion, a chosen and precious Cornerstone, and the one who trusts in Him will never be put to shame." 1 Peter 2:4-6 NIV

As she read the scriptures for herself she said that it was like God's love was speaking to every fear she had been thinking about in relation to making Jesus the Lord and Savior of her life. After that we unpacked the rest of the vision together as both of us stood in awe of God's love and how such a simple series of images could communicate so much truth! The path that she saw in her vision stood for Jesus as well. Jesus is referred to as "the way" (John 14:6). That way lead to a mountain which in a positive context in the Bible stands for a meeting place with God and encountering His presence we see this with Abraham (Genesis 22) and Moses (Exodus 19) in the Old Testament and with Jesus in the New Testament (Matthew 17). The flowing river she saw coming out the side of the mountain has great meaning as well. Jesus referred to the Holy Spirit as a "river of living water" that will flow out of those who believe in Him (John 7:38). Also on the cross after Jesus had died He was pierced with a spear in the side to ensure He was dead and out of His side flowed water and blood which was a clear sign that Jesus was in fact already dead. These images can have other meanings as well, depending on what God is showing you and the context of what you're asking Him about. In this case God was making it clear to her that Jesus Christ is the way to salvation and the transformation of her life. Later that week she gave her life to Jesus Christ based on the personal encounter she had with God!

God also loves to use metaphors and similes. A metaphor is a figure of speech that is used to make a comparison between two things that aren't alike but do have something in common (YourDictionary). For example one of the times I asked God how much He loved me I saw a beach scene in my mind. As I was looking out at the sea and at the sand on the seashore I got the following thought "more than all the water in the ocean and all the sand on the seashore" God was metaphorically describing His love for me. Other images I have seen God use frequently are triangles, which are 3 sided just like God is 3 in 1. God the Father, God the Son and God the Holy Spirit. Crowns; which symbolize God calling you into His royal family, favor and sonship. A red heart standing for the love God. In beach scenes God is often communicating that He is a place of peace, joy, love and rest. Various forms of water a river, spring, ocean and lakes are images for the Holy Spirit, refreshing of your soul, a body of Believers and provision. These images can be very defined or very faint within your mind's eye depending on the circumstance either way ask the Holy Spirit what the images you're seeing mean as well as take the time to research what the images could mean Biblically, literally and figuratively.

A simile is a figure of speech that directly compares two different things. The simile is usually in a phrase that begins with "like" or "as" (Your-Dictionary). An example of this is when I asked God who He was and I saw this flaming fire and then I got the flowing thought "I am like a flaming fire of love that never burns out! I am your Daddy!" The Bible is full of this type of figurative language so it only makes sense that as God speaks to us actively He would use word pictures, word associations, symbolism and other metaphorical images to communicate with us. People often ask me, "Sterling, why does God not just give me a straight answer? Why does He use a lot of figurative images and sometimes symbolic vague language?" I use to ask God that same question and then He showed me that throughout the Bible God uses imagery, symbolism, word plays, puns, parables, prophetic pictures and figurative language, it is a pattern within His nature. He is also inviting us to discover and experience Him in a real and personal way that takes faith, trust, and intimacy within a daily relationship. God is looking for sons and daughters that will follow Him on a daily basis and allow their lives to be guided by faith through the Holy Spirit. We see this same thing modeled in the life of Jesus. He often spoke in parables which are stories that illustrate moral and spiritual lessons. These can seem like riddles or puzzles in story form in which the listener has to think about, ponder and seek God for the meaning and application to their lives. Jesus used and still uses these parabolic stories to culture people hearts. For those of us who search for the message within the story God is trying to convey to us, and seek Him for the meaning and application to our lives will get understanding and insight into what Jesus is truly saying to us individually and collectively today. So when you think about God's voice and activity through that filter it makes sense why God's active voice would be full of the same kind of imagery, symbolism, figurative language and why by our human estimation God can be somewhat vague in His guidance. Because all of those things take effort to search out the meaning, faith to believe and daily reliance on Him. However, to God He is speaking clearly for those that have spiritual ears to hear, spiritual eyes to see and the faith to continually seek after Him!

Inner auditory is the realization and acknowledgment that you hear a voice inside of you, a voice that is smarter than you that brings wisdom, hope and peace through very wise thoughts, you know it is God speaking to you in an inner auditory way through your conscious. As you seek God's active voice you will hear in your spirit a still small inner voice that comes with a flow to it of love, hope, peace and wisdom. That still small voice may just be a phrase such as "Follow Me" or "Trust Me" or "I've got you", or it may come to you more directly. In my personal experience, God has rarely spoken to me in an audible voice. It is not the normal way I have seen Him communicate with most people on a regular basis, but as we have stated previously, all relationships with Him are different. When we look at the life of Jesus as our model we see Him spiritually hear, see and sense what God is saying internally through the Holy Spirit on a daily basis. In the New Testament we only see God speak three times audibly two were to the people around Jesus and only once to Jesus directly in an externally audible way. However, Jesus spiritually communicated with God on a constant and continual basis internally through a Spirit to Spirit exchange. I would suggest this be the model you seek to follow and pattern your spiritual life after. It is also the model and pattern we will will spend the majority of this book covering. So even when you don't sense anything on a subject in an inner auditory type of way, by faith, expect an answer to come to you by being watchful for God's activity to speak to you, and for Him to answer you in other ways.

There may be kinetic manifestations of God's presence and physical confirmations that people experience in prayer such as: the goosebumps, feelings of heat, warmness and electrical sensations in certain areas of your body, sensations of coolness and wind, tingling sensations, your forehead itches or tingles, a feeling of peace, eyes watering, tears, eyes burning, the top of your head tingles, a sense of someone touching you or pressure on certain body parts like God is putting His hand on your shoulder to comfort you, nose tingling, joy rushing over you and even crying. Other physical senses people have experienced is a sensation in their spirit of uneasiness, this feels like something almost vibrating, or scratching you from the inside like anxiety or a lack of peace about something. On the other hand an intense spiritual laughter and joy can manifest in a time of prayer and worship with God. There is also a sense of an inward knowing such as when an idea or a wise thought comes to your mind or you read a scripture and you feel like God just winked at you like He is saying "I got you My child"! During your daily personal conversations with God so often when you pause and listen what you will receive is a kinetic inward knowing that He is listening to you and you may have a sense He is with you which both these senses are always true and this sense from God while simple can also be your answer and your comfort from Him. Knowing inwardly He is guiding and directing you. You can also experience a sense of lightness in your spirit like a weight just got lifted off of your shoulders or chest. Another example is when you get a flowing wise thought after you ask God a question or ask Him to give you His perspective on a situation that comes with a sense and feeling of peace. God is always present with us and as a Believer in Jesus the Presence of God lives within us through the Holy Spirit. So you are a carrier of the very Presence of God! In addition, when we refer to "God's Presence" in this book we are often referring to a sense of knowing that you are personally experiencing the "manifest Presence of God" which comes in various forms depending on the person. Such as the kinetic and physical experiences listed above, God's Presence can also be described as an inward knowing or heightened awareness of God being present with you and within you. Sometimes the room or the space that you are in seems to be spiritually charged in a way that you can sense God's energy around you. Where the atmosphere can become almost electric, charged with peace, love and power! *"You will show me the path that leads to life; Your Presence fills me with joy and brings me pleasure forever." Psalm 16:11 GNT* Personally when I sense the Presence of God I often experience goosebumps from the top of my head going down my back and on my arms and warm sensations of peace in my chest area. I also have a heightened sense of awareness of God being there with me and I sometimes even sense a weight of God's Presence tangibly resting on various parts of my body usually on my shoulder like the Father is comforting me and resting His hand on my shoulder. I have encountered and experienced just one of these sensations or a combination of them, or other manifestations of His Presence depending on how God wants to show Himself within the situation. Throughout this book we will cover these 3 main categories of hearing God's active voice through personal testimonies, exercises and other practical applications.

It's also important to know what the enemy's voice sounds like. When we refer to the enemy throughout this book we are referring to the demonic spiritual realm of the devil, evil spirits and demons. It is essential to understand that the devil himself, also known as satan, is NOT equal whatsoever to God. He is a created being. Meaning similar to humans God created him as a beautiful angel, but at one point he chose to rebel against God, was cast out of Heaven and is now a fallen angel. Unlike God, satan can only be at one place at one time but he does have an army of evil spirits and demons which fell with him. However, don't let that scare you at all for God is greater and much more powerful than all of the demonic forces combined! The army of God that is for you is much more vast and powerful than the demonic realm against you. *"For we are not fighting against human beings but against the wicked spiritual forces in the heavenly world, the rulers, authorities, and cosmic powers of this dark age" Ephesians 6:12 GNT.* There is a supernatural unseen realm in operation all around you. God is real and is at work all the time in and around your life. Angels exists and are ministering spirits sent by God and they are sent by Him to guard you and help you achieve your purpose and destiny in this life. There is also an enemy, a demonic realm of the devil and his demons that hate you and are trying to destroy your life and the entire world, through: evil, fear, shame, lust, confusion, isolation, unforgiveness, greed, pride, idolatry, depression, worry, unworthiness and sins of all kinds. They have the power of evil temptation and persuasion through demonic suggestion. Often times it is so subtle that people don't even know the enemy is talking to them and they are actually following the suggestion of demons.

It is important to understand a little about the enemy forces we are battling and the tactics they use. *"To keep satan from taking advantage of us; for we are not ignorant of his schemes." 1 Corinthians 2:11 AMP* There are so many people who don't even realize they are hearing the lies of the enemy through the demonic temptations of the spiritual forces of wickedness upon this earth which come from demons and evil spirits. They take these demonic temptations often in their most common form of negative thoughts, until eventually the way they personally think, speak and act towards themselves and others are affected by the lies they believed. This is often combined with the negative words of other people in our lives that the devil uses to create fear and unworthiness in our hearts. Oftentimes the people being used by the enemy do not know their own true created value in Christ as a son or daughter. They are often hurt themselves, are struggling with personal strongholds and are in some level of emotional pain so they in-turn are easily manipulated by the enemy through these hurts and therefore hurt others. If you don't speak faith filled words over yourself and to the negative voices, eventually you will begin to believe what they say!

Just like faith comes by hearing the Word of God (Rom. 10:17), fear, shame, anxiety, doubt and unworthiness comes from hearing the lies of the enemy. The enemy's voice usually comes with an accusatory or demanding type of tone. A tone that does not create the fruit of the spirit, like we covered earlier; it does not produce love and faith. God's voice is not demanding but innovational. On the contrary, the lies of the enemy produce fear, self-will, doubt, shame and guilt. These statements from the enemy usually start out with "you" type statements. "You are never going to get out of debt. Your kid is never going to turn around. You are a bad parent. You don't really matter. You have a dead-end job. No one likes you. You are unloved." The enemy also like to use "what if" statements to create doubt and unbelief. "What if it does not happen? What if God does not come through? What if it does not work out?" Demons also like to use "yeah but" statements in order to minimize, dismiss and devalue God's Word and activity in your life and who you are in Christ. "Yeah the Bible says you're valuable but no one really cares about you. Yeah, you are supposed to be a Christian but you know what you did the other day. Yeah, you experienced God in a powerful way but look at you now it didn't change anything you are still acting the same way. Yeah, you prayed, but nothing is really going to change. Yeah, God's Word says He will provide for your needs, but you don't have enough money right now look at your bank account." One of the schemes of the devil and his demons is to reduce the significance and impact of God's voice, Word, Spirit and activity in your life from having their maximum influence by coming in with various kinds of doubts and fears, which they know over time will subtly erode and hinder your faith in God's Word, your interaction with the Holy Spirit and your overall relationship with God.

After some time of the enemy speaking to you, at some point you actually start agreeing with them. You are never going to get out of debt, changes to I am never going to get out of debt. Your kid is never going to turn around and you are a bad parent turns into my kid is never going to turn around, and I am a bad parent. Why do people make bad decisions? They are based on lies that the enemy has told them, others have told them and the words they have told themselves. You are not going to be anything, you have no purpose in life, God is not gonna change anything in your life, you are on your own, God does not love you, you are a disappointment, your parents are ashamed of you. These "you" statements if they go unchecked and unchallenged change into "I" statements of ownership; I am a bad kid; I don't have a purpose in life; I am not liked; I am not smart; I am a disappointment; I am a failure; I am not good enough; I am on my own God does not care about me. See how after a while the ownership and the identities shift to false identities!

Thoughts of: I am a worrier; I am depressed; I can't forgive them; I am not going to be healed; I never get any good breaks; it is too late for me; become false identities, beliefs and perceptions. The enemy always tries to create doubt and fear in subtle ways. Even if he can just create a little fear, doubt and shame he knows over time he can create a wedge in your relationship with God. It's like a boat that during a journey gets a couple of degrees off course and it will soon be miles off course the longer the trip goes on without the boat being corrected. The devil comes after your identity. The reason why he originally fell from an angel to who we now know as the devil is that he wanted to rise above God. God speaking about satan in the Bible confirms this very truth, ***"You said in your heart, "I will ascend to the heavens; I will raise my throne above the stars of God; I will sit enthroned on the mount of assembly, on the utmost heights of Mount Zaphon. I will ascend above the tops of the clouds; I will make myself like the Most High."*** **Isaiah 14:13-14 NIV** That is why he tempted Adam and Eve in the garden of Eden he wanted to get the authority God had given to them because he figured with the blessings and authority God had bestowed upon them by making mankind in the very image of God that he could combine that with his own, then rise above God and take God's Throne. Of course we know that did not happen.

The devil started his temptation of mankind in the Garden of Eden by asking Eve a simple question ***"He said to the woman, "Did God really say, 'You must not eat from any tree in the garden'?"*** **Genesis 3:1 NIV** The devil used that simple question to place doubt in their hearts and minds which made them begin to question their value and their identity of who God had already made them to be and if God was in fact holding out on them with something they didn't yet have. In this case it was eating from the tree of the knowledge of good and evil which God instructed them not to eat from. Of course God was not holding out on them they were already like God made in His image and filled with His Spirit the only difference is they did not yet know sin and evil in their world. So in essence God's command was made to protect them, not to hinder or to hold out on them like the devil was suggesting. The devil will also try to ask you questions to make you question God's goodness, love and faithfulness as well as your personal value, identity and worthiness. This tactic is to get you to agree and partner with spirits opposite of the Holy Spirit such as the spirit of fear. In which you actually hand over your authority and power to the demonic influences of doubt, shame, anxiety, depression and unworthiness. The same authority and power Jesus sacrificed His life for us to get back that we lost because of the sinful fall of mankind. Garden of Eden type of questions such as: Does God really love me? Am I good enough? Am I wanted? Am I liked? If God's good then why did this happen in my life? Will God's Word really change my life? If you think about it in this context the whole world getting messed up started out with one question from the devil "Did God really say?" then he brought all kinds of misinformation, false accusations and fear. He is still using the same type of tactics today so be aware of the "what if, does God really, am I, why me, will God and did God really say" type of questions that can create doubt, fear and any number of unwanted consequences within your life. For me personally the questions of; "Am I good enough? Will I ever be good enough? Why does it feel like nothing I do is good enough?" have caused a great deal of fear, hurt, shame and pain in my life until those questions were answered through my love relationship with Jesus. Not to say I still don't have those types of questions come up in my mind and heart and try to trigger me and trick me into believing lies about God, myself and others but now I know how to battle and how to respond to them, with who God says I am and that in His eyes I am and have always been good enough! The key is to just be mindful and aware of fearful, devaluing and disempowering questions, thoughts, feelings and words. Then responding to them through the filter of God's Word, love and Holy Spirit.

If you look when satan tempted Adam and Eve he attacked their identity and value by saying ***"For God knows that when you eat from it your eyes will be opened, and you will be like God, knowing good and evil." Genesis 3:5 NIV*** Then when he tried to tempt Jesus the Bible shows us how he did it, ***"And the tempter came and said to him, "If you are the Son of God, command these stones to become loaves of bread." Matthew 4:3 NIV*** Then Jesus goes on to correct the devil with the Word of God and leaning on His identity and value as God's Son. You see Jesus always knew who He was and never had a case of mistaken identity. So, many of us suffer with the enemy speaking to us often unknowingly. I pray that these short examples will help you discern when the enemy is talking to you. The devil's intentions are still the same, he wants to rise above God but now he tries to do that within the human heart and mind by making our fears, worries, desires, needs, sins and problems seem bigger than God. The devil still wants to take God's Throne, except now the throne he wants to take over influence of and have power over is the throne room of your mind, will, emotions and life. The devil also tries to convince us that God is mad at us, that God does not want a relationship with us and that God does not care about us as His sons and daughters.

I have discovered once you recognize how the enemy sounds it is fairly simple to spot demonic activity because they usually try to create some type of fear, doubt, guilt, shame, unworthiness and demands that lead you away from God. The enemy's voice, like we stated earlier, is often in the accusatory second person, "you" are just talking to yourself; God is not speaking to "you"; "your" not worthy of God's love; your prayers are not going to change anything; you are not going to make it; God is disappointed in you, you can't go to Him after what you did. Before you know it, if you are not careful the enemy's voice becomes your inner dialogue, your identity, value and thus your personal reality. Such as I am not worthy, I am not going to make it, God does not speak to me, I can't hear Him. I suggest to people who are struggling with negative thoughts that as they start hearing negative things from the enemy if you want to hear the actual truth of God just flip what your hearing to the total opposite. By creating positive, faith-filled statements based on the opposite of the negative thoughts your having and begin to speak them out loud and you will, most of the time, be hearing what God's Truth is and what He says about you and the situation! It really is empowering to do a ninja flip on the devil in this way and it's very effective!

Do not allow the enemy to create doubt with thoughts like "Oh, you are just talking to yourself, that is not really God". That is the number one question and probably the number one struggle that people have is how do I know I am not just talking to myself? Remember, God's voice that comes from within you, His still small voice, the inner voice of God often sounds like the inner voice of your own conscious but it will come with a flow of peace, wisdom and love to it that will not be your own. The more you develop your daily communication with God, the better you will be able to tune into His frequency and hear His voice. It is important to know that hearing God will always be an everyday seeking and pressing into His Presence. Make sure when listening for God, default on the side of right-eousness, meaning you are listening for God's voice and seeking His guidance so default on the side of it being God's voice. As long as what you are hearing matches up with His Word, character and nature accept it as God speaking to you because God will always confirm what He is saying to you in various other ways as well which we will cover throughout this book.

Keep in mind that as we train up in discerning between the 4 voices we generally hear which are: 1) God's Voice 2) Our Voice/Self Talk/Con-scious/Self Narrative 3) Our Flesh (what our hormones and body want) and 4) The voice of the enemy; we grow in that ability to discern the differences and we enable the Holy Spirit to guide and direct us. The more we yield to God's voice, will and activity in our lives and the less we rely on our own self-will, the greater the sensitivity of our hearts will increase to make God based choices daily. We literally have thousands of choices a day to live on self-will and self-reliance or walk by the guidance of the Holy Spirit. Which is making choices based on God's will and Word making us God reliant and God dependent by using the Holy Spirit that lives inside of every Believer as our guidance and navigation system. So we live more by the Spirit and less by the flesh if we are paying attention and practicing hearing and submitting to God's voice and guidance.

"Praise breaks" throughout the day are a great way to practice staying in constant awareness of God which is often called "Practicing God's Presence". I say daily phrases like "thank You Jesus", "Holy Spirit I trust You", "Jesus I love You", " Holy Spirit guide me in this", and ""Father I love You" all day long, on an average probably 20 to 30 times. These acts of acknowledging, welcoming and celebrating God's Presence continually throughout your daily life is powerful and transformative. Thanksgiving and giving God praise is one of the highest forms of worship to God and something that brings you into the Presence of God having your awareness of God heightened continually throughout the day and as Believers it should be a way of life and a language to us. The Bible encourages us that, **"God inhabits the praises of His people!" (Psalms 22:3)**

The language of praise and thanksgiving is powerful and creates joy, peace, freedom, faith, love and so much more in your heart. I often start out my day with the Lord and especially in my quiet time with Him by thanking Him and praising Him for who He is, who I am in Him and what He has done for me! I will thank Him for His Holy Spirit in me, the precious blood of Jesus, His powerful Word and the beautiful Name of Jesus. I will thank Him for what they currently mean in my life and the power that they have over my circumstances. I will say "Lord I thank You for the precious blood of Jesus, I thank You that it has power to defeat any enemy, that it takes away all my sin, that it gives me bold access to You!" I do that throughout my day to reinforce an attitude of thanksgiving and praise which in turn creates joy and strength within me. Confessions and thoughts of praise and thanksgiving lift your heart, mind and emotions by developing and cultivating the fruit of God's Spirit in you which is love, joy, peace, patience, kindness, goodness, faithfulness, gentleness and self-control, and keeping the fruit of the Spirit alive and energized in your life. Understanding spiritual fruit has to be cultivated and grown. Think of yourself as a musical instrument of the Lord and when you praise Him you give off these beautiful sounds for everyone to hear and experience. These sounds continue to spread out into the whole earth, then they rise up to the atmosphere and reach up into the heavens. **"Rejoice always, pray continually, give thanks in all circumstances; for this is God's will for you in Christ Jesus." 1 Thessalonians 5:16-18 NIV** Notice the Scripture says God's will for you is to give Him thanks and praise all the time no matter the circumstances you are facing. You are not necessarily thanking Him "for" the circumstances, you're choosing to thank Him "in" the circumstances and choosing to praise God no matter what. Many people want to know God's will for their life, well here is the answer right here in the Bible! You want to live out God's will for your life? Then the foundation of living out God's will for your life is living a life of praise and thanksgiving to God!

You can and will experience God's voice, activity and presence as you practice involving Him in every aspect of your daily life. Especially inviting Him into things you enjoy such as music, artwork, working out, sports, video games, and outdoor activities. For instance if you play an instrument, draw or cook, practice praying to God thanking Him for His favor being upon you and what you're doing such as, "Jesus thank You for Your favor and blessings upon this time of playing and making music", "Father thank You for giving me Your creativity as I draw and paint", "Holy Spirit thank You for supernatural focus and strength in my sports game". Through inviting God's Presence into what you're doing you will experience God giving you new levels of creativity, focus, wisdom and strength. You will sing and make music with a level of empowerment you have never experienced before, artwork will seem to flow from your heart to your hand and your cooking will seem to have an extra special flavoring of love in it. No matter what it is you're doing in life, be purposeful to invite God into it through affirmative thankful prayer. I have found everything in my life is richer, fuller and better when you invite and involve God in it!

I encourage you to give God your racing, intrusive, negative or prevailing thoughts of lack, wants, worries, fear and stress. You do this through affirmative thankful prayer. Such as, "Lord I thank You for providing the resources I need for my bills, my car, my house, my kid's college fund. Lord I thank You for Your favor over this conversation with my spouse, boss, coworker, child. Lord I thank You for guiding me in this text, email, or presentation. Lord thank You for Your wisdom, favor and peace while I am taking this test or while I am doing my homework." This kind of affirmative thankful prayer can often be based on the opposite thoughts of whatever is causing stress, fear and worry. People often tell me they don't know how to pray I advise them to just pray the opposite of the negative thoughts you're wrestling with. This invites God's favor, blessing and peace in as well as keeping you focused on God's love, power, promises and presence. At the same time reducing your stress level in a major way. Plus the results that you experience on the things you involve God in and pray over on a daily basis are a wonderful way to encounter God's favor, love and activity in an intimate and personal way.

Realize whatever you focus on, you empower in your life. When you focus on negative things, those are the very things you empower in your life and they will affect you in negative ways. When you choose to focus on your relationship with Jesus and practice a lifestyle of praising, thanking and thus worshipping God on a daily basis you receive the joy, peace and love of the Kingdom's empowerment. Meaning you begin to know and experience the power of God at work in your life and you focus on the most powerful change agent in existence which is God's love, Word, Presence and Holy Spirit. Praise and thanksgiving lead to joy which is a huge weapon of warfare in the life of any Believer. This type of daily living filled with thanking and praising God has radically changed my life and keeps me free from the bondage of stress, fear, worry, anxiety and depression which I use to suffer from and it will do the same thing for you if you put it into practice in your daily life!

The Bible says, *"Through Jesus, therefore, let us continually offer to God a sacrifice of praise--the fruit of lips that openly profess His name." Hebrews 13:15 NIV*. When we offer praise and thanksgiving like that, it is a continual sacrifice. Think about it, we are to be a living sacrifice and in the Old Testament when they offered a sacrifice it took effort. You had to raise or buy the animal, take it to the temple, the priest had to prepare the animal according to God's Law, get wood, make a fire and burn the offering. It took effort to give a sacrifice to God. Today it still takes effort to be on fire for Jesus! Romans 12:1 says that we as Believers in Jesus Christ are called to present our bodies (our animal and self-willed nature) as living sacrifices which is called our reasonable (rational and intelligent) service, spiritual worship and act of worship. So in the Old Testament what did they do with flesh sacrifices? They always burned them with fire! Today we are called to put our bodies and minds under the influence of the Holy Spirit who was likened to fire throughout the Bible, and our lives are to be "on fire" for Jesus! *"In view of God's mercy, to offer your bodies as a living sacrifice, holy and pleasing to God--this is your true and proper worship." Romans 12:1 NIV* God is actually saying that to live as a living sacrifice is your reasonable, rational, intelligent and logical service, spiritual worship and act of worship to Him. God is calling all of us to be on fire every day for Jesus through intimate prayer, interaction with God's Word, having an attitude of praise and living in loving friendship with the Holy Spirit!

As we choose to be motivated by our loving companionship with God and worship Him we offer back to God the free will He so graciously gave to us by subjecting our freewill to the Lord's will for our lives. This offering of our will, compelled by our love for Him, is really ALL we can truly offer to God. As you come into daily fellowship with God and are led by His Word and guided by His Holy Spirit your life becomes a sweet smelling offering and a living sacrifice unto the Lord!

WAITING ON GOD IN PRAYER

Wait on the LORD: be of good courage, and he shall

***strengthen thine heart: wait, I say, on the LORD. Psalms 27:3
ESV*** Pausing, waiting and expecting the Lord to speak to you is a crucial part of hearing God. Sometimes I tend to hear or see something and jump out in front of Him in the midst of our conversation within my mind and heart, instead of waiting on the whole message and asking Him for clarity on what I hear, see and sense. It's like when we're kids and we would only listen to half of what our parents said to us and then we start doing it saying "I know, I know" "I got this", maybe some of us listened to our parents all the time but we all have probably done that at some point in our lives to someone. Unfortunately, I do that to Jesus quite often, even still, but God is patient with me and He will be patient with you too! So ask the Lord and wait for Him to speak and allow Him to get finished with what He is saying to you. Keep in mind nothing is ever wrong with God's broadcasting system it is always on and operational. God's voice is generally at the same volume and frequency it is just when something rises above that sound level or disturbs the frequency that you cannot hear God's voice. Sometimes it's our own thoughts, the cares of the world, the enemy's temptations, our fleshly wants and desires or just the reality of life in general can be loud at times, that is why it's so important to practice hearing God's voice on a daily basis in your life in things big and small. Remember God's heart desire is to have two way communication with you and for you to hear His voice, know Him and follow Him relationally on a daily basis; so be expectant!

EXERCISE #1: HEARING GOD'S ACTIVE VOICE

We are going to take you through a simple exercise on listening and hearing God's active voice. We have done this exercise with many people and time and time again they have experienced God in powerful ways! We are going to go through some practical examples of how God speaks actively so when these things happen you will know it is God speaking to you. You can think of this like God's voice as a flow of water and the pipe that the water of His voice flows through is partly clogged and needs to be unclogged and widened. What this exercise and steps are designed to do is pour Holy Spirit Drano down that clogged pipe and open it up so the water flow of God's voice and presence can flow freely through it.

There is no formula for hearing God, and God can choose to speak in a combination of various ways and often does. Our aim and goal is to give you practical examples of how God speaks the most often when we help people tune their hearts to hear God's active voice. Let's review the three categories of God's active voice that we covered earlier:

1. Visual, this can be an image, series of images, video, vision, text or words that you see within your mind. These inner visual experiences can

range from being extremely vivid to very faint. They can also be visual in the sense of experiencing an outward projection of your mind and imagination upon the physical world around you kind of like you seeing a faint hologram. This is often referred to as "seeing in the spirit" meaning God is utilizing your mind and imagination to project these hologram like images on to the physical world around you to show you spiritual realities through His divine perspective and insight. These internal visualizations can be interpreted literally, figuratively or metaphorically depending on what God is trying to communicate to you. This is an aspect of what the Bible refers to as having eyes to see, it is talking about your spiritual eyesight and perception.

2. Inner auditory, which often come as flowing thoughts in your mind that are usually accompanied by a sense of peace, hope and wisdom. The series of words, impressions and thoughts from God is also known as the *still small voice and the delicate whispering voice*. This is an aspect of what the Bible refers to when it talks about having ears to hear, it is talking about your spiritual hearing and perception.

3. Kinetic, which comes through senses of peace, joy, comfort, goose bumps, tingling, warm sensations, eyes watering and other types of physical senses that come through spiritual experiences and encounters with God's presence. These senses can also come with an inward knowing or an impression you get about what you are feeling and sensing.

Many people will experience inner auditory, flowing thoughts that come with a peace and wisdom to it. This is often referred to as the still small voice of God. They will often sound like the inner voice of your own conscience; however, it will come with a flow of love, peace and wisdom to it that will be from God. God will sometimes speak to you in the context of how you speak, it is as if God chooses for His voice to flow through your personality but there will be a slight difference in the flow of His active voice and your own conscience. Your inner voice will often have the subtle difference of feeling slightly unsettled within your mind and not come with a flow of peace and wisdom as God's active voice does. God frequently communicates with people daily in this way. These thoughts also come as impressions, where you get an inward sense of what God is saying to you, like God's Spirit wirelessly downloads something to your heart. It's as if something inside of you is telling you something without words. We have all made the statement "something told me to do this" or "I just felt this is my heart". That "something" is a person His name is Holy Spirit. I have found these thoughts often rise up and flow from your inner being to the middle of your mind. So positionally the thoughts from God often come from within you rising up to your mind. This is a pattern I have experienced and not a guideline or a formula it is just something for you to be aware of as you develop your spiritual ears to hear God's active voice. I have also seen God use music or tones for people that are musically inclined, for example I have had people hear trumpets, wind chimes, pressure in their ears, sense wind blowing in their ears or a particular song will play in their minds over and over again. There will be an inward knowing that this is not your voice but God is speaking to you. Having doubts as to whether you are talking to yourself or it's God speaking to you through these flowing thoughts are common things that people battle.

Keep in mind the 4 measurements earlier in this book that you can refer to as a gauge if it is God speaking.

1. Does what I hear, see and/or sense line up with the scriptures as well as the ways and nature of God which is love? God's voice and activity will always be in line with His Word, character and nature.

2. Does His inner voice come with flow to it, a sense of peace, love, hope and wisdom? This inner voice will often sound similar to your inner voice but it will come with a realization and flow to it that will be slightly different from yours.

3. Does it produce the "Fruit of the Spirit" as defined in Galatians 5:22-23? *"But the fruit of the Spirit is love, joy, peace, patience, kindness, goodness, faithfulness, gentleness and self-control ESV"*

4. Does it have the result of producing freedom and releasing you from bondage i.e. fear, worry, shame, anxiety, insecurity, depression, doubt or unworthiness? All divine truth has the ability to set people free and where the Spirit of the Lord is there is freedom (2 Corinthians 3:17).

As you practice listening to God and expecting Him to speak to you it will get easier to discern when you are talking to yourself and when God is speaking to you. Remember this is a NO FAILURE ZONE God is so joyful and pleased that you are making the effort to tune into His frequency! He is so excited and He wants to speak to you more than you want to hear from Him! God desires a relationship with you more than you want it and He is just waiting for you to open your heart to listen to what He wants to say to you! Creating a healthy relationship requires active listening and valuing what you are hearing from the other person. The same principle holds true for a healthy relationship with God.

During these listening exercises, many people experience a form of visual communication from God in the form of videos that play in your mind and images that you may see within your imagination that bring a sense of joy and a sense of peace. This visual communication will connect your heart with God and be personal to you. The images and videos will often be word associations, metaphors and word pictures and scenes that are object lessons for what God is saying to you. So ask yourself what do the images communicate to me, what does it make me think of and what do I sense God is saying to me through these images? When I first started listening and hearing God speak to me I saw words, phrases and script that came across my mind like a page on a computer screen. I still get a lot of my communication from God this way. I encourage you to pray into the images or videos you get and write them down especially when you don't understand what He is showing you. Asking God for further clarity is awesome in the sight of God, He is all about building a trusting relationship with you! You can ask Him, "Lord what are You saying about what I am seeing or sensing?" Then listen to what you sense He is telling you and showing you. It helps me if I journal down what I hear, see and sense from God in the notes section of my phone or make an audio recording of it. However, you choose to write it down or record it wither it be hand written, typed out or an audio or video recording I would encourage you to journal your experiences with God whenever possible.

Think about this naturally. In your everyday life you ask for further clarity when you don't understand what a friend is saying to you, why not ask God? Just like you ask a teacher in a classroom to explain something further to you or even go to a tutor for additional help. The Holy Spirit is our teacher, counselor, helper and standby! As you get words, images, visions or the inner video tapes in your mind these are answers. You may also want to pray into those answers to see if you can get additional guidance, clarification and confirmation from God. Also looking up what certain images mean Biblically will illuminate and often times clarify what God is saying and showing you. A couple of websites that I often use are John Paul Jackson's Dream Dictionary and Christian Dream Symbols which are free to use. As you look up anything God shows you using Biblical resources there will often be something that is highlighted to you and it will set well in your heart with a feeling of peace and contentment. It will be like your heart is saying, "yes that is it, that is the meaning" and it will come with a sense of accomplishment and peace. Sometimes you will not come to an understanding of what you're hearing, seeing and sensing until you begin to research what God is telling you and showing you. Don't dismiss what you're hearing, seeing and experiencing with God. Seek out the meaning by asking the Holy Spirit more questions and researching the meaning behind the words and phrases He uses as well as the images and visions you will see. Act as if it is God speaking to you, until you can prove otherwise, because most of the time it will be God speaking in ways you never thought of! God loves when you faithfully chase after His voice, activity and Word!

God is looking for a two way dialogue and for us to engage Him in conversation which builds intimacy and relationship which brings love, revelation, healing, value, worthiness and power! I also suggest asking God open ended questions because they leave more room for Him to communicate what He wants to share with you. For example: Lord what are saying about this situation? Lord what do You want me to do in response to these circumstances? Jesus what is the truth about this challenge I am facing? Then listen and allow Him to speak to your mind and heart.

People also experience God's active voice kinetically. They get a feeling of peace that seems to come through their body in the form of goosebumps, warmness or heat in various parts of their bodies, the feeling of wind on their skin, waves of joy, eyes burning, tears, a sense of lightness to them that almost is a floating feeling. Faint sensations of electricity and tingling within their bodies. An inner sense of knowing God is listening to you and what He is communicating to you. A lot of times people who have racing thoughts, or their mind seems to run constantly, will have a sense of peace over them. Their minds will be at rest and the racing thoughts seem to be quieted and stilled.

These examples are just that; examples of how we have seen God speak to people most frequently. These examples are given to heighten your awareness of God's activity so you will recognize it as you begin to do these exercises and live a daily lifestyle of talking to, listening and hearing God speak to you. This exercise is to get you activated in listening and hearing God's active voice and the more you turn your heart to listen to what God wants to share with you the more abundant your relationship with Him will be. This is a lifestyle, a daily practice and a yearning to want to hear from God knowing He wants to speak to you.

Now that you know some examples of how God is going to speak to you we can get started with the process of getting your heart into a place to listen to and hear God's voice. That way when you do experience God's active voice you will not dismiss it as you just talking to yourself, or your just causing yourself to think of those images within your own mind or your body just so happens to be sensing the certain kinds of kinetic feelings we described earlier in this book. Through my experience in helping people hear God's active voice this type of thinking is the most common hindrance to people hearing the voice of the Holy Spirit. After engaging in the exercise I often ask people what they experienced and so many times they will be in conflict, wondering if it was them talking to themselves and just making those things up or was it God. In those cases I will often ask people, to get them out of that mind frame, "Are your thoughts usually that wise, do you usually talk to yourself like that, do you usually experience those types of images playing within your mind or having sensations such as you're feeling now?" The answer to all of those questions is usually "no, I don't", it can be challenging for your mind to process the spiritual communication that is happening especially when you first start hearing God's voice. Self doubt is a common struggle. This is why we practically describe what God's active voice sounds like so when you encounter it you will be more aware of what you are experiencing and what God is communicating to you. Those types of questions above are ones you can ask yourself as well if your struggling with doubt about what you are experiencing as you engage your faith in hearing God's active voice. Remember God's voice is like a flow of water and the pipe which the water of His voice flows through is now getting unclogged, widened and will be totally unclogged. This exercise and steps are going to pour Holy Spirit Drano down that partly clogged pipe and open it up all the way so the water flow of God's voice and presence can flow freely. Even right now the pipe of your heart is expanding to hear God's voice in new and wonderful ways!

STEP 1: YOU WANT TO READ THE WORD OF GOD CONCERNING HEARING HIS VOICE OUT LOUD OVER YOURSELF.

This step will help bring more faith to this specific area of your life because the Bible says that faith comes by hearing the Word of God (Romans 10:17). The Bible also says the Word of God is alive and active sharper than any two edged sword and will divide the soul and the spirit (Hebrews 4:12). Reading what Jesus says about hearing God's voice is going to build your faith, divide your spirit from your soul (mind, will, emotions) and is part of the unclogging process so God's voice can flow into your heart. Jesus made it very clear in the Bible that it is God's will for us to know His voice and hear God's voice right now today. For more than 15 years of my life as a Christian, I had no idea that God actually still spoke to people but that was a lie I believed. God not only speaks to people everyday but He yearns to have relationship with us where we walk with Him, talk with Him and listen to His voice every single day of our lives, all day everyday!

Read these scriptures over yourself out loud. I encourage you to personalize them putting your name in them and changing the "you" to "I or me":

Jesus said, *"But He who enters by the door is the shepherd of the sheep. To Him the doorkeeper opens, and the sheep hear His voice; and He calls His own sheep by name and leads them out. And when He brings out His own sheep, He goes before them; and the sheep follow Him, for they know His voice." and in the same conversation Jesus declares, "I am the good shepherd." John 10:2-4,11 NKJV*

Jesus went on to say later in the Book of John speaking about the Holy Spirit: *"He will Speak whatever He hears [from the Father--the message regarding the Son], and He will Disclose to you what is to come [in the future]. He will glorify and honor Me, because He (the Holy Spirit) will take from what is Mine and will Disclose it to you. All things that the Father has are Mine. Because of this I said that He [the Spirit] will take from what is Mine and will Reveal it to you." John 16:13-15 AMP*

We know from these scriptures it is God's will and purpose for you to know His voice and to hear His voice. Notice it says the Holy Spirit will speak, disclose and reveal. These terms all denote God directly communicating with you. It is also important to know that Jesus gave His very life so that God's Spirit the Holy Spirit could live, inhabit and indwell each and every person who puts their faith in Jesus Christ as their Lord and Savior. Jesus paid with His very life so you can hear God's voice. Isn't about time we take advantage of and utilize what He paid for us to have?

STEP 2: PRAYING IN FAITH TO GOD AND CONFESSING HIS GOODNESS WITH THANKSGIVING AND PRAISE IS FOUNDATIONAL TO RECEIVING ANYTHING FROM GOD INCLUDING YOUR SALVATION.

All of God's promises are conditional on you doing something, even salvation. It is a free gift from God but the Bible says to receive Jesus Christ as your Lord and Savior you have to confess with your mouth Jesus is Lord and believe in your heart that God raised Him from the dead and you will be saved (Romans 10:9). So in this exercise we are going to do a confession to continue the process of opening up and unclogging that pipe so the water of God's voice can flow freely!

Pray this prayer in faith: "Jesus I thank You that I am your sheep and that I know Your voice and I hear Your voice. I thank You Lord that I have eyes that see, that I have ears that hear and I have a heart that receives, understands and is open to You. Holy Spirit I thank You that You are speaking to me in Jesus Name. I declare that I am a child of God and that I hear Your voice, that I know Your voice when I hear it and that I sense Your activity working in and around me. Thank You Heavenly Father! Amen."

STEP 3: LISTENING TIME!

Now that we have poured some Holy Spirit drain unclogger into that pipe the water of God's voice is going to flow freely into your heart! Before you start this last step you may want to go back and review some of the examples of how God speaks so they are fresh in your mind if you feel comfortable go ahead and let's start listening and hearing God's voice!

You are going to want to get in a relaxed position and in a place that is quiet so you can focus on God. As you develop an ear for God this will not always be necessary, but in the beginning for me it took a lot of practice to learn how to focus in the midst of noise or distractions. As you get in this relaxed position take a couple of deep breaths to relax your body and remember God really wants to speak to you, He loves you no matter what, because you are His child!

Then close your eyes and say out loud or under your breath *"Jesus I love You"* and then just relax and listen. Give God a couple of minutes to speak to you. During this exercise people often get a flowing thought back from God "I love you too" but again I have seen God speak in all kinds of ways during this activation. I want to caution you not to overthink it. You don't have to keep saying Jesus I love you over and over again; He heard you, He sees you and He wants to speak to you! This is a listening and hearing exercise so give God a chance to speak to you. If you find yourself not being able to focus just give yourself some grace, take a couple of deep breaths, relax, close your eyes and say the phrase again, pause and listen again. Keep in mind God is usually not going to talk over you, so if you keep on asking the question, thinking about what is gonna happen next, is God going to speak to me, what if He does not speak to me, and so on, that type of "mind chatter" is going to hinder you from listening and hearing Him so just relax, pause and listen. We suggest people close their eyes when they first start these exercises because we have found it helps most people focus and visualize what God might be showing you. Now I pray and listen to God with my eyes closed or open depending on the situation and what I feel God is leading me to do. Another suggestion that we mentioned earlier in step 3 is asking these questions out loud or under your normal voice tone. You can pray to God with the inner voice of your conscience and that is something I encourage people to do on a daily basis. However, asking questions and talking to God out loud or under your normal voice tone will help you focus and build relationship with God. So in these exercises we suggest that you start with that. You also want to ask God open-ended questions and try to stay away from asking God "yes or no" questions because they don't build a great amount of intimacy and the questions, by nature, box God in, instead of allowing Him to give you His perspective. A lot of the time I still speak to God out loud or under my normal voice tone; then I pause and listen. I have found this helps me to focus and hear Him with more clarity. I encourage you to try various methods and go with what works the best for you depending on the day and circumstances.

STEP 4: LISTEN, EXPECT TO HEAR GOD SPEAK TO YOU AND SENSE HIS PRESENCE. AFTER YOU DO THIS EXERCISE JOURNAL WHAT YOU EXPERIENCED AND WHAT YOU SENSE GOD IS SAYING TO YOU.

Always open your spiritual eyes, ears and senses to what God is doing and cherish it in your heart. What does it mean to live by every word that proceeds out of the mouth of God? It means to base your thoughts, feelings, emotions, words and actions off of the written Word of God and also the spoken Word of God which is what God is speaking personally to you. I have lived in His Word for years now and some are Bible promises while others are personal Words God he has given me about my relationships, finances, future and ministry through His active voice, dreams and visions.

Once you have tuned into God's frequency you can continue the exercise and ask:

Jesus how do You see me?

Then pause and listen, as is the case for the following 2 questions. This question is amazing because you get to hear from God's heart on how He sees you and what He relates to you. When I have done activations using this question people often experience images, scenes, words written in text within their minds and flowing thoughts are common.

Next question: *Jesus what gifts do you see in me?*

During this part of the exercise you may receive flowing thoughts and experience seeing words come to your imagination like text would on a computer screen. Your experience may be totally different and that's ok, this is the beauty of having a personal relationship between you and God. Continue to journal what you hear, see and sense God is saying to you.

Lastly ask: *Jesus what do You love about me?*

This will give you a chance to hear from your Heavenly Father's heart. What He says about you and the riches He sees in you. Remember what you continually hear, see, say and think, you become. So guard what you allow access, into your ears, eyes and mind! We all need to be built up and Fathered by God. This part of the exercise gives God a chance to speak fresh encouragement directly to your heart and give you the gifts He sees in you!

This exercise will help instill in you, your identity and value as sons and daughters of God through asking God what He loves about you, who He says you are, how He sees you and what gifts He has placed within you.

It's important to connect to God's frequency of love early and often. I do some form of this exercise most mornings before I get out of bed. I try to tune into God's frequency before I do anything. It helps get that snowball effect of faith going and it gets your heart in-tune with God's heart. I have found this practice helps me hear God and sense His activity with more ease during the day. It is important to relax and don't let the thoughts of life and what all you need to do that day overtake you.

Often a combination of life's demands, my mind wondering off and the enemy's subtle distractions try to rush me through my time with God so that my mind and heart get unfocused and easily distracted. This makes it harder to tune into God's frequency and sense what He is telling me. Let yourself have this time and don't let thoughts of your day take control. Schedule and give yourself at least five minutes where you and God can get connected first thing in the morning. We were made to connect with God, as well as other people, that is why social media has been such a huge phenomenon because that yearning to be connected is hard wired into our hearts.

People sometimes ask me, "Sterling what if I don't hear, see or sense anything from God while doing this exercise?" These cases do happen at times, for various reasons people will have trouble unclogging the pipe and allowing the flow of God's voice into their heart and mind. I suggest if this happens actually ask God this question. "God what is blocking me from receiving and hearing Your voice?" So many times God will actually reveal the answer to you through a flowing thought, or by some other means, what it is that's blocking the flow go His voice. Unforgiveness and unworthiness is probably the biggest blocker of the flow of God's voice in those cases. So at that point I take people through a confession that they are worthy and that they forgive whoever they are holding unforgiveness for, including themselves and God.

I also suggest you go back and read the scriptures above about hearing God's voice several times because faith comes by hearing and hearing by the Word of God. The more you hear the truth that it is God's will for you to hear His voice and that He loves you, died, defeated death and was resurrected just for you personally, the more faith will come. Remember to stir yourself up in faith and boldly begin to declare by faith "I hear from God, Jesus loves me, I command my heart to be open to the voice of the Holy Spirit in Jesus name!" Use these faith-filled declarations to change your negative confessions and thinking such as I can't hear His voice, God does not want to speak to me or this does not work for me or any other lies that your own self-doubt or the enemy will try and get you to believe.

The other thing is practice, practice, practice! Make listening and hearing God a lifestyle! How do you get good at anything? Repetition is key to getting better at anything you do. You train to hear God's voice, not just trying, don't just try every once in awhile but train up in the things of God on a daily basis!

It is just like when I started running long distance. At first I could barely jog a mile without wanting to collapse, but did I say running does not work for me? No, I knew if I kept training than it would work and that I would continue to build up my endurance. God's Word will always work no matter what you experience if you continue to do God's Word. Listening and hearing God's voice is similar to eating healthy and exercising. If you continue to work out and eat right you will eventually see results. It works for anyone that is willing to keep practicing and putting in the daily effort to do it. In your love relationship with God it is important to continually put yourself in a path of faith its just like if you keep going to the gym on a daily basis you have a better chance of working out than if you stay on the couch. I would rather be the big guy at the gym trying to get in shape, than the big guy on the couch wanting to get in shape but not taking any positive action to change my circumstances. At least when I go to the gym I am putting forth the effort to better myself instead of just accepting living in an unhealthy way that does not match up with what I want out of my life. Can you work out (going to Church, reading your Bible, talking to God) once a week, four times a month and expect to lose weight and tone up your body? No. You would have to work out 3 to 5 times a week and eat a balanced diet on a daily basis if you want to see powerful results. Would you only eat one time a day or a couple of times a week? No. You eat several times a day on a daily basis to keep up your physical energy. Likewise you have to feed your "spirit person" within you every day, just like, or even more than, you feed your fleshly body. You don't live off of yesterday's breakfast or lunch, you eat again the next day. It is always wise to be connecting with God, feeding your faith with the Word, training your soul to be under the power of the Holy Spirit and growing in your spiritual relationship with Jesus everyday. You want to stay in and on the pathway of God's Presence and Word.

In Mark 4:24 Jesus talks about what I refer to as the measure principal and the law of use. Jesus taught on this principle throughout the New Testament, to pay attention to what you hear for the measure you pay attention to and use what you heard, the more of what you pay attention to and use, will be given, or measured, back to you in a fuller measure. This can work positively or negatively depending on what you are thinking, saying and doing. So make sure what you are thinking, saying and doing is what you want more of. For example if you constantly are saying and thinking I don't hear from God then you will talk yourself right out of a relationship with God. Even though He wants one so bad with you that He was willing to be tortured, crucified and died and was resurrected in order to defeat death for you. So that He could have a daily, intimate and healthy relationship with you through the indwelling of His Holy Spirit within your spirit.

People who don't sense they are hearing from God may also want to practice relaxing, being still and not overthinking it. Don't let the enemy convince you that you are broken or that God does not love you. In other cases, if you hear anything fear based that does not sound like love that is either unbelief and doubt in your soul or the voice of the enemy or it could be a combination of both. If you do hear something fear based like that confess over yourself, "That is not the way I think anymore, God loves me and Lord I thank You that I am hearing from You." Then send the enemy on his way by confessing the truth of God's love over yourself. When I first started listening and hearing God it was hard for my mind to be still and for me to focus on God, I would get easily distracted. My mind would wander off on tangents to all kinds of places past, present and future. It would be everything from what I did last weekend, to some random thought about what I presently need to do, or it may be thoughts about what I needed to do at work or do in the near future. Even today I have to be intentional about being still, focusing in on God and listening to His voice. Then when my mind does get off track, I often pray His name saying "Thank You Jesus" lovingly giving myself grace and refocusing in on God's voice and presence. I would also get negative intrusive thoughts of all kinds. The enemy was often trying to put me into shame for having negative and often sinful thoughts and at first I even accepted the shame and guilt but then I realized I was accepting defeat. Then I began to say out loud or under my breath "I refuse those thoughts, I thank You God that You are protecting my mind and I am hearing Your voice and Your voice only!" I have confessed that saying 100's of times in my years of hearing God's voice. Command your soul to be still and listen and thank God that you hear His voice. Being still, focusing in on God and stopping racing and intrusive thoughts in your soul realm (mind, will and emotions) is a daily practice and takes time, attention, commitment and determined daily action.

As you train up in this on a daily basis more and more, over time it will get easier and easier to tap into God's active voice. However, even today I still have to intentionally strain, focus, and seek God to hear His active voice. I have learned how to listen and it has become easier because of practice and the intimate relationship I have developed with God over the years. We experience the same thing in our lives when we meet people. After a while we know their voice even if they were to call us from a different number we did not recognize or call us out in a crowd the closer we are to that person relationally the easier it is to know their voice.

For example, I can be in a crowd of 100 people and my mom can say my name and because I know her voice I will be able to tell that it is my mom calling my name because of the intimate knowledge I have built with her over the years. It's the same thing when it comes to hearing God's voice. The more intimate knowledge you develop by practicing listening to His voice on a daily basis the easier it will be to recognize His active voice and activity in your daily life. Believe that God wants to speak to you on a daily basis because that is what He longs to do! He lives inside you as a Believer so He is closer than the air you breathe (1 John 4:4).

I want to encourage you with a short testimony about the goodness of God, about His love and how much He wants to speak to you. I was working with a young man one night on hearing God's voice. He was seventeen years old and he had just given his life to Jesus: God had given me the honor of leading him into salvation. As I often do with new Believers, I talked to him about talking, listening, and hearing God's active voice and sensing His activity in his daily life as a vital part of building a relationship with God.

Salvation I often say is the first date with God; it gets the relationship started but there is so much more! The cool thing about God is that there is always more with Him! So, I take the young man through a series of exercises (like the questions we had you go through above). He was not getting anything that he could spiritually hear, see or sense. We did five rounds of questions and then he told me "maybe I am broken. Maybe God does not speak to me, Sterling." I told him, "God loves you so much: You are not broken, this does work and God wants to speak to you even more than you want to hear Him. Something right now is blocking your flow. Let's try another exercise." So, we do another exercise on listening to God and this time I ask God, Lord, I know you love this young man, I know You want to speak to him and I know he is your beloved son. So, Lord, please give me a vision or tell me something that I can tell him that he will know how much you love him and care for him.

I have my eyes closed as I am praying this prayer and talking to God about the situation because the enemy was telling me things such as "see God does not love him, you see it didn't work this time, this kids gonna be so disappointed and it is all your fault!" However, I know the enemy's tactics and I know what fear within my flesh sounds like and I know not to be moved by either one of those things, but talk to God and stand on the truth of God's Word and what He tells me personally. You cannot control what thoughts come to your mind and the enemy will try and get you to feel guilty and shameful about even having those thoughts.

However, you do have full authority, power and accountability on how you respond to those fear based thoughts and you respond with the truth of God's Word and seeking God and saying "God give me some truth to defeat this lie" and then listen to what the Lord says to you and shows you.

I am declaring and believing the truth of God's love throughout the whole time that I am doing these exercises; knowing and being fully assured by God's love and Word. As I am talking to God about this, I see in my mind a vision of a baby with a red heart shaped ornament like you would put on a Christmas tree. I say to God in my mind, Lord what does this mean? That he has a new heart in You because he is born again? Then the vision fast forwards and I see this young man as a kid about ten years old and he is holding this same heart shaped ornament and he is putting it on a Christmas tree. I am sitting here trying to figure out what God is saying to me and then I get the flowing thought. "You asked for a vision I gave you one just tell him the vision and it will mean something to him."

So, I was obedient to what I sensed God told me and I explained to the young man what I saw. Then I said "does that make sense or mean anything to you?" He looked at me puzzled and said "no, that does not mean anything to me". My heart sank into my stomach and then I heard the voice of the enemy; "See, now you look like a fool. You did not hear God. You are just talking to yourself. This stuff does not work." I refused those thoughts in Jesus name and said to him, "Well, bro, that is what I sensed God was showing me. This is not an exact formula or science maybe I heard wrong." This can happen; do not get so prideful that you think that you can't miss it. I have misunderstood God plenty of times, in the same way I have also misunderstood what people have told me at times in my life. That miscommunication does not stop me from communicating with people and the same goes for God! When you do miss it God will always get you back on the right track when you continue to seek Him daily. At the same time realize that sometimes what you are seeing and hearing may be something God is trying to show you and them for the first time or in a new way. When that does happen I let people know I am still learning how to hear God. I encourage them with how much Jesus loves and values them which is always 100% accurate! I will often talk to God again to see if He will give me any clarity on what I am hearing and seeing. I share with them anything I sense the Lord wants to say to them. It may be a scripture that comes to my mind or an encouraging word that seems to be on my heart to share with them. This all takes stepping out of your comfort zone by taking faith based risks.

Oftentimes people are just really amazed and honored that you are trying to hear God for them. I can also promise you this; God is never disappointed in your efforts to hear Him! He loves your effort because it is coming out of a place of love. Besides you can't ever let God down because He is looking for persistence and effort and not performance and perfection. Remember hearing God takes risk and is a no failure and no pressure zone. I want to encourage you to get as close as you can to Jesus, talk to Him and listen and expect Him to speak to you knowing that it is His will and good pleasure for you to hear His voice! So I am talking to God about what I sensed He was telling me to communicate to this young man as well as what I had seen in my mind earlier. Trying to get some truth from God to combat all of these negative thoughts I was getting and doing my best to stay in faith knowing God loves me and him. Before I can get a response from God the young man jumps out of his seat.

"Oh that can't be! That is crazy! I can't believe that! How could you know that! This is so weird!" I looked at him and said "Bro, help me out here! I don't know what you're talking about!" He said, "I was thinking about the vision you said God showed you and now it all makes sense!" I leaned in and listened intently on the edge of my seat. I said "Well, tell me!" He said, "I was thinking about the vision you told me about and when I was 8 years old I made a red heart shaped ornament at school and I put it on our Christmas tree that year!" I exclaimed, "That's amazing!! Go Jesus!!" He said, Even more crazy is that every year since then my mom always has put it on our Christmas tree and even at 17 years old it is still on our tree right now! My mom said that she is going to keep the tree up till I get home for Christmas in a couple of weeks! That is so crazy bro!!"

I smiled and lovingly responded, "No bro, that is not crazy, that's not weird, that's the love and favor of Jesus on your life! Your Heavenly Father loves you so much! He knows everything and not only that He experiences everything with you down to the most intimate detail!" His mom found out later that week about him giving his life to Jesus Christ and about what God had shown me and she started to weep at the goodness of God's love for her son. She even brought a picture to show me of the heart shaped ornament on their Christmas tree that very year! God speaks and He wants to speak to you and He wants you to want to hear His voice and listen and wait on Him expecting to hear Him!

This story is an example of God's love and an encouragement to you that if you don't get anything at first, continue to seek His active voice and communication with Him. It will happen! Keep on trying, listening and expecting God to speak because He will. I have seen it time and time again with vast amounts of people. I have done these exercises countless times in all types of individual and group settings with people of all ages, backgrounds and spiritual maturity levels. Such as the in-treatment drug rehab facility for young people God had me at for a season. Over time, I have seen breakthrough after breakthrough and incredible increase in people's relationships with God and hearing His active voice. If I can see God pour out in some of those challenging situations where the young people I am ministering to are struggling with all kinds of issues then God can, does and will speak to anyone, anywhere.

If God seems to be silent maybe you are asking the wrong kind of questions; such as "Why me?" God questions. I don't get a lot of answers to those because I am usually asking out of fear and being irritated or frustrated with myself, God or others. Maybe He wants to show you and talk to You about who He is and Who you are! So, ask Him God, "What are You saying about this situation that I am facing?" He wants to give us His Truth about who you really are! He wants to reveal Himself and His love for you! I also pray and ask God "Lord what do You want me to pray about and then I lift up whatever comes to my heart". I call this praying from Heaven down. This is a great way to pray more effectively and in line with God's will for your life. I have found God really likes when you seek Him out to lead you in praying from Heaven down.

Also, oftentimes people are expecting clear, direct, and specific answers from God on a situation. This may seem strange but God does not want you to just follow the directions He gives you. He wants a relationship and He wants a partnership and to be involved in your everyday life journey. Often times when I pray and ask God about a situation I get phrases like "Trust Me", "Follow Me", "I've got you, son", "Let go", "Forgive", "Have faith", "Be patient", "Be still", "I am here", "Step out on faith", "Just believe". I have found God loves these one liners! There can also be an impression that comes with these one liners where you get a sense what He is communicating to you. It's as if God uploads information to your heart through an inward knowing you receive from His Spirit. Within these short one line phrases God is letting you know that as you trustingly follow Him, He will show you what you need to do. Oftentimes He brings it about in such a way that explaining it to you would not make a lot of sense to you anyways, at least from a natural mind standpoint. He wants to show you as you follow Him. These are words of encouragement and guidance to continue on in faithful reliance on His Spirit, Word and love. He is letting you know that He has you in the palm of His hand and to keep living in an everyday relationship that allows Him to guide you and lead you into victory!

I have come to an understanding that I know will bless you in your daily walk with God. That God does not often just give you detailed instructions because He wants you to Follow Him in a daily relationship. He is all about leading you and speaking to you in the context of a healthy relationship based on two way communication, trust, praise, thanksgiving, intimacy, partnership and teamwork. God is not solely interested in you following instructions like so many people assume. He does not want slaves, He wants daily fellowship with you and for you to follow Him as a son or daughter of His.

I have often foolishly "told God" if You would just tell me what You want me to do I will do it. I think this is probably a thought process and conversation we all have experienced at one point or another with God. Lord if You would just tell me plainly and give me a plan or a map I will do it. I have found out this truth about Him, God wants a relationship before anything else and to develop your character to be more like Him. He wants to cultivate your heart with His love, voice, activity, Word and presence.

God is always looking to draw you into a deeper relationship with Him. Life with Him I often think of as a Holy Spirit treasure hunt, a huge puzzle and a wonderful riddle that is continually unfolding as I seek God. The Kingdom of God is built on you asking, seeking and knocking. *"Ask and it will be given to you; seek and you will find; knock and the door will be opened to you. For everyone who asks receives; the one who seeks finds; and to the one who knocks, the door will be opened." Matthew 7:7-8 NIV* When you live from this place of knowing, experiencing and receiving from God on a daily basis He will continually keep you filled with His love, peace and presence. As I was writing this God began to speak to me through a series of flowing thoughts and word pictures and He said: *"I want their hearts, minds and emotions to get in line with My Love I want them to become! BECOMING: LOVE, LIGHT, WORD, ME."*

EXERCISE #2: HEARING GOD 2 WEEK CHALLENGE

For the next two weeks ask God at least one question every day following the listening exercise we did above or a variation depending on your clarity of hearing. Then write down what you experience, what you sense God is saying to you and showing you. As you practice this you will become more acquainted with God and His active voice. Remember when you start doing anything new (a new job, position at work, a subject in school, a sport or workout routine) you are not going to be the best at it when you start are you? No, you become better at it as you practice, train and develop your skill level over time, effort, repetition and commitment. If your job asked you to do a new process or take on a new position that was going to pay you twice what you are making now would you give up after the first couple of tries and say, "oh well that does not work for me". No, you would practice, stay late, get to work early, ask for help, get some additional training, whatever you needed to do because more money and its benefits are at stake. Well here your happiness, peace, joy and relationship with God are at stake, how much more should we be willing to practice and train up in hearing God's voice which is the most important relationship that anyone can have. Because out of your personal relationship with Jesus Christ all of your "Kingdom Benefits" like health, love, joy, peace, prosperity and blessings will flow.

EXERCISE #3: MORE QUESTIONS YOU CAN PRACTICE ASKING GOD AND LISTENING TO HEAR HIS HEART ON THESE THINGS. (Notice these are open-ended questions which we discussed earlier)

- What's on Your heart, God?
- What do You want to do today, Lord?
- How do You see me?
- God, what do I need to change?
- What gift can I offer You today?
- Is there anything in my life that makes You sad?
- What in my life brings You joy?
- What should I do about this situation, Lord? (School, Work, Family, Relationship, Business)
- Where should I go today? Can You please help me plan out my day?
- Lord what are You saying about this situation?
- God what are You saying right now?
- Lord how do You see this person?
- God who are You? Would You tell me what You are like?
- What were You thinking about when You made me?
- What would the Love of Jesus do in this situation?
- What people group are You calling me to love and minister to Lord?
- Holy Spirit are there any steps of faith I need to take to receive breakthrough and manifestation in this area of my life?
- Lord is there a verse of Scripture You want to share with me? God how can I apply this Scripture to my life this week?
- How are You doing God?
- Where were You in the room when that happened to me, show me Lord? (Because Jesus never leaves our side so you can ask God where He was in certain situations in your past like trauma and difficult life circumstances)
- Lord what are You saying about this?
- God what is my purpose in life? What are some practical steps I can take towards that purpose in the next month Lord?
- When reading the Bible if you sense you're not understanding it and it does not feel alive to you ask: Lord, I thank You that I have Your Spirit of Wisdom. God, what do You want to say to me about this scripture? How can I apply this scripture to my life in the next week?
- Jesus, if my heart were a house, is there any room You would like to redecorate? Why?
- God which of Your character traits would You like me to consider today? Why?
- God what can I do to partner with You to receive my healing?

When you are having two way conversations with God you will inevitably get distracted and off track in your mind. This still happens to me all the time and others whom I have spoken to about talking and listening to God. When you have racing thoughts, your mind seems to get off track, go off on tangents or your head tripping; pause and refocus on asking God questions then listening. When you begin talking to yourself instead of God, it's like you are seeking wisdom from the tree of the knowledge of good and evil, which can be described as seeking your own self-will, desires and you defining what you think is the right and wrong way of being and doing. This allows your bodily desires, false perceptions based on past experiences, fears, as well as the world system and demonic forces to easily influence you. ***"There is a way that seems right to a man and appears straight before him, but at the end of it is the way of death." Proverbs 14:12 AMPC***

It is like you lose your frequency with God. As this happens give yourself plenty of grace, forgive yourself and thank God for His love and then start your conversation right back up with Him. Sometimes I have to do this several times within a conversation because our minds tend to be easily distracted and wander off as God speaks to us. Remember God is not disappointed with you in any way. The enemy will try to shame you and convince you otherwise but he is a liar! God is so happy, joyful and excited that you want to talk with Him as well as listen and hear what He has to share with you. Just like any loving and supportive dad would, God is so much more because He is love Himself. Just as a father loves his children, ***"So the Lord loves those who fear and worship Him [with awe-filled respect and deepest reverence]. For He knows our [mortal] frame; He remembers that we are [merely] dust." Psalm 103:13-14 AMP*** In other words God made us, He knows us and He is aware of our limitations and shortcomings but knowing all that He still constantly pursues a loving relationship with us!

We often ask ourselves questions like why is God not listening? Why does God feel so far off? Why is He not speaking to me? Why can I not hear Him? I hear these complaints all the time and they use to be some of my own words before I came to realize that He does speak and what His active voice sounds like. Then I began to listen for God and expect Him to speak to me. Let me give you an example of what many of us do. It's as if you are asking your friend (God) for advice and they (God) are sitting right beside you and you just keep talking and never give them (God) a chance to answer or pause and let them (God) answer the question you have for them (God). Then you walk away and come back later and do the same thing. So instead of listening you keep talking to them (God) with no chance for them (God) to answer then you walk away again. Then you go over to your other friend and say I don't know why our other friend (God) never talks to me, I feel so disconnected from them (God). I know this sounds kind of funny right, but how often have most of us done that to and with God? I did that to God for more than 10 years of my Christian life and did not even know any better! I would just pray and then get up never taking the time to listen, not even knowing that God actually has an active voice and can, will and does want to speak to you. In fact Jesus gave His very life so God could once again walk with you side by side like He did in the Garden of Eden through His Holy Spirit that now lives inside of you as a Believer in Jesus Christ. I just didn't know, my parents didn't know themselves, the Church I was raised in didn't know either and never taught on the things I am sharing with you now about God's active voice through a daily relationship with Him and I did not search it out for myself until years later in my walk with God. To be transparent I still talk over God and don't listen from time to time but like all of us I am still "in process"!

In those times He lovingly reminds me when I say to Him, "Why are You not talking to me Lord?! Why can't I seem to hear You?" He graciously reminds me, "I am right here" it may be through a flowing thought, an image I see within my mind or a subtle sense that He is with me all of these things no matter how subtle are God speaking. Then I give myself some grace saying, "God I love You and I forgive myself". Then I refocus back on Him and say, God what are You saying about this situation and then I listen and hear the voice of My Father!" So many of us are just like I use to be for so long. We feel like God is far from us, we feel disconnected like He does not want to speak to us or that He somehow left us. When the truth is that He lives inside of us. God is in a relentless love pursuit of our hearts if we will step out on faith and begin to realize that He loves me and wants to speak to me. Then as you talk to Him, pause and wait on God to speak to you and expect Him to answer you. Don't stop pressing into, practicing and straining on a daily basis to listen and hear His voice, it will happen! If it can happen for me and millions of other people it can happen for anyone, God is no respecter of persons (Acts 10:34) He wants a healthy, intimate and thriving relationship with all of us, and that includes you.

When you're praying and asking God for His wisdom on a specific question and you don't sense a clear answer on what to do, be patient and be watchful for God to answer you over the next couple days and weeks through His active voice and various kinds of confirmations. Such as your daily reading of the Bible, your daily devotional, a sermon you hear, a sense of peace about the decision you're thinking about making, a dream you have and circumstances that you sense God speaking to your heart through. There often will be a theme and a flow to the confirmations that will lead you to your answer. Remember God is always working, guiding and speaking to us throughout our daily lives it's up to us to pay attention and be open to His communication with us. Always allowing the Holy Spirit and the Word of God to be the filter we hear and experience God through.

Keep in mind there are many things you just have to experience with God. Sometimes His response to you is "Follow Me"! Meaning as you live with God in a daily love relationship He will show you, tell you and experience with you, the answer to your prayer. As we stated earlier God often is not going to give you the whole plan, instructions and details because He wants a daily relationship and partnership with you not as slaves but as His son or daughter, not as robots but as freewill children of His to worship and love Him by our own choosing. I have learned the hard way not to box God in, don't expect Him to speak in just one way or His normal ways that He communicates with you the most often. Sometimes I have gotten so focused on how I want God to speak to me that I miss what He is doing right in front of my face and I miss God's voice and activity. He often graciously points it out in a way that is corrective but never condemning. I apologize to Him and forgive myself which is usually the hardest part because giving myself the same grace as God gives me is still a work in progress for me but as I practice it I get better; just like I know you will too!

Remember these exercises are just to get you started. I practice talking to God and listening in a continual dialogue all day long 30 to 40 times a day which keeps my mind focused on Him, which the Bible says creates life and peace (Isaiah 26:3). God always wants and is speaking to you, the real question is are you listening and paying attention to His voice and activity? I still have to make the determined decision everyday to press into the Holy Spirit in me and connect with God, sometimes really having to strain over and over again to hear Him. Some days it seems so easy and I hear Him and see His activity so clearly. Other days I feel like I am almost spiritually deaf, blind and senseless but what I do is give myself grace, keep pressing in and seeking God because I know He loves me, He wants to build an intimate relationship with me and He wants to speak to me. The good news of the Gospel of Jesus Christ is that through His Holy Spirit God wants the same for everyone in this whole world including you! Even as you are talking to God conversationally it is important to stay God inside minded by having the inner knowing that He lives inside of you and is your ever-present help and Father. So many times when I am just talking to Him and pouring out my heart to Him the truth of knowing He is listening and He hears me is so comforting. Even if I don't sense Him answer inner audibly or visually however, kinetically there is a deep sense and inward knowing of peace coming from my awareness of His Presence and that He lives in me and is listening to me, that sense as simple as it may seem to you, is God speaking.

EXERCISE #4: COMMUNICATING WITH AND PRAYING FOR OTHERS

I want encourage you to make it your aim and goal in life to involve God in whatever you do on a daily basis. We spend a lot of our lives interacting with other people our spouse, kids, family, classmates, coworkers and others that are in our life's path. That is a huge opportunity to see and experience God working in you and then God working through you, to bless others around you. On a daily basis I ask God to guide me in every conversation that I have with other people. I usually say short prayers in my mind or under my breath such as, "Holy Spirit guide me in this conversation". When someone asks me for advice or a question before I answer I pause for a second and say in my mind or under my breath "Holy Spirit guide me and give me Your wisdom to answer this". This is a mindset and a lifestyle I would encourage you to practice daily. I began, and still do meditate, on a couple of scriptures in the morning before I start my day, that have to do with giving people wise answers and having God guide my conversations.

[The Servant of God says] The Lord God has given Me the tongue of a disciple and of one who is taught, that I should know how to speak a Word in season to him who is weary. Isaiah 50:4 AMPC

Gentle Words are a tree of life. Everyone enjoys a fitting reply; it is wonderful to say the right thing at the right time. Proverbs 15:4, 23 NLT

A Word fitly spoken and in due season is like apples of gold in settings of silver. Proverbs 25:11 AMPC

As I developed this heart position there began to be a wise and loving flow to my conversations, interactions on my job, emails, texts, posts on social media, and advice that I would give to family, friends and others. I began to see the love and power of God flow through me as I asked God to guide my daily conversations with others around me. I began to get feedback from others that what I was saying was exactly what they needed to hear. My words changed their outlook on the situation and imparted hope and peace to them, over and over people would say I was so easy to talk to, that my words came with a godly wisdom to them. It was not that I myself had gotten any wiser or that I give that great of advice it was that I made a conscious heart decision to ask God to direct and guide me to think like He thinks and speak like He speaks over every person in my life. This decision and commitment has radically changed my daily life, conversations and the communication that I have with people. Thus changing and affecting the lives of everyone God puts into my path. This is such an empowered and restful way to live because you're doing it in God's wisdom, strength, love and power by asking the Holy Spirit to guide your mind and tongue. As you practice this exercise I know it will radically change your daily life as well. You will begin to experience God's wisdom working in you and through you. The Bible says in the Book of James that "no man can tame the tongue" James is saying in our self effort alone we cannot tame our tongue but the Holy Spirit can and will, if you make the daily decision to allow Him to guide and direct your words (James 3:8).

In praying for others during my personal prayer times with God which can be anytime you turn your heart to communicate with God. I will often ask God what do You want me to pray about for this person or situation. Then I listen, as God brings things to my heart. I then pray for them following the flow of thoughts that come to my mind for them. After that I become still and wait for the next instruction from the Holy Spirit. If you sense that God is finished then go on to the next person or situation. This is how I pray for my wife, family and other people, as well as praying about situations for others. Many of us have experienced God bringing someone to our minds which we often chalk up as this person "randomly" came to my mind the other day, in actuality this is often God's way of having you pray and intercede for a person you may know.

As I began to do this God would give me more insight to other people's hearts and lives including my own. So now when I think about someone instead of chalking it up to some random thought I take it as an invitation from God and I will often pray whatever is on my heart for them even if I don't have any natural factual basis for my prayers I will just pray whatever is on my heart for that person. Usually it's just a 10 to 45 second prayer, but small things in God's Kingdom have great power. Then so often, I will end up seeing them within a couple of weeks, or we will connect on social media, other times I am praying by faith alone knowing God is calling me to pray for a certain person and for me that is enough. I have gotten so many reports from people that God brought to my heart that have shared with me that at the time I was praying for them that they were going through a difficulty of some sort. When I am able to share with them that God had me praying for them and that He brought them to my heart and I was obedient to pray for them their whole perception on God and their circumstances often change to one of encouragement and being known and loved by God. I have experienced the same thing in people praying for me as well. During the writing of this book I went through a very challenging season in my life and I had more than 7 people in less than two months text me or call me to say they were not sure what was going on with me but the Lord had put me on their heart and that they had been praying for me. I can tell you that personally I felt known, loved and encouraged by God and to God prayer matters! Prayer has great power and it causes reactions and manifestations in the seen and unseen realms in Heaven and on Earth. I cannot tell you exactly how all aspects of prayer work, but I know it's important to God in operating on this earth in the lives of His people. That as His people pray for one another, God moves in miraculous ways and I have seen powerful breakthroughs, encouragement, increase and blessings because of the prayers I have prayed for others and prayers others have prayed for me! The Lord is just looking for those that care enough to listen and believe that He wants to speak to us about our lives and the lives of others!

When you do get negative thoughts, perceptions and feelings about other people don't use it as an opportunity to tear down the person in your mind or be judgmental. Instead pray the opposite of anything that does not line up with the love of Jesus in their lives; call things that are broken fixed, things that are shattered put back together in Jesus Name. Pray, claim, call and say what you want to see in people's hearts and lives. See them with the eyes of God through the lens of God's love, Word, goodness and destiny. God will even at times give you a sense about someone or an inward knowing about some personal aspect of their lives. He is showing you these things so you can pray and intercede for these people based on His love for them.

I do this all the time when I get judgmental thoughts about people. To combat those negative thoughts I will pray the opposite of the judgments using the thoughts I am getting as a call to release my faith in prayer for them. For example at work we all have certain people that seem to get under our skin at times and we have a tendency to tear them down within our minds. When I get these types of thoughts I will repent and say God forgive me for these thoughts and then I will begin to pray for the person opposite of the negative thoughts I am getting about them. This stops the landslide of negative thoughts that can continue and so often increase if these resentments, irritations and frustrations go unchallenged and unchecked by God's love, Spirit and Word in us.

This happens to me oftentimes as I walk through a store or anywhere there is a lot of people. During which I often will do quick "drive by prayers" for people. In the past I would get some kind of judgmental thought about them and then just shrug it off and keep moving. Now I use those negative or judgmental thoughts as a call to prayer for them. It is often just a simple 5 to 10 second prayer under my breath or in my mind and then my heart feels better and I have given the enemy and my flesh no place for judgments to set in. God convicted me of being judgmental years ago and this is a tactic I have found that has over the years transformed my heart to love God, myself and other people at a higher level. The great commandment of Jesus was one of loving your fellow person as He loves us! Thinking negatively about others, making unkind comments in our minds and tearing people down even in your own mind is not demonstrating the love of Jesus.

Remember this; what you think will eventually come out of your mouth and becomes your beliefs and perceptions. I have spent years changing my way of thinking because of what, I thought at the time, were harmless negative perceptions about others. These thoughts had cultured my heart in a way that was in opposition to the love of Jesus that now rules and reigns in my mind, heart and body!

Become the move of God, become the revival this world so desperately needs to experience! BECOMING the MOVE OF GOD starts with you living out THE GOSPEL on an everyday basis. Praying for your spouse, kids, family, friends, coworkers, classmates and people you encounter everyday for bodily healing, financial blessings, increased love and harmony within their life and family, deeper intimacy with God where they may hear His voice more clearly than ever before, these are the types of things we all need prayed into and over our lives. It is really important to manifest and model Jesus on an everyday basis and praying for, over and with your family, kids and co-workers. Stepping out and laying your hands on people in prayer for them. Becoming and being a praying family that you show Jesus at home and model love for your family and friends walking out the love of Jesus in your daily life! Become the move of God wherever you go! I want to encourage you to pray for others all the time in your mind, out loud, in your quiet time with God and over them and hear God's heart for them. This will transform your heart and the people around you and the Word of God says you will fulfill the Royal Law, do well and be blessed!

"If you really fulfill the royal law according to the Scripture, 'You shall love your neighbor as yourself,' you are doing well." James 2:8 ESV

QUALITY AND QUIET TIME ALONE WITH GOD: THE SECRET PLACE, THE THRONE ROOM, SITTING WITH THE LORD

In a healthy relationship it is important to have quality time, times of solitude, intimacy and closeness. Jesus often demonstrated this in His life and ministry He would often go to a place of solitude in order to be alone with His Heavenly Father and have some quiet alone time with Him. *After leaving them, he went up on a mountainside to pray. Mark 6:46 NIV* This helped Jesus to operate out of the overflow of God's love, wisdom and power in His life. Jesus not only came to die for our sins giving us eternal life in Heaven and get His Holy Spirit inside of us as Believers, Jesus also came to earth to model what a love relationship with God looks like. He is the model of how to have a daily intimate relationship with our Heavenly Father empowered by the Holy Spirit. One of the ways He often modeled this relationship was quality time and times of solitude with the Lord." *But Jesus Himself would often slip away to the wilderness and prayed [in seclusion]. Luke 5:16 AMP*

As you enter into this intimate time of prayer with God, especially your quiet time with Him or what is often referred to as the "Secret Place", "Sitting with the Lord" and the "Throne Room", you want to ask and thank the Holy Spirit for opening up and communicating with your heart. This type of heart posture positions and opens you up to hear and receive from God. I will often start out with a prayer like this "Father, I thank You for Your awesome and loving Holy Spirit that lives in me. Holy Spirit I open my heart to You and I am desperate for Your presence and voice please guide me and direct me in our time together and in every area of my life. In the name of Jesus I declare that my heart is fully open to You Lord!" There is no formula for encountering God during this time, it is all about seeking more of Him; knowing He loves it when you set aside time to talk and listen to Him, just you and God! This alone time with the Lord is going to be rooted in seeking and encountering God's presence, worshipping God and coming to know God by experience through this intimate time together with Him. I try to do this in a quiet place in my house. Some people choose to make prayer rooms or prayer closets. Practically it can be any place that is comfortable for you and quiet with limited distractions. This is a time to intimately connect with God and being intentional about investing your attention, time and energy into your personal connection with Him. Some people feel more connected to God in nature so their quiet time is spent outside or maybe they take a walk with God. Whether you sit, kneel, stand or take a walk with the Lord is a personal preference and it is good to mix up your positions of prayer. Giving God your undivided attention and focus through worship, praise and thanksgiving, talking with Him and most importantly listening to Him expectantly, waiting on God to speak to you is what this quality time with Him is all about. *After Jesus had dismissed the crowds, He went up on the mountain by Himself to pray. When it was evening, He was there alone. Matthew 14:23 AMP*

I often play worship music of all kinds. Depending on how I feel I may be sitting, standing, lying on the floor or even dancing around the room it can be instrumental or non-instrumental worship music, it is between you and God how you choose to spend this time with one another and it can look a variety of different ways depending on the person and the day. In this section we just want to give you some practical ideas and examples. Such as if you play an instrument and/or sing like my wife does, you may want to spend some of your time playing music and singing to the Lord. A lot of the time I read my Bible and a daily devotional "Jesus Calling" by Sarah Young, is one of my personal favorites. I often use this time to meditate on the

Word discussing it with God and asking Him questions. Spending time praising and thanking God for His goodness, blessings and love is a great way to worship the Lord during this time. If you don't know where to start I would suggest praying some of the Psalms out loud, they are full of praises to God and you can even personalize them by putting them in the first person to make them read like they are from you to God. Psalms 21, 96, 100, 145-150 are ones that I would suggest you start with. Taking communion is also something you can do during this time. You can hold the elements of the bread and the grape juice in your hand, one at a time, and begin to thank God for the blood Jesus shed for you and His body that was broken so you don't have to be broken but filled with God's Spirit. Then just began to praise and thank God from your heart for His goodness as you take communion in remembrance of what Jesus has done for you!

Other times I will ask God, "How is Your heart Lord? or what's on Your Mind today God?" Then I will just sit there, be still and listen. Often at this time I will get a series of flowing thoughts, mental pictures and images, a sense of God's presence and others forms of God's active voice that we have discussed earlier. On some occasions I will do most of the talking just pouring out my heart to Him, knowing He is listening to me. At other times I just sit in silence with Him just being present with Him and waiting on Him to communicate with me. During quiet times like these of just sitting with the Lord, soaking in His Presence, being still, waiting and listening I will sometimes even fall asleep for a moment, it does happen. When it does give yourself some grace and begin to sit with Him again, you can get up, walk around if you need to or change the flow of your time with Him to something more high energy. I have even slipped into a short dream at times so even falling asleep during your quiet time, though not ideal, can lead to an encounter with God. I also use this time to write down dreams I had that night, discuss them with God and receive interpretations to their meaning and what God is communicating to me through them. There are times that God and I laugh, have fun, and it is so light hearted I feel like I am hanging out with my best friend. Other times I find myself crying and weeping, overcome by His love and His Presence. No matter what you experience and choose to do during this time of solitude and intimacy with God, always keep in mind this is about being with God, spending quality time with Him, so that you may know Him through experiential heart knowledge. I can assure you there is a supernatural transformational power just within the act of intentionally and continually taking the time out of your life to be alone with God and getting to know Him intimately!

This is a great time to talk with God about your issues, sins, struggles, failures and strongholds that are robbing you of your current peace. Also if you're mad, upset or frustrated with God about something, be transparent with Him and talk it out, because He already knows how you feel so this is a good time to get things off your chest and pour out your heart. I want to encourage you to take these situations and feelings into this intimate time with God besides if you tell on yourself and talk it over with God the devil has nothing to hold over your head anymore! I cannot tell you how many times I have gone into my quiet time with God stressed with the weight of something on my shoulders or heavy on my heart. Even when I have had times of great sadness and tragedy, such as the grief of someone close to me dying, I take that process of mourning into my alone time with God. Then as I sit with the Lord, He supernaturally lifts the burdens off of me, enlightens me, gives me His wisdom to know how to handle whatever has been weighing me down and comforts my soul. This is a great time to get healing for your heart through confessing sins and struggles to God, asking God to show you the root causes of why you think a certain way or do certain things you want to change, but seem to keep on doing. Allow the Holy Spirit to bring things to the surface and heal your heart. Ask God to show you His perspective on certain struggles you're having or situations you need guidance on. For example I have asked God, "Why did I get frustrated and irritated with my wife yesterday which caused me to react defensively towards her?" Then as I listen I have had God show me mental pictures and visions of scenes from my childhood and other life experiences that have misshaped the way I think and act towards myself, God and others that were root causes of negative mindsets that I was currently struggling with. Just knowing where the root of something in your heart started, comes with such a sense of empowerment and self-awareness. Then you can repent and break agreement with those negative mindsets and ask the Holy Spirit to change your heart in regards to what you spiritually hear, see and sense God is saying to you about yourself. My life has been remarkably transformed by God's Presence in my secret place time with Him. God has supernaturally transformed and healed things in my soul that only He could accomplish by His Spirit. God has supernaturally made changes in me I knew I could never make on my own. I have experienced so much freedom and deliverance from fear, self-esteem issues, stress and past hurts during my quality alone time with God, that has allowed the Holy Spirit to continually shape my heart and life.

At first just to sit still and quiet with the Lord for 5 or 10 minutes was really hard for me. I felt like I was wasting my time and His. Because my mind would drift off and be all over the place, except focused on God. I would not sense that I got anything out of my quiet time with Him. However, I kept on pressing into my secret place time with God by putting into habitual action what I knew the Bible said and promised about quiet alone time with God, and how Jesus Himself modeled this in His personal life. As I continually did this by faith I began to sense more of God's love, voice, presence and power in real and tangible ways. It is the intimacy I have built with God in my quiet time reading His Word, encountering His Presence, talking and listening to Him that has been one of the most important aspects of transforming my life and developing my personal fellowship, companionship and relationship with God. Spending time alone with God is foundational and paramount to having a healthy relationship with Him.

This is about having quality time with your Heavenly Father and having intimate fellowship with Him. How this time looks and what happens is ultimately up to you and the Lord. I want to encourage you to be open, creative and keep it fresh and exciting. There are times that what I am doing during my quality time with God does not feel fresh or I feel unfocused. During these situations I pray to God "Lord what do You want to do during this time? What do You want to show me?" So often a thought of what to do will come to my mind for a different position of worship, praise, prayer and connection. You may also want to have access to a list of some sort where you can write down things that come to your mind which you need to do that day or later in the week. This helps me so when things do pop into my head I can just write them down and refocus on Jesus. I especially use this in the morning time because I seem to be able to keep my mind on task much easier, instead of telling myself I will remember that later and then having my mind trailing off to what I needed to remember to do instead of focused on God. Practically, this list helps me to not get sidetracked and to keep my focus on Jesus. I often bring my journal with me to write down my questions and what God is telling me and showing me. This helps me focus and build on what He is revealing to me. I like to use the note section on my phone for journaling, some people like to hand write and draw pictures, for others typing on a laptop works better for them. Use whatever works for you. This allows me to go back and experience what I journaled while in these intimate meetings with God. We have a journaling section in this book that I would suggest you put into practice during your quiet time. I have had some of my most powerful and profound encounters and conversations with God using this journaling process during my quiet time with Him. I also pray in my supernatural prayer language during this time as well, which we will cover later in this chapter. Sharing with a spouse, family member or a close friend what you are experiencing with God in your alone time with Him is a great way to build intimacy with others and to have someone you're accountable to. This also allows others to learn and be inspired by your personal relationship with the Lord.

Just like we schedule activities with our spouse, family and friends it is a good idea to schedule your quiet time with God. You can look at it like scheduling weekly date nights with Jesus. Sometimes during my alone time with God I just get lost in His presence, His voice, His Word and His activity. Before I know it has been an hour or two but it feels like I just sat down with Him. Other times it feels labored where 20 minutes seems like an eternity or I cannot seem to get focused on God and so I just try various ways to get centered. Sometimes I put on praise and worship music and just soak in the music and sing to God. The key is to press in and spend some intimate alone and quiet time with Him. *Very early in the morning, while it was still dark, Jesus got up, left the house and went off to a solitary place, where he prayed. Mark 1:35 NIV* The times I do this throughout the week varies depending on what I have going on but I try and get at least 5 to 10 minutes of quiet time with God when I first wake up in the morning before my day gets started as well as scheduling at least 2 to 3 times a week where I have an hour or more to spend alone with God.

No encounter is the same with God, just like no encounter with another person is the same. It is always different. So don't try to put God into a box by attempting to go after the same exact experience, sensation or encounter you had previously, because just like with another person, every meeting and encounter is different with God. I have seen this frustrate so many people that are trying to chase or base their success in connecting with God on a previous feeling, sensation, revelation, flow or encounter with God. Every encounter with God you have will be different, so embrace the newness and freshness of His Presence and love!

A practical caution to consider is not allowing the busyness of life to make you feel guilty, rushed or shameful for setting this secret place time aside for yourself and the Lord. This is a trap I have fallen into before and one I have to fight my way out of every so often but it is easier now that I know how valuable my intimate time alone with God is for me and for others around me. *"Then, because so many people were coming and going that they did not even have a chance to eat, Jesus said to them, "Come with me by yourselves to a quiet place and get some rest." So they went away by themselves in a boat to a solitary place." Mark 6:31-32 NIV* Busyness is probably one of the greatest silent killers of intimacy with God, yourself, your family and those closest to you. It is just as big as any addiction, idol, habit or self destructive cycle that we can have and for most of us busyness is socially acceptable and sometimes even celebrated. However, to God He calls busyness idolatry and being focused on the world system, the seen, on things passing away and not on Him. It's important to understand being busy and busyness are two different things we all have busy lives that is not sinful, it's good to be productive. Busyness is when we mistaken constant activity and work, for healthy progress and productivity. We allow "doing things" to subtly become an idol in our lives. It happens when we lose focus on connecting with God throughout our day, neglect taking time to care for ourselves and struggle with being emotionally present with other people we are in close relationship with.

Jesus explained to us that when we make intimate prayer time and intentionally staying connected with our Heavenly Father a priority in our lives, there are great rewards that come with it. *"When you pray, go into your [most] private room, and, closing the door, pray to your Father, Who is in secret; and your Father, Who sees in secret, will reward you in the open." Matthew 6:6 AMPC* Rewards such as guidance the on decisions you make; experiencing God's voice and presence in intimate personal ways; peace in your mind and heart; reduced stress levels; the wisdom of God to understand how the Bible applies to your current situation; there are a countless number of rewards that come from quality time spent between you and your Heavenly Father! One of the rewards that was so profound for me is when I realized as I spent time alone with God and had times of solitude with Him, the less lonely I felt and the more connected I felt to God and others in my life. There is a big difference in being alone and being lonely, as well as having times of solitude versus isolating. Having alone time and times of solitude with God is all a part of developing an intimate relationship with Him. While loneliness and isolation are tactics of the enemy to keep you disconnected relationally from God and other people. What is one of the oldest tactics of warfare? Divide, isolate and conquer. You counter and combat this through intimacy with God first and then by having healthy God centered relationships with other people.

I want to share with you a revelation that came to me from the Lord on busyness. One night as I was finishing a movie I felt the presence of the Lord and my eyes began to tear up and burn. This is a prompting I get from God sometimes when He wants to speak me, oftentimes about something powerful and impactful. So knowing this I got my phone out and went to my notes and waited for God to speak to me. At first I wrote down the phrase "Behold I show you" which I saw in my mind in blue block letters. As I wrote that down God gave me the rest of this in pieces through a series of flowing thoughts, mental pictures and images. **"Behold I show you the great deception My son the great deception is reality and the seen realm, busyness and lack (scarcity) thinking that this World (system) is all there is and focusing on life (this worldly life) instead of LIFE (John 10:10 Life abundantly lived in relationship with Me) many have been deceived. Do not see with the natural eyes that is the deception "seeing is**

believing", NO, see Me and See everything! Your EYES ARE NOW WIDE OPEN. SEE."

I am not telling you nor am I suggesting that you neglect your duties of life because we all have a lot going on. We all have to live in reality and take care of our responsibilities and obligations. I am only cautioning you about the dangers of busyness and suggesting to you to consider your quality alone time with God necessary to your everyday existence, effectiveness and productivity. Try to do your best not to allow the things that are important in your life like taking care of your family, working and school to become more important than the most important thing in your life which is knowing God and having intimacy with Him. Because the empowerment to be the best version of yourself and living from a place of peace, wisdom, love and power will overflow out of your relationship with Jesus.

I have found when I am intentional about connecting with God especially first thing in the morning that my stress level is drastically reduced. I make better decisions throughout the day. I have much more patience, kindness and love for my spouse, family and coworkers. It is easier for me to be led by God's Word and the Holy Spirit in me. Thus I am much more connected to God throughout my day and even when adversity comes it is not able to overcome me it is like I have a Holy Ghost bullet proof vest on or like a forcefield of faith is surrounding me. I have found when I don't connect with the Lord early in my quiet time and often throughout my day, I feel disjointed and scattered in some respects in my thoughts, words and actions. At the least bit I will wake up and even before I get out of bed I will say, "Jesus I love You" and then just listen. I will often get the flowing thought of "I love you too son" or I will ask, "How is Your Heart God this morning?" "God what do You want to do today?" Then I listen and connect with God's voice, love and presence before I even get out of bed to brush my teeth. I thank God He still loves me even with morning breath! So make sure you are making quiet time to sit with the Lord, in the Secret Place, in the Throne Room, in solitude just like Jesus did when He was on this earth because if Jesus Himself needed this alone time with God and modeled it for us then how much more do we need to connect with the Father's heart in the same way.

PRAYER AND FASTING

Fasting has been a huge part of my walk with God. It has been vital to building my spirit man up and tearing the self-willed flesh down; thus allowing my mind, will, and emotions to be governed and under control of the Holy Spirit that is within every born again child of God. There are increases and breakthroughs that fasting brings to your life to which nothing else can compare. Fasting is not about getting God to move, getting Him to answer some of your prayers or getting Him to love you more. Fasting is about demonstrating your sacrificial love for God, by abstaining from things such as eating, drinking and social media out of your loving devotion for Him. Fasting is withholding something from your body or your mind for the purpose of building up your spirit. It can be anything God leads you to give up for a specific period of time in order to focus on your spiritual growth with the Lord. Fasting throughout the Bible is about humbling yourself before the Lord, giving God access to more of your heart through faithfully seeking to experience more of His goodness and His presence. Fasting is about moving away from solely using self-effort and self-will to control your fleshly wants, desires and habits. To putting the Holy Spirit in control over your flesh, thus putting the Spirit of God in charge over your fleshly wants and desires. I love how the Passion Translation breaks this truth down about being led by the Spirit of God instead of our own self-will. *"As you yield freely and fully to the dynamic life and power of the Holy Spirit, you will abandon the cravings of your self-life." Galatians 5:16 TPT*

Fasting is about being desperate and hungry for God, for more of Him and for more of His Presence. Fasting pours living and refreshing water into your heart and soul through the power and love of the Holy Spirit, it will literally reposition your heart towards God to receive more of Him. Fasting, when done with the right heart intent of seeking more of God, will set you on fire for Him by His Spirit and you will be able to literally feel God's love and power working in your mind, will, emotions and body. It is an amazing thing to sense the power of God at work in your body in real, tangible, ways. *"That is why the Lord says, "Turn to me now, while there is time. Give me your hearts. Come with fasting, weeping, and mourning. Don't tear your clothing in your grief but tear your hearts instead." Return to the Lord your God, for he is merciful and compassionate, slow to get angry and filled with unfailing love." Joel 2:12-13 NLT*

Fasting is not about what you eat or give up, but it is about seeking God and focusing on Him. When you fast, everyone is different. I personally like to fast off of solid food. I often will drink milk, honey, water and broth which I call The Promise Land Fast. Especially on long terms fasts! For example, when my family and I do a 40-day and 40-night fast once a year I often will give up all solid food and go on a Promise Land Fast. I also fast in shorter terms throughout the year as God directs me and they vary from 3 days to 21 days. Additionally, I fast once a week as a spiritual practice.

During this time, I will pray and listen to God about what day to fast, on the 1-day fasts I usually drink water only. Often on the weekly fasts I go from dinner time to dinner time the next day.

When fasting you can choose to give up anything you want or feel led to abstain from. A lot of people think fasting is just drinking water and not eating, but that's not the case. Fasting is the giving up of anything in your life that would be a stretch for you, that you believe you would need God's help and empowerment to obtain from. Something that would add more time and focus on God in your daily life. You could give up or cut back and fast from playing mindless games on your phone, TV, internet, sodas, coffee, sugar, bread, video games, social media, limit meals to 1 a day, eat vegetables only and so on. There are countless ways to fast. Whatever you give up needs to be something that would be a stretch for you to do. Then you can experience God's power and love at work during your time of prayer and fasting. If you're a vegetarian and you say, "Hey! I am going to fast from meat" that's not a fast. If you say, "I am going to give up sodas", but you drink one every couple of days that's not fasting. Whatever you give up or modify your intake of needs to be something that will make a noticeable difference in your daily life. I often suggest for people to pray and then listen to God about what they should fast from. Mine is usually solid food because for me I really like food and I eat a lot. Allow the Lord to lead you in this. That can be as simple as you praying and asking God what you should give up and then as you start thinking about how you are always snacking at work or how you could not live without coffee that would be a form of God speaking to you regarding what you should fast from. A lot of times when God is speaking to us it comes as thoughts or as impressions; an inward knowing that is accompanied by a flow of peace and wisdom. A good sign in this case is if you're praying about what to fast from and the thing you're thinking about giving up causes your body to start to get uneasy and you say to yourself I could never do that, or it would be really hard to give that up. This is a good sign whatever that "thing" is most likely is the very thing God is calling you to fast from. Even now as you read this there are some things that are popping into your mind that you're saying to yourself that would be way too hard for me to give up and fast from. You're right, it is too hard for you to do in your own strength, that is why God wants to give you His strength and His power to do it through Him!

Fasting heightens your awareness of God and draws your attention closer to God and it moves your heart closer to Him because you are focusing on putting your mind and flesh under control of the Holy Spirit in order to fast. Fasting is not something you want to tough your way through. It is not something you do in your own strength and self-effort. Fasting is about you humbling yourself before God, seeking God and focusing on God to overcome the temptation or the want for whatever you are choosing to give up. If you find yourself irritated, frustrated, losing your peace and joy then you are most likely trying to fast in your own strength, self-effort and self-will. This is really not spiritual fasting and you're not going to see the benefit of growth in the spiritual side of your life that you are looking for. In turn, when you attempt to fast in your own strength you will most likely get frustrated and thus frustrate the people around you! That's not what Jesus intended for you to do and that's not fasting. God speaks through fasting by giving you tangible strength to withstand temptation and the wants of your physical body, mind, self-will, and emotions. You can actually feel God working in your body and you can experience the power of prayer within your own body which is really amazing. Fasting shows you the Holy Spirit's power to help you walk by the Spirit of God and not by your own self-will and fleshly desires.

Let me share a couple of testimonies with you about the power of fasting so you can see how it can benefit you and how God speaks through fasting. After I began fasting from time to time, one day I was reading in Matthew chapter 6 Jesus was teaching about giving, praying and fasting and He would begin each teaching by saying "when you give, when you pray and when you fast" and I caught on to something that God illuminated for me. Meaning I had a thought, almost an observation, that came to my mind that seemed to give direction to my mind and illumination to my understanding of the scriptures even though I had read it before. That day God opened up a deeper personal meaning to me. This was God speaking to me. It did not say "if you do these things", but "when you do these things"; meaning these elements are the foundation of a healthy relationship with God and a normal Christian lifestyle. Fasting in so many ways has been a lost spiritual practice and many of us, like myself for many years, did not understand the value of fasting. I really just thought *I like food too much I can't just stop eating!* I didn't understand even the basic principles of fasting, that I could fast from basically anything the Lord lead me to give up and that I was not going to do it by my own strength and self-will anyway, but that I was going to pray and "faith my way through it"! So when I saw this in the scripture I said to myself *I need to add this element of fasting into my relationship with Jesus and make it part of my lifestyle.* I started out fasting solid food, drinking water and herbal tea only for just 6 hours. At first I thought I was going to die from not eating! I was trying to "tough my way through it" instead of faith and pray my way through it!

Then I worked my way up to a 1-day fast and realized when I got hungry I would pray and the hunger pains would go away shortly after I prayed or sometimes immediately! I was like wow I can feel the prayers physically working in my body. It was really cool! I also took the times I would be spending at meals to read the Word of God and I found that my mind was more clear and the scriptures seemed to come alive. Then I went on my first 3-day fast and I thought "Oh, my Lord, I am going to die from starvation!" To be totally transparent, I was scared and didn't know if I would be able to make it. I had prayed and I sensed God was telling me to just drink tea, honey and water because when I prayed about how to fast those 3 items came to my mind several times. I had learned on my other shorter fasts to pray early and often for peace so I would start my day off in prayer saying "God, I thank You that Your Peace is upon me and I will hunger for You and not for food." I would repeat this prayer sometimes 5 to 10 times a day as the hunger pains tried to creep in on me. I read the Bible in place of my food when I would get hungry and I would talk to God about how I felt and say "God, I am really hungry right now, but I am casting my cares on You Lord and I am releasing them over to You." As I did this throughout those 3 days over and over again and stayed connected with God through prayer and listening to Him, devotional time, journaling what I sensed God was telling me and reading the Bible I was able to have peace in a time when I didn't know how I was going to make it. The truth is that I had to pray and faith my way through it! I continually called upon the Spirit of God that lives in me and every Believer to help me in my fasting efforts. Did I have struggles? I sure did! Did I have thoughts of pizza and cookies dancing around in my head at times? Of course! At the same time, I gave those thoughts over to God and prayed for peace and comfort then commanded God's peace to come upon my stomach and my mind. This is one of the most awesome parts of fasting. When you seek God for peace and comfort over your mind and body, He gives it to you and you feel Him working in very tangible, physical ways!

When I fast and counsel others on fasting, especially on longer term fasts of 3 to 40 days, I suggest that people make two lists which I usually keep on the notes portion of my phone. One list is a prayer list of what they sense God wants them to lift up to Him and the other list is what they personally would like to get out of the fast. Even making these lists is an awesome faith building exercise to do with God. I actually pray for God to give me these items on my list and for Him to bring them to my heart. I usually start working on my lists with God a couple of days before I go on a long-term fast. God uses all kinds of ways to speak to you! It can be a burning desire of your heart, a flowing thought, a mental picture of something or someone God brings to your imagination, or something someone says in a conversation to spark an idea. A good rule of thumb is if you think God wants you to put it on your prayer list then go ahead and do it! You can always add to the list during your fast and you want to journal during your fast about how you sense God is answering the items on your prayer and fasting list. You will be amazed that by the end of your fast He will have addressed all the items on your list in some type of way.

I remember when God called me on my first 40 day and 40 night all liquid fast I thought God had lost His mind! I thought to myself there is no way I can do this. I was right, I could not, but through God's Spirit and my daily relationship with Him I could! You may be asking, how did God call you on this fast? That's an awesome God story and one which involves several ways God speaks. I was on a 7-day fast where I was drinking tea, water and honey only and I was working out with one of my buddies and he said, "Sterling, I think God is putting a 40-day and 40-night fast on my heart. I am trying to quit smoking and I was reading about Jesus fasting for 40-days and 40-nights." I realized that God speaks through other Believers and people around us so I paid attention to what my friend was saying; especially because I had just had the thought that morning, I wonder how a 40-day and 40-night fast would be? I remember shaking my head and saying to myself, "I could never do that!" Then a couple of hours later my workout partner was talking about the same godly thing I was thinking about. I recognized that God's activity was all over this. I told my buddy I would pray about it but I was not too sure about this whole 40-day thing! So, I prayed about it and listened for God and felt peace about going on the fast, but my mind and flesh were saying, "Oh no you better not! You are going to shrivel up and die from not eating!"

I said to God, "Lord, if You want me to go on this fast I want to know it is Your will and that I am not trying to do this in my own strength or making this up in my head, because this is kind of scary." After I pray I often listen and this time I felt a peace come over me. Which is a way God actively speaks and this sense of peace often is a positive confirmation in relation to what your praying about. However, I was not all the way convinced yet, but I was very watchful for how God was going to further answer and confirm my prayer. The next week I went to Church and the preacher was preaching out of 1 Kings 19:8 about how Elijah, a prophet in the Old Testament, went 40 days and 40 nights on one meal and how God sustained him and gave him strength! Have you ever been in Church and you felt like the preacher had been reading your mind and he was talking directly to you? Yeah, that would be God speaking to you!

To be transparent I was still not 100% convinced, but God now had my half-hearted commitment to fast for 40 days and 40 nights, but I was still not totally in. Mostly because of my fears and the massive commitment I knew this would take and I wanted to be sure God was calling me into this. Then two weeks later, I attended a Christmas service and a different preacher then the one before, gets up and says, "I don't know who needs to hear this, but I am not going to preach the typical Christmas sermon about Jesus. God has continually put it on my heart to preach Jesus in another light, so I hope this blesses all of you". I was really excited. I was thinking "Whoa, whoever this is for is going to get rocked by the love and power of Jesus!" The preacher went on to say, "I am going to be preaching about God's provision and about how Jesus fasted for 40 days and 40 nights in the wilderness under the power of the Holy Spirit." Remember that guy that I said was going to get rocked by God's love and power? Well, as you probably guessed by now that guy was me! As he spoke my eyes began to burn and tears began to form in my eyes. I heard the still small flowing inner voice of the Holy Spirit ask me, "Is this confirmation enough for you to fast 40 days and 40 nights with Me?" I answered right there sitting in Church "Yes, God, You have my full commitment and attention!" Thank God for His grace and patience!

When I went on this 40-day and 40-night fast I was so interested in how my body would respond and I wanted to work out and lift weights for as long as I could, but I figured from my years of training and working out that at about day 20 I would most likely hit a wall and would be too weak to work out. I had discovered the power of praying and meditating on previous fasts when I worked out that would literally give me supernatural strength and energy and then God showed me I could access this physical power and strength even when I was not fasting to just pray and seek Him during my workouts for power, strength, and endurance. Let me be very transparent with you: I have tried all kinds of pre workout mixes, boosters to boost your energy, loud music to get me pumped up, yelling and jumping around, trying to get angry to do more weight; you name it I have probably tried it over my years of training and working out and being a high school, college and eventually pro athlete. Nothing has worked more effectively and had greater long-term benefits than prayer and meditation on the Bible before and during my workout. I was shocked! I never knew before fasting that God would give you physical strength and power to do something like working out, but I have learned that there is nothing in your life that God does not want to be involved in. He wants all of you, all the time, in everything you do. He wants to bless you abundantly! This is a very powerful and tangible way God has spoken to me and wants to speak to you is giving you physical, emotional and spiritual strength and endurance to fast and pray.

I discovered this truth even more on my first 40 day fast, as I was saying, I thought I would be too weak to workout by the end of my fast because, after all, I was not going to eat any solid food for 40 days and 40 nights. During that time I would drink water, milk, honey and broth the Promise Land Fast as God came to call it. So I started my fast by taking measurements to see how my body would respond to the fast and to see if there was some way that I could maintain or not lose any of my muscle mass or endurance and strength. I had the wild thought that maybe I could gain those things during this fast, but I dismissed that thought based on the 15 years of training and workout experience I had. During those next 40 days I did what I knew to do; I prayed and listened constantly, devotionals with God, spiritual journaling, prayed over my prayer and fasting lists, read the Bible and did whatever I could do to connect with the power of God on a continual basis. I was amazed at what happened! My energy level, as I prayed and confessed that "I have the strength of God" during my workout and between sets, was still at a high level. By the end of my fast, I was stronger and had more muscle endurance than I did when I started my fast! It did not make any sense in the natural, but supernaturally it was so amazing to feel God working in my body and giving me physical strength every day to hit the gym like a man possessed with the Holy Spirit power of God! Then on the last day of my fast, I took measurements and I was in shock. I had lost body fat but supernaturally gained lean muscle mass! I was so thankful and God was more awesome and more real to me personally than ever before! It is one thing to believe in God from an intellectual knowledge such as "I know there is a God and I know information about God" but God wants you to know Him by experience and enter into intimate knowledge of Him, the heart level kind. To say, "I know God because I have experienced His love, power, goodness, and sweetness in my own personal life. I have experiential based knowledge of God which is the highest form of knowledge!" That is where God wants all of us to get to, by experiencing His goodness, love, power, and compassion. Fasting is a great way to do that!

Jesus taught His disciples in the Book of Matthew that fasting also removes unbelief.

And Jesus rebuked the demon, and it came out of him; and the child was cured from that very hour. Then the disciples came to Jesus privately and said, "Why could we not cast it out?" So Jesus said to them, "Because of your unbelief; for assuredly, I say to you, if you have faith as a mustard seed, you will say to this mountain, 'Move from here to there,' and it will move; and nothing will be impossible for you. However, this kind does not go out except by prayer and fasting." Matthew 17:21 NIV

A lot of people think that Jesus was only talking about the demon here in this passage and for much of my life I did too. However, Jesus was actually teaching about unbelief and lack of faith. His disciples asked Him a question, why they could not cast the demon out and His response was because of your unbelief and lack of faith. He was saying this type of unbelief and lack of faith only comes out by prayer and fasting. I never understood this passage until I fasted myself. Then through fasting and prayer I saw some unbelief and lack of faith come out of me that I didn't even know I had through seeing God's Word and Spirit work in my own body.

I experienced this first hand when I would have hunger pains and I would pray and they would go away sometimes instantly, sometimes taking a little longer. I prayed for energy and strength during my workouts and before I knew it; it was like I got supercharged! There were times I would feel irritated or not at peace and I would begin to say, "Lord I thank You that Your peace is covering me and I release all irritation and frustration to You in Jesus Name." I would speak to my body and it would obey me, I would command it to get in line with the Word of God and be at peace and be full of joy and energy. Then those very things that I spoke by faith would happen over and over again! It was amazing! I got to experience Jesus work within my life and body in personal and tangible ways that I didn't even know were possible! This experiential knowledge of God purged and removed a certain amount of unbelief and lack of faith out of my life.

The 40-day and 40-night fasting is now something that me and my whole family do once a year and everyone now looks forward to experiencing God in really powerful and personal ways. At first my family and my friends thought I had lost my mind, but then they began to see my life radically change and they saw the fire in my heart for God come alive in a new way. They saw transformation and they saw the prayers that I was praying being answered in undeniable and powerful ways. I have seen so much increase in my life and the lives of others who have put this amazingly powerful spiritual practice into play in their lives. It is especially awesome to see one item after the next be somehow touched on and answered over your time of prayer and fasting. Then, when you go back and look at the lists after a couple of months or years you will see so many things God has brought to pass in your life based on the prayer and fasting lists you've made and prayed over. I have seen families restored, children come back to the Lord, addictions broken, bodies healed, marriages restored, financial breakthrough, job promotions, an untold amount of blessings in the spiritual, physical, mental and financial realms through fasting. I want to encourage you to start small and work your way up to longer term fasts. Give yourself plenty of grace and celebrate what you can, will, and did do. No matter what you did, even if you did not accomplish the goal you set out for, celebrate what you did accomplish even if it was trying to fast for a few hours. If you begin fasting by giving up social media for a day or just drinking water until dinner time, celebrate what you did do! The same truth goes for your whole life especially in your relationship with God.

Make sure you are acknowledging and celebrating the small daily victories; this is one of the keys to living a victorious life! Even when you don't realize it, you are being changed and transformed daily by the little victories with God! God sees your effort and your heart's intent. He wants to be involved in every area of your life; if you will just let Him into those areas, begin to expect Him to speak to you, listen for Him speaking, and be watchful and attentive for His activity! I pray that the peace, power, and joy of the Lord be upon every fast you go on! In Jesus Name, Amen!

TAKING THOUGHTS CAPTIVE: HOW DOES THAT REALLY WORK?

This section will give you some practical tools in responding to intrusive thoughts, stopping racing and obsessive thoughts, changing negative self talk, transforming the negative self narrative in your head and building up your self esteem. Stop worry, anxiety, depression and being overcome by fleshly desires and destroying thoughts of fear, doubt and temptation from the enemy. This is all about controlling your thought life through spiritual based weapons! This is vitally important in hearing God's voice on a daily basis because it makes it challenging to hear God say the right things to you when you are often thinking and listening to the wrong things. It starts with changing and challenging your thinking! Your life will go in the direction of your predominant thinking in essence whatever direction your mind, will and emotions go, on a consistent basis, so will your life. There is a saying, "whatever you focus on, you become, for better or for worse" and in life I have found that principal over and over again to be true. As you keep your life focused and centered on the nature of Jesus and His Word you will become like Him. You become Christlike by fellowship, friendship, communion, and intimate relationship with God. As your mind is transformed by God you begin to live out the very nature of Jesus, which as a byproduct will render negative thoughts and the demonic forces that try to influence your life ineffective.

Have you ever heard the statement "Let go and let God" or "leave it at the foot of the cross" and wondered to yourself yeah that sounds great but how do you practically do it? Have you ever wanted to stop worry and anxiety from having place in your life? Have you ever wondered how you practice forgiveness for yourself, God and others? Have you ever heard you have to walk by "the Spirit" to not be overcome by the flesh? Have you ever wondered what does "walking in God's love" practically look like and mean? Well this next section will help you understand the practical application of these things and how to put them into action within a simple three step process. Together we will unpack some of those spiritual sayings and questions such as how to let go and let God, how to stop worry and anxiety, as well as what it means to walk in God's love.

The Word of God says above all things to put on God's love like a garment. Walking in God's love is an every day decision and a choice; not an emotion. These 3 steps when put into action will empower you to take your thoughts captive and walk in the love of God! You have to put love on and choose love 100's of times a day in your thoughts, words and deeds but it all starts with your thinking. This process will radically change your life, as well as how you hear from God, if you will make the decision to practice this in your life on a daily basis. I have often said getting free is an awesome thing but staying free is everything! This process will empower you to maintain the victory that Jesus Christ obtained for you!

2 Corinthians 10:3-6 speaks of taking EVERY thought captive, punishing the negative thoughts and making them obedient to God by His Word and through your prayers; this is how you keep your heart clean! **"For though we walk in the flesh, we are not waging war according to the flesh. For the weapons of our warfare are not of the flesh but have divine power to destroy strongholds. We destroy arguments and every lofty opinion raised against the knowledge of God, and take every thought captive to obey Christ, being ready to punish every disobedience, when your obedience is complete." 2 Corinthians 10:3-6 ESV**

STEP 1: CHALLENGING NEGATIVE THOUGHTS THROUGH; REFUSAL AND CORRECTION; GIVING THE ENEMY THE HAND AND THE SPIRITUAL STIFF ARM AND SLAPPING DOWN THE THOUGHTS:

When a negative thought comes into your mind you say, **"I refuse that thought in the Name of Jesus, that is not my thought, I have the mind of Christ and I am not taking it!"** You can also use the words refuse, reject, rebuke or the phrase **"I cast that thought down in the Name of Jesus! I have the mind of Christ!"** If possible you want to speak these words under your breath or out loud. This act of verbalization will help you to break up the thought. If you don't feel comfortable doing this, or it is not appropriate at the time, you can also do this within your mind. We are defining a "negative thought" as any thought you have that is not in line with God's nature, ways, Word, love and the Holy Spirit. Thoughts of irritation, frustration, defensiveness, stress, fear, doubt, worry, unforgiveness, lust, shame, envy, jealousy, regret and guilt would all be categorized as negative thoughts.

A great place to start reading and meditating in the Bible in order to help you identify negative thoughts and to understand a good definition of God's love, is 1 Corinthians Chapter 13 specifically in the Amplified Classic Bible translation (AMPC). I like this translation when it comes to this chapter because it explains God's love in a detailed way that will help give you a measuring device when it comes to your thoughts, words and actions. Use it as your love gauge and meter. Take 1 Corinthians 13:5 AMPC for instance **"Love (God's love in us) does not insist on its own rights or its own way, for it is not self-seeking; it is not touchy or fretful or resentful;"** based on this verse if you have any thoughts that are "self-seeking" (self-centered, self-absorbed or only looking out for what you want), "touchy" (overly sensitive or irritable), "fretful" (stress or frustration), "resentful" (offense, bitterness or indignation) you are going to identify those thoughts as negative or unwanted. Then challenge those thoughts and respond to them by utilizing these 3 steps. I suggest first starting out reading this passage 5 to 7 times a week and any thought contrary to God's love take it captive and cast it down using this 3 step process!

This step stops the temptation from gaining momentum and turning into worry, doubt, and confusion; like a snowball effect of negative thoughts. This step keeps the negative seeds and fiery darts from landing in your heart and mind and taking root. Because how many negative thoughts does one negative thought lead to? A lot more, right? 10 or 20? Or if you're anything like I use to be, maybe more! During this step we like to encourage people to use physical anchors for what is happening emotionally, mentally and most of all spiritually. For example in this step I often will put out my hand in a stop motion depending on where I am if I am by myself I might do a full on stop motion, if I am around other people I will just put my hand down to my side and put my hand in a stop position. What am I doing? I am using a physical motion or anchor to remind myself that I am refusing this thought in the name of Jesus, that it is not my thought, I don't think this way because I have the mind of Christ and I am not going to take it. Being a former football player, I feel like I am giving those thoughts and temptations the stiff arm you would see a running back use where he uses the hand he is not carrying the football with to fight off would be tacklers. Some people like to envision themselves slapping down the thought, or they imagine the negative thought being burned up and being blown far away from them, whatever works for you. I often do a combination of things depending on the situation. I have found that physical anchors reduce my stress level and tie a physical action to what I am doing by taking thoughts captive, which is a fundamental part of spiritual warfare!

You cannot stop the thoughts of temptation from coming into your mind, but once they are present, then you have full accountability, authority and power on how you respond to those temptations. The Bible even tells us that Jesus Himself was tempted in every way yet without sin. (Hebrews 4:15) So we know through the Word of God that to have thoughts of temptation is not sinful in itself. However, it's when we entertain, mediate and act on those temptations giving them place in our minds and lives that we fall into sin. These negative thoughts come from several places. Negative perceptions, strongholds, and mindsets you developed during your lifetime from all kinds of places, from the way your parents raised you, to how other kids treated you and what they said about you as you were growing up. Painful or hurtful life experiences often lead to negative and fearful subconscious thinking. Other causes are your fleshly desires, reliance on self-will, limiting core fears and beliefs, the demonic realm or the negative words of others that have been spoken to you and over you. *"When you are tempted don't ever say, "God is tempting me," for God is incapable of being tempted by evil and He is never the source of temptation. Instead it is each person's own desires and thoughts that drag them into evil and lure them away into darkness." James 1:13-14 TPT* These thoughts attempt to frustrate you by trying to make you feel negatively such as guilty, shameful and fearful. They lead to additional accusations by the enemy with thoughts such as "how could you think like that, you should be ashamed of yourself". However, that is when you refuse even those additional thoughts and temptations in Jesus Name and give yourself some grace. Remind yourself that it is not the actual temptations that will arise that you can control, but how you respond to those temptations and negative thoughts! How you respond is within your full power, authority, and control. Always remember to call on the name of Jesus and to plead His blood over your mind. For we have the mind of Christ. (1 Cor. 2:16)

STEP 2: THE RELEASE AND REMOVAL OF THE NEGATIVE THOUGHTS FROM YOUR HEART OVER TO THE LORD. THIS STEP IS THE "FORGIVENESS EXCHANGE" WHERE YOU RECEIVE FORGIVENESS AND GIVE FORGIVENESS:

"If we [freely] admit that we have sinned and confess our sins, He is faithful and just [true to His own nature and promises], and will forgive our sins and cleanse us continually from all unrighteousness [our wrongdoing, everything not in conformity with His will and purpose]." 1 JOHN 1:9 AMP

After Step 1, you want to confess to God the negative thought of fear, worry, irritation, etc. and repent (repent means to change your way of thinking to the way God thinks, speaks and acts) of the negative thought by saying:

"Lord, I confess my thoughts of (irritation, worry, shame) _____ about (the situation: a person, your finances, or the past) _____ to You, I repent and I receive Your forgiveness, I thank You that I am forgiven in Jesus' Name."

Then you give Forgiveness: "Lord, I forgive by faith and choose to release and cast _____ (any negative thoughts, feelings, or person(s) that may have wronged you), on You and I choose to love and forgive. Amen."

Let's use an example that we can all relate to at some point in our lives, of a classmate or coworker that has said or done something to irritate, frustrate or offend you; we will call him Bill. This is an example of the model prayers above with the blanks filled in so you get a better picture of how step 2 flows. Remember these prayers are just a model for you to use and adapt to your specific needs and circumstances.

"Lord, I confess my thoughts of irritation, frustration and unforgiveness about Bill and how he treated me this morning, as well as the way I reacted to Bill out of my irritation with him. To You Lord, I repent and I receive Your forgiveness. I thank You that I am forgiven in Jesus' Name."

Then you give Forgiveness: "Lord, I forgive by faith and I choose to release and cast all irritations, frustrations and resentments that I have for Bill over to You God. I thank You that You have taken the offense that I had for Bill from me! I also forgive myself for allowing myself to get angry with him. I choose to love and forgive myself and Bill and I let the situation go into Your Hands. In Jesus Name. Amen"

The physical anchor that I like in this step is flicking my hand like I am physically getting water off my fingers. This gives me the sense of release and is the physical anchor that I use on a daily basis. If I am by myself I will sometimes hold my arms out in front of me or to the side of me and flick my fingers against my thumbs in an outward flicking motion. If I am around others I usually hold one of my hands or both down at my side and flick my hands a couple of times as I forgive and release these thoughts over to God. I physically feel and sense something is being taken off of me. Another effective physical anchor is deep breathing. Taking a couple of deep breaths out as you forgive will help you come to a place of peace and slow your heart rate down. This helps especially if you are really irritated or frustrated with a person or situation. As I do this I envision blowing the negativity out and breathing in God's goodness and peace. I use physical anchors frequently throughout the day.

When taking thoughts captive I encourage you to use visualization techniques. For example when a fear based thought comes into your mind encase it in a large red stick of dynamite and then blow it up! Visualize putting the thought into a cage with a whole bunch of prison bars surrounding it and then throw it at the foot of the Cross of Jesus that is floating over a beautiful blue ocean. Next, picture it sinking into the sea and then say in your mind, "you cannot come back to bother me ever again"! You can also imagine that the thought gets covered by the Blood of Jesus and then is totally removed or melts away! Visualization has helped me many times as a great tactic to overcome negative and intrusive thoughts. This technique works very well for people that tend to be visual learners.

The first step stops the negative thoughts and temptations from gaining momentum and leading to more unwanted thoughts. Step 2 releases and removes the negative and unwanted thoughts and stops them from taking root in your heart and mind. This release and removal is likened to tending a garden and pulling the weeds out of the garden of your heart. This is the way you are able to keep any negative seeds or weeds from taking root in your mind and heart, no matter how small the seed. Because any seed or unwanted thought that does land in your heart and mind, produces after its kind. Who wants all of these weeds of frustration, fear, shame, worry, unforgiveness and irritation to grow in their hearts and minds on a daily basis? None of us want that! However, you have to make a determined response to remove them, otherwise by default they are planted and take root and then we water them with worry and anxiety because one negative thought usually leads to more! Why would you feed and water something you don't want to grow? The answer is you don't, but so many of us allow this to happen on a daily basis. I know for years, as a Believer, I allowed myself to be overrun with unwanted and negative thoughts. Comparing taking thoughts captive to tending a garden makes a lot of sense. If you pull the weeds up in a garden a little at a time on a daily basis then the garden stays in good shape, but if you go two or three weeks without pulling the weeds out then your garden will most likely be overrun with weeds! Just like our hearts and minds get overrun with thoughts of fear, worry, irritation and we wonder why we are anxious, depressed and frustrated by the end of the day or some of us on a daily basis.

You can also think about this process and these unwanted thoughts as pebbles. How uncomfortable is it to have one pebble in your shoe? This is something that we can all relate to. We all have had a pebble in our shoe at one time or another in our lives and it is so nagging and uncomfortable until you stop, take off your shoe and shake the pebble out of your shoe! Likewise our minds get bombarded with unwanted thoughts everyday that by the end of the day they leave us feeling worn down, anxious, frustrated and tired. I also have realized this truth: worry is administering or feeding fear to yourself and fear is faith in what your false perceptions, fleshly desires and the demonic realm say. I also like to use the example of a smoke alarm. Most often anxiety, worry and depression are a byproduct of an untended heart and it is your body and spirit's way of saying, "Hey there are some spiritual and emotional issues here! There is some hurt, pain, unforgiveness and fear we need to deal with and give over to God!" So ignoring them would be like ignoring a smoke detector that is going off in your house even though you smell smoke. The smoke detector is not your "issue or problem" it's the fire in your house! In like manner trying to medicate those things away or suppressing them with busyness, work, video games, television, food, drugs or whatever means you prefer to use, is like getting up in that same scenario and hitting the smoke detector with a hammer until it stops beeping and then going back to whatever you were doing. Again the issue is not the smoke alarm it is the fire in your house; the hurt, pain, fear and unforgiveness in your heart. These steps allow you to stop those unwanted thoughts and fight against them by using them as calls to prayer to release and practice your faith and prayer life with God; thus hearing His voice and experiencing His activity in your daily life.

"Therefore humble yourselves under the mighty hand of God [set aside self-righteous pride],... casting all your cares [all your anxieties, all your worries, and all your concerns, once and for all] on Him, for He cares about you [with deepest affection, and watches over you very carefully]." 1 PETER 5:6-7 AMP

Notice God told us to humble ourselves and for us to do the casting of our cares. So we have to do the humbling, releasing, forgiving and casting! So if it is a seed of frustration, worry, doubt, or confusion, it will produce those same things in your heart and mind. It is kind of like playing a game of basketball or football, nothing happens in the game until the ball is released. Likewise, this release of negative thoughts; the receiving and giving of forgiveness is a vital step to winning the battlefield of your mind and thus the game of life! This is exactly why you want to immediately release and remove any unwanted thoughts that are trying to be sown into your heart and mind. Once you surrender those thoughts over to God, letting them go by releasing them over to Him, make sure you rest in and trust in the truth that you have surrendered those things over to Him, you are forgiven, you are free, and you are loved by God.

You see, God has given you directions on how to defeat the enemy and put your mind and flesh under the control of the Holy Spirit. The issue is a lot of us are not taking advantage of the power provided to us through Jesus Christ. The Bible says YOU resist the devil, you give him no place, you put on the whole Armor of God, you have the authority to trample on all the power of the enemy, you are called to put your faith into action and to use the power that God gave you through what Jesus has already done for you, you have to flip the switch! The power of the Holy Spirit is there but you have to utilize it! You do the praying for your enemies and people that irritate you, you do the forgiving, you do the casting of your cares on God. He gave you the access to His grace and love and He gave you the power of free will to act on His Word, His love, His name, through His own Holy Spirit that lives in you as a Believer, but you gotta flip the switch every day putting the Word to work in your life!

STEP 3: STANDING ON AND IN THE TRUTH OF WHO YOU ARE AS A SON OR DAUGHTER OF GOD AND BY FAITH RECEIVING, DECLARING, CLAIMING AND PLANTING THE GOOD AND LOVING THINGS OF GOD INTO YOUR HEART AND LIFE AS WELL AS INTO THE LIVES OF OTHERS.

In Step 3, you want to pray the opposite of the negative or unwanted thought to which you are being tempted. It can be a thought about God, yourself, another person or a situation. People often tell me they don't know what to say in this third step so I suggest that they take the negative or unwanted thoughts they are getting and turn them around in the opposite direction into a positive faith filled prayer. You bless and pray for the person who you are worried about, frustrated with or holding any unforgiveness for. As well as declare God's Word over your life, the lives of others, and the situation. Jesus commanded that you not only forgive your enemies but love them and bless them by praying for them (Matthew 5:44). If God wants you to do that for your enemies, what about the people who have the most opportunity to irritate, frustrate or worry you on a regular basis: your spouse, kids, family, friends, coworkers, classmates and yourself? To be transparent, I have used these three steps on myself countless times because for most of us the one who we are the hardest on and teardown the most is ourselves. I have worked these 3 steps regarding my wife, daughter, family and coworkers a countless number of times as well! Because as we can all attest to in life, close relationships and family can be messy! I have also made the commitment to continue to work these steps on a daily basis so that I can live from a place of love and forgiveness for those closest to me. I would encourage you to do the same and even more importantly so does God!

Jesus says, *"You're familiar with the old written law, 'Love your friend,' and its unwritten companion, 'Hate your enemy.' I'm challenging that. I'm telling you to love your enemies. Let them bring out the best in you, not the worst. When someone gives you a hard time, respond with the energies of prayer, for then you are working out of your true selves, your God-created selves. This is what God does.*

"In a Word, what I'm saying is, Grow up. You're kingdom subjects. Now live like it. Live out your God-created identity. Live generously and graciously towards others, the way God lives toward you." MSG Matthew 5:43-48

For instance, if the negative thought is frustration and worry about your spouse because of something they may have done or said that irritated, worried or frustrated you, you would instead pray for them the opposite way of the temptation. These prayers and steps are usually prayed in your mind or under your normal voice tone or out loud if you are by yourself. These prayers are not for others to hear you, they are for yourself and God although, they do benefit other people.

BLESSING THE PERSON:

Say, **"Lord, Jesus, I thank You that I treasure my spouse's heart. I pray blessings of wisdom and peace upon their life! Thank You that they are so valuable to You Lord, that they are Your child and that they come to know their true value and worth and so do I! I thank You Lord that they are loving and kind and that our relationship is full of love and blessings."**

BLESSING THE SITUATION:

Begin to bless your marriage, and call by faith what you positively see and want in your spouse by declaring blessings over them. **"Lord thank You that Your peace and understanding are covering my marriage and that You Lord are at the head and in the middle of everything we do! I thank You my spouse and I are quick to forgive and make peace with one another!"**

BLESSING YOURSELF:

Then pray for yourself, **"Lord I thank You that I am the righteousness of God in Christ Jesus, that my value is in You, that I am worth the blood of Jesus, that I am loving, caring, patient and kind towards myself and my spouse!"**

BLESSING GOD:

Then praise and worship God, **"Lord thank You for loving me, thank You for my spouse! Father thank You for Your goodness and faithfulness to me and my family!"**

So now, using these three steps, your taking the negative thoughts that were robbing you of your peace and using them as a call to pray and connect with God. You use them as a springboard propelling you forward to bless your life and the lives of others, as well as an opportunity to praise, thank and worship God! As you practice praying this way it will begin to bless and transform your mind, heart and life as you stand on God's Word about His goodness, yourself, other people and situations. ***Jesus said: "For this reason I am telling you, whatever you ask for in prayer, believe (trust and be confident) that it is granted to you, and you will [get it]." Mark 11:24 AMPC*** When you continually choose to speak life and blessings you and your family will live in freedom and prosperity (Deuteronomy 30:19). Some people will say to me, "Well these things are not true about me, my life or the person I am praying for, I feel like I am lying, I feel like am being a hypocrite." and I ask them, "How can you lie and be a hypocrite by saying and praying what God says and calling forth what you want just like God does?" You're not a liar nor a hypocrite if you have any desire, intent or motivation to become more like Jesus. The sheer fact you're reading this book and seeking God means you have a desire to know Him and become more like Him! When you keep on doing the same negative things which you really don't want to do anymore, this just means you need to continue in the Word of God, continue being in close fellowship with the Holy Spirit and continue to say what God says about you, your life and others, till breakthrough and change comes! God promises in His Word that if you continue to do these things then you will experience change and transformation! I tell them the same thing I am encouraging you to do, "You have to see and speak blessings over yourself and others by faith through God's love, Word and Spirit just like Jesus did, and just like He commanded you to do!" ***"God who gives life to the***

dead and calls things into existence that do not exist."
Romans 4:17 CSB

You are calling by faith the blessings and changes you want to see happen in your life and the lives of others that line up with God's TRUTH. That is why it is important for you to get into the Word of God and allow it to transform and renew your mind to what God says, as well as listening to His active voice on a daily moment by moment basis. By making the commitment, decision and daily choice to the practice and the training of taking thoughts captive, repenting, forgiving, and releasing your faith in prayer, will help you keep your heart clean of negativity, fear and unforgiveness and keep your life blessed and prosperous!

The first two steps were defensive in nature, but you cannot win a sports game by only playing defense. In order to win, you have to play the game with some offense as well! The first two steps you were responding to the temptation and keeping your heart clean by resisting unwanted thoughts and the enemy's temptations and removing whatever might have landed on your heart! This third step is where you become offensive, and you bless your life, the situation and the lives of others. When you pray and speak the Word of God over your life and others, God supernaturally causes things to move in the spiritual realm on your behalf. This will in-turn eventually affect the natural realm of your life causing breakthrough, change and blessings to occur! The Bible tells us that God actively watches over the prayers we pray for our lives and the lives of others to ensure they are carried out as we pray in faith by His Word! So we can be assured even when we don't see how God is going to bring it to pass through our prayers, God is working on our behalf behind the scenes in the spiritual and natural realms of our lives and the lives of others, kind of like on a movie set. *Then said the Lord to me, You have seen well, for I am alert and active, watching over My Word to perform it. Jeremiah 1:12 AMPC*

The Bible tells us that Ministering Spirits and Angels work on our behalf as we pray and release our faith in praying and declaring blessings over ourselves and others. (Hebrews 1:14, Psalms 103:20). God honors our faith, love, and hope. You also allow the Word of God to transform and renew your mind and heart on a daily basis to be more like Jesus! We like to use the illustration of a palm tree on a white sand beach and it's filled with all this amazingly beautiful and tasty fruit of whatever you want for your heart peace, value, joy, freedom and as you declare these things through prayer you pull down these tasty fruits into your heart and you are filled back up with God's love, Presence and Word!

In this step the physical anchor that I like to use is, as I pray for others or certain circumstances in my life, I imagine and envision in my mind that the prayers I am praying for them or the situation are working and having a powerful impact. When I am praying for myself I will sometimes pretend I am picking fruit from that palm tree and as I claim who I am in Christ and thank God for His love for me, I pull those things down out of the air like I am pulling blessings down from Heaven itself, which spiritually speaking is a true statement, and I place my hand over my heart as to say I am putting these fruits of: value, identity, love, peace, worthiness, prosperity and healing inside my heart, soul and body! I also practice what I call "Running to the Throne Room" meaning I use this third step as a call to praise, thank and worship God. I claim God's blessings over my life through who I am in Christ. If I am having some prevailing thoughts that I am struggling with that won't seem to stop and that keep almost bouncing or swirling around in my head, I will write down the negative thoughts I am having so I can look at them and talk them over with God. I will ask God to give me His perspective and truth on these thoughts and then I listen. There is something powerful about getting thoughts out of your head by writing them down and then giving them over to God that brings clarity and freedom.

You want to make sure you fill the void that was made by the negativity that you gave over to God and that He took from you in the second step. When you released whatever it was over to Him and are receiving and giving forgiveness. In Matthew chapter 12:43-45 Jesus speaks of a person that had a demon cast out of them. In the parable after a time the demon came back and found the house (the person's heart) empty, clean and in order and Jesus said that the demon came back with 7 other spirits more wicked than the first demon and the state of the person was worse than before. What is the key here? Do not leave your house, your heart and mind, empty. Fill yourself up with God's love, Word and Presence!

The enemy recognizes this truth so when you begin to put these three steps into play, you render the enemy's attack ineffective in a lot of ways. You are in essence becoming much harder for the enemy to tempt and frustrate. You will find that the longer you have been putting this into practice in your life, the easier it will be for you to defeat the enemy's temptations. You will begin to learn how to dominate the enemy, your self-will and fleshly desires by controlling your thought life through these spiritual weapons of prayer, worship and praise. Thus controlling your mind, will, and emotions instead of allowing them to control you. **So humble yourselves before God. Resist the devil, and he will flee from you. James 4:7 NLT** These three spiritual steps empower you to put this scripture above into action in your life; humbling yourself by acting on God's Word, submitting your thoughts to God, resisting the devil through affirmative thankful prayer and praise to God which causes the devil to flee from you! Living like this will cause you to walk in the power and authority that

Jesus gave us in His finished work on the cross. As you live this out as a daily practice and choice of lifestyle, you will experience the Fruit of the Spirit: Love, Joy, Peace, Patience, Meekness, Gentleness, Kindness, Faithfulness, and Self-control overflow in your life by leaning on the Holy Spirit in you through these three steps (Galatians 5:22-23). This type of lifestyle is one of freedom and victory in, with and through Jesus Christ!

I have been practicing these 3 steps for years now, so sometimes I don't work the steps in order. I may go straight to releasing, forgiving, using physical anchors and praying opposite of the temptation, or a combination and variation of the 3 steps. Most of my focus now is spent doing the 3rd step; praising and thanking God for how awesome and amazing He is and who I am in Him as His son. Then praying Bible based blessings over myself and other people. However, if you are just starting out it is best to get comfortable with the 3 step process and then from there you can use variations of the 3 steps. I use these steps or a variation of them at a minimum of 10 times a day, every day. On other days it may be 50 to 60 times, and on the really challenging days it feels like I am working these steps hundreds of times, because I have made the commitment to no longer give the enemy or negative thinking place in my mind or heart! After years of practicing these steps, I find myself at times working the steps in my mind as an automatic response to negative or unwanted thoughts coming at me. Still other times, I find myself having to be very intentional and focused on working these steps through continual prayer. Remember this is not a works based process that you're trying to do in your own self-effort and self-will. On the contrary this is a God-centered spiritual victory based process where you are engaging your faith in the Word of God, through prayer, by the power of the Holy Spirit. Thus surrendering, trusting and resting in God's Word and in all the finished works of Jesus. Since I have made these steps part of my daily walk with Jesus I have been completely delivered from worry, anxiety, depression and fear. I have also overcome the doubts I use to have about God, His promises, His goodness and His Word being completely true. What does that mean to be completely delivered and free? Do those types of thoughts still come? Of course they do, and do I still have to contend daily to keep my peace and joy? You better believe it! The difference is I use to allow my mind to run wild with fearful thinking and anxiety. I use to entertain worry and allow it to rob me of my peace. I use to read the Bible and allow thoughts of doubt to race through my mind. I use to slip into days of depression but now no longer! Now I know how to respond to these thoughts! Now I fight back and I am winning the battlefield of my mind on a daily basis! Now I know how to, lean on and press into, the Holy Spirit through these 3 steps and keep the garden of my heart free of the weeds that use to weigh me down! That is deliverance and freedom! These 3 steps can and will do the same for you and even more! I have seen these steps when applied, radically change lives, stop anxiety, worry and depression; restore marriages; improve the way people parent; increase job performance and cause financial breakthrough. I have seen children's hearts, behavior and lives turned toward God and families who were in disfunction totally reconciled by coming into right standing with one another and more loving than ever! This 3 step process when put into practice will enable and empower you to hear the active voice of God with greater clarity and sense His activity in your daily life by heightening your awareness of Him.

I would like to share with you a couple of tips about living these steps out. First of all, give yourself plenty of GRACE always, but especially when you first begin to do this because you are probably going to find out that you have a lot more negative, fearful, unloving and doubtful thoughts than you assumed you had. I know I did when I began to live this as a lifestyle.

Secondly, do not let this process of renewing your mind and heart frustrate you or get you off track into shame, pride or guilt. Instead, let yourself off the hook, forgive yourself, give yourself some grace, and realize that you, as well as all of us, are continual works in progress! Remember that you cannot stop the thoughts of your fleshly desires, self-willed soul and demonic temptations from coming into your mind because that is the work of your fallen flesh, fear based strongholds, soulish perceptions and the enemy. What you do have within your control and have accountability for as well as full authority over is how you respond to these thoughts and desires. When taking thoughts captive don't be pushed around and intimidated by the enemy or by the fearful thoughts of your flesh and self-will. As Moses encouraged the children of Israel as they were going over and taking new territory called the "Promised Land" which is a Biblical example of living in a loving intimate relationship with God that produces freedom and blessings. I encourage you also to be strong and full of boldness now as you are taking new territory in the Promised Land of your heart, mind, will and emotions! *"Be strong. Take courage. Don't be intimidated. Don't give them a second thought because God, your God, is striding ahead of you. He's right there with you. He won't let you down; He won't leave you." Deuteronomy 31:6 MSG*

The Bible says, *"For God has not given us a spirit of fear, but of power and of love and of a sound mind." 2 Timothy 1:7 NKJV*

The enemy will always try put a little doubt or a little shame or unworthiness on you. He is trying to land as many shots as he can, like "You should not be thinking that. You are no good. If people knew what you were thinking no one would like you. I can't believe you are having that thought about that person. Yeah I know what the Bible says but you know what you did. You should be ashamed of yourself. What about this in your life that you did wrong or that time things went wrong? What if it happens again?" the list goes on and on of accusatory statements by the enemy. Even today when I meet someone the enemy will often give me a slight thought of judgment about the person and then blame me for thinking that way! The enemy is a liar!! Cast that thought down, shake off the guilt and shame, it is not yours to carry! Give it over to Jesus! The truth is you were not created to carry stress, worry, shame, guilt and fear. It can and will kill you if you choose to carry it and not cast it on Jesus as the Bible commands us to do (1 Peter 5:7). These 3 steps are how casting your care on Jesus is practically done!

When intrusive thoughts come at you remember, don't just let the enemy get over on you. Cast those thoughts down and replace them with God's truth by bringing them to God and speak the Word of God over these thoughts. In addition, I suggest getting a fresh "Rhema Word" from God, which is a personal and timely word from God to your heart. What does getting a fresh Rhema Word from God look like? When these thoughts come, I often will ask God, "Lord, what are You saying about this lie? Lord, give me some truth to combat this lie," then I listen.

The Holy Spirit will often bring a scripture, parable or phrase to my heart in the form of flowing thoughts, mental images, inward impressions or a video playing within my mind of the Rhema right now truth God wants to share with me. He will also often give me kinetic feelings of peace that we spoke about earlier in the book, regarding God's active voice of the Holy Spirit. He may remind me of one of His promises, His nature, one of His sayings to me like, "I got you son, don't give the enemy any place, I love you, follow Me." God will often bring Biblical stories, spiritual principles and spiritual laws to my heart. For example, He will bring to my heart that as I think, speak, and act on His Word it has great power. As I speak faith filled words it is causing things to happen in the unseen realm, that my prayers do change things! That if I continue to speak His Word, I will see breakthrough and walk in the reality of His promises to me, as His son. God will also bring to my remembrance spiritual markers of prayers He has answered in the past, as well as previous dreams, breakthroughs and encounters I have experienced with Him. These experiences are like your own personal "Gospel" message of what God has done in your life, it is like He takes out the "scroll" of the personal testimonies He has done in your life and shows them to you. It is so comforting hearing some fresh words and encouragement from God and getting some, right now, Holy Spirit spoken truth! His active voice adds layers of intimacy to your personal relationship with Him and so many times, will break the back of the enemy's attack against you.

Remember, when you are in a daily relationship with God and you're meeting heightened levels of adversity, you're often close to victory, breakthrough, blessings and seeing the glory of God manifest in major ways in your life. When you are on the verge of blessings, new seasons of increase and breakthroughs you will often sense opposition from the enemy. This also happens when you are doing things that are going to position you for increase such as prayer, reading the Bible, spreading God's love and becoming more like Jesus. I often practice doing the opposite of what that voice of doubt says "Oh reading the Bible is not doing anything for you. You can't even remember the scriptures you are reading", "Don't pray for that person, what if they think you are weird", or "There is no use in praying, it is not going to change anything anyways. It is just some words you are speaking into the air".

These are all lies of the enemy and fearful mindsets that still try to come against me but now I know where they come from! Now I know to do the exact opposite! The truth is, if the enemy is fighting what you are doing then there must be some activity and power going on in the spiritual realm that he does not want to happen.

The enemy will even try to use condemnation for having negative thoughts, to try to bring guilt, shame and unworthiness, because some of those thoughts entered your mind. I fight this battle all the time but now instead of taking those thoughts and letting them land in my heart I cast them out by the Name and Blood of Jesus! I declare "They are not my thoughts and I don't think like that I think like Jesus! I have the mind of Christ! (1 Corinthians 2:16)" The great news is the more you practice these 3 steps and declaring God's Word over your life, situations and others the less power negative or unwanted thoughts will have over you. You will also begin to recognize and experience more God inspired thoughts in your daily life. Thus your life will be transformed into the victorious life Jesus paid for you to live!

Any time you feel condemned just know that is the enemy and your own self-doubt trying to get you to accept feeling guilty, shameful and less than your true value as a son or daughter of God. There is a huge difference in conviction and condemnation. Conviction can be described as a "godly sorrow" that you experience when you sin or do anything contrary to what you know is right based on God's Love, Word and Spirit. ***"For the kind of sorrow God wants us to experience leads us away from sin and results in salvation. There's no regret for that kind of sorrow. But worldly sorrow, which lacks repentance, results in spiritual death." 2 Corinthians 7:10 NLT***

Conviction is from the Holy Spirit about something you need to look at changing, repent of, let go of and give over to God. Conviction will come with a sense of encouragement, love and wisdom it draws you closer to God. It's an inner knowing of remorsefulness that what you did was not right and needs to be changed, repented of, forgiveness needs to be given and received between yourself, God and others. Conviction is an invitation to connect with the Holy Spirit so whatever needs to be corrected can be addressed, repented of and changed. Conviction, while it may be uncomfortable, will always draw you closer to God and He wants you to respond to His voice, activity and guidance. Experiencing conviction means your heart is already changing and you are not who you use to be in the past the fact that you want to do better and be closer to God already is proof your changing and being transformed.

Condemnation is of the enemy and your own negative self talk. It is designed by the enemy to push you away from God through guilt, shame, unworthiness and fear. God does not operate in those areas, meaning He does not use fear based feelings like guilt, shame and unworthiness to communicate with you. The Bible says, ***"There is therefore now no condemnation for those who are in Christ Jesus, who walk not according to the flesh, but according to the Spirit." Romans 8:1 NIV*** If you find yourself feeling any of those ways or having those types of thoughts of thinking "God does not love me, I can't go to God after what I did or He is ashamed of me", that is not God's activity or voice, that is the voice of the enemy and negative mindsets that fear has caused in your life because of life experiences and lies you have believed about yourself, God and others.

In Philippians 4:6-7 AMP the Apostle Paul encourages us, ***"Do not be anxious or worried about anything, but in everything [every circumstance and situation] by prayer and petition with thanksgiving, continue to make your [specific] requests known to God. And the peace of God [that peace which reassures the heart, that peace] which transcends all understanding, [that peace which] stands guard over your hearts and your minds in Christ Jesus [is yours]."*** Paul is writing this encouragement to us from his prison cell. Although, he was physically locked up in prison mentally and spiritually he was experiencing freedom and peace in his heart, by putting his faith in Jesus into action, through putting a variation of these 3 steps into practice in his daily life. We all have had "prison experiences" of some type in our lives where we have felt trapped, stuck, locked up and imprisoned in some way. It could be a challenging living situation, school, financial difficulty, an unhealthy relationship, health issues or a challenging season of life that you feel stuck in. No matter what we are facing the grace, love, peace and freedom found in a daily relationship with God will empower us to overcome!

It's time to start winning the battlefield of our mind! It's time to expose and be delivered from the things that keep hooking you negatively, hurts from your life experiences, hang ups that keep limiting your life, unhealthy habits and relationships, intrusive thoughts, negative cycles, unhealthy patterns, destructive behavioral cycles and limited mindsets and beliefs, so you can live God's best for your life now! It's time for you to start living the victorious life Jesus Christ has already bought and paid in full for you to possess! It's time to start hearing, experiencing and focusing on what the Lord is thinking and saying about you! The way you think and the thoughts you entertain and focus on will greatly impact hearing God's voice and sensing His activity in your daily life. If you will make the decision to put these 3 powerful steps into action in your daily life you will see your whole life transform, remember the choice is yours!

UNDERSTANDING SIN AND HOW TO STOP SINFUL THOUGHTS AND BEHAVIOR PATTERNS THROUGH CONFESSION, REPENTANCE AND PRAYER:

Sin is missing the mark by thinking, saying and doing things that don't line up with God's Word, nature, character and love. Sin is also not doing what we know we are supposed to, based on what the Word of God says and how the Holy Spirit is leading us in our lives. The Bible refers to sin as disobedience towards God. Habitual sin is often an area of our lives that God does not have Lordship in and has not been invited to take control of by His Holy Spirit.

When you're confessing and repenting of your sin as a Believer in Jesus and giving it over to God, realize He has already forgiven you through the blood of Jesus. Your confessing and asking for forgiveness from a place of knowing that Jesus has already paid for that specific sin as well and that His blood removed all of your past, present and future sins from you. In the mind of God, through the blood of Jesus, the forgiveness of your sins is a finished work and a settled transaction. So you are confessing your sins to God from a place of affirmative thankful prayer because through what Jesus has already done for you He prepaid for any sin you will ever commit! That is a huge part of the "Good News" of "The Gospel of Jesus Christ" and God's love for us demonstrated through Jesus! Repenting of your sin means to turn away from sin and turn towards God from a heart condition of being sorrowful or remorseful about your shortcomings. Repentance implies changing direction, changing your actions, behavior and changing your way of thinking about anything you are doing that is contrary to God's Word, nature and character of love. In essence you're saying, "God I messed up, by faith, through Your help Jesus, I am choosing to turn away from this sin and change my way of thinking about it to Your thinking Lord." The Bible tells us it is actually knowing and experiencing God's goodness and kindness that leads us to repentance. ***"Do you realize that all the wealth of His extravagant kindness is meant to melt your heart and lead you into repentance?" Romans 2:4 TPT*** It is important to understand that sin damages your soul and causes trauma to your thinking patterns, mindsets, perceptions, emotions and twists your self-will to be more prideful and less God dependent. We will spend our whole lives in the process of becoming more like Jesus within our mind, will, emotions and intellect, which is what the Bible calls sanctification.

The steps and process of confessing and repenting of sin does several things for us. First, it conditions your soul; which is your mind, will and emotions; to live in a continuous place of humility and forgiveness for God, yourself and others around you. Confession and repentance of sin detoxes your soul from impurities and cleanses your consciousness. It removes sin from your soul and God cleanses your mind, will and emotions removing all unrighteousness that has tried to come into your heart thus keeping your heart tender and sensitive to the Holy Spirit's voice and guidance. Because how you hear God's voice and sense His guidance has to flow through your soul and conscious for you to gain understanding of what God is communicating to you. So the less impurities and strongholds in your soul the more effective the filter will be through which you hear God's voice and sense His leading. It keeps your relationship and fellowship with God healthy and growing. This practice also exposes the darkness of sin to the light of God's love. It brings sin out into the open so it's not hidden in your heart by guilt and shame. Confession and repentance of sin applies the blood of Jesus and God's grace to your shortcomings and removes the legal rights the devil can use to gain access into your life through your own willful sin and disobedience. The enemy will exploit this to manipulate and influence your life through your personal sins, strongholds and fears. Thus through the confession and repentance of sin you are appropriating and applying part of the provision of the finished works of Jesus Christ to your life which is destroying the works of darkness within your life (1 John 3:8). Lastly confession and repentance of sin is a spiritual realignment. It helps stop sin patterns, closes open doors and footholds that the enemy will use as legal consent and grounds to kill, steal and destroy in your life. This allows the hedge of God's protection around your life to stay strong. Unconfessed and unrepented of, sin, habitual sin patterns and sinful choices made that are contrary to God's Word do have negative consequences. ***"People who conceal their sins will not prosper, but if they confess and***

turn from them, they will receive mercy." Proverbs 28:13 NLT

Sin in your life can affect your relationship with God in negative ways and can cause natural consequences that will negatively impact your life and how well you hear God's voice. It does not mean God loves you any less. At the same time God hates sin, that does not mean God hates or dislikes the person. To God every person is redeemable and worth saving. The most vile and evil person you can think of God loves them and Jesus died for them. He does not like their sinful actions and lifestyle but He does love them. It's important to understand the enemy's plan when it comes to sin. The devil's scheme is to entice you with sin, then he shames you and blames you for the sin he enticed you with and lastly he attempts to convince you that God does not love you and is ashamed of you. Thus trying to separate you relationally from God so that you will be discouraged from having a healthy relationship with God because of your sin. This way when you tell on yourself the devil has nothing to hold over your head anymore! ***"If we confess our sins to God, He will keep His promise and do what is right: He will forgive us our sins and purify us from all our wrongdoing." 1 John 1:9 GNB***

So many times I hear people say I can't go to God I have done this or that or I don't feel worthy. They might have some sin in their lives they are not ready to let go of or they think they have to clean themselves up first before they go to God. The sad part is you can't clean yourself up on your own self-will, Jesus has to do that for you through a relationship with Him. Saying I am going to clean my life up and then have a relationship with God is like having a huge bleeding wound and saying I have to stop the bleeding and heal up the wound before I go to the emergency room. No, you go to the hospital to get care so your wound can be appropriately treated and cared for so your wound will heal properly. You can't be right-eous, forgiven or even truly changed on your own, you need a daily love relationship with Jesus, awaken to what He has done for you and receive the empowerment of the Holy Spirit. Jesus said it best in John 14:6 " I am the way, the truth and the life" meaning in this case of trying to "clean your-self up" before you can come to God I believe God is showing us the order that transformation happens in. You come to Jesus and surrender your life over to Him and get on the right "way", then as you learn the "truth" of the Bible by reading, listening and becoming God's written Word through the power of His Holy Spirit then He transforms you and cleans up your "life" in the process!

When you are confessing your sin you do it from a mindset of knowing you are already forgiven through the blood of Jesus for past, present and future sin. When you were born again Jesus made you His righteousness.

"He made Him who knew no sin to be sin on our behalf, so that we might become the righteousness of God in Him."2 Corinthians 5:21 Meaning no matter what you do or don't do, your legal access and right standing with God is secure. It is not based on what you do now or in the future, nor what you did in the past, but it is instead based on what Jesus did for you. That's grace, getting that which you did not earn. Once you surrender your life over to Jesus and confess Him as the Lord of your life you are made the righteousness of God through Jesus Christ!

It's very important to understand that the Bible says to awaken to righteousness and sin not; meaning to possess a righteousness consciousness (1 Corinthians 15:34). Knowing that no matter what you do, have done or will do, you as a Believer in Jesus, have the same legal access to God as Jesus does. The Bible makes it very clear Jesus was sinless, tempted in all ways just like we are but without sinning, so He could be the perfect offering for our sin. At the same time Jesus did not go around trying not to sin, His focus was not on sin. Jesus was so in love and focused on His relationship with His Heavenly Father and He knew His value and identity as God's Righteous Son and that focused loving devotion compelled His actions. We likewise are to focus on our value, identity and righteousness within the context of a devoted relationship with God. These truths are foundational to living a life of freedom from sin and in moral excellence and holiness. *"He Himself bore our sins" in His body on the cross, so that we might die to sins and live for righteousness; "by His wounds you have been healed." 1 Peter 2:24* The Bible says through what Jesus did for us on the cross we have died to sin and we live unto righteousness. It would not have said we can live for righteousness if it were an impossibility for us to do so.

As you develop this kind of *righteousness consciousness* as a mindset, perception and identity based on an intimate relationship with God, it will make sin powerless over your life. Now your focus is on your position of right standing with God and a healthy daily relationship with Jesus and not on the guilt, shame and fear of your sin. Thus confession and repentance of sin, receiving and giving forgiveness, becomes a daily part of your life. Humbling yourself and being quick to repent from a place of righteousness is one of the greatest truths in staying in a healthy relationship with God and hearing His voice. Tending the garden of your heart by pulling up the weeds of sin that try to entangle you on a daily basis and to rob you of the peace, joy and love that Jesus paid for you to have, is and should be the lifestyle of every Believer.

I want to give you an example that we can probably all relate to in some way, which is getting upset, irritated or frustrated at someone you work with, let's call them Billy. So I am at work and Billy does something to irritate me and I start thinking all these negative thoughts about Billy, even though I might feel like some of them are justified that is still sin, and I need to get it out of my heart and give it over to God. To do that I would use a variation of the 3 step process that we covered earlier.

I am going to give you a prayer that I would use in that situation as a model and guideline you can follow:

Step 1: (Refusing the thoughts and feelings) "In Jesus Name I refuse those negative thoughts about Billy and I don't want to think or feel like that about Him because I have the mind of Christ."

Step 2: (Confession and Repentance) "Lord I confess my irritation and frustration with Billy's actions and I repent for those feelings and thoughts against him and I release them over to you in Jesus Name." (Forgiveness Exchange) "Lord I forgive Billy by an act of my will I don't care how I feel because Your Word says to forgive and love other people so by an act of my will I forgive him and I forgive myself for thinking those thoughts about him."

Step 3: (Pray for yourself) "Jesus I thank You that I am forgiven and that You love me Lord. I praise You for Your goodness and that Your Spirit of joy and Your peace floods my heart." (Pray for Billy) "Lord Jesus I thank You that Billy comes to know You at a deeper level and Your love will guide his thoughts, words and actions. I bless Billy's life and family with joy and peace! In Jesus name. Amen."

You may have to use these 3 steps several times on one person or situation depending on how upset you are, but as you keep releasing it over to God He is cleansing your consciousness and keeping your heart free of offense, unforgiveness, irritation and all the other sins that try to rob us of our peace on a daily basis. The amazing thing is these 3 steps often take less than a minute to do and will save you so much time from stewing on the situation and keep your heart clean of negative thoughts and emotions throughout the day!

So often after we release a situation over to God or forgive someone, we will find ourselves picking back up again what we just gave to God within our minds through our thought life. Before we know it the negative and sinful thoughts start coming at us again and that is when you have to relax, stand on the grace of God and surrender those thoughts and feelings over to God again as many times as it takes, knowing the Holy Spirit will help you. Depending on the situation you may also need to humble yourself and approach the person and apologize if you acted unlovingly or defensive towards them. You may even feel like your actions towards them are justified and that you're in "the right" but the real question is were you acting out of love and righteousness? Meaning did you speak and act in such a way in which the person receiving it recognized the love of Jesus within you? If not then default on the side of love and righteousness, humble yourself and apologize. A great gauge of irritation and frustration with someone is defensiveness. If you sense you are being defensive about something even if it is within your own thoughts that is a good indication you may be irritated or frustrated with someone or something. This type of self protection and self preservation based on being offended and irritated with someone or something resulting in defensiveness as subtle and as harmless as it may seem is sinful and not God's best for your life or others. In this example, if my irritation leads me to have an attitude of defensiveness with Billy or to say something to him contrary of God's love as defined in 1 Corinthians Chapter 13 in the Amplified Bible then I would need to either apologize to Billy immediately or at a later time. In those type of situations I either try to apologize right then or if I need time to cool down I will ask the Holy Spirit to prompt me to apologize at an appropriate time later on that day. Remember these steps are a model and a guideline for you to follow. You can use variations of this 3 step process on a daily basis depending on the situation and how you sense the Holy Spirit is having you address it.

I want to share a quick testimony of how I applied this process of confession and repentance of sin in my own personal life that allowed God to work within me to break sin patterns, change my behavior and transform my life. For years I used curse words all the time as part of my daily vocabulary. I tried several times in my own self effort and did not see any lasting change. Then I decided I would do it through God's power and spiritual weapons. So made a commitment that whenever I cussed I would confess my sin of using profanity, repent and thank God for my forgiveness, and then I would pray Psalms 19:14 over myself ***"Let the words of my mouth and the meditation of my heart be acceptable in Your sight, O LORD, my rock and my redeemer." ESV***

Lastly I would worship God by thanking Him that the Holy Spirit lives within me and is changing my mind, will, emotions and personality to be just like Jesus! Over time my cussing got less and less until it was no longer a sin pattern in my life and I did it through God's Spirit, Word and power and not my own self-will and self-effort! As you live this kind of lifestyle of confession, repentance and humility you are able to maintain a peace, joy and love that will allow you to cultivate a healthy relationship with God where you hear His voice and sense His activity in your daily life.

It is important to note, do not let your emotions of "not feeling forgiven" get the best of you. Remember you're confessing and repenting from the position of being righteous before God. You are already forgiven. Forgiveness is not a feeling or an emotion it's an act of submitting your will to God and appropriating the forgiveness Jesus paid for you to have. Confessing and repenting of your sins through these steps and having a righteousness consciousness will allow you to walk in the reality of having true freedom from sin; which Jesus gave His life for you to experience!

WHAT DOES IT MEAN TO BE STILL, REST, RELAX AND BE PATIENT BEFORE GOD?

When most of us hear **"Be still and know that I am God Psalms 46:10"** we think of being quiet, resting and being patient which has some context to it. However, this concept has an even deeper meaning that is important to understand from God's perspective. The Hebrew meaning behind rest coupled with this statement is broken down into three main parts (Strong's 5117). One is to stop striving in your own self-will and self-effort, two is to let go of "the thing" you're holding onto or fighting with and three, is to surrender whatever that "thing" is to God through prayer thus accessing and leaning on the spiritual power and effort of God and not your own self-will. Then look to God and know Him intimately by experiencing His presence, voice and activity in a personal and relational way. Resting and relaxing in God is a confident trust knowing God is good and you are leaning into and relying on His goodness, Spirit and Word. Practically speaking it could look like you surrendering unforgiveness over to God in prayer, instead of striving and fighting in your marriage in self-effort start involving God in your marriage by praying for and with your spouse. This also looks like in your personal prayer time relaxing in God's presence, not allowing the cares of life to pull at your mind and knowing God wants to speak to you. Not striving trying to get God to love you because He already does and wants to talk to you more than you want to hear Him. Another aspect of being still could be letting go and releasing your cares over to God as they come and refocusing on what He is saying to you through His active voice, activity and Word. Then surrendering on a daily basis your will and life over to God. Not allowing your positive or negative circumstances to control your decisions and choices. Instead allowing God's voice, Word and Spirit to be your guidance for all of your thoughts, emotions, words and actions. All these examples sound simple and for the most part they are simple. However, when challenges come, the storms of life roll in and the reality of life begins to speak very loudly these things can be very hard to do. That's why it's important to be intentional about making them a daily lifestyle choice.

Resting, relaxing and being still in the Lord is something God has really been working with me on for the last several years. I want to share with you what resting, relaxing and being still in the Lord looks like to me practically. Consistently spending alone time with God, being secure in my identity and value as a son of God by reading and speaking God's Word over my situation, giving my issues and thoughts over to Him by using the three step process we teach in this book on a daily moment by moment basis. Then surrendering my cares over to God and trusting that God has me through thanking, praising and worshiping Him everyday. There is a quiet power and peace that comes over you as you cast your cares upon Him in trust and total surrender. As issues come up I seek His wisdom first, take the necessary action and trust Him that His plans for me are good and they are to prosper me (Jeremiah 29:11). I rest in the memory banks of what God has already done in my life by thinking about past life experiences and spiritual markers of where God's promises came to pass in my life and it gives me faith to trust Him right now and in the future. Resting, relaxing, and being patient are not inactivity they actually call you to take action by doing the things listed above like taking negative thoughts captive, trusting in the Lord and communicating with Him on a daily basis thus staying in a healthy loving relationship with Him. The Bible says there is a "labor" to enter into the rest of God (Hebrews 4:11). I have found out through experience that this labor consists of a lot of affirmative thankful prayer, alone time with God, taking actions by faith and in faith, continuously surrendering your will over to God and trustfully following God on a daily basis like we will talk about throughout this book. There is an internal trust and peace in understanding we live and we fight from a place and position of rest, grace, faith and our intimate alone time with God. So essentially you do what you can do by faith taking the necessary actions and leave everything else in God's hands. Resting is trusting and relying on God to be good to His Word and to do His part.

4

THE HOLY SPIRIT

THE ACTIVE AGENT ON EARTH

THE HOLY SPIRIT IS THE SPIRIT OF GOD AND HE IS ONE OF THE TH-ree Persons of God: God the Father, God the Son Jesus Christ, and God the Holy Spirit; Three Persons, All One God. The Holy Spirit is the active agent on the earth that inhabits, empowers and energizes the Believer and the Word of God.

Jesus said speaking of the Holy Spirit: ***"But I tell you the truth, it is to your advantage that I go away; for if I do not go away, the Helper (Comforter, Advocate, Intercessor—Counselor, Strengthener, Standby) will not come to you; but if I go, I will send Him (the Holy Spirit) to you [to be in close fellowship with you]." JOHN 16:7 AMP*** God speaks through the Holy Spirit that lives inside every born again Believer. That is why when understood and lived out correctly, Christianity is not a religion at all, it has been taught and lived out in that way at times but that was not God's original intent for Christianity. All religions you look at throughout the world are about you working harder, you doing better, you being a good person through your own self-will, you doing the right thing, you attaining some type of enlightenment or mystic wisdom so that they will possibly become good enough or accepted by the god they serve. ***And you did not receive the "spirit of religious duty," leading you back into the fear of never being good enough. But you have received the "Spirit of full acceptance," enfolding you into the family of God. Romans 8:15 TPT*** Christianity is not about being a "good person" and it is not about what "you do", it's about receiving what Jesus has done for you on your behalf. Jesus did not come to make you a "good person" He came to make your spirit on the inside of you spiritually alive and connected with God again and to give you the power to transform your life into His, by putting His Holy Spirit inside of you and therefore connecting you back to God's nature and Spirit. Christianity is not a life enhancement course, behavior modification or a religious system; it is the total restoration and transformation of your entire life!

It is God's eternal life-giving Spirit being imparted to you and living inside of your spirit and flowing through you on a daily basis. It is not about you working hard enough, keeping a set of rules or laws, being good enough, serving more, or attaining a certain amount of wisdom and enlightenment to try to get God to love and accept you. God already loves you and accepts you because you are His child, and He wants a daily relationship with you that is real, personal, powerful, and intimate. Christianity is at its core, a spiritual relationship with God, based on God living inside of you. It is God coming to inhabit you and living in you now, on earth and causing you to live with Him forever; which gives you eternal life in Heaven, once you leave this earth. This is Christianity it is the indwelling of the Holy Spirit, Christ in you the hope of glory! Jesus came to live, suffer, and die for you. He did this not only to get all of us into Heaven, but to get Heaven, God's Spirit, into us. Which imparts eternal life into all who would believe and call on the name of Jesus Christ, the only name that saves! God made us His residential address! We are God's address and residence because the Holy Spirit lives in us! We are carriers of God's Presence! We are the Temple of the Holy Spirit, *"Do you not know that your body is the temple (the very sanctuary) of the Holy Spirit Who lives within you, Whom you have received [as a Gift] from God? You are not your own, You were bought with a price [purchased with a preciousness and paid for, made His own]. So then, honor God and bring glory to Him in your body." 1 Corinthians 6:19-20 AMPC*

The Holy Spirit is God coming to live in you so that you can have a constant and continual spiritual fellowship with Him. God's desire is for you to live out what He has called you to in His Word which is: to love God with all your mind, body, soul, and strength. To love yourself by receiving God's love for you and in turn giving that love back to Him in a love and worship exchange which looks like a daily intimate relationship with Him. Then out of the overflow of your love exchange with God go out and love others as Jesus loves you! Christianity is not just about getting something out of you like: sin, fear, worry, guilt, shame and unworthiness. Christianity is about getting God; Who is love, Who is light and

Who is the Word inside of you. It is about the blood of Jesus totally removing your sin by Jesus taking it upon Himself, and being completely possessed and inhabited by God's Spirit! God is bigger, stronger, and more powerful than any sin or fear; and therefore, nothing can overtake you when you live in relationship with God! In Him, you are no longer a slave to sin or this world, but you become a joint heir with Jesus Christ and are made His righteousness. ***"For we are the temple of the living God; even as God said, I will dwell in and with and among them and will walk in and with and among them, and I will be their God, and they shall be My people. [Exod. 25:8; 29:45; Lev. 26:12; Jer. 31:1; Ezek. 37:27.]" 2 Corinthians 6:16 AMPC***

As you become aware of God living on the inside of you and begin to lean on the Holy Spirit in you to guide your thoughts, words and actions, you become love, you become light, you become the Word of God on flesh and bones for everyone to be able to experience the love of Jesus, through your life! Thus, destroying the kingdom of darkness all around you by walking and living through the Holy Spirit who is Christ in you the righteous expectation of God's glory being shown through your life. Living in the truth that when you were born again you received the same Holy Spirit that Jesus had as He walked on this earth and there is no difference, the Holy Spirit that was in Him, is now in you as a Believer in Christ. This means you have the same access as Jesus had to the Kingdom of God which He said lives inside of you, the Holy Spirit. Therefore, you base your life on God being good to His Word and you allow the Holy Spirit to guide your thoughts, emotions, perceptions, words, and actions on a daily, moment-by-moment basis. Jesus said speaking of the Holy Spirit: ***"But when He, the Spirit of Truth (the Truth-giving Spirit) comes, He will guide you into all the Truth (the whole, full Truth). He will take of (receive, draw upon) what is Mine and will reveal (declare, disclose, transmit) it to you." John 16:13-14 AMPC***

Through this process you become more like Jesus everyday by being led by the Holy Spirit, then your behavior and what "you do" (your actions) becomes a byproduct of "who you are" (in Christ) with the transformational change coming through you being in close fellowship, friendship and companionship with the Holy Spirit. So instead of you trying "to do good things" in order to become a "good person" based on your own self effort, you become like Jesus taking on His very nature, character and Spirit which in-turn causes you to behave differently, being compelled by your intimate relationship with the Holy Spirit and His love.

The Holy Spirit allows you to be a constant worshipper of God.

Constant worship is what God seeks from us; which is free will worship, love, and relationship. ***But the time is coming—indeed it's here now—when true worshippers will worship the Father in spirit and in truth. The Father is looking for those who will worship Him that way. John 4:23 NLT***

As humans, we were made to worship and be joined to God in a marriage covenant like a groom (being God) and the bride (being us as Believers) and as the Bible says the two becoming one flesh (Genesis 2:24). We were made to connect, and we were actually made to live in and walk with God on a daily basis. So, if you don't worship God, you will worship things of this world such as people, money, career, children and material possessions. If you don't connect with God, then you will find yourself needing to connect and get validation from other people, social media and the world system. If you don't live in and walk with God, on a daily basis, you will find yourself trying to fill that void in your heart with all kinds of other self made idols: status, television, busyness, food, your job, your kids, your spouse and any other things you look to get life and peace from, as your source besides God. An idol is anything in your life you hold back from God or choose over God either directly or indirectly. An idol is also anything you look to get your needs met by when it comes to your value, identity and peace instead of God.

Be aware of this spiritual truth, satan and evil spirits are after your worship of God. Their aim is to get you to subtly worship and serve anything else besides God, thus getting you into sin and trying to hinder your relational growth with God. Even the "good things" and blessings from God, satan will subtly use to try and create modern day idols of worship in your life such as; a promotion you want at work or a business you own which overtakes your life, allowing wanting more money for you and your family to drive you to take on too much, seeing your children succeed to the point where they become the center of your life instead of God, putting stress on yourself to purchase or payoff a house, or doing work "for God" at the expense of having a vibrant relationship with God. The concerning thing is that the enemy needs your service and your cooperation in this world to get things done. The demonic realm has the power of suggestion and persuasion to tempt us. If you do not resist their subtle temptations to worship other things besides God, they will create fear, pride, guilt, shame, unworthiness, greed, isolation, doubt, and sin within you. This will cause you to be a detriment and an ungodly influence to yourself and others around you. God has a purpose and destiny for your life. The devil also has a purpose and destiny for your life as well. The question is whose report are you going to believe? Because whoever's report you believe and follow will be the purpose and destiny that you live out. It sounds really simple, and it is, but when the stresses, trials, storms and hardships of life come will you forgive when it is not convenient or easy? Will you love the people that are hard to love? Will you believe in the promises of God when your life looks like the exact opposite of what God's Word says? Will you choose to put God at the head and at the center of your life when the reality of life seems to be pulling on you from all different directions? I want to encourage you to follow and pursue a love relationship with God no matter what the enemy and this world system tries to shout at you and throw your way. Remember the enemy needs your cooperation and consent don't give him place! Don't allow fear, shame, busyness, worry, worldly desires and unforgiveness to separate you from the purpose and destiny God wants for you. The daily intimacy we can have through the Holy Spirit, transforms you into God's love, peace, glory, power and Word. It also delivers us from the powers of darkness and translates us into the kingdom of Jesus Christ! (Colossians 1:13)

When we look at people in the Bible, the ones that the Bible says, "Walked with God" they were all people who had relationship with Him, intimately. Their lives had the mark of transformation and God's glory upon them. Experiencing this intimacy, is when my life radically changed. I became a worshipper and a lover of God through intimately experiencing Him, on a daily basis, through interacting with the Holy Spirit, who lives inside of me as well as each and every Believer in Jesus Christ. For so many years, I was stuck in religion and did not spiritually interact with God by way of the Holy Spirit. Meaning religiously I did "good works", I went to Church, I prayed a couple of times a day for a minute or two, I served at my Church and other community organizations. I was even a motivational speaker mostly to young adults but I had little to no intimate relationship with the Holy Spirit where I experienced hearing God's active voice and sensed His activity in a real and personal way in my life on a daily basis. When that did begin to happen, my life radically changed, and God began to personally Father me and His Word came alive in my life. I began to become the Word of God, instead of just reading it. I began to sense the Holy Spirit's leading and hearing His still small voice inside of me! I received my supernatural prayer language and began to pray in other tongues on a daily basis. This was the catalyst for reaching places of real, personal intimacy with God that I never knew were possible. This kind of God lead life is available to every single person that will believe on Jesus Christ and receive the infilling of His Holy Spirit!

As you partner with, yield to, and interact with the Holy Spirit, you move from knowing about Jesus with head knowledge, to the experiential heart level knowledge of Jesus that brings transformation where you become like Jesus who is the Word, Light, and Love. Who, now lives inside of you through His Holy Spirit! Living a Presence driven life, is key to an abundant life of victory, peace, and joy no matter your circumstances. God's Presence is referring to living a daily life driven by an intimate love relationship with God that is powered and guided by His Spirit, Word, and Love. That relationship comes through an intimate and continual two-way dialogue where you communicate with God on a daily, moment-by-moment basis, through the Holy Spirit. This is where you talk, listen, and yield to God's Spirit within you. God's activity and voice are imprinted and embedded throughout your daily life, in a vast amount of ways. The aim of this book is to help you identify and join God in His activity and understand His communication with you, as well as what He is doing in the lives of others around you. Thus, you are partnering with and encountering God! Through those daily interactions, you build a healthy relationship based on trust, intimacy, experience, respect, reverence, love, and worship. These encounters happen as you lean into, rely on, and put your trust in the God that lives inside of you, as a Believer in Jesus Christ, on a daily moment-by-moment basis.

Let me give you an example of what has really happened to you in the unseen spiritual realm that I think everyone can quantify and grasp. When you give your life to Jesus Christ and make Him the Lord of your life the Bible says you become a joint heir with Him and that you are adopted by God and we are given a "Spirit of Adoption" that we not only call God Father but "Abba" which is equivalent to the term "Daddy" in the English language (Romans 8:17). So in essence it is kind of like Bill Gates, the owner of Microsoft (or you can use your favorite billionaire or celebrity), has adopted you into his family and now you have access to his entire fortune and he wants to partner up and team up with you on a daily basis to make all of your daily life experiences peaceful, blessed and joyful and he is going to use all of his resources to insure that your purpose, destiny and calling are fulfilled. It is as if Bill Gates wanted to hang out with you all the time to ensure your success in life. If Bill Gates wanted to do that for you and adopt you, would you accept that free gift? I think most of us would easily and with great excitement say yes to accept that free gift! Why? Because of the influence, money, power and wealth that is behind Bill Gates; we would be ecstatic at the thought of having access to all that comes with being adopted by Bill Gates and given instant access to his entire multi-billion dollar fortune.

In the grand scheme of things Bill Gates, compared to God, is just a mere man; but because of the reality of his wealth on this earth we would count being adopted by him as something wonderful and great. God is the source of all love, power, wisdom, resources and He has given you something money can't buy, the peace of being in relationship with the Holy

Spirit now here on earth and eternal life which guarantees your place in the Kingdom of Heaven when you leave this earth. When you think about it in those terms why would we not want to partner up, team up, lean on, rely on and trust in the most powerful and loving Father that we could ever have? Many people are thinking, "Yeah Sterling, but I can see Bill Gates and his bank account is something that in reality can change and empower my life, I can't see God". You are right you can't see God tangibly in the way you could a normal human being but you can experience God in ways that far outweigh any human interaction! You can hear His active voice and sense His activity to where He becomes so real to you, like He is in my life and the lives of everyone who have come to develop an intimate daily loving relationship with Him. I hope and pray that this example shifts your thinking to know and believe how loved, cherished and blessed you truly are and can be through a relationship with the Holy Spirit.

Knowing that the God of the universe is living inside of you, that He wants to guide you and direct you on a daily basis into peace, joy, love and your purpose and that He has picked you to live forever with Him in Heaven is an amazing and free gift from God! What it takes for this to become as real as Bill Gates adopting you is for you to receive the Holy Spirit, begin to live "God inside minded" and tap into God's active voice and begin to sense and celebrate His activity in your daily life! As you live a lifestyle of love in Christ, as a joint heir you come to know God by experience and you come to know the peace, joy and love that no amount of worldly provisions or possessions can buy!

We are to be in constant communion with the Holy Spirit. When most people hear the word "communion" they often think of participating in the "Lord's Supper" also called "Holy Communion" by partaking of the bread and some type of red wine or grape juice. Christians do this in remembrance of the body and blood of Jesus being broken and shed for us to enter into the New Covenant where we are made the righteousness of God in Christ and God's Spirit comes to live within us. However, in this sense "communion" with the Holy Spirit means to engage God in heart level conversations where intimate thoughts and feelings are exchanged between you both. This interaction transforms our conscious and our subconscious by the leading of the Holy Spirit, which causes an inward knowing and a leading of God's Word in our hearts. It is a process to be led by the Holy Spirit in both realms. It takes daily practice and training. ***"My conscience [enlightened and prompted] by the Holy Spirit bearing witness with me" Romans 9:1 AMPC***

God wants you to seek Him and lean on the God in you (1 John 4:4) on a daily basis so He can transform and renew your conscious and subconscious mind. This glorious transformation in our lives, of God making us more like His Son Jesus, comes from pursuing a daily relationship with the Holy Spirit and is a lifelong process. As we choose to be led by the Holy Spirit and choose not to try to make our own self-driven way in life, day in and day out, God can do His work within us of conforming and molding us into the image and essence of Jesus. This moves us from running on self-will, self-effort, self-desires and trying to be self-reliant, to living our lives leaning on and being guided by the Holy Spirit in us. This Biblically refers to "denying ourselves", "crucifying the flesh", "dying to self" and laying aside the "old self" meaning putting to death the fallen animal nature of our fleshly desires and self-will by putting God's Word first place in our lives and walking in a close loving fellowship with the Holy Spirit (Romans 6:6, Ephesians 4:22-24). You may be saying to yourself "Whoa Sterling those terms sound really intense!" However, in actuality living by the "old self" is much more intense and detrimental to our lives. Because the old self is influenced by fleshly desires, negative life experiences, the demonic realm, current challenging circumstances, pride, all kinds of fears, hurt, unforgive-ness, self-seeking ambition, idolization of people and things, guilt and lust of various kinds. Living by the old self in combination with these influences produces; worry, anxiety, depression, shame, anger and grief which I think we can all agree are intense and unwanted. So instead God is calling us to "lay aside the old self" through daily communion with the Holy Spirit, knowing God intimately through a loving relationship and renewing our minds with the Word of God so we can become transformed into what we were originally designed to be, which is just like Jesus. So by forsaking our self-will for God's will all we have to lose is the "old self" something we were never meant to be in the first place! This happens as we choose to lay down our old-self and pick up our new life and nature in Jesus. Thus running on God's will for our lives and being God dependent and God reliant as the dwelling place of the Holy Spirit which is how God originally designed and purposed for us to be. Jesus modeled this for us by dying daily to what His soul wanted and instead He chose to be lead by the Holy Spirit. Then He took it one step further by actually dying a physical death on the cross for you and me so we could have the Holy Spirit live within us, so we could be empowered to put the old self to death by living through the power of the Holy Spirit. Some practical examples of dying to self can be: forgiving others when it's not east to do so, humbling ourselves and apolo-gizing to others when we are in the wrong or even when we think we are in the right, repenting and admitting our short comings to God and being willing to act in love even in challenging situations.

You have heard the expression "error on the side of caution" which means being careful about what you're thinking, saying or doing. I have another terminology and mindset that I use and say that has helped me in my daily walk with the Lord. I now "default on the side of righteousness" and I "train in righteousness" everyday. From glory to glory and faith to faith, I make it my goal to increase everyday in my relationship with Jesus. Being guided by the Holy Spirit, is a moment by moment mindset, choice and determined action. Being so possessed by God's love that it becomes who you are. So in essence I let God's Word, Spirit and Love be the filter, lens, mindset and perception that I view and conduct my daily thoughts, words and actions through. This is what it practically means to "walk by the Spirit" and live from "glory to glory" and "faith to faith" as the Bible calls it. *"So I say, let the Holy Spirit guide your lives. Then you won't be doing what your sinful nature craves." Galatians 5:16 NLT* I want to encourage you to default on the side of righteousness and walk by the Holy Spirit! Which will empower you to deny yourself and follow God's will more closely as well as hear God's voice more clearly. Ask the Holy Spirit to get all up in your business on a daily basis!

There is no pressure to transform ourselves. Religion may have taught you that you have to be "cleaned up" to be a part of a local Church family or that you are not worthy of God's love and acceptance just how you are now. That you have to strive to be better and be "good enough" for God through your own self-will, self-effort and performance before you can have a relationship with Him. How exhausting is it to try to pretend to be something you are not? Aren't real relationships based on truth, vulnerability and trust? A healthy relationship with God based on the Bible and the life of Jesus shows us that God wants us to come to Him just as we are, and that just by being in close relationship with Him, interacting with the Holy Spirit on a daily basis through prayer, worship, applying and reading the Word, that He does the work in you! *"For it is God who works in you both to will and to do for His good pleasure." Philippians 2:13 NKJV* Think about it this way. If you were all dirty, would you clean yourself off before you take a shower? It sounds silly to think about, but a relationship with God is the same way. We do not have to walk in shame or hide from God like Adam and Eve did in the Garden of Eden after they sinned. I am not saying sin in our lives is ok, because it's not ok and God does not like sin. Not living a godly life has consequences and a sinful lifestyle will hinder you from maximizing God's best for your life. What I am saying is that sin does not change the way God feels about us, God loves you. Sin also does not change the plans He has for us if we will come to Him and allow the Holy Spirit to relationally transform our lives! God sees all and He really enjoys the transformation process! He is known for making beauty out of the ashes of our mistakes. Taking broken people and making beautiful stories of healing, purpose and destiny out of them!

Let me give you an example. When I first started walking with the

Lord, seeking Him and pursuing relationship with Him, I had areas in my life that the enemy had a foothold in and patterns of sin that were ungodly, that the enemy had used to keep me in bondage. God did not deal with some of these patterns right away. When I cried out to the Lord in distress because I was sad that I could not stop sinning against Him, He spoke to me very clearly through the inward voice of the Holy Spirit and taught me something very valuable. He said, "You are my responsibility. I have seen the end from the beginning. I am greater than any situation that you will ever face and have met you in the darkness to show Myself strong on your behalf. Trust Me." You see, God wanted me to know that He loved me anyways. That I could not make myself better on my own time and performance. But in His perfect timing, He would move and bring transformation in those areas. The condition of my heart was pure towards the Lord, but I was still unable to free myself. I was completely reliant on my relationship with God and because of His loving response to me, I pressed into Him deeper, I clung to Him for life, and eventually He brought freedom, deliverance and new life in those areas of sin and struggles and so much more! He continues to do this! A relationship with God is a constant process of growth and we never just arrive! It is like a mountaintop that leads to Heaven, it is the journey of a lifetime! He is always building our character, transforming our soul and continuing to shape us to be more like Jesus. That is why the lesson He taught me was so important. He wants us to trust and rest in Him while He works in our lives. All of our strength, refinement, transformation, ability, and freedom comes from being in relationship with Him! But you have to be willing to do it His way by being obedient to the Holy Spirit's leading and trusting Him in the process.

The Bible says that, ***"Unless the Lord builds the house, the builders labor in vain. Psalms 127:1 NIV"*** God has the original blueprint for our lives. When we submit and are obedient to His ways, which is giving Him permission to move freely in our heart and lives thus choosing His way over ours, He is able to start building based on the original design and intended purpose He created you for! In order to become like Jesus and live God's best for our lives, we have to do things God's way. This means living in obedience to His written Word and being obedient to His spoken words through His Holy Spirit.

David said in the Psalms 119:104, ***"Your Word is a lamp unto my feet and a light unto my path."*** In this scripture, David is referring to both God's written Word and His spoken Word through the Holy Spirit. You might be wondering what this looks like in everyday life. It might seem like a huge task, but the truth is, it starts with one decision at a time. Just like with any relationship, trust and communication builds a strong foundation.

It is important to trust God's love for us and know He is faithful to keep us safe and on the right path as we step into the process of learning to hear His voice and follow His Spirit.

As we continue to lean on God, in every decision, and turn our thoughts towards Him, whether it be looking up some scriptures that relate to circumstances we need God's wisdom and guidance on, or thanking Him for little things throughout our day in short prayers, we begin to develop a pattern of communication with God. We begin to be God inside minded leaning on God's Spirit within us. God's Word says, "to ask, and you shall receive"(Matthew 7:7). So, ask God to lead you by His Spirit, and thank Him for making His ways in your life plain to you, that there would be no confusion or distraction. When you ask these things in Jesus' name, scripture says they will be given to you (John 14:14)!

Communication from the Holy Spirit comes in many forms. His leading often comes with a sense of peace you get along with flowing thoughts of godly wisdom you receive about what God is saying to you or about the situation you're seeking His perspective and guidance on. Sometimes it feels like a stirring of excitement in your spirit or a leap in your heart! We have all made the statement "something told me not to do that, or something told me to do that" well the something that told you not to do something that does not line up with God's love and Word and to do and take positive action on things that do line up with God's love and Word was the Holy Spirit. This can be an unction, inward knowing, thought or impression you get from the Holy Spirit within you. *"For all who are led by God's Spirit are God's children." Romans 8:14 ISV* The key is to follow the inner knowing and keep your Holy Spirit unction soft, keep your heart tender in the little things, stay sensitive to His leading with the impressions that we sense in our spirits. Often times it is as simple as something we feel God is putting on our heart for someone or about something we are experiencing in our lives that come as impressions or thoughts. When I first started walking close with God He would train me in keeping my heart soft by prompting me in small acts of integrity. Such as picking up a piece of paper on the ground, cleaning something up that I could have left for someone else to do and correcting myself in conversations when I found myself exaggerating a story I was telling or being incorrect when communicating with others which I use to just blow off as "little white lies" but it was the small acts of integrity that God used to start transforming my heart to hear His voice and sense the prompting of the Holy Spirit. God really does want to interact with us in all things. There are many times I get an impression on my heart that this person needs a kind word or I feel that I am being prompted to say or do something that matches God's love and nature. I have found when I act on these promptings that myself and others experience God in powerful ways.

The Holy Spirit has also been called the voice at the back of your mind. The truth is the Holy Spirit's voice will often sound a lot like your inner voice or conscious but it will come with a slightly different flow and tone to it, one of peace, love and wisdom. You will sense God is putting something on your heart; it's like an impression, idea, feeling and thoughts that you get. It can even seem like a swirl of words or swirling thoughts that come to your mind that come with an inward knowing and a sense of I need to think, speak or take this certain action in this way. It is important to practice hearing God in your everyday life in various decisions throughout your day. For instance, I encourage you to discuss all kinds of things with the Holy Spirit; what shoes to wear; what purchases to make; where to go to lunch or dinner; what compliment to give your spouse; what upbuilding words to give to your child; how to answer a question someone asks you; what business decisions to make at work; what book in the Bible should I read today? That way when the larger decisions come, you're trained up in hearing the Holy Spirit's voice when there is little to no pressure. This will also allow you to build trust, intimacy and friendship with God coming to experience that He wants to be involved in every area of your life. God truly is practical. So many people miss this truth. God wants to bless you with creative solutions and Godly wisdom to strategically guide you in your daily life such as business ideas, financial guidance, creative ideas, inventions, divine connections, school and education, wisdom for your homework and tests, decisions at work, solving family issues, wisdom with your spouse and kids. Invite the Holy Spirit into these areas of your life by asking Him questions about these various areas and then listen and write down or take a mental note of what you sense He is saying to you. Reading scriptures that relate to what your asking God about is a great way to get a personal revelation from God where His Spirit brings practical application to His Word. Also using affirmative thankful prayer as you do your daily tasks, inviting God's favor, wisdom and presence in to team up with you. When I came to understand that God truly wants to be involved and help me with every area of my life and in every decision I make, there was a sense of love and fullness that I came to experience where I finally did not feel lonely or empty anymore. My whole life became richer and fuller as I began to team up and partner with God on a daily basis!

In sensing and being guided by the Holy Spirit in you, remember God's love, nature and Word is always the context you base everything on. The Holy Spirit is God's power, love, and Spirit, placed into your spirit by the Greater One who now lives on the inside of you, but it is still up to us to inquire of, lean on and trust in the love, power and Spirit of God in us. Guidance, relationship and transformation does not happen automatically you have to be intentional about engaging the Holy Spirit by faith on a daily basis.

For example, when you are praying about something and wisdom comes to your mind that gives you a sense of peace or a phrase that God brings to your heart like "I've got you", "follow Me", "trust in Me" He is speaking to you. He has said those kinds of phrases to me, and I have heard others testify to that as well. This is the still small inward voice and the wise whisper of God that rises out of your inner being. That voice will always be peaceful, calming, and in line with the Bible. While these nudges and communication can sometimes be very subtle please don't discount the simplicity of the phrases, mental pictures or the senses of peace you receive because there is a great amount of love and wisdom behind this communication between you and God. Which will lead you to greater revelation of His love, purpose and leading for your life.

In contrast when you are praying about God's will on something, and you do not have the leading of God's peace on a decision; which is something I call "getting a check in your spirit." It is almost like the Holy Spirit is sending up a red flag and removing peace through a sensation that feels like a discomfort in your chest or a sense of uneasiness in your stomach. This is what women, moms especially, often call their "6th sense" or "mother's intuition". It's when you just know, that you know something, is not right. It could be described as a spiritual understanding and supernatural direction known as discernment.

Often when I have a knowing of something God is telling me through the Holy Spirit, it feels like a deep knowing in my heart and spirit. It feels as though God has stamped this information on my heart or downloaded it to my spirit and my mind. I know it is true by faith and there is a peace about what I am sensing. The Holy Spirit will lead us as we allow for it; meaning seeking God's perspective and yielding over to what we sense He is telling us by faith. Remember as you take risks and step out on faith in what you sense God is telling you and showing you, there is always grace for the process! Part of being a son or daughter of God, is learning through experience. This means sometimes we miss what God is saying to us, we make wrong decisions and we don't hear God correctly. Instead we hear out of our own conscious, the voice of others or the voice of the enemy. In those times, which will happen to everyone, it is important to humble ourselves by admitting when we may have missed it, accept being corrected and be teachable and willing to learn from our mistakes. Do not let this create a fear of failure in you. God has an abundant amount of grace for your personal creative process of hearing Him and being lead by His Spirit.

Hearing God and being led by the Holy Spirit is a lifelong journey and process done by faith, so there will be a continual element of uncertainty and tension at times because you're acting by faith. That is all part of using your free will choice to trust, seek and have a relationship with God on a daily basis which in-turn will help you develop your own love language with God that will eliminate some, but not all of the uncertainty and tension you have at times. In the process of being led by the Holy Spirit and hearing God, know that God loves you, that He is for you and that as you seek Him He will cause any mistakes that you might make to work out for your good and that He can and will always graciously get you back on the right track!

The Holy Spirit is our divine counselor and guide. **There are 3 major places that we can take guidance and counsel from, that we need to consider, that can cause us to get off track in our daily lives.**

1. We take counsel and guidance in our souls (your mind, will and emotions) instead of your spirit by the Holy Spirit. This is called running on self-will instead of God's will for your daily life. ***How long must I take counsel in my soul, Having sorrow in my heart day after day? Psalm 13:2 ESV*** This is where we often allow our life experiences, self-perceptions, good intentions, self-centered desires, materialism and core fears in our soul to guide and direct our thoughts, emotions, decisions and actions. It is easy to develop a false sense of "perceived control" having a mindset of "oh I am good, I have things under control" when really we are being influenced and molded by all these other life circumstances and factors instead of taking the counsel of the Holy Spirit in the light of God's Word, nature and being shaped by a daily relationship with Christ.

2. We often unknowingly take guidance from satan and his realm of demons, in the form of temptations like certain sins, negative intrusive thoughts, suggestive lies, fear, shame and other demonic influences of the devil. The enemy is also working against us through others often without them really being aware that they are being used by the enemy against us. ***"Put on the whole armor of God so that you may be able to stand firm against the Devil's strategies." Ephesians 6:11 ISV*** The guidance you take needs to be healthy and based on what God's Word says about you and not

what the enemy, other people or the world say about your value and identity.

3. Another place counsel and guidance can come from which can cause us to get off track in hearing God's voice and living out His best for our lives is the spirit of this age. This can be defined as worldly normalities that go against the Word of God. We are exposed to this type of guidance on social media, television, news programming, movies and other people's worldly counsel. If we are not careful these resources become our source and the lens and filter in which we see ourselves, our values, our identity and our very lives through. Then what society calls acceptable, which God calls sinful, we begin to accept as ok and our "new normal". Society also often calls what is good and acceptable in the eyes of the Lord, "religious extremes" that they will argue don't really apply to today's society. The flip side of that is when we choose to take the guidance and counsel of the Holy Spirit and the Word of God. Our "normal life" as Believers in Jesus Christ should be based on the context of God's love, nature and Word lived out supernaturally through the Holy Spirit! *"I will bless the Lord, Who has given me counsel; I shall not be moved. Therefore my heart is glad and my glory [my inner self] rejoices." Psalms 16:7 AMP*

This being the Holy Spirit chapter of the book we wanted to cover briefly the "Baptism of the Holy Spirit" what it is, what it means for you and how to receive it for yourself. Ask yourself this question, "would you like to receive everything God wants you to have and be filled and over-flowing with more of God's love, intimacy, presence and power?" If you are taking the time and effort of reading this book then the answer to that question is yes! The Bible tells us and shows us clearly that the Baptism in the Holy Spirit is a separate experience from Salvation. *"The Holy Spirit had not yet come UPON any of them, for they had only been baptized IN the name of the Lord Jesus. Then Peter and John laid their hands upon these Believers, and they received the Holy Spirit." Acts 8:14-16 NLT* When you receive Salvation you are now IN Christ, the Holy Spirit IS resident IN you. The Baptism in the Holy Spirit is the total submersion into the Holy Spirit and an additional supernatural empowerment you receive from Jesus. When you receive Jesus Christ as your Lord and Savior you get Baptized into Jesus, you are now IN Christ and the Holy Spirit lives IN you and you are Heaven bound! When you are Baptized in the Holy Spirit by Jesus you are filled with and totally submerged into the Holy Spirit (John 1:33). Once that happens you are now infilled with the Holy Spirit, He is UPON you and you are clothed in His Power. In this wonderful act of faith you are choosing to receive the Divine Person of the Holy Spirit.

Some practical benefits of receiving the Baptism in the Holy Spirit is He will dramatically increase your spiritual senses in various aspects of your life, especially hearing God's active voice and sensing His activity in your daily life. When I received the Baptism of the Holy Spirit it was like everything in my spiritual life got the volume turned up on it to new levels that I had never experienced before. It magnified the Word of God in a way that gave me more understanding, it gave me a hunger for God I did not have before, my dreams became more vivid, my spiritual discernment increased, wisdom seemed to flow from me at greater levels, God became more real to me personally than ever before, I was more sensitive to God's guidance in my daily life and I began to personally experience the gifts of the Holy Spirit working through me in greater frequency such as the Gift of Healing. I began praying for people and seeing them healed by the power of God at a greater frequency. Divine healing has become something I no longer just read about in the Bible and wondered if it was possible, but it has become something I now experience on a continual basis. I now have seen countless healings and miracles some of which I share in this book.

These things either started happening to me after Jesus Baptized me with the Holy Spirit or it greatly increased in what I was already experiencing in my relationship with God. These things did not happen instantly, for me it was a process of stepping out on my faith, putting what the Bible said into action and a continual development of my daily relationship with the Holy Spirit. However, there was a definite shift in my life especially now that I look back years later I see how the Baptism of the Holy Spirit marked and changed my life forever! Jesus can and will do the same for you because of the great love He has for you! "John answered them all, saying, ***"I baptize you with water, but He who is mightier than I is coming, the strap of whose sandals I am not worthy to untie. He will baptize you with the Holy Spirit and with fire."*** Luke 3:16 ESV

It is important to note that the Baptism in the Holy Spirit is mentioned in all four Gospels Matthew, Mark, Luke and John in similar fashion of Luke 3:16 quoted above and Jesus Himself promises the Baptism of the Holy Spirit to His disciples in the Book of Acts (Acts 1:5) which is fulfilled later in the Book of Acts on the day of Pentecost (Acts 2:4). The Baptism of the Holy Spirit is now available and active in the Church age of today to every born again Believer in Jesus Christ! Jesus proclaimed to His Disciples,

"For John baptized with water, but you will be baptized with the Holy Spirit not many days from now." Acts 1:5 ESV

Jesus said Himself that He wants to baptize you with the Holy Spirit to endue you with dynamic working power and to empower you to be supernatural witnesses for God upon this earth (Acts 1:8). Evidently Jesus thought having the divine personality and power of the Holy Spirit come upon you and infilling you was really important and vital to following Him and being His witnesses otherwise He would not have said it and provided the Baptism in the Holy Spirit for us. So how do you receive the Baptism in the Holy Spirit? Well you receive it just like you received salvation (Romans 10:9-10) you ask God in faith for the Baptism in the Holy Spirit, believing in your heart and confessing with your mouth that you want Jesus to Baptize you with the Holy Spirit. Then you begin to thank Jesus for Baptizing you in the Holy Spirit and thank the Holy Spirit for totally submersing you into Himself! We have a whole teaching series dedicated to this subject as well as my testimony about how Jesus Baptized me in the Holy Spirit that you can check out on our YouTube Channel and Website. If it is something you want to do right now by faith we have included a prayer below that you can pray to receive the Baptism into the Holy Spirit. Many people have practically sensed various things as they prayed for the Baptism in the Holy Spirit and everyone's experience is different just like everyone's salvation experience is different.

While sensing or feeling something during prayer is not what we are after or what we should be solely seeking there are sensations that people experience when they encounter God that we want to share with you so if they do happen to you than you will have a context for what you experience. People that get Baptized in the Holy Spirit have commonly experienced: a sense of peace and lightness, goose bumps, tingling, burning or hot sensations over some areas of their bodies, eyes watering or tearing up, feeling light headed and faint, a welling up of peace and joy in their hearts that's tangible, a sense of the Presence of God upon you which is a weighty glory in which you have an inward sense of God being near you, or you feel compelled to speak and proclaim about the goodness and love of God which the Bible refers to as "prophesying". As well as Biblically in the Book of Acts this is when many Believers begin to speak and pray in tongues as the Holy Spirit gave them utterance, which we will discuss later in this chapter. There are times during the Baptism in the Holy Spirit where many people receive their supernatural prayer language and speak in tongues, sometimes this can also be a separate faith experience. Everyone is different. Personally, because of my own fear and false judgment about praying in tongues, when Jesus baptized me in the Holy Spirit I did not speak in tongues until years later but the Baptism of the Holy Spirit marked me and caused a spiritual transformation in my life. I just want to encourage you to yield over to whatever Jesus wants to do in and through your life including praying in tongues!

Again you don't have to have a physical, emotional or tangible manifestation or feeling to receive the Baptism in the Holy Spirit it is by faith alone, we just want you to be aware of what some of the common experiences are so if they happen to you then you have some context for what you experience. The type of experience people have has nothing to do with how much God loves them, their value or if what they did "worked" or not. So many people base the value of their faith decisions on what they feel or sense and so they are left seeking feelings, emotions and some tangible experience instead of seeking God realistically by faith. This kind of emotional and feeling based seeking sets you up as an easy target for the enemy and his lies like: "oh it didn't work", then you don't "feel saved" or "you don't feel like you really got Baptized in the Holy Spirit". The enemy will say to you "Yeah you got Baptized in the Holy Spirit but you know what you did last week", "nothing has changed about you", "see you're still acting the same way", don't believe those lies! So as you pray this prayer by faith know that God loves you already and it is Jesus's pleasure to Baptize you in the Holy Spirit! Even if you think you have already been filled and Baptized in the Holy Spirit remember there is only one Holy Spirit but many fillings because with God there is always more! Therefore, I want to encourage you to ask Jesus to fill you anew and Baptize you afresh in the Holy Spirit that you may receive and experience the Holy Spirit in a deeper and fuller way!

Pray this prayer with me: *"Lord Jesus I thank You that Your Word says that You would Baptize us with the Holy Spirit so right now I ask that You Baptize me in the Holy Spirit. Lord Jesus I receive the Baptism of the Holy Spirit. Holy Spirit I thank You that I receive You right now in full and I am totally baptized and submersed into You in Jesus Name. Thank You Jesus. Thank You Holy Spirit! Thank You Daddy God! Amen."* (Then begin to thank Jesus for His goodness and praise Him for what He has done!)

Congratulations if you prayed that prayer in faith Jesus just baptized you with the Holy Spirit and you will never be the same again! Even if you don't "feel different" I want you to know that your spiritual life just got super-sized and filled with more love, intimacy and power! As a Believer in Christ the Holy Spirit lives within you and now that you are Baptized in the Holy Spirit He rests upon you and overflows out of you in a new supernatural way and power! I invite you to watch our teaching about this subject for more in-depth information and practical application about the Baptism in the Holy Spirit. If you prayed that prayer I would invite you to just stop and praise God right now and just thank Him for His goodness and let the Holy Spirit just flow out of you with thanksgivings and praises to God! Also we would love to hear about your decision and experience in receiving the Baptism in the Holy Spirit so please email us with your testimony at info@sterlingharris.org and we would like to celebrate with you and send you a free gift.

PRAYING IN TONGUES; RECEIVING YOUR SUPER- NATURAL PRAYER LANGUAGE; IN-FILLING OF THE HOLY SPIRIT:

Receiving the gift of your supernatural prayer language, also known as praying in tongues and being filled with the Holy Spirit, is a gift from God that every Believer can receive. Although there has been much misinformation and sometimes a weird stigma about the subject of praying in tongues, let me assure you it is a wonderful gift from God. The Apostle Paul writes to us, ***"The one who prays using a private "prayer language" certainly gets a lot out of it." 1 Corinthians 14:4 MSG***

Like the gift of salvation in Jesus Christ, receiving your supernatural prayer language and praying in tongues is done by faith through confessing with your mouth that you want the gift and believing in your heart that you have received the gift from God by faith. There are whole books written on this subject! We have videos on our website and YouTube Channel about how to receive this gift and grace into your life as well as how to use it effectively in your daily prayer life.

When it comes to God I think we can all agree there are various features, sides, layers and levels to God's love, grace, power and thus your overall relationship with Him. There are so many ways that God speaks, operates, and increases your relationship with Him. Just like a mansion has many rooms, a car has many features, a cake can have several layers, and a building can have many floors and levels to it, so it is with God there is always more! Speaking in tongues and receiving your supernatural prayer language is likewise a wonderful and powerful feature of what the Bible refers to as the Baptism in the Holy Spirit (Acts 1:5) or being filled with the Holy Spirit (Acts 2:1). Which is a topic we covered earlier in this chapter under the Baptism in the Holy Spirit. Speaking in tongues is a feature and aspect of being filled with the Holy Spirit which every Believer in Jesus Christ can receive by grace through faith because of God's great love for us.

I was raised in a very conservative Christian denomination that did not believe that this gift of the Holy Spirit was for today and that it had somehow ceased and passed away, but the Bible says God's Word will never pass away and thus praying tongues has not passed away or ceased to be available to any Believer in Jesus who wants to receive it (Mark 13:31). We see throughout the New Testament that after the Holy Spirit was poured out on the Believers in Jesus at Pentecost, that the gift of speaking in tongues is evidenced by the early Church and all of the apostles. The apostles wrote the New Testament under the direction and through the power of the Holy Spirit. Those same apostles also spoke in tongues and practiced their supernatural prayer language frequently and put great value on it. The Apostle Paul writing to the Church of Corinth in *1 Corinthians 14:18* *writes* **"I thank My God that I speak with tongues more than any of you." NKJV** He was saying that he prayed in his supernatural prayer language more than everyone in the whole Church put together! That is a lot of praying in tongues! Not many would argue that the Apostle Paul is one of the greatest Christians of all times. When I saw that he had a gift that I could have by asking God for it and receiving it by faith, a gift that he valued so much, that he used and practiced it all the time, I said, "Yeah! I want that!"

I heard all kinds of things about praying in tongues growing up and none of it was good, nor was most of it true. I thought it was weird, fanatical, non-Biblical, not of God, passed away with the 12 Apostles, not real, faked by people just trying to show off and just plain strange. I actually use to make fun of people who did practice it. I had a whole little rant I would go on that would have people laughing; at least people like myself who did not know any better. Now I am sure that there have been people who misuse and fake this gift over the years, but that's people. That is not the Holy Spirit and it is not of God, but don't throw out such a great gift because of what you might have seen or heard that others have misrepresented. God has poured out His Spirit on us and in us: Speaking in tongues is part of your Christian Benefit Package! If you look at the day of Pentecost in the Book of Acts which is one of the most important days in Church history it is the day Jesus baptized His followers with the Holy Spirit. On this foundational day in Church history one of the first gifts Believers in Jesus Christ experienced was speaking in tongues, that is a powerful Bible truth.

You might be asking yourself, how did you come to receive this gift and exercise it on a daily basis in your life, when you were so far away from it in the opposite totally negative direction? Well, I am glad you asked. I began to read the Bible for myself a number of years ago and began to listen for God to guide me in the Scriptures. I allowed the Holy Spirit to guide me and I began to walk out of my religious belief system and into a daily spiritual love relationship with God the Father, Jesus Christ and the Holy Spirit. That is when God began to reveal things to me in the Bible I had never seen or known before, because I had always went off what I heard at Church and what I heard others say about the Bible instead of getting in and doing my own research. Like we all do when we love and are interested in someone or something, we find out more about them or it, by doing our own research.

When I first started looking at and researching praying in tongues for myself, I still had my old religious filter and glasses on from my upbringing so I had judgment in my heart that this speaking in tongues business was not right and was not real. Your perceptions will often affect the way you view God's Word. Without God's perspective on a matter, your true potential in God's Word will not be manifested and shown forth in your life, meaning you will not live out the reality of God's best in your life even though it is available to you through His Word and His Spirit. God began to change my perception and sent a man named Calvin into my life who is still a dear friend of mine today. He was a person that was a "Full Gospel" Believer meaning he believed that whatever the Bible says you are, you are, whatever the Bible says you can do, you can do, and whatever the Bible says you have, you have it. It seems simple and it really is, but for so many of us we don't live like the Bible is true and powerful with our everyday lives. Now it is my aim and great hunger in life to have a Full Gospel mindset in every area of my life and to be on fire for Jesus! God told me to trust Calvin and that he had been sent into my life to show me some things that God wanted me to know. When I received this flowing thought from God I was with Calvin in my room talking about God's Word and there was a sense of peace that came with the flowing thought, at the same time I experienced something supernatural I was not expecting. At almost the same moment I received this flowing thought; within my mind's eye, I saw a bright metallic silver and green circular halo flash just for a second or two over Calvin's head which came with an impression from God of, "I am confirming what I said about this man, trust him". Then, when I was around him, I felt a peace in my heart as if God was confirming and approving of our friendship. We seemed to have this God connection between us. After we had several Bible studies together where we would share the Word of God with one another and discuss the goodness of God, He said to me, "I feel like God wants you to pray in tongues and receive your supernatural prayer language."

I began to squirm in my seat and for the first time in our relationship, I felt uneasy. This was a different feeling; one of strongholds and religious mindsets that were shouting at me all the negative perceptions I had ever believed about this subject. I told him I had prayed to God to receive this gift and if it was "God's will" for me to have it God would just give it to me, but at the same time I was not sure if it was for me. My false assumption was that this gift would some how just come upon me and God would cause me to start praying in tongues all of the sudden, whenever He was ready for me to have it. Truthfully, I was full of false judgment and unbelief over this subject and was not in faith over receiving it from God. At the time I didn't realize that. He said, "well, let me walk you through the scriptures, but I am going to need you to take your judgments and religious teaching and set them aside to let the Holy Spirit lead you." I smirked at him and then reluctantly agreed based on what God had told me to do previously which was to trust the man He had sent to me. He walked me through the Biblical teachings. I saw that all these people in the early Church in the Book of Acts, Corinthians, Romans and Ephesians had this gift and that it was still available for today. I could have it and after all, I was hungry for God's best! I wanted it! I want to share with you some insight that I received before telling you the rest of my testimony.

Jesus said in Mark 16:17 that these signs will follow them that believe In My Name they will...Speak in new tongues. So Jesus taught that this sign, after the Holy Spirit was poured out, would follow the Believer in God. That is every born again child of God who wants this gift!

The Apostle Paul, when talking about this subject within the Church, gave us some guidelines in his letter to the Corinthians. A lot of people misinterpret this passage of scriptures. Paul was referring to and addressing order in the Church assembly he was basically wanting the Church members to conduct the Church services in an orderly fashion. When he spoke about his own personal prayer life he said he spoke in tongues more than the whole Church combined! Paul addressed this in his letter to the Corinthians because they were doing various things in their Church assembly that were out of order and not right before God. Therefore, Paul was instructing them on how to have an orderly and fruitful Church service.

The Holy Spirit, speaking through the Apostle Paul, said to the Church...which means God is saying this to you too...

"I wish you all spoke with tongues" 1 *Corinthians 14:5 NKJV*

"Therefore, brethren, desire earnestly to prophesy, and do not forbid to speak with tongues." 1 Corinthians 14:39 NKJV

"For if I pray in a tongue, my spirit prays but my mind is unfruitful. What am I to do? I will pray with my spirit, but I will pray with my mind also; I will sing praise with my spirit, but I will sing with my mind also." 1 Corinthians 14:14-15 ESV

What did the Apostle Paul say? He said I will pray both ways! I will pray with my spirit, in this case meaning in tongues, and I will pray with my mind as well. Notice he did the praying. He said I will pray with my spirit: He had to use his mouth and do the praying, he had to yield his tongue over to the Holy Spirit in him that would provide the utterance and supernatural language.

For one who speaks in an unknown tongue does not speak to people but to God; for no one understands him or catches his meaning, but by the Spirit he speaks mysteries [secret truths, hidden things] 1 Corinthians 14:2 AMP

People ask me all the time, "do you know what you're saying?" and I tell them "yes, sometimes God does give me an impression of what I am saying or praying about and by faith I receive the interpretation." However, I also know what the Bible says I am praying and saying which is *"by the Spirit he speaks mysteries [secret truths, hidden things]"* so I always know that I am speaking mysteries, secret truths and hidden things of God by His Holy Spirit that lives in me. So, what will I do, like the Apostle Paul, I will do both. I pray in tongues off and on throughout the day and I also pray with my understanding as well throughout the day. I listen for God to answer me and watch for His activity in my daily life. So when someone asks you "do you know what you are saying?" you can always say," yes, I am speaking and praying the mysteries, secret truths and the hidden things of God and His perfect will over my life and the lives of others." That's a powerful and truthful statement based on God's Word.

According the Book of Romans, you are in-essence praying the perfect will of God for your life and the lives of others when you pray in your prayer language. This profound truth has taken a lot of pressure off of me and it can do the same for you. When I am praying about something, I usually will tap into my prayer language and pray over it in tongues. I also use it when I don't know how to pray about a particular situation. I often hear people say, "I want God's will for my life". To that I say, pray in tongues and you will be praying God's perfect will over your life and the lives of others. *In the same way the Spirit [comes to us and] helps us in our weakness. We do not know what prayer to offer or how to offer it as we should, but the Spirit Himself [knows our need and at the right time] intercedes on our behalf with sighs and groanings too deep for Words. And He who searches the hearts knows what the mind of the Spirit is, because the Spirit intercedes [before God] on behalf of God's people in accordance with God's will. Romans 8:27 AMP* In addition the Holy Spirit knows what you need in the future to fulfill your goals, dreams, purpose and destiny. He knows what you will need 5 hours, 5 days and even 5 years from now and beyond and when you pray in tongues you pray out God's perfect will for your life and in the lives of others.

One who speaks in a tongue edifies and improves himself; 1 Corinthians 14:4 AMP This is one of my favorite scriptures about this subject. It says when you pray in your supernatural prayer language you improve, edify, and build yourself up. A modern word picture for the word edify would be the charging up of a battery. So when you pray in tongues you charge yourself up by the Spirit of God! I really like that! I have never met a person who said, "Oh no, brother, I am too built up in God. I don't need to improve anything in my life I am too charged up in God already. I have too much faith, confidence, and joy. I don't want any more of God's peace and power in my life". No, we never say that because life on this earth; no matter your background, race or social status, is painful and challenging in some sort of ways for everyone, because we live in a world where there is evil, sin and bad things happening. So why not allow God to give you a gift that would help you build yourself up in Jesus? The obvious answer is of course I want and need a gift like that! Well, that is why your Heavenly Father offers the gift of having their own personal supernatural prayer language to every Believer. The truth is when you choose to receive your supernatural prayer language you are choosing to receive and exercise a feature and a personality trait of the Divine Person of God the Holy Spirit.

If you choose to not receive this gift from God then I want you to know you are still saved, the Holy Spirit still lives in you and your sins are still forgiven. You are still going to Heaven and God loves you just as much as He always has! The only difference is that you are choosing not to receive a wonderful gift from God that Jesus paid for you to receive and to exercise in your daily walk with Him. Let me give you a picture of what taking advantage of and utilizing all of the finished works of Jesus in your life looks like. I think this will illustrate the point of praying in tongues. Life, in, with, and through God, is abundant; with God there is always more to be experienced and known. I think we can all agree with that last statement, or do you think God is limited to one sided love, glory and power? No, it's manifold, meaning it has many sides and elements to His love, glory and power just like an amusement park has many rides. Let's say you had full access to a beautiful mansion and it has many rooms. Do you want to stay in the entryway or just the living room, or do you want to enjoy all the other rooms in the mansion you have access to? You would probably say you want to see and experience everything you have access to within the mansion. God is offering you the same opportunity with speaking in tongues. He is offering you supernatural intimacy with Him.

Here is another example: if you had the opportunity to fly in a jet airplane with the best pilot in the US Air Force flying you around, would you want to go as slow as the jet could safely fly and just experience the minimum the jet had to offer or would you want the pilot to show you all kinds of cool moves and various speeds? You would probably want to get all you could out of this opportunity. Do you want to go deeper with God and get all you can out of your relationship with Him or do you just want to do and get the minimum? I think we can all say that we want more of God and we want His best for our lives. For those who want more, and want to speak in their own personal supernatural prayer language with God, the opportunity is available to everyone who has received Jesus as their Lord and Savior and wants this wonderful gift! After all why not receive and utilize the full benefits of what Jesus paid with His life for you to have?

My life has radically changed and increased since I received this gift. This brings me back to my testimony of how I received the ability to pray in tongues. So, my friend and I went through the scriptures, which I shared above as well as some others (if you would like more information about receiving your supernatural prayer language you can also go to our YouTube channel and website for extensive teaching and additional scriptures). As Calvin and I went through the Bible together my friend pointed out some of the truths I have shared with you. Through those Biblical truths I realized this is for me and I wanted this! Immediately I moved from my unbelief and false perceptions to being spiritually hungry for this gift. It was as if a light came on in my spirit. I said to my friend, "I want this, I need this, I have to have this! I want all God has to offer me, and I want His best for my life!" I said, "Will you please pray with me to receive this?" We began to pray. I asked Jesus to Baptize me in the Holy Spirit like He did in the Book of Acts and for my supernatural prayer language, then I began to thank Him for receiving it by faith. I said, "Lord, I thank You that You have Baptized me in the Holy Spirit and that I am speaking in other tongues, in Jesus Name!"

At first, nothing happened. However, I was not moved by that I just I kept thanking God and praising Him by faith that I am a receiver of this and I have this gift in me, in Jesus Name. Then between my praises I would pause, listen and wait on God to speak to me. Then, I felt something begin to bubble up in my stomach and on the inside of me, I could hear words and flowing thoughts that were not in English! As they seemed to travel up near my mouth, I began to speak them out! At first, the enemy tried to hand me thoughts of "oh, you're just talking gibberish. You're not saying anything. You don't even know what you are saying. You're just making words up this is not real." But see, I know when the enemy comes at me like that I must be doing something right! Otherwise, he would not be bothering me about it. My friend and I were so joyous! I had broken through false teachings and religious mindsets into the supernatural! He encouraged me to practice speaking in tongues on a daily basis and at that moment I felt a joy, peace, and a love that I had never experienced in God. Because God is infinite, there is always more to experience with Him. In Him there is always more and He wants us to get more of Him all the time. Since then through exercising the gift of praying in my supernatural prayer language on a daily basis my relationship with God has been magnified and increased in various ways. Such as hearing God's voice more clearly and with greater confidence, it has helped me to experience God living on the inside of me in a real and tangible way thus, staying God inside minded which has in-turn eliminated loneliness in my life and the feelings I use to have like God was so far from me. Praying in tongues also will strengthen your defenses to withstand temptations, sin and fear of all kinds and so much more!

Are you ready to receive God's gift of a supernatural prayer language and to speak in other tongues and pray the perfect will of God for yourself and others in your life? Good! Here is a short exercise to receive this amazing gift. Remember God loves you so much and wants you to have this, so it is as simple as praying and asking for it and then by faith beginning to speak in something besides your native language, in my case something besides English!

EXERCISE #5: PRAYING IN TONGUES AND RECEIVING YOUR SUPERNATURAL PRAYER LANGUAGE FROM GOD: IN-FILLING OF THE HOLY SPIRIT

Step 1: You have read some of what the Bible has to say regarding this subject already so your faith by hearing the Word of God on the subject of receiving this amazing gift has already grown because the Bible in ***Romans 10:17 says that faith comes by hearing and hearing by the Word of God***. That means your faith has already been built up on the subject and hopefully after reading the scriptures, the teachings and my testimony you are hungry for more of Jesus!

Step 2: Get in a relaxed and somewhat quiet area where there are limited distractions so you can position yourself to receive from God. If you have someone you know and trust that has already received this gift from God it may be a good idea to have them come and pray with you, but it is not necessary.

Step 3: Ask God *"Lord I thank You that Your Word says if I ask that I will receive, that if I seek then I will find and if I knock the door will be open to me, I am asking right now in faith for You, Jesus, to Baptize me in the Holy Spirit, for the gift of speaking in tongues, Holy Spirit I ask You to infill me with Your Power! I receive this right now by faith in Your Word. In Jesus name. Amen."*

Step 4: Then thank God by Faith: *"Lord I thank You that I have received what I have asked for in Jesus Name, thank You Jesus, thank You Father, thank You Holy Spirit."* Sometimes I have seen it help the process to just give God whatever praise and thanksgiving that comes to your heart for a couple of minutes. As you do this pause and listen for your supernatural language to begin to come to your mind and heart.

Step 5: Then open your mouth, yielding it over to the Holy Spirit and speak words that are not known to you. It helps some people when they begin to roll their tongues and begin to make sounds with your mouth moving your tongue and lips by faith. Remember the Holy Spirit is not going to force you and make you speak in tongues, it is not just going to happen like I use to think. You open your mouth and you do the speaking by faith. You will often sense a bubbling up in your stomach area, a warmness in your chest, a peace or a joy come over you, maybe tingling feelings in your body, or possibly like me you will seem to hear words on the inside of you or words that come to your mind that are not known to you. Everyone's experience is a little different so if these things are not happening to you it's not a big deal. I am just sharing some of the typical responses I have seen, but God is not cookie cutter nor is He a formula, your experience will be different than mine or anyone else's for that matter.

Step 6: Keep going and speak the words you sense that you are hearing internally, no matter what your mind or the enemy is trying to tell you. So many people run into problems receiving this amazing gift from God because they get stuck in their head, or they believe the lies of the enemy. You, my friend, are not going to fall for that trick. If the words you are thinking about, sensing or hearing inwardly don't make logical sense, that's a good thing! It is a supernatural language you are not supposed to logically understand it! I want to encourage you to speak out whatever you're hearing or sensing by faith and God will give you the grace to receive even more!

Step 7: Practice and enjoy your newfound spiritual language on a daily basis! Paul and Jude both remind us of this truth and the importance of praying in tongues, which the Bible often refers to as *praying in the Spirit*. I want to encourage you to practice and train yourself to fully utilize this wonderful gift from God. I would suggest exercising your gift of praying in tongues at least 20 minutes to an hour a day and sometimes much more if you can. Practically you can pray in tongues anytime throughout your day. Such as; while you are getting ready in the morning, on your way to and from work or school, under your breath throughout your day and before bed at night or whenever you have something you need guidance on. You can also start out praying in tongues about important decisions you need to make for a minute or two, then ask God open ended questions and listen. A lot of people experience hearing God more clearly when they practice this method. Sometimes as I pray in tongues and often times before I begin to pray I will practice confessing by faith that "I believe that everything I pray about in the Spirit brings praise and honor to You Lord and I receive what I pray about in the Spirit, that God's perfect will for my life will come to pass." This type of prayer and heart position will help you to become and stay motivated about praying in tongues and by faith receiving everything you pray about in the Spirit into your life and the lives of others. I would also encourage you pray for your spouse and your kids in your supernatural prayer language because when you do the Bible says you are praying God's perfect will for them. It's hard to always know what those closest to us really need but God does know and praying in tongues allows you to pray the Holy Spirit's will for their lives. A model prayer you can use is saying, *"Lord by faith I am praying for (name the person) in my supernatural prayer language and I believe by faith I am praying Your perfect will for their lives because You know what they need Holy Spirit and by faith I am partnering with You in what You want to do in their lives. Amen."* Then pray for them in your supernatural prayer language in whatever time frame you feel lead to. I would suggest praying in tongues for about 3 to 5 minutes a day for your spouse and your children or until you sense a feeling of accomplishment or a sense of release that often comes with an inward knowing like what you needed to partner with God on in prayer has been accomplished. Praying in your supernatural prayer language all throughout the day is a daily lifestyle choice and one that can bring so much enlightenment and intimacy with God into your life.

"Praying always with all prayer and supplication in the Spirit." Ephesians 6:18 KJV

"But you, beloved, build yourselves up on [the foundation of] your most holy faith [continually progress, rise like an edifice higher and higher], pray in the Holy Spirit," Jude 20 AMP

When the Bible speaks of *praying in the Spirit or pray in the Holy Spirit*, it is most often referencing praying in tongues. If you do have any issues receiving this gift from God relax. God loves you and wants you to have this gift. Most of the time it is a faith blockage issue, which are usually some questions, concerns or misconceptions that you still have that are blocking your flow of receiving from God. I would encourage you to read some additional scriptures and watch some of our teachings on the subject which you can find on our website and YouTube Channel. Within our teaching entitled "How to Pray in Tongues: Understanding, Receiving and Exercising Praying in the Spirit" there are about 15 scriptures that we cover as well as answering a lot of common questions, misconceptions and false religious ideas that are not Biblical, like I shared in my earlier testimony. This will help you build up more faith in receiving this wonderful gift as well as remove doubt from your heart. You might also want to ask God to reveal to you or tell you what is blocking you from receiving and listen to what you sense He is telling you and showing you. Write it down, talk it over with God and release whatever is blocking your flow. Most of the time after reading the scriptural teaching in the Bible on praying in tongues we provide in this book and within our video, you will receive it because faith comes by hearing and hearing by the Word of God. When you read the whole teaching on this subject from the Bible through the perspective of the finished works of Jesus Christ and the age of the Holy Spirit living in us it is so apparent that God wants you to have this and it is a gift you can and will receive. Keep thanking God for it and by faith receive it and begin to open your mouth and speak out your supernatural language!

I pray that God blesses you abundantly in receiving and exercising your own personal supernatural prayer language through the Holy Spirit and may praying in tongues take your relationship with God to new levels of increase! Even right now as you read this book, the Holy Spirit inside you is bubbling up and there is a shift in your thinking and in your spirit to receive this amazing gift from God! Speak it out and receive!

EXERCISE #6: SPIRITUAL JOURNALING

Journaling has been a huge key for me in receiving flowing communication from God. Spiritual journaling will help you to focus more on what God is saying and allows you to receive little bits of His voice at a time which often lead to a flow of communication from our Heavenly Father's heart. It's important to write down what you spiritually hear, see and sense God is saying to you. Because His voice is infused and embedded with hidden, deep and secret meanings which you will not always catch until you write them down, re-read them, think about what God is truly saying, talk it over with Him and listen allowing the Holy Spirit to download and impart His thoughts into your mind and heart.

JOURNALING EXERCISE:

"I will climb up to my watchtower and stand at my guard post. There I will wait to see what the Lord says and how He will answer my complaint.

Then the Lord said to me, "Write My answer plainly on tablets, so that a runner can carry the correct message to others.

This vision is for a future time. It describes the end, and it will be fulfilled. If it seems slow in coming, wait patiently,

for it will surely take place. It will not be delayed."
Habakkuk 2:1-3 NLT

Notice what happened. He watched and waited on the Lord to speak, knowing God would answer his "complaint" or his prayer. Then God answered him and instructed him to write down the answer He gave him making it plain to see on tablets so that he could carry the correct message to others. This is a great Biblical pattern to follow as you journal your experiences with God and what He is saying to you. Watching for God's activity, waiting on Him, expecting Him to communicate with you and then writing down what you sense God is telling you, showing you and His activity that you experience, is paramount to developing an intimate, real and personal relationship with God. Where you internally hear, see and experience His communication with you. When you write it down you value what God is saying, showing and doing in and around you and it opens the door for deeper communication and revelation of God's plan, purpose and destiny for your life and the lives of others.

1) Get to a quiet place where you can focus on God and concentrate. Don't allow yourself, other people, society or the enemy to bring feelings of guilt upon you concerning taking time for you and God. This time with the Lord is vital to you becoming more like Jesus; which will in-turn benefit you and everyone around you.

Try to keep your mind focused on God during this time and what He is saying and doing. Try not to allow your mind to run with racing thoughts or drift off in random thoughts. When it does, because it will eventually if not immediately happen, lovingly refocus on God and your conversation with Him. Choose to give yourself plenty of grace, forgive yourself and bring your attention back to God. These types of things happen quite often to everyone, so just give yourself a lot of love and grace and say "Thank You, Jesus that I am refocused on You, I love You Lord and I know You love me" and adjust your focus and heart back on God. During these times it is also somewhat normal, especially first starting out, for your mind to be restless and for the enemy to try to disrupt you hearing from God with all kinds of thoughts in order to get you sidetracked and frustrated.

Thoughts range from worry, fear and distractions, to all kinds of sins, to what you need to do tomorrow at work or school. Your soul (mind, will and emotions) have to be transformed and conformed to God's Word, Spirit and nature over time. It takes patience and daily practice to focus on God and overcome random and negative thoughts. This is also done by the devil to create frustration and shame so you will give up or believe the lie that God does not talk to you or that you are the only person who struggles with these thoughts when trying to pray and hear God. I have found after interviewing and counseling with people of all kinds that everyone struggles with the same types of things because the enemy uses the same kind of tactics on everyone with just a little different variation depending on the person. The truth is God loves you, always wants to communicate with you, and is so proud of you that you are seeking to listen to His guidance and perspective. He made you and He understands better than anyone how your mind works and the opposition you face in your thought life and in trying to keep your focus on Him. He knows it's challenging but He will help you and God loves your effort to communicate with Him!

2) Open up the notes section in your smartphone, laptop, tablet, or get out a physical writing journal. When starting out, sometimes it is better to use a physical journal and do your spiritual journaling within it.

The physical act of writing it out by hand, seems to help some people with their spiritual creative process and those who are more artistically inspired and inclined enjoy drawing what they are spiritually seeing from God. Plus, when you use a physical journal, you are less likely to get distracted. Personally I use my phone and computer for most of my journaling. I would encourage you to just try a couple of different ways and use what works best for you. To be transparent there are many times I go to use my phone notes section, to get a word of guidance from the Lord, and someone calls or texts me or I just end up getting distracted and checking my email or social media instead. In those times I give myself grace and refocus back on God as soon as I can. The Bible says God understands our weakness and chooses to love us in the midst of them. Regardless of what you choose to use, give yourself plenty of grace and keep pressing into Him!

3) Posture your heart to hear and receive from the Lord. I start by confessing the Word of God and declaring that I am God's sheep, and I hear His voice and I know His voice. In John 10:2-5, Jesus speaks about Himself as being the Good Shepherd and that His sheep know His voice and hear His voice.

"The one who enters by the gate is the shepherd of the sheep. The gatekeeper opens the gate for him, and the sheep listen to his voice. He calls his own sheep by name and leads them out. When he has brought out all his own, he goes on ahead of them, and his sheep follow him because they know his voice. But they will never follow a stranger; in fact, they will run away from him because they do not recognize a stranger's voice." John 10:2-5 NIV

I make a confession based on this scripture. This is commonly referred to as "standing on God's Word." I use to hear people say, "I am standing on the Word of God," and I would to just shake my head yes or say, "Amen to that!" At the same time, I didn't know practically how to do it myself. What this phrase means, is to base your thoughts and confessions (your words) off of what the Bible says about that particular situation. So in essence it is the Scriptures that you are "standing on" and using to base your faith and confession upon. So, my confession for this exercise in hearing God is based on what Jesus said in John 10:2-5; that, I could and would hear His voice, and I would be able to tell the difference between His voice (the Shepherd) , my voice (the sheep), and the enemy (the stranger).

Here is the confession that I use a lot of times when doing this exercise with others. I still use this confession sometimes personally, but over the years, I have built a lot of faith in this area so I don't necessarily say it every time. There is also no formula for this. Our goal is to give you some examples that will help you along this journey of hearing from your Heavenly Father!

Pray this confession with me: "*Lord Jesus, I thank You that You said that I would hear Your voice, and know Your voice, and that the enemy's voice I would not follow. Heavenly Father, I confess and believe right now that I hear Your voice, and that I sense Your communication with me. Holy Spirit, I claim that I have ears that hear, eyes that see, and a heart that is open to Your voice, and receives Your Love. I thank You Father that I hear Your voice. In Jesus' Name. Amen.*"

Notice I am using affirmative thankful prayer as discussed in previous chapters to get my heart into a position to receive from the Holy Spirit. After the confession, I listen for a moment and write down anything I spiritually see, sense and hear God is saying and showing me. The way in which we listen for God to actively speak to us when we journal is similar to our prayer exercises earlier in this book which you can refer back to for review. We are listening for the Holy Spirit's active communication with us. In spiritual journaling you are often able to get more clarity on what God is saying to you because you are writing it down and reviewing it with God. As you go through this process God tends to build on what He is saying to you and showing you. Often patterns will emerge and you will see things more clearly when you spiritually journal while engaging the Holy Spirit in conversation. Then, after the initial pause to listen, I usually start journaling about the situation I need clarity on and I will write out some open-ended questions I may have for God to get His perspective and guidance on. During this process, sometimes God will begin to speak to me while I am journaling about the situation. I will stop, listen and journal what I sense God is saying to me. You want to keep your heart in a position of praise, thankfulness and faith knowing God's favor, power and grace is upon you and your circumstances regardless of the situation. That kind of heart posture is not always easy to maintain especially when you are coming to God in the midst of challenges and hardships. However, when you stay in a mindset of gratitude it will put you in a receiving position to hear God's active voice more effectively. I have found that writing a question down, asking God the question out loud, and then listening for Him to speak to my question allows for a greater level of focus.

Knowing when God is beginning to speak to you often comes through a prompting in your spirit where you can sense God is beginning to speak with a flowing word, phrase or a thought seems to start. This can also come visually as a mental picture or God using your imagination to create imagery in your mind that He uses to communicate with you. Sometimes while I am writing down the situation or the question that I need some clarity on, I will often sense that prompt in my spirit. It will often start with a word or phrase that I see inner visually like block text or script within my mind or a flow of thoughts and impressions begin to come to me. This prompt in your spirit can be experienced in various ways as a welling up in your chest, eyes watering or burning, a sense the Holy Spirit is saying something to you, a sense of God's presence comes over you, a boldness or confidence seems to rise up on the inside of you, mental images begin to form within your mind or it can be a combination of things. When you experience God personally and practice hearing Him through spiritual journaling you will come to know that prompting and when He is speaking.

As you develop your relationship with God the sense that you get will be personal to you and after awhile you will know the prompting through your experiential knowledge of interacting with the Holy Spirit. Visually you may experience seeing well defined or very faint images, pictures, scenes and videos that play out on the television screen of our minds. It may begin with only one word or a simple phrase you seem to hear internally within your heart. The key is to keep your heart open and expect to spiritually hear, see and sense God speaking to you.

As you write down what you sense God is telling you, remember to also be listening for more. Then, what I call "a flow of words" will often begin to happen. These impressions, thoughts and visual communication will come with a flow of peace, hope and wisdom. During this process, don't try and figure out the full meaning behind what God is telling you. Just write it down and then begin to read it once you sense the flow of words, images and communication has stopped.

The flow of God's active voice looks different for everyone and often will vary even for the same person. God may choose to communicate in a variety and combination of ways as He answers you. Remember some common ways are flowing thoughts, ideas, intuition and images of the words or phrases that you see in your mind like written or typed text on a digital screen. This is how I get a lot of my guidance and downloads from God.

Sometimes you experience an inward knowing and impressions of what you sense God is saying to you. While other times you see images, a series of images, a scene or videos that seem to play in your mind like a memory of a life event that we can recall to our imagination. The key is to write down what you are experiencing, discuss it with God, as this happens you will begin have more clarity and God will build on what He is saying to you. Then engage the Holy Spirit by asking Him how you can apply the revelation of what He is saying to you and showing you to your personal life and your circumstances? After that listen and then write down and take action on what you sense God is saying to you. This guidance can be very simple such as you sense God is telling you to follow Him more closely or it can be more detailed and complex, it just depends on the situation and the person.

4) There may be times when the flow does not start as you are journaling and getting your heart in a position of praise, thanksgiving and faith. When those times happen at that point, relax, write down the question you have for God. Next, ask God the question and then listen for His response.

It may come in the form of flowing thoughts or maybe you see the words come across your mind like on a computer screen or other ways we have discussed that God actively speaks. As this flow starts, write down what you sense God is telling you or showing you until you sense that the flow has stopped. Sometimes, God will say "Amen" at the end of these thoughts, words or images that you are receiving from Him or your mind will go still momentarily and you will know the flow is over. God also seems to sign the end of some of the answers He gives with a characteristic of His personality that He wants us to tie to this experience; for example, The Lord of Glory, Your Heavenly Father, The Holiest of Ghosts, Your Daddy, and The King of Kings. Then the flow of thoughts will often stop until you ask Him something else. When I first began spiritual journaling at the end of journaling down what I sensed God was saying to me I would see Bible verses in my mind such as the name of a specific book in the Bible and then the number, which appeared to be written in blue block lettering within my imagination, for example "Ephesians 4:13". To be totally transparent; oftentimes I had no idea what these verses said or if they even existed in the Bible. I would go to the book and then find the chapter and the verse and read around it and it would more often than not correlate and confirm what God was telling me. Sometimes these verses would not even be in the Bible, but I refused to get frustrated and back up into performance, which is easy to do.

I would rest in knowing God loves me and He loves the fact that I am trying to hear Him. Then I would read around the area I sensed God told me to go to and see if something seemed to touch my heart. So many times it did. God is in the confirmation business, so if He tells you something and you want scripture to confirm it, ask Him to give it to you. There are times I got something right away or I went to research or Google the topic and God led me to a deeper understanding that would come with a peace in my spirit of satisfaction with an inward knowing of "this is what I was looking for", "that is what God was trying to communicate with me." There are other times I am reading in my Bible two weeks later and the answer seems to jump off the page or be highlighted to me with a sense of that's God's *answer and guidance*. I might hear a preacher I am listening to explain the very thing God was saying and showing me in an earlier conversation I was having with Him that comes with a sense of enlightenment and wisdom. It seems as if God gave the preacher the sermon just for me! The key is to ask Him, listen, look at and research what you sense He is telling you and showing you and be expectant, hopeful and watchful for His answers because they will come in all kinds of amazing ways!

5) When you are training up in hearing God, command all other voices and thoughts to stop and cease. Ask God to quiet all other voices and thank Him that you hear His voice and His voice only in Jesus' name.

You may have to do this several times as you practice hearing His voice. When I first started journaling and trying to hear God's active voice I had to cast a lot of thoughts down. The enemy would try to take my mind all kinds of places to get me into shame, guilt and fear so that I would give up on trying to hear God. You name it, I had to cast it down, from sexual images to cuss words and everything in between. The key is to keep pressing into God's voice knowing that He loves you and wants to speak to you no matter what the enemy or your mind is telling you. I would sometimes have to say 10 to 20 times "I refuse that thought or image in Jesus name and God I thank You that I hear Your voice and Your voice only, I command all demonic influences to stop in Jesus Name! Mind, I command you to be still." Then I would get still and ask the question again. Some of these thoughts were just from my own mind not being renewed and trained to hear and listen to God's voice. I use to suffer a lot from racing and obsessive thoughts.

In times of racing, random, or excessive thoughts I began to confess out loud in prayer *"Lord I thank You that I hear Your voice and I thank You that I have Your thoughts because the Bible says I have the mind of Christ, mind, I command you to be calm and still in Jesus Name. Amen"*

There were times at first when I had to do that cycle so many times that I got frustrated and took a break or just quit. Then I would give myself some grace and say to myself I am not going to allow the enemy or my own thinking to defeat me, and I would try again. It will help you to journal what you sense God is telling you, especially about a question you have for

Him or encouragement and guidance that you need. As you write down and journal what you sense God is telling you, your focus, concentration and spiritual flow of thought will tend to be more effective, clear and the revelation of God's wisdom is more deeply developed within you.

Remember to become still and quiet. At first you will need to go somewhere quiet, but as you train up in this you will be able to get still any time. Like anything else, it takes practice. The enemy will tell you: "but what if you don't hear God right?", "you are not hearing anything; you are just talking to yourself", "God's not real", "God's not here with you", "this is stupid", "crazy" or "weird". I have a saying when you are meeting the most adversity, you are often the closest to your victory! The enemy does not want you hearing from the Holy Spirit and developing a relationship with God, because that is when lives change for the glory of God and are radically transformed! At that point, people begin to develop a personal relationship with God that is real, intimate and powerful and as that happens the enemy's strongholds and lies in your life are systematically destroyed by the power of having a relationship with the Holy Spirit!

Personal intimacy with Jesus is the key to living a victorious life and walking in the fullness of the purpose and destiny that He has for you. There is nothing more fulfilling and freeing than that! Jesus came that we would have life, and have it more abundantly in Him! (John 10:10) The enemy hates that Jesus has won the victory. The enemy has no authority over those who are in Christ Jesus because of Jesus' death, resurrection and the indwelling of the Holy Spirit within us. We have authority and power over the demonic realm that tries to attack us on a daily basis. The enemy only has the authority and power over us that we choose to give him by coming into agreement with the lies used to keep us in bondage such as shame, fear and doubt. When we declare God's truth over these lies by hearing from God directly and declaring scripture in every situation, we are breaking free of and defeating the enemies' tactics! We are destroying the lies of the enemy by using the "Sword of the Spirit" which is the Word of God! (Ephesians 6:17, Hebrews 4:12)

Remember that prayer is a two-way communication. You have to listen, as well as talk. God is a gentleman and generally is not going to talk over you. People often keep talking or saying, "God, speak to me" over and over in their minds or out loud. They also often keep asking the question over and over again in their minds or out loud and don't give God any room to speak. Have you ever been in a conversation with someone who seems to always be talking? Even when they ask you a question, they somehow keep talking or don't give you enough time to answer and they talk over you? We all have had those conversations and they are not as fruitful as they could be because the one person is dominating the conversation and not listening.

Listening and giving God time to speak to you is key to hearing God's voice and sensing His active communication with you, which as we talked about comes in various ways. I still struggle with this sometimes. I will be doing all the talking or I will not be actively listening to God. I will ask God something, but then I don't get still and listen because my mind keeps on running or I literally keep on talking. At times, I will catch myself wondering why I have not sensed God say anything to me. Then God lovingly reminds me to "listen My son". Then, I quickly apologize to God, forgive myself and refocus on Him and what He wants to say to me. Sometimes I even laugh at myself, because even after years of spiritual journaling and hearing God's active voice I still seem to run out ahead of Him in our conversations.

Practice these steps and remember, this is a *no performance and no failure zone*. You are writing down what you sense God is telling you personally. Open your heart up, take risks, and enjoy hearing from your loving Heavenly Father! He loves you so much and wants to talk to you more than you want to hear from Him. He delights in you seeking out His voice and counsel.

Jesus encourages us to follow the flow of the Holy Spirit within us! ***"Have faith in me, and you will have life-giving water flowing from deep inside you, just as the Scriptures say." John 7:38 CEV***

"But no one who drinks the water I give will ever be thirsty again. The water I give is like a flowing fountain that gives eternal life." John 4:14 CEV

The FLOW, follow the FLOW, out of your belly will FLOW rivers of living water, follow flowing thoughts, the images and sensations from the Holy Spirit to your spirit and to your mind. They will come with a sense of wisdom, hope and love infused within them!

6) The last part of this exercise is going back and reading what you wrote out or what you journaled about hearing, seeing and sensing, then asking the Holy Spirit to help you get a deeper sense of what God is communicating to you.

We covered earlier how you will know it is God speaking to you. It will always line up with His Word, His Nature, His character and His love. God will never tell you anything opposite or in contradiction to the Bible. Have fun and enjoy stepping out on this wonderful faith and love journey with God! This process and practice of spiritual journaling has radically transformed my life into one of godly wisdom, peace and knowing my Heavenly Father intimately in a deep personal way. I pray as you practice this way of life that your life too will be cultured and transformed by the Father's love for you!

EXERCISE #7: UNFORGIVENESS PURGE

The Spiritual Principle of Forgiveness happens when I/we forgive people by faith and obedience through the Word of God. There is a blessing by OUR Father in Heaven that comes from that; as well as peace and prosperity for OUR Souls and Lives.

Keeping your heart tended from offense and unforgiveness, taking thoughts captive, and living a lifestyle of forgiveness everyday is what living in victory and hearing God speak to you and through you is all about! Be quick to forgive. Live as a forgiver. Declare everyday, "I am a *Forgiver!*" Let that daily declaration become a part of your identity in Christ. Forgiveness is a supernatural spiritual force and an intentional act of your will by faith in God's Word which calls us to forgive. Forgiveness is a lifestyle and a continual process. Forgiveness is not a one-time event. Forgiveness does not excuse what was done to you. Forgiveness does not release someone of the accountability and the consequences that they have for their actions. Instead, forgiveness releases you from bondage and gives your power back to who it belongs to, YOU! Forgiveness does not mean you have to trust and have a relationship with the person who wronged you. Because trust is earned and having a relationship with someone is a personal choice. However, forgiveness is a command of God acted upon by the choice of your will. Forgiveness does not mean you have to forget what was done to you.

Forgiveness means healing is consistently happening in you, as you forgive. Where you continue to heal to the point where the hurt and pain no longer have control over any areas of your life. People ask me *how do I know when I am healed of unforgiveness, unfair situations and traumatic life experiences?* I like to use the comparison between an open wound and a scar. If you have an open wound, such as a burn, on your arm if you bump it even lightly it will hurt and cause immediate pain. If someone were to just touch your arm to get your attention and accidentally touch that open wound, you would have an immediate reaction of pain because it is not healed which makes it very sensitive. A scar, on the other hand use to be an open wound but because of the healing process, now if you were to bump it on something or someone were to touch it there is no pain because it's healed and now it is just a scar, a reminder of an injury you suffered.

So it is with the spiritual, emotional and mental healing process. When you have an open wound it is easy to get offended and for pain to come from that area of your life. The saying "time heals all wounds" is a lie and a deception of the devil because we all have personally experienced or know someone who still has an open wound and is suffering from wrongs done to them years ago. However, when forgiveness has taken root in your heart and the healing process has taken place, the pain is lessened and eventually removed. Lastly, forgiveness is not about the other person or anyone else. Forgiveness is about you living free and empowered. WHO do you need to FORGIVE TODAY? Yourself? God? Mom or dad? A brother or sister? A current or former spouse? A family member? A company? A friend? A boss or co-worker? A neighbor? An enemy? Someone who has wronged or hurt you? An unfair situation? An injustice?

1 Peter 5:7 AMP says, "Casting the whole of your care [all your anxieties, all your worries, all your concerns, once and for all] on Him, for He cares for you affectionately and cares about you watchfully."

Ask the Holy Spirit to bring to your heart and mind who you need to forgive. Whoever He brings to your heart and mind, forgive them by faith. Do not rob yourself of the opportunity God has shown you by saying or telling yourself, "I have already forgiven them, or I don't have unforgiveness for that person, or I am good, I have dealt with that." Holding unforgiveness often gives people a false perception of control, power and safety. Don't be deceived by these false perceptions. Humble yourself and forgive by the power of the Holy Spirit!

For the Kingdom of God is not just a lot of talk; it is living by God's power. 1 Corinthians 4:20 NLT

We all need to engage the supernatural power of the Holy Spirit to continually stay in a place of love and forgiveness, especially for those the closest to us like our spouse, kids, family, friends, classmates and coworkers.

God sees things you don't see. God knows things about you that not even you know about you. Remember, forgiveness is a PROCESS, NOT a one-time event. Following His leading in who you need to forgive and release over to Him will allow God to fulfill the promises in His Word. Your heart will be blessed, and your life will be prospered. Forgiveness is NOT about the other person or agreeing with the wrong that was done to you. Forgiveness IS about setting yourself free of bondage and giving yourself back the power in your life that was stolen by unforgiveness. So allow the Holy Spirit to help you to take your POWER back!

When I practice the Unforgiveness Purge, there are two people that God usually brings to my spirit, heart, and mind. The first is God, the second is myself. The rest of the people that are brought forth to me differ at various times, but these two are usually consistent. The reason for God always bringing Himself up in these unforgiveness purges is contrary to what most people think it's actually very easy to get offended at God. From what you think He should be doing, to what you think He should not be allowing and everything in between and it's often so subtle people don't recognize it as small offenses against God. Ever thought to yourself why am

I going through this God, why hasn't God answered this prayer, why does this person seem to have it so easy and I am struggling, why is God allowing this to happen? We all have asked these questions at some point in our lives often internally within our minds. While subtle these thoughts and beliefs create little frustrations and resentments towards God. So God wants to remove all of that out of your heart to make more room for you to receive His love, power and joy. I practice this forgiveness process several times a week sometimes even several times a day depending on what God presses upon me and what challenges I am having. Some purges are more in depth than others, but it is a constant practice and a continual way of living. Forgiveness is a lifestyle!

God will communicate with you in various ways during this process. In addition to some of the examples we have covered on God's active voice, you may experience the following; seeing the image of the person's face in your mind's eye; a video or memory of a certain situation may play in your mind; you may get an impression of the person's name in your mind or spirit; flowing thoughts with people's names or situations you need to release; you may see words come to your mind that remind you of someone or of a situation that requires some forgiveness. You may see an image of a scene like a snapshot memory from your life of a person or situation. When this happens there is often an inward knowing of who and what you need to forgive and release over to God. Also it is not just people that the Holy Spirit will bring to your heart and mind. Sometimes it is a corporation or business, life situation or circumstance, a Church, a certain people group, an economic unfairness, a particular injustice in the world, a hurt or pain you suffered spiritually, emotionally or physically.

Whatever God brings to your heart, mind and spirit do yourself a big favor, don't argue with God about it just forgive and let it go into His hands knowing you can never "over forgive" but any unforgiveness has the power to keep you in bondage and torment your soul. I say that, and most of us would think to ourselves, "I would never argue with God" but if we think about it we all have done it at one time or another. I still catch myself trying to justify why I don't need to forgive someone or something that God brings up. Here is a good rule to go by, if you have to justify it then that is a red flag right there that you need to forgive and release it over to God! The important thing is not to argue with the Holy Spirit and what He is bringing up to your heart and mind. Instead forgive, release it over to God, ask the Holy Spirit to take the unforgiveness from you and supernaturally heal your heart, soul and body!

You may be asking yourself, "What do I say?" There are no formulas with God. We have a teaching on "Walking in Love and Forgiveness for Yourself, God and Others" on our website and Youtube Channel that you can check out to learn more, and we encourage you to do that. In addition, let me give you what I use in a short version, so you can start hearing from the Holy Spirit right now!

Step 1: Start out with a simple prayer get still and say, *"Holy Spirit bring to my heart and mind who or what I need to forgive and release over to You."* Then listen for the Holy Spirit to speak to you and bring things to your heart and mind in ways we described above in this exercise.

Step 2: As the Holy Spirit brings people, situations, and circumstances to your heart say, *"Lord, I forgive_____ in Jesus' Name, and I release that person and situation over to You, Lord, Holy Spirit thank You for cleansing my heart. Amen."*

During an unforgiveness purge, you are turning your will over to God in trusting that you can NEVER go wrong when forgiving anyone or anything. We can always use extra forgiveness as there is no such thing as giving out too much forgiveness. The worst thing that can happen is that you just give out more forgiveness; which in-turn makes your heart even more loving, peaceful, and powerful! You can also use some of the physical anchors we talked about in the taking thoughts captive section here to help you release the unforgiveness. Such as: Deep breathing, blowing out the offense, hand flicking, writing it down on a piece of paper, crumpling it up and throwing it away, or burning the paper, drawing a picture with the blood of Jesus covering and removing whatever you're giving over to God and using visualization techniques.

Step 3: After an forgiveness purge then ask the Holy Spirit to fill you back up and fill the void that those things left in Jesus Name! Say, *"Holy Spirit I thank You that You are filling me back up with Your peace, joy and presence!"* Again there is no formula, just begin to call into your heart what you would like to be filled up with by the Holy Spirit. Praying opposite of what you released is a good place to start. *"Lord fill my heart back up with forgiveness, Your love, worthiness, the Spirit of Adoption, and the Blood of Jesus!"*

Step 4: This last step may be the hardest for a lot of us. Bless the people you forgave like Jesus said for us to do. You are to pray for your enemies and bless them so in turn you will be blessed and allow God to fight your battles for you. Jesus said: **"When someone curses you, bless that person in return. When you are mistreated and harassed by others, accept it as your mission to pray for them." Luke 6:28 TPT**

Practicing forgiveness, training in forgiveness, and living in a perpetual mindset of God's love and forgiveness is NOT easy. It takes practice, honesty, love, humility, and courage on a DAILY basis, but when you experience the joy of living in a state of forgiveness, you realize that your peace and prosperity are worth it!

The first time I did an unforgiveness purge with the Holy Spirit I had been walking with the Lord for a while and even taught classes on how to forgive and let go of unforgiveness for several years. I thought to myself "I am good" this will only take a couple of minutes "I have dealt with my unforgiveness issues", so 45 minutes later I am sitting in a field crying and confessing all of the unforgiveness I had in my heart that I did not think I had. I share that experience with you to encourage you to allow the Holy Spirit to clean out and heal your heart. A close family member of mine was having various issues in his life with anxiety and depression, along with not being able to hear God's active voice on a regular basis. I had him practice this exercise 3 times a day for 2 weeks. In that short amount of time the anxiety and depression stopped and he began hearing God like never before! He also experienced what I had experienced which is the Holy Spirit began to bring up memories he had forgotten about from his past and began to show him how those people and events of his life were still negatively impacting his life years later. What was happening? He had retained the sin and the wrongs that were done to him in his past along with the ones that he had committed. This caused unforgiveness in his heart. Which was negatively affecting his life and his ability to hear God's active voice. So many of us do this and don't even realize it. The Bible says, **"If you forgive people's sins, they are forgiven. If you retain people's sins, they are retained." John 20:23 ISV** Like my family member you don't want to retain unforgiveness and sin in your soul by holding onto it for yourself, for God or for others. So he forgave, released it over to God and experienced a new found freedom and relationship with the Lord and you can too!

Allow yourself to be blessed so that you can, in turn, be a blessing to yourself, others, and most importantly, to God. For we are to show forth His glory in our lives on a daily basis, and in order to do that, you have to live free by walking in love and forgiveness. We suggest this exercise be lived out on a daily basis, but especially if a person feels like their flow of God's voice is being blocked. Often times unforgiveness for ourselves, God, and others will hinder our flow of His communication with us. The Bible tells us in Mark 11:25 that anytime we pray if we have anything against anyone we must forgive. Forgiveness is a command, not a suggestion. Jesus said in John 14:23 that "if you love Me you will keep My Word and do what I say". If you truly love God then you will do His sayings and forgive. I want to encourage you to live as a forgiver. Your peace, joy and life are worth it. Do not allow unforgiveness to have any more place in your life! Take your power back and let the Holy Spirit shine His light and joy into your heart!

5

THE INWARD WITNESS

YOUR SPIRIT CONNECTED TO GOD'S SPIRIT

THE INWARD WITNESS IS YOUR SPIRIT ON THE INSIDE OF YOU THAT is connected to, inhabited and led by the Holy Spirit after you give your life to Jesus Christ. ***"The spirit of man [that factor in human personality which proceeds immediately from God] is the lamp of the Lord, searching all his innermost parts." [I Cor. 2:11.] Proverbs 20:27 AMPC***

People refer to it as your gut feeling, but in actuality it is your spirit, what the Bible refers to as the inner person of the heart (1 Peter 3:4). As humans, we are triune, three part beings. We are a spirit; that lives in a body; and we have a soul. When the Bible talks about the heart of a person, some of the time it is actually referring to the human spirit. Your spirit is what is "born again" when you receive Christ as your Lord and Savior. When this transpires your soul, which is your mind, will, emotions, intellect and desires, has to be renewed and transformed by the Word of God and an active relationship with the Holy Spirit. Your spirit acts as an internal compass, navigation system, GPS and a "Holy Ghost Google Maps" and your spirit will continue to lead you by an abundance of peace or by a lack of peace in accordance to your thoughts, words and decisions. It is like an internal navigation system for your daily moment by moment life. Because God wants to be involved and guide you in everything you ever do if you will choose to listen to Him, He wants to guide you into love, peace, joy and blessings! ***"You will indeed go out with joy and be peacefully guided." Isaiah 55:12 NIV***

In my experience, if I find that I do not have peace about something I have said, done or that I am thinking about doing, I know that something is wrong and somehow I have gotten off the track of God's best path for me. That is when I go to God in prayer. At the same time, I also do a spiritual inventory based on the Word to see how I might have gotten off track. For example, when you do things that you know are not right, you will often get a sense of uneasiness and lack of peace in your stomach or a tightness in your chest area. That is your spirit alerting you to something that needs to be addressed, brought to the Lord in prayer, so certain actions can be taken or avoided. We all have ignored this leading at different points in our lives. At some level it has ended up costing us at the very least, unwanted negative consequences. Other indicators that you have lost your peace could be: your mind is continually running, your heart is racing, palms getting sweaty, a sense of heaviness, a feeling of uneasiness, anxiousness, depression, worry, you feel like a heavy weight is on your shoulders, an unrestful vibration type of feeling in your stomach, confusion and irritation are all signs you may have lost your peace.

In direct contrast, when we do follow that prompting in making positive faith-filled decisions; like giving to someone out of love; through an encouraging word or an act of kindness, the feeling we have when we lovingly serve someone; or after leaving an uplifting Church service, we experience the approval in our spirit from the Holy Spirit within us. We sense a warm peacefulness in the midsection area of our bodies or a lightness, like a weight just got lifted off of our shoulders. This is your spirit bearing witness to the positive choices that you are making. ***The mind governed by the Spirit is life and peace. Romans 8:6 NIV***

When I lose my peace about something, I immediately begin to try and figure out what I need to do to get back into a place of love and peace. If I do not immediately know the answer, I ask God to reveal it to me. This can be done by simply praying and asking God, "Lord why did I lose my peace?" then listen and respond to what you spiritually hear, see and sense God saying to you. Most of the time, I know immediately what is troubling me. This is because I have developed an understanding of my spirit through my daily interactions with God in our relationship and by staying steeped in the Word of God and yielding myself over to the leading of the Holy Spirit. Generally, I find that I need to forgive someone, I need to pray about a certain situation and release something to God, or I need to repent (change my way of thinking) about something I should not have thought, said or done. I allow myself to be guided by this inner peace throughout my day. But when I do things contrary to God's Word, I oftentimes will begin to feel anxious, or my spirit begins to almost vibrate, and I sense a heaviness about me. It is in those times that you will come to know by experience that you need to address something that you are thinking, saying or doing.

This kind of spiritual sensitivity will become possible as you choose to involve God in EVERY aspect of your daily life by constantly communicating with Him, focusing your mind on Him, and seeing your daily life through His eyes. There are 2 different types of knowledge. There is a *factual head knowledge* with "I know God exists and I believe in Him." Then there is a *heart knowledge* with "I know God and talk with Him about my life every day because I have experienced His power, love, and favor in a personal, real, and intimate way!" Both are important however, it is the experiential knowledge of God's love every day that separates religious duty from relationship and the works of our flesh from a life led by God's Holy Spirit within us. For example I believe in airplanes, I know factually that an airplane will fly, I have flown on a lot of airplanes and I even know a little bit about how they fly and about the law of lift and aerodynamics. In other words I have factual head knowledge about flying an airplane but I don't have the intimate working knowledge it takes to actually fly the airplane myself as a pilot. I use to believe in God and believe He existed. I even went to Church and served at the Church.

However, I didn't have a daily working relationship with God where I was intimately trained in following Him and involving Him in my everyday life, thoughts, decisions and actions. As Jesus told His disciples, "Follow Me". That phrase in the original Greek language speaks of following the same road, mimicking or becoming like the person you are following (Strong's 3101). The word picture is of disciples and students of that day accompanying their teachers on their walks and journeys in order to learn from them and become like them, in essence: an apprenticeship. So how can you become like Jesus or mimic Him when you don't know Him that well and don't follow Him? The answer is you cannot, that is why it is so important to come to know the inward witness of the Holy Spirit personally and intimately. Just like fans of a music group often times mimic and emulate that music group's style, behavior and speech patterns. I use to do this with various rappers I followed when I was growing up. Now I mimic and live out the style, behavior, actions and speech patterns of Jesus! *Jesus said "I am leaving you with a gift—peace of mind and heart. And the peace I give is a gift the world cannot give. So don't be troubled or afraid. John 14:27 NLT*

I now follow and yield to the inward witness and the peace of Jesus, and I act on His guidance and direction. When you practice this, things will work out in your favor and for your good, and you get to experience God in a real, personal, and intimate way, and your faith is built up to greater strengths. Even in challenging and negative situations, that will and do come into all of our lives because of the choices of others, the enemy, and sometimes our own poor choices as well; God still promises us in His Word that He will make everything work out together for our good (Romans 8:28). Even when negative things happen to you and the enemy tries to come into your life to kill, steal and destroy your hope, love and faith. Because you love God, and involve Him in your daily life and you are led by His Word, Spirit and inward witness, you will overcome any and all challenging situations that the enemy or anyone else tries to hinder your life with. You will overcome through God's power that is at work within you!

"Let the peace of Christ rule in your hearts" Colossians 3:15 NIV

When you get in your emotions and feel like God is far from you always remember to stay God inside minded knowing that the Holy Spirit actually dwells, lives and inhabits you on a daily basis and never leaves you. Thus you will stay God inside minded. Which will empower you to hear God's voice with greater frequency and clarity.

George Muller said something that has been my heart cry for so long. It has blessed me abundantly and I pray it does the same for you. He said, "How to ascertain the will of God: I seek at the beginning to get my heart into such a state that it has no will of its own in regard to a given matter. Nine-tenths of the trouble with people generally is right here. Nine-tenths of the difficulties are overcome when our hearts are ready to do the Lord's will, whatever it may be."

Based on this truth, my personal declaration has been, "I make it my aim and goal in life to get my heart to a place where it has no will of its own, except for the will of God." I have lived by that principal before I read that quote, but it crystallized my thinking. It became my heart's desire to want the will of God in every area of my life! Even when it means sacrificing something that I may want based on self desire and will. This is the ultimate act of surrender and trust. You might be saying, "If I am just doing God's will all the time then I won't be my own person. What if I don't like what His will is for my life?" However, when you follow and surrender to God in a daily relationship you stop being led and influenced by selfish desires and fears, such as the fear of not being accepted, fear of failure and the fear of unworthiness as well as shame, worry and stress. Instead you start being led by God's Spirit, love, peace and power. So you actually become a more empowered, dynamic and authentic you in the process! In addition God's will for your life is so much more abundant and amazing then you could ever imagine! God created you so He knows all of your true heart desires, gifts, talents and purposes that are going to bring you and God the most joy, peace and fulfillment!

Being guided by God's love in you (Romans 5:5) is partnering up with God to fulfill the most important commandment in the Bible; which is the love commandment which Jesus said everything in the Bible hangs on. If you fulfill the commandment of love then you have fulfilled all of the commandments in the Bible. Walking in love is the principal thing. Jesus said: *"And you shall love the Lord your God with all your heart, all your soul and all your mind and with all your strength." Mark 12:30 NIV Jesus went on to say in John 13:34 ESV "A new commandment I give to you, that you love one another: just as I have loved you, you also are to love one another."*

When you are walking and living your daily life in the love of God there is a sense of peace that is resident in you. If you sense you don't have peace about something then you have most likely have gotten out of God's love in some way. Meaning you have gotten outside of the love commandment and violated it. Ask God, "Lord what have I done to get out of Your love and peace?" and then listen allowing God to bring things to your mind and heart. Then say, "Lord I choose Your love and I release those things over to You and I choose to love, I choose You, Jesus!"

It is most often something you need to let go of and put into God's hands and under the blood of Jesus. This practically looks like putting the *taking thoughts captive* and the *confession of sin* sections of this book into action through prayer. The other hindrance to your love walk is unforgiveness which can be addressed and removed using the same sections as well as utilizing exercise #6 the "unforgiveness purge."

To put these steps and practical applications into action in your life on a daily basis can be challenging, but like anything of high value it takes effort, determination and sacrifice. Being guided by the love, peace and wisdom of God in you can sound simple, which in truth it is, but it can be very challenging to maintain as life's circumstances and the actions of others are rude, hateful and inconsiderate. That is when you have to make the determined decision that I am not going to let the sin around me or done to me produce sin within my heart and rob me of my peace, joy and intimacy with God. Peter speaking by the Holy Spirit reminds us: *"Don't repay evil for evil. Don't retaliate with insults when people insult you. Instead, pay them back with a blessing. That is what God has called you to do, and He will grant you his blessing.*

For the Scriptures say, "Search for peace, and work to maintain it. The eyes of the Lord watch over those who do right, and His ears are open to their prayers. 1 Peter 3:11 NLT

Notice in the scripture it says "search for peace and work to maintain it" so you have to labor to maintain the peace and the love of God within you. This means it takes effort; daily godly decisions; communicating with the Holy Spirit and putting your faith into action; oftentimes when it is not easy to do. We are not talking about working harder and doing better to get God to love you and be forgiven and righteous; that is religion. Christianity is not a *performance based faith*. This is a *victory based way of living life*. You were already loved by God, even before you loved Him. When you gave your life to Jesus you were made and given His righteousness and all of your sin; past, present and future, was totally removed and nailed to the cross (Colossians 2:14). Working or laboring to enter into God's rest and keep your peace is not about self effort. It is about utilizing the spiritual tools such as the ones listed above and discussed throughout this book that God gave us through the Gospel of Grace to live in and to *live from* a place of trust, faith, rest and daily victory through the finished works of Jesus Christ. Laboring to live from a place of Godly rest is about *living out* and living in what Jesus has already done and already provided for you through His righteousness, wisdom and holiness which He has freely made you to be and given to you in Him. (1 Corinthians 1:30)

As you live out your daily life leaning on the inward witness of the Holy Spirit, God will guide you. He will do this by: putting things on your heart, impressions, an inward sense you get about something, an unction, a subtle nudge, a quickening, spiritual and mental downloads, prevailing thoughts, flowing thoughts and flashbacks of a prior memories, all of which God will use to speak to you, guide you and most importantly develop a personal relationship with you. Spiritual markers, which are times you have experienced God in the past that God will bring to your remembrance in order to direct your path in your present circumstances. A sense you need to say or do something that matches up with God's love, Word, character or ways. That sense will often come with a peaceful feeling you get about what God is putting on your heart. You also can sense God's heart of compassion for someone, a situation, a group of people or a cause. This is God allowing you to feel His heart. This often comes with a sense of needing to help in a certain situation which is usually accompanied by a sense of peace and fulfillment in your heart. This is God speaking to you. For example if you have a burning desire or compassion for a certain people group then God is most likely calling you to minister to that people group in some way. The key is talking it over with God and taking some actions to minister to the group of people He has highlighted to you. God loves for us to step out on what we sense He is telling us. This takes great faith and as we put our faith into action He will guide us and direct our path as we learn to lean on the Spirit of God in us! Always know, as a Believer in Jesus Christ...the Greater One, God lives in you (1 John 4:4). He speaks from inside you and from the

Kingdom of God that is within you! Jesus said this about the Kingdom of God living in you. *"For behold, the kingdom of God is within you [in your hearts] and among you [surrounding you]."* *Luke 17:20-21 AMPC*

The Apostle Paul says that this truth of the Holy Spirit living in us is the mystery of the Gospel. *"And this is the secret: Christ lives in you. This gives you assurance of sharing His glory." Colossians 1:27 NLT* This truth reminds us to live God inside minded. Allow the Kingdom of God to come out of you, leaning on God's Spirit living on the inside of you to guide and direct your daily thoughts, words and decisions. This kind of interaction with the Holy Spirit will allow the Kingdom of God to come out of you and flow into your life and the lives of others around you. Every day as I live being God inside minded I am constantly checking in with the Spirit of God within me about various decisions that I make and things that I say, to ensure that I am operating by God's Word and in God's will for my life and not self-will which is very easy to fall into. I fall into self-will, often unintentionally, on a daily basis. Meaning what I am thinking, saying or doing is not lining up with God's love, will, Word, nature and ways. When I realize it I apologize to God and I say "Thank You Jesus, for guiding me" I give myself some grace that Jesus already provided for me and let myself off the hook knowing that my daily walk with God is built on progress, not perfection. That no matter my actions I am forgiven, loved and liked by God along with being made righteous and holy by the blood of Jesus and being in Him as His son, no matter my conduct this is who I am and who you are in Christ. This is your true selves in Christ. Checking your Spirit is a means to ensure that the decisions you're making are bearing witness to your inner peace of God's Spirit within you. This is a continual checking in with God just like you often glance at the speedometer on your car from time to time while you're driving to check to make sure your going the correct speed or checking your navigation to ensure you are on the right track when going to a new destination.

This is "pressing into" the Spirit of God within you by praying into senses that you get and ensuring that what you are doing and the decisions you are making are coming with a sense of peace and bearing witness to the Spirit of God within you. You can do this by asking God open-ended questions for example "Lord what are You saying about this? Lord how do You see this through Your eyes? How does this look through the lens of Your Word?" Then listen to what you sense God is telling you, showing you or what you sense, in the way of having peace about what you believe God is saying to you. This process is not and will never be an exact formula with God, because with God there are no formulas. We are giving you more of practical guidelines to follow and patterns in God's nature and ways to watch for in order to create a greater sense of awareness in how you can be led by God's Spirit within you. This ensures that you are continually leaning on the Spirit of God within you and not your own carnal understanding but God's understanding and wisdom.

Discernment can often be part of the inward witness as well. Discernment is a positive or negative perception, feeling or sense you get about someone or a situation in the absence of worldly, fleshly, self willed judgment, where you obtain spiritual direction and understanding through God's love and the Holy Spirit. Discernment is not an opportunity to be judgmental, isolate ourselves or get into self condemnation for sensing something about someone or a situation, instead it is an invitation from God to hear His heart and release His love over a person or situation through prayer and the Word of God. Most of us have experienced discernment before, where we get a sense, feeling or impression about someone or something. It's an inward knowledge or intuition. Almost everyone has thought or made the statement "I have a feeling about that person or situation" that is often discernment where God is inviting us to pray and listen to Him about a particular person or situation.

For example I use to get these negative senses about certain people I would even sometimes get insight about them from the Lord. I would see visions from their childhood in my mind, have an inward knowing about their life or be able to discern something about their character. So when this happened and it was negative I would avoid them, or reach negative judgments about them. Then one day the Holy Spirit spoke to me through that inward voice and said, "I did not give you this discernment to avoid and judge people, I gave it to you so you can pray over them and have compassion for them". As I was obedient to do what the Holy Spirit told me to start doing God began to give me encouraging prayers to pray over these people and even more spiritual insight. These prayers could be something I prayed over them out loud in their presence or to myself between me and God. What you do depends on the situation and what you sense God is leading you to do. God also began showing me more things about their lives through visions, dreams and His inward voice. This does not always mean that God is calling you to have a relationship with the person, pray for the person face to face or share with them what He is telling you and showing you. Sometimes God is just looking for you to agree with Him in prayer about the person or situation privately between you and Him. You will know when God is prompting you to share and do certain things just stay open to His leading. However, this does, always mean, He is calling you to pray for them and listen to His heart about the person or situation. Discernment can also be a positive sense of peace and an inward knowing about a person or a situation. No matter what you're discerning a good practice is to take it to the Lord in prayer and ask Him "Lord what are You saying about this person or situation?" and then listen to what He tells and shows you; then act on what you spiritually hear, see and sense.

Some people kinetically tend to feel and sense things very strongly. These types of people are often termed as "Feelers". It's important to be aware of this if you are a person who feels from God very strongly to know that what your sensing is not always yours to accept. Some of the time your kinetically sensing what is going on with other people around you or in the spiritual atmosphere. These kinetic senses can often times be experienced in your emotions, thoughts and feelings. When people do have these experiences they tend to feel certain emotions in which God is actually communicating with you based on what you kinetically sense. Such as you may have an emotional burden on your heart, or you may sense a certain emotion for someone around you. Which God may be trying to use to communicate with you about how that person is feeling and a possible need they have, for prayer and encouragement. For example you may get around a person and all the sudden you sense sadness and anxiety or on the other spectrum compassion and joy. You also may experience God's emotions for a person or a situation such a deep sense of compassion and love or even sadness and concern.

Your reaction to this can simply be asking the Holy Spirit how He wants you to respond to what your sensing. He may want you to pray the opposite if what your sensing is negative, other times He may highlight a specific person He wants you to pray for under your breath between Him and you or He may even invite you to personally encourage them by praying for them face to face. The key is being aware of what your sensing and being open to talk with God about it by simply asking Him "Lord what am I feeling and how do You want me to respond to what I am sensing?" then listening to what you spiritually hear, see and sense He is saying to you.

Remember there are a lot of the ways God speaks to you. His voice can come as an intuition which is a deep inward knowing written on your heart, imprinted and made alive on the inside of you. The Bible also refers to this as a spiritual truth being "quickened" or made alive to you (Strong's 2227). These are impressions God puts on your heart, feelings God gives you about a certain person or situation, wise thoughts and wisdom that you seem to get about prior spiritual markers and past life experiences that seem to speak to your current situation and seem to impart some divine guidance to you. You also can get impressions and thoughts about Bible parables and stories that God seems to bring to your heart. Staying God inside minded and focused brings you back to being aware of this type of activity and it will help develop and train your senses to follow God's peace within you on a daily moment by moment basis. This will help you stay on the path of peace and running your life on God's will instead of self-will. ***"For in him we live, and move, and have our being" Acts 17:28 KJV*** Thus you will be constantly leaning on, following and being sensitive to the inward witness of the Holy Spirit living on the inside of you!

6

CIRCUMSTANCES

HAPPENINGS THAT DECLARE GOD'S VOICE

C IRCUMSTANCES ARE SITUATIONS, EVENTS, SIGNS AND ACTIONS that line up with the Word of God, His nature, character, voice and ways thus confirming God's activity in your daily life. God uses circumstances and answered prayers to confirm His Word and show Himself to us; we often refer to these as *golden breadcrumbs* from Heaven, spiritual markers, confirmations, clues and Holy Spirit grace trails. God leaves us clues in our daily lives in which His voice is embedded in the details. His confirmations and activity will fit together like pieces of an amazing God inspired and directed puzzle. I also call these *Jesus' Fingerprints*. I look for God's confirmations and activity within, around and on the things I am experiencing on a daily basis and especially things I am praying about. When a detective is trying to solve a mystery and figure out who has been in a room or area they look for fingerprints, likewise we should look for God's fingerprints on our circumstances, prayer requests and our daily lives in general because God is always looking to speak to us and confirm Himself and guide us in His Will for our lives. As a follower of God you want to live your life as a spiritual detective looking for God's "love clues" as God leaves His fingerprints throughout your day. This will help you solve the mystery of what God wants to say and show you by finding and discovering God's voice embedded throughout your day and life! ***"If you look for Me wholeheartedly, you will find Me. I will be found by you, says the LORD" Jeremiah 29:13-14 NLT***
   These things will almost seem to be coordinated together because God is the best coordinator, conductor and confirmation specialist of circum-

stances ever! I want to encourage you to look for God every day, everywhere you go. Always be on the lookout for His voice and activity, because He implants and embeds it all around you. These are love languages God wants to establish within your relationship with Him. God wants you to discover Him. He weaves a beautifully designed multicolored tapestry of His activity and voice together within your daily life. God wants you to be watchful for His activity, searching it out like hidden treasures, then acknowledging His activity and experiencing His goodness. This process of searching out what God is saying through all of His various activities in and around your life creates a sense of awe, wonder and intimate experiences that cultivate your heart to acknowledge and celebrate the personal love languages that God wants to develop with you. *There is nothing concealed that will not be disclosed, or hidden that will not be made known. Luke 12:2 ESV*

God is always speaking. The question is are we watchful, listening, paying attention and expecting God to speak to us? These confirmations, signs and spiritual markers are used to create a personal story line between us and God, reminding us of ways we have experienced Him in past circumstances, as well as what He is saying about our present and future. They reveal His nature, character and voice. God is always in the confirmation business. He loves leaving confirmations all throughout your day of His activity and communication all driven by His great love for you. Remember this is God's love language with you and He will speak through all kinds of activity, signs, details and confirmations with His purpose always being to draw you into a deeper intimate love relationship with Him so that you can know Him by experience. *"It is the glory of God to conceal a thing, but the glory of kings is to search out a thing. [Deut. 29:29; Rom. 11:33.]" Proverbs 25:2 AMPC*

God has themes, a flow to His implanted voice. It will seem that things and circumstances begin to build on themselves. A dream you have in the morning or something you have been dealing with lines up with your daily devotional, then a song you hear on the radio comes as an encouragement to your heart and seems to line up with the other things. Later on that week you hear the same song at Church or the preacher seems to be preaching on exactly what you need to hear that builds on what God has been saying to you in subtle ways all week long. It's God's love language. Don't miss the details of His daily love language with you. He loves to show Himself in the details of your daily life. You may think to yourself as I often have, "Why is God not speaking plainly to me? why all the mysteries, puzzles and figurative communication?" I have come to realize it is because to believe and follow God in those things it takes faith, which pleases God and will culture your own heart in the process to know God's nature. Throughout the Bible God speaks in mysteries, word puzzles and figurative communication it is a pattern with God's nature and an invitation to enter into the mysteries and solve them with Him. His intention in this is to draw you into a continual conversation coming to know Him and experiencing Him in various ways. In God's reality He really is speaking clearly. You just need to have eyes to see and ears to hear by faith. Be intentional, watchful and willing to search Him out! I refer to these types of flows of God's activity as "this has been coming up in the spirit" meaning God has been inner weaving certain themes into His communication with you through specific confirmations and circumstances. *"Every matter may be established by the testimony of two or three witnesses." Matthew 18:16 NIV* I want encourage you to interact with God throughout your day by asking Him "Lord what are You saying about this confirmation or circumstance?" Then listen and often you will get a flow of wise thoughts or an inward knowing where you will sense what God is saying to you through these confirmations. Other times it is a sense of being known by God, you feel like He sees you, that He is leaving clues to let you know He cares for you and that He is acknowledging His love for you. This is God speaking.

There is also an important truth we have to realize when understanding how God speaks through circumstances. We must realize that everything that happens in our lives is NOT "God's Will" for our lives. Every action we take or don't take, there is a reaction and consequences that will either be positive or negative, depending on our choices. This is coupled with the enemy's attack against us trying to destroy the Word of God within us, our hope, faith, love and thus, our lives. As well as the positive and negative choices of other people around us that do affect our lives in both direct and indirect ways.

WHEN YOU BREAK DOWN THE CIRCUMSTANCES THAT HAPPEN TO US IN OUR LIVES TO THE ROOT CAUSES THEY ARE CONSEQUENCES AND COMBINATIONS OF THE FOLLOWING 4 ACTIVITIES:

1. God's activity towards us. Which is for the development and advancement of His love, hope, joy, peace, healing, faith and grace in our lives. God's activity will always be to continually call us into a deeper personal relationship with Him. God's activity by nature is invitational, directive, corrective and loving.
2. Our choices, actions or inactions positively or negatively.
3. The activity of the enemy against us. Which is always to kill, steal and destroy using things such as: unforgiveness, pride,

anger, shame, fear, worry, sickness, lust, unbelief, doubt, guilt, sin, isolation and the world system.

4. The choices of other people around us and their actions or inactions for positive or negative.

So the circumstances, situations and life experiences we have are a combination of these four activities. I want to encourage you to practice discerning between these four activities by asking the Holy Spirit to reveal to you which of these four activities are at work in the circumstances you are experiencing or what combination of these activities are at work. Often just by being aware of the definitions of these four activities God will enable you to discern what combination of activities are affecting the circumstances you are experiencing.

A lot of times, people will think God is speaking to them through signs or circumstances that go against His nature and His Word. Please understand that He will NEVER do that because God will never compromise His Word, He will only affirm it. God literally cannot contradict His written Word. He is perfect, sinless, and He cannot deny Himself. **"God is not like people, who lie; He is not a human who changes His mind. Whatever He promises, He does; He speaks, and it is done." Numbers 23:19 GNT** That is why it is so vitally important to get the Word of God into your heart on a daily basis as well as pray and get God's direct guidance on signs, confirmations and circumstances that you're experiencing.

There is a truth that when I came to accept it as truth, it set me free to experience the favor of God upon and within my life. I realized there is no such thing as luck, coincidence, happenstance or chance. God is sovereign, meaning He has the power to control everything if He wanted to but in His sovereignty He chose to give mankind free will choice. This means that there is nothing outside of His knowing and control. The Bible tells us that not a bird will fall from the sky apart from our Father in Heaven's knowledge and that the very hairs on our head are numbered and known by Him (Matthew 10:29-30). At the same time, in our lives, because of mankind's free will choice to act upon our own self-will and the four activities that we discussed above not everything that happens to you is God's will for your life, nor is it His best for you. So being able to sense what is God's activity and what is the activity of the other three influences in our lives, is key to effectively following God. God is a God of details and He is always speaking. It is up to us to be prayerful, watchful, expectant, and looking to how God is working throughout our day and throughout our lives, because He is always communicating with us in various ways.

"Now faith is the substance of things hoped for, the

evidence of things not seen." Hebrews 11:1 NKJV As we follow God in a love relationship, we come to know Him by experience and the substance of our faith grows stronger and larger. Hebrews 11:1 comes to life in our personal lives. The evidence of things not yet seen become more evident and the weight of evidence becomes very heavy. Don't let the enemy or your intellect rob you of God's activity by saying "oh, that's just luck or a weird coincidence" or "man, that's crazy or weird" when you see God's activity or when you see Him answer prayers in ways you never expected. It's not weird, it's not crazy, it's not a coincidence, it's not luck, it is God working and speaking and showing Himself to you. So that the substance of your faith may grow and the evidence of His activity may be built up like the evidence in a legal case so that you may believe in and experience God, the One you can't see with your physical eyes but the One you can experience and see with your eyes of faith! Good luck can be described as the devil taking credit for God's handiwork which is a scheme of the enemy.

I hear people say all the time, "I prayed about this and then this happened and it came to pass. Man, it was crazy and weird. I can't figure out if that is just a coincidence or luck or God actually answering my prayer." I understand. I use to be the same way. Between my self-doubt and the devil I was so confused and sitting there thinking, "Is this luck or coincidence? Or is this God speaking to me or is this God answering my prayer?" "Would this have happened anyway or is this God?" The enemy would hand me thoughts such as "oh, this was going to happen anyway. Your prayers don't make a difference and they don't have any power." Or "that's just luck", "that's just coincidence, that's not God answering your prayers."

This bothered me so I began to ask God questions about this subject and if what I was experiencing was Him. Then in His grace and love God began to speak to me on this subject. In my mind and within my heart God asked me through a series of flowing thoughts, "Sterling, do you believe that I'm a sovereign God? Meaning, do you believe that I have the power to control everything upon this earth and that nothing happens without My knowledge?" I said, "Yes, Lord, I believe You are sovereign. I believe that You can control everything and that by Your own Will You have given us the power of free will choices and that is why evil happens because our free will choice to choose good or evil, blessings or curses, life or death, to accept You or reject You, to worship You or something else in this world." And God began explaining to me that there's no such thing as luck, coincidence, chance or happenstance and that the enemy often uses these tools to create doubt within us, steal God's glory and to hinder our faith in order to cause us to pray less, communicate with God less and use our faith in God's Word less. Therefore, robbing us of the very power that God has put inside of us as Believers in Christ and hindering our relationship with God.

The Lord began to show me this truth in several different places within the Bible, how Jesus' disciples casted lots for the 12th disciple after Judas betrayed Jesus and killed himself (Acts 1:26), how the priests prayed and rolled die in the Old Testament and how God spoke through, David saying, "Lord You even control My Lot" (Psalms 16:5), I also found out that the word "luck' is not in the Bible. Throughout the Bible, we see examples of God "controlling the lot" or as we would call it chance, coincidence, random, and luck.

I want you to know that if you have struggled with this subject before, you are not alone. There are millions of Believers that struggle with this very thing. You see the devil tries to divide and conquer as one of his war tactics. It is designed to get us isolated in our minds and make us think we are the only ones that struggle with this. He often ends up convincing Believers, both new and more mature Believers, that the things that happen in their lives are by chance, luck, or coincidence. There are so many times I have heard people, myself included, talk about how they prayed about something or thought about something and it came to pass in ways that really stuck out to them; in ways they never thought could happen. Their responses to God's activity is "that's weird", "isn't that crazy"? "I was just randomly thinking about this and then that happened." "Man, I got lucky!" "That is kind of a crazy coincidence, right?"

No! That is God hearing, working, watching, performing, and loving on you through His power in your life! That is God's grace; His willingness to use His ability and His power on your behalf, even though you did nothing to earn His grace. It is based on His love for you and is founded on the abundant promises and the Word of God. So, free yourself of even using the terms; luck, coincidence, chance, weird and crazy when it comes to positive circumstances that happen to you! Start realizing and giving God praise for His goodness and His work in your life. ***"Every good and perfect gift is from above, coming down from the Father of lights, who does not change like shifting shadows." James 1:17 CSB*** Give God the credit in your life for His goodness and favor! Credit is due! All good and perfect gifts come from God.

In direct contrast all evil, sickness, destruction, murder, sexual assault, molestation, condemnation, unworthiness and all fear and all evil-based activity comes from the demonic realm of satan and his demons. Combined with people coming into agreement with evil and their own sinful fleshly desires through their thoughts, words, choices and actions. When you have experienced "bad things", "unfair things" and "traumatic things" realize those "things" were not God's activity in your life it was most likely a combination of the enemy's activity and the negative free will choices of other human beings. Bad things that happen to us in our lives come from the activity of the enemy and the negative choices of others, as well as our own negative and poor choices at times. God is a good and loving God. He is a healing God. He is a God who has walked in our shoes and who died so that we can have freedom and victory in our lives from sin and death. He died so that we could put the enemy underneath our feet as a defeated foe. This is the victory that overcomes the world system and the enemy our faith (John 5:4).

Giving God the credit for His work in your life is a key to developing and building up your faith! It can be likened to a relationship with a friend. When a friend is attentive to your needs and responds to your requests with loving support, you continue to build trust with them and increased confidence in their faithfulness and commitment to your life. However, if your friend was continually being supportive and you never acknowledged their efforts or returned the love in some way eventually the intimacy and deepness of your relationship with them would be affected. Our relationship with God works in the same way, it is an exchange of acknowledgment, love and trust. As we continue to acknowledge and celebrate God's consistent attention and activity in our lives, His faithfulness to answer prayers and to "show up" in mighty ways, we are stepping into faith as the foundation of our relationship with Him. We are also recognizing and experiencing special parts of God's nature. God longs to be acknowledged in His passionate love for us. These subtle yet miraculous happenings are actually God wooing us into His love! Each experience is God's way of speaking to your heart. God is saying, "Look! Taste and see My goodness. I love you so much. I want to show you the depths of My love for you. See Me and see My love for you. My love is all around you. I want you to experience My love on a daily basis so We can have a vibrant relationship with one another!" As we believe God for more in our lives, we position our hearts to receive the fullness of all God longs to bless us with. He wants to bless His children in abundance. Standing in faith and thanksgiving is a necessary part of inheriting those blessings.

Our faith works by God's love within us. With the measure we use it, that love is measured back to us in abundance. As your love walk grows, your faith will grow. So walk in love and increase your faith and overall prosperity and victory in your life! Always remember we wage a war in which the battle has already been won for us on Calvary's Cross. So, step into victory, step into prosperity, step into life by having a love relationship with Jesus Christ. Jesus is the victory! Therefore, we have and can live in the victory because we are in Christ.

We also have to realize that the enemy comes to kill, steal and destroy, but Jesus came that you might have life and be blessed in all that you do (John 10:10). God is not the author of evil. Evil upon this earth is the work of the devil and his demons. This demonic evil is coupled with people using their free will choice to choose and yield to evil, sin and their own self willed desires. I have heard so many well meaning Christians say "I would not be who I am today if those bad things had not happened to me, they have made me who I am today." No! That's not true. It is not the storms, trials, traumas, negative situations, demonic attacks and bad choices by others and even our own bad choices in life that have made you into the person you are today. It is God's goodness and compassion to see you healed and prospering coupled with how you responded to those things in, with and through faith in Jesus Christ and His precious Word that has caused God to be able to bring good out of negativity, evil and bad situations because of His relentless love for you!

God is the author and developer of your faith, love, and blessings. So, if negative things are happening to you, there are a couple of ways you can look at them to gain a more clear understanding of what is actually happening. It is often the enemy coming to kill, steal and destroy your faith during these times. Jesus explains this using the parable of the sower that persecution, affliction, and tribulations arises for the "Word's sake" (Mark 4:13-20). This simply means the devil comes to steal or render less effective the Word of God living in our hearts; satan wants to destroy God's activity within our daily lives and our faith by hindering our daily relationship and communication with God through things like doubt, unbelief, offense, unforgiveness, shame, regret and sinful desires. For example, as you experience confirmations from God the enemy will often come for the "Word's sake" with thoughts such as "that was going to happen anyway" or "that is not God it's just coincidence" of course we now know those are both lies but the enemy will try to create whatever doubt he can to render God's activity less effective in your life. When he comes for the "word's sake" if he can reduce the impact of God's voice, Word and activity in your life from 100% impact to 50% impact by coming in with various kinds of doubts and fears then he knows over time he can subtly errode and hinder you from having an intimate relationship with God. The other issue that could be happening if you are experiencing a lot of negative circumstances is that somewhere along the way, you have opened a door and given legal right to the enemy through sin. The best way to get back on track and close that door is talk to God and ask Him to reveal any "place" you have given to the enemy in your life. This process of taking a spiritual inventory is a good and helpful thing to practice as a regular part of your relationship with God. Ask the Holy Spirit, "Have I done anything to give the enemy a foothold in my life?" Then listen and confess to God anything you spiritually hear, see and sense God is telling you, repent of any sin or legal place you gave to the enemy, release it over to God and then accept His forgiveness and grace. Talk to God about the situation. Especially if you need to get any thoughts, feelings or emotions off of your chest. This will help you to keep your heart open and in right relationship with God. You are always, as a Believer, in right standing with God; meaning you are righteous and you are in Christ. We are talking in terms of maintaining a healthy and open relationship with Him and closing any open doors or legal places created through sin, fear and unbelief that the enemy may be using to bring negative circumstances into your life.

God loves to leave a trail of clues in our everyday lives and circumstances and it is important to note them as He weaves them through our day. We want to encourage you to be watchful, attentive and discerning about the circumstances around you. God's fingerprints, puzzle pieces, golden breadcrumbs from Heaven, spiritual markers, confirmations and Holy Spirit grace trails, where God leaves us clues in our daily lives in which His voice is embedded are everywhere, all around us, all the time. This is all part of Him revealing this beautiful mystery of the personal relationship He wants to develop with you. This is all part of God's activity and as I have found is paramount in developing your daily walk with God, following Him and hearing His voice. He speaks through all kinds of various ways and circumstances. His voice is implanted all around us. Let your daily prayer be "God open up my spiritual eyes and ears so I can find You everywhere!" I have seen Him use billboards, street signs, yard signs and even people's T-Shirts that seem to say what you are and have been asking and talking to God about. Times of the day or night that correlate with scriptures. This happens a lot with dreams and the times God wakes you up out of them. Numbers that have Biblical meanings to them that often seem to have a continual pattern of showing up on store receipts, in dreams, license plate numbers, phone numbers and Bible verses. For example the number 7 stands for completion and the number 3 for resurrection, new beginnings as well as the Father, Son and the Holy Spirit often referred to as the Trinity. Physical signs and manifestations in your body such as a sense of peace about a situation or a lack of peace. Emails and texts that seem to come in at just the right time and say the right things. Daily devotionals that seem to speak to your very heart and circumstances. You open up your Bible and a certain text seems to be highlighted and stand out to you. Dreams, which God speaks through all the time will seem to give you direction and guidance. Colors that seem to stand out to you within a dream or within your daily life, such as blue which often stands for revelation of God's truth. Red can be symbolic of God's love and pink can represent childlike faith. The important thing is for us to look for God everywhere because His voice is implanted all around you and He is always speaking in various ways!

The images that we see can be God speaking to us, for instance I have been driving along talking to God about a situation then all the sudden it's as if a rainbow appears across the sky and I sense it is God reminding me that He is good to His promises because in the Bible the rainbow was a sign of a promise that God gave to His people. God also uses answered prayers, but so often I see a pattern of Him answering our prayers in a way or in ways we never thought of or considered. Jesus using a child smiling at you to bring a smile to your face, someone shows care to you by opening a door for you, you sense God's affection through a hug from a friend. All these things can be God using other people to love on you and that love can break things within you, such as stress and feeling isolated.

God has so many gifts for us throughout the day, don't miss them! He uses conversations with other people or maybe a sermon we listen to, that confirms something God has told us or answers a question we had. Marketing and advertising that we have seen come on just at the right time and it seems as if God is speaking through it. Through nature God often reminds me that the same God who spoke the sun into existence is the same One who loves me and wants to guide and empower my life. Seeing certain animals, for example I have been praying then immediately after I sense an answer in my spirit from God a dove flew over my head which Biblically is symbolic of the Holy Spirit. It was as if God was confirming what He spoke to my heart. Other times I have been talking to God about a situation that seems impossible and yellow butterflies will begin to fly past me and I sense God encouraging me to have hope because yellow is the color that represents hope and courage. I also sense God is saying that a beautiful transformation and change is going to happen, the same as when a caterpillar emerges from their cocoon as a colorful butterfly. That type of encounter with butterflies has happened numerous times. It often came with a sense of peace and an inward knowing that God was encouraging me and confirming something I was talking to Him about.

God can use social media posts that speak to your heart in a godly way. When certain inspirational songs come on the radio just at the right time, and they seem to say just what you need to hear, it's as if God wrote the song just for you in that moment! These examples of confirmations and signs of God's daily activity could go on and on. The key is to look for God's voice everywhere and look at your life like a Holy Spirit treasure hunt for God's activity! Don't chalk it up to luck or coincidence but to God speaking to you through His activity in your daily life. You want to live with the expectation of knowing that His activity is progressive in nature and that these circumstances will build upon one another throughout your daily life and fit together like a masterfully designed puzzle!

You want to practice asking God about the signs and circumstances you are encountering, because sometimes He wants to give you more insight into what you're experiencing. I often ask God, "Lord what are You saying about this circumstance or sign? What are You communicating to me through this?" Then I listen to God's active voice of the Holy Spirit to get more revelation and insight on what God is saying to me about these circumstances and signs. I have had God say things through flowing thoughts as simple as "I love you" "I thought it would make you smile" or I get a sense of peace of His love for me and an inward knowing that He has me! When making important life decisions you don't want to make them solely based on the circumstances and signs your experiencing, such as leaving your job, starting a new business or starting or ending a close relationship. While business decisions, job offers, moving, financial investments, friendships and making educational decisions are all positive life experiences, you want to make sure you have God's guidance on them so you can make an informed decision based on God's wisdom. You want to make sure you ask the Holy Spirit what He thinks about the decision and what He wants you to do. Then listen and journal down what you sense He is showing you and telling you.

Before I came to know and experience the active voice of the God I lived my life solely on signs and circumstances and a lot of times I missed opportunities and didn't make God's best choice for me. I also believed everything that happened in my life was God's Will for my life which was incorrect and I did not yet know my life was a combination of the four activities I shared with you earlier. It was like I was feeling my way around in a dimly lit room banging my knee and stubbing my toe on things because of my lack of vision, when all I had to do was turn the light of God's active voice on! Then I could receive His perspective on what I was experiencing. Instead I interpreted the signs and circumstances through my own soul and not through the Holy Spirit. I would pray about various decisions I would make but I never took the time to listen to what God had to say mainly, because I didn't know that God would speak back to me and I didn't know how to listen for His active voice even if God did speak to me.

Make sure you are seeking God's perspective on the signs and circumstances you're experiencing even when it is something good and positive such as leaving your current job for one that is offering you a higher paying and seemingly better position. That decision may seem to be a no-brainer and a clear sign from God, but without engaging and asking the Holy Spirit the decision to take the job could lead you out of the will of God for your life. Maybe God has something better set aside for you in the near future.

There may be a possibility God knows something going on behind the scenes at the company offering you the job that you don't know about and that you don't see. God may want to protect you from harm and lead you in another direction. You want to make sure that you make decisions by seeking the Holy Spirit for guidance. The good things in life can sometimes be in opposition to God's best for us which is why it's so important to know Him and allow Him to guide you in everything so you don't miss His best for your life!

Also recognize that you can hear God correctly on certain life decisions, but your timing can be off such as in this example of a new job. God may be putting on your heart and showing you that He is going to move you into a new season and a new job soon. The important thing is not to just take the first thing that comes along assuming *oh this must be from God*. There will often be a flow of God's voice, confirmations and activity. It can be as if you sense God is "releasing you" into the next opportunity which often comes with a certain amount of *grace* on it, where is seems somewhat smooth and fluid. As you relationally experience God's grace and favor being upon things you will get a personal sense of what I am referring to. If there seems to be a lot of continual resistance and you don't have peace about a decision you're making, even if it's a good thing you sense God has told you to do in the future, or something He is saying will happen, be careful you may be trying to make it happen in your own strength and self-will. Instead go to God for clarity and follow the flow of the Holy Spirit realizing God may in fact be leading you to do something or make a certain decision, but it may just not be in the timing you are thinking of.

In this example, as you go to God for clarity you may hear, see and sense He is telling you to be patient and wait on the job He has set aside for you. God may also use the circumstances you're experiencing to make His path for you clear by eliminating other options you were prayerfully considering. For instance, in this scenario if in the process of considering a new job the company you were looking to move to hires someone else or you interview with them and you don't feel peace about working for the new company, this may be God closing a door of possibility in order to guide you into His best for you. So even when things in your life don't seem to be happening fast enough, or doors of opportunity seem to close or they are taking longer than expected always remember this truth you cannot lose time waiting on God! Be diligent, but at the same time don't force it and follow the flow of God's voice and activity closely.

That's why you want to practice listening to God as circumstances happen to you throughout your daily life. It will help you to develop a sense of what are *signs and activities of God* versus what are not. You will also get to personally experience what a confirmation in your spirit from God feels like for you, such as a *sense of peace* and an *inward knowing* as we explained in earlier chapters.

You want to make the choices that align the most with God's Word, nature, and the active voice of the Holy Spirit. When you are having trouble making a decision a good mindset to have is to choose whichever is the more abundant life in God and has the stronger confirmations. I like to compare my previous relationship, or lack thereof with God, where I use to credit a lot of God's activity to luck and coincidence to an unhealthy marriage in which one spouse does all of these little things to make the other spouse's life richer, fuller and smoother. Then the spouse that is having all these little acts of love, service and kindness done on their behalf in-turn takes for granted or does not appreciate all the little things their spouse is doing for them to make their life richer, smoother and better. I was the unappreciative spouse when it came to my relationship with God. Now that I know that God wants to be involved in every area of my life and is constantly speaking to me, I am watchful and appreciative of all the little things He does to show Himself to me. He communicates with me through various details, signs and circumstances in what has now developed into my own personal love language between God and me. Part of the good news of the Gospel is that God wants to develop a personal relationship and love language with all of us! ***"Trust in and rely confidently on the Lord with all your heart, And do not rely on your own insight or understanding. In all your ways know and acknowledge and recognize Him, And He will make your paths straight and smooth [removing obstacles that block your way]." Proverbs 3:5-6 AMP***

Stewardship, Biblically, can be defined as utilizing and managing all the resources God provides you with for His glory and the advancement of His Kingdom. His Kingdom is within you (Luke 17:21) and having a healthy and intimate relationship with you is one of the most important things to God's heart and thus is a huge part of the advancement of His Kingdom. He created us because He wanted a family built on love and freewill worship. The stewardship of God's voice and activity is valuing what He is saying to you, writing it down, praying into what He is showing you, following Him in loving obedience, changing what He is calling you to change and continually transforming your character to become more like Jesus. Practically this stewardship of God's voice can look like Exercise #6 in the earlier Holy Spirit chapter on Spiritual Journaling. Making Spiritual Journaling apart of your lifestyle will help you to build your faith in you hearing God's voice in various ways, in relation to this chapter it will help you to recognize how God is putting together signs, circumstances and confirmations of previous things you journaled about because you can go back and read what you previously heard, saw and sensed God was saying to you. There will be so many times where you will see how things God told you have come to pass and fit together through circumstances, signs and a flow of God's confirmations. Prayers and things God told you that you may have forgot about when you go back and read it you realize God brought your prayers and what He told you to pass in some amazing ways!

When I personally was doubting if I was hearing God's voice or just having a rough day in general I would often go back and read my Spiritual Journal from the previous month or two. This would always energize me and build my faith because I would always find something in there that God told me or that I prayed about which I realize fit together with something I experienced that at the time it happened I didn't realize it was a confirmation or God showing Himself to me and it would be in ways I could have never orchestrated, but God did! This would in-turn encourage me, build my faith in the fact that I was hearing God and often times give me some clarification on a certain direction I needed to go or decision I needed to make. I still go back and do this from time to time and without fail I aways find some Holy Spirit golden treasure or part of a God mystery that was right there in my journal waiting for me to uncover, in which God was answering my prayers, concerns, needs, wants and dreams in some type of loving and relational way.

It's so important to respond to God's voice and activity in and around your life on a daily basis. So many times I would believe the lies of the enemy and the doubts in my head that God was not speaking to me, that it was just me thinking that, that it was just luck, coincidence or something crazy or weird that happened to me. I suggest that as you make this decision to live a lifestyle of listening to, hearing and experiencing God on a daily basis that you live by this rule of thumb if it matches God's Word, ways, activity and nature then by default recognize, acknowledge and celebrate it as God speaking to you!

Circumstances and situations in our lives can often cause us to dwell in the past or project ourselves into the future. This can leave us feeling anxious, stressed, worried and not focused in the present on Jesus and what He is saying and doing in and around our lives. When this happens make sure that you project Jesus with you. Meaning when you are thinking about past, present and future circumstances and situations, make sure you consider and imagine that Jesus is there with you empowering you. He is always with you and He loves you, so make sure when you are thinking that you perceive and project God there as being present with you to guide you, direct you and love on you.

For example, I have a tendency to project myself into future circumstances by myself without God's guidance, help and resources. This type of thinking creates anxiety, worry and racing thoughts of excessive planning for me if it goes unchallenged and uncorrected. Some people call this future tripping and I use to call it my everyday life. It got so bad I had trouble sleeping for several years before I learned this practical tactic. My mind would just run at night and spin around over and over again like a hamster on a wheel. So now as my mind starts to jump to all kinds of future events, meetings or who knows what else, I pray "Lord I thank You that You are going to be there with me with Your love, Your power and Your resources. Lord I thank You that You will guide me on what to say and do." I also ask Him, "Lord what are You saying about this situation?" then I listen for guidance and wisdom. I also pray over the situation, circumstances and people. I cover them all in prayer by releasing my faith. Remember if you don't know exactly what to pray for, just start with praying the opposite of the negative thoughts that you are getting or you can begin to pray for what you would like to see happen in the situation. Both of those are good places to start. I may have to do this numerous times throughout the day and night but when I do it peace comes and it will come to you if you will apply and practice this tactic!

When you apply this Biblical truth, you will feel less anxious and confused about the past, more motivated and empowered in the present, as well as hopeful and expectant in the future. This will free your mind up to be more aware of God's activity around you. ***"To whom much is given, much is expected" Luke 12:48 NIV*** We are called to be good stewards of the presence of God that rests on our lives because of our adoption as His children through our salvation and the precious blood of Jesus Christ. Act as if Jesus is watching you, celebrating you, loving on you, living inside of you, and speaking to you, through circumstances all around you, because He is!

I want to share with you an awesome God story about how God uses circumstances to speak and how His voice is embedded in our daily lives through clues, detailed confirmations, themes and Jesus Fingerprints! When I met Leah, who is now my wife, God had been speaking to her in His Word about how a three cord strand is hard to break, how when she meets the man God has set aside for her that it will be three hearts in unity together. Our two hearts and God's heart. ***"A person standing alone can be attacked and defeated, but two can stand back-to-back and conquer. Three are even better, for a triple-braided cord is not easily broken." Ecclesiastes 4:12 NLT***

She had also had several people tell her that they felt like her husband was coming soon and the scripture she felt like God was speaking to her heart was Jeremiah 33:3, again the theme of 3's. ***"Call to me and I will***

answer you, and will tell you great and hidden things that you have not known." Jeremiah 33:3 ESV

The number 3 in the Bible stands for the number of completion, the number of resurrection and the number of new beginnings because Jesus was raised on the 3rd day. The night I was introduced to her at a Church leadership conference which her Church was hosting, we were talking and getting to know one another. She told me God had been impressing on her heart about the significance of number 3 in the Bible and that it had been coming up in various ways in her life lately, but of course at the time we were speaking she left the husband detail out. As I complimented her on a powder blue purse she had with a golden lion on the front she said, "Thank you". Then she said, "You have a lion on your shirt", which I did, then she said, "Hey you have the number 3 on your right arm sleeve!" which I did. I commented smartly that I was marked just for her and I winked at her and we both laughed about it not knowing how true that statement was. On a side note when I am picking out my clothes in the morning I often ask God what to wear because I am always training in hearing His voice even in the small daily things. This time listening to His fashion advice really paid off!

There were many more confirmations that God used which included a dream that I had the night after I met Leah where God spelled out her name for me using various metaphors and symbolic images within the dream confirming our future relationship. Two dreams that my mom had about my wife months before we even met which ended up coming true when I first met Leah. My wife and I both sensed an inward peace about our relationship. God answered so many prayers that we both prayed for one another by faith even before we met. Years before I met her God told me through a series of flowing thoughts that my wife would be "stunning" "stellar" and "out of sight", although she is all of those things and more I didn't know it but God's words to me would also be a figurative play on words because her maiden last name is Starr! God is so fun! When I met her I went back through my spiritual journal to all the words God had given me about my wife and I realized so many of the things that He told me matched Leah perfectly and in ways like above with her maiden name that only God could put together! Leah and I both heard the active voice of the Holy Spirit confirming what we were experiencing and what God wanted for our relationship. As well as other people who felt like God was also telling them that we were set apart for one another. Those are just some of the confirmations, signs and Holy Spirit breadcrumbs that we followed and received as God speaking, along with having the practical basics you would think of. For example we both love Jesus, we have a lot of the same likes and dislikes, similar values, good chemistry and we have so much fun together!

God's confirmations of 3's continued throughout our relationship when we got engaged we decided to get married at 3:33 p.m. in honor of the Word out of Jeremiah 33:3 that God gave her. That same scripture had a huge significance to me as well because it was one of the verses God used to invite me into an intimate relationship with Him and into ministry. When Leah and I sent out our wedding invitations we used a savings code and looking at our receipt, to our surprise and joy, we saved $333.00 It was like God saying to our hearts "My fingerprints and approval are all over this marriage." When we went to get our marriage license we had been running around town not paying attention to the time. As the court clerk was processing our marriage license my wife said "hey babe look at the time" it was 3:34 p.m. When we got back our marriage license the time stamp on it was, you guessed it 3:33 p.m.! There were times, in between these, that texts, emails and calls would come in at exactly 3:33 p.m. that were totally unplanned by either one of us. These were all confirmations by God to encourage, guide and confirm to us that we were making the right decision. As we prayed into these circumstances and signs God would give us various thoughts and impressions that we were doing the right thing and making the right decisions and a peace would come with the inner active voice of the Holy Spirit. We have leaned on these confirmations to help guide us at various times, encourage us in challenging situations and inspire us to love one another no matter the circumstances in our marriage. These confirmations and circumstances are the spiritual markers and a supernatural stamp of approval upon our relationship. They confirm to us we heard the active voice of the Holy Spirit correctly and God confirmed His word to us with signs and wonders! Since that time even our daughter Gracie joined in on God's calling card to us popping her head out into this world at 3:33am and was born on 12/6/18 numbers all divisible by 3! This was another sign and circumstance which confirmed and assured to us that we are in the will of God and that He cares about every detail of our lives! God has also brought this to our remembrance to encourage us as parents through good times and really challenging ones!

I want to encourage you to stop negatively questioning and discounting God's activity and start counting and celebrating it! God's activity is a sign of His goodness, presence and love so when you experience anything good big or small acknowledge and recognize it as God's activity of love towards you, thank God, praise Him and take it as His goodness showing forth and manifesting in your life! Don't fight it in your head with your intellect and your logical mind. Instead receive it by faith as His activity, His voice and as a personal message to you! Remember God is in the confirmation business all the time and He will always confirm His Word and Himself! Look for God everywhere in your daily life and celebrate God's activity in your life as God speaking to you! God often has you follow Him on these pathways of circumstances so it is not often a direct answer or direction because God is looking to cultivate a healthy Father-child relationship with you by knowing Him through personally experiencing His love. So often it's as you follow the trail of confirmations that God gives you your answers. That is why it is so important to recognize and acknowledge His activity in your daily life. So you don't miss out on God leading you to your blessings, plan, purpose and destiny!

7

THE CHURCH AND OTHER PEOPLE

GOD'S VOICE THROUGH HIS BODY

GOD SPEAKS THROUGH THE CHURCH WHICH IS EVERY PERSON around you that is a born again Believer in Jesus Christ as well as the Church assembly which would be your local Church family. God even speaks through non-Believers at times. One of the missions of this book is to help you be aware of God's activity in your daily life and for you to be expectant of Him communicating with you in dynamic ways. When I am talking to God about the various aspects and happenings in my life, I have discovered there is a certain flow of confirmations that God uses to guide and direct us. God using others around us to speak to us in a confirming way is a pattern of His throughout scripture. God will confirm Himself by various witnesses and various means. *"This will be the third time I am coming to you. 'By the mouth of two or three witnesses every word shall be established.'" 2 Cor 13:1 (NKJV)*

The Bible is also very clear about seeking good, godly, and wise counsel. I have several people that I know live a lifestyle of worshiping God in wisdom, spirit, and truth. Those are the type of people I seek for counsel when making certain decisions in my life and as a confirmation that I am hearing God correctly in certain circumstances. If you don't know anyone like that, seek out a person that has the type of relationship that you would like to have with God or a person that you sense a certain peace and joy over their lives that you respect and admire. I know several people like this that I allow to speak into my life. I give them permission and authority to be transparent and loving with me on what they see in my life positive or nega-tive. As you identify these people in your own life you want to allow them to be open and honest when they give you feedback. You also want to be intentional about making time to fellowship and spend time building community and spiritual family with them. It's also important to fellowship with other like minded Believers within your local Church family and in your local community. God created human beings to be in family, to have close loving relationships and to enjoy community together with our unity being rooted and grounded in the Heavenly Father's love, the righteousness of Jesus and the joy of the Holy Spirit.

There are many times you will be praying about something, and when you speak to another Believer, it will be a confirmation or guidance from God on what is needed. Most of the time, this type of confirmation will be a witness to your spirit and what God is already telling you. Such as when someone is talking to you and you sense God is speaking through them, you almost think to yourself, have you been listening to what I have been thinking in my head or talking to God about? When you feel like God is speaking through another person, talk to God to verify what you sense He is saying to you through them. You will often get a peaceful feeling about the situation so that you can be assured that God has indeed spoken to you about that particular situation. This is what we mean when we say "a witness to your spirit". God will always confirm Himself, meaning He will often communicate with you using the same themes over and over again in various ways and means. You just need to be expectant and watchful for God's activity, because He is constantly communicating His love and His will to us for our lives. God speaks through the loving actions of others as well. For example someone smiling at you or giving you a hug and you sense the loving encouragement of God, or they are opening a door for you as if God is saying I see you and want to help you, or perhaps someone graciously lets you over in traffic. This can also be when God uses another person to help you when you have a need of some kind, a divine connection where God uses a person to connect you with another person they sense will bring you an opportunity to grow or bless your life, God uses the actions of others to speak to us and communicate His love to us all the time. God also wants to use you to speak to others as well through your love inspired actions. Our job is to pay attention and seek Him within our daily interactions with other people.

Practically, it is also a good idea to have one or several accountability partner(s) to share with relationally that can point out God's activity and voice in your life. There are so many times that I will be processing my day with my wife or one of my friends and they will say, "Hey I sense God is speaking to you about this through these circumstances". This may be a blind spot that I totally missed God's activity on or they see a certain perspective that expands my thinking and that adds value to my life. Then I will pray into this and take what they say into consideration and seek God for my clarity. Sometimes I get a feeling of peace about it right then and I know God is speaking through them. Other times you can point out patterns of God's activity that you see in one another's lives. People say that, "God works in mysterious ways" that is not entirely true, God does often bring about things in ways we never considered and that are beyond our understanding so in that way God is totally mysterious. However, if you look at scripture God does work in certain behavioral patterns that flow throughout the Old and New Testaments based on His Word and His nature of love. So having someone who recognizes God's behavioral patterns, who you can trust, that you know who loves, worships and has a relationship with God can be a great blessing to your life and your personal walk with the Lord. It is really comforting to have people in your life who are open to actively listen to you, who will allow you to just share your heart with them, that are a safe place to process life's journey and even at times go on a good rant about life with! During these times of just sharing hearts I have seen God use those times to radically heal hearts, change mindsets and provide divine guidance to both parties. There are also times and situations I sense "I am not sure I am hearing God clearly on this" or "I need some additional guidance from God" then I will have my wife or one of my friends pray with me listening for the Holy Spirit's active voice in regards to me and the situation. Then they will sometimes hear, see and sense God is moving in my life in a certain way or as they pray get an uplifting word from God about me. Sometimes this happens right away and other times they will come back to me days later with insight about something God showed them in regards to me and my situation. I cannot tell you how many times I have had that happen to me. I have also been the person God uses to give encouraging words and counsel to other people.

Becoming God's love in the lives of other people is a great way the love of God can flow through you and you can experience the power of God in your life and in the lives of others. Wherever we go, we take Jesus with us!! One of the keys to kingdom living, meaning to live by faith from the place of God's grace, power and love, is to model a kingdom lifestyle by having an intimate relationship with God and spreading His joy and love to others. *For the Kingdom of God is not a matter of what we eat or drink, but of living a life of goodness and peace and joy in the Holy Spirit. Romans 14:17 NLT* It is important to always represent Jesus wherever you are and wherever you go by living a lifestyle of radical love and generosity.

God wants to speak to you about others, as well as have them speak into your life. There are times we all have probably experienced where God puts someone on our heart, a person seems highlighted or stands out to you in some way. You see something good about them that you sense you need to share with them. This is God speaking to you and wanting to speak through you. Just like we talked about earlier how He uses other people to speak to you, God also wants to use you to encourage others around you. The Bible says *"Do not withhold good from those to whom it is due, when it is in your power to act. Do not say to your neighbor, "Come back tomorrow and I'll give it to you"— when you already have it with you." Proverbs 3:27-28 NIV* That means if you have some encouragement and love to give to someone, give it freely and don't let the fear of people and the fear of rejection rob you of being used by God to encourage some of His children. You could be robbing someone of something they really need to hear at that exact time, day and season of their lives. I see God doing that all the time with me He uses people to encourage and lift me up with compliments and calling out talents, abilities and gifts they see in me.

When you get encouraging words from others it is often God calling out the gifts in you through them and vice versa. It is important to share with people the talents, gifts, abilities and good you see in them as well as keeping your heart open to receive the same blessings when they come. God wants to use us and others around us to bless one another in various ways and speak words of encouragement on His behalf. He is just looking for us all to be available to be used by Him. I use to get these uplifting, loving thoughts about sharing something positive with people that I knew or would meet throughout my day but often the fear of rejection and the fear of judgment would hinder and keep me from sharing what God had put on my heart. I would think "Oh what if they think I am weird?" or "What if they don't like what I have to say?"

The Bible says that *"Every good act of giving and every perfect gift is from above" James 1:17 NIV* So we know that when we get flowing thoughts, impressions on our hearts or a nudge to give someone positive praise or to share the love of Jesus with them that prompt is coming from God and is Him speaking and acting through you. Now I realize that God is wanting to speak and act through me! This wonderful truth motivates me to share His love with the person no matter how uncomfortable I may feel. It also reminds me to keep my heart open to receive from others as well, knowing God is using them to act on His behalf to speak to my heart, by giving me some encouragement and calling out seeds of greatness that God sees in me. When I got this revelation the fear of people and the fear of rejection began to break off of me. I still struggle with thoughts of doubt or fear sometimes but I try my best to go against them and step out on God's love and faith. I have been so blessed by living this kind of lifestyle now and you will be too!

Jesus has called us to become His love and Word. You may be asking yourself *ok what does that look like and how do I put that into practice in my life?* I would suggest as you meet people you can ask God practical questions about them:

Father God, what's one thing that You want me to share with this person?

Jesus, how do You see them?

Holy Spirit, what do You Love about them?

Then listen and share what you sense God is telling you and showing you. Ask God what's on His heart for your spouse, children, family, friends, classmates and coworkers. Then begin to pray into what He gives you, asking Him more questions about them and to reveal to you more about His love and destiny for them. See the Holy Spirit working within the hearts of your spouse, kids, family and loved ones with your eyes of faith knowing God is working on them even when you don't see it with your natural eyes! Then sow into them, which can look like: calling out greatness over their life, when they do mess up react in a way which builds them up, when you mess up take accountability for your actions and apologize, giving others positive praise, supporting your kids in sports, band and academics, being emotionally present with your family as you spend quality time with them. Practicing active listening in your close relationships where you give them your full attention. Telling your spouse how much you appreciate them, taking them on a date night, and sharing what God has been showing you about them, praying over them in person when you are with them based on what God has put on your heart for them and also praying for them in your own personal prayer time. As you ask God about His heart for them, listen then write down and speak out what He tells you and shows you. The transformation you will see in your heart, life and in those around you such as your spouse, kids and coworkers will be amazing! The legacy of love you live out has the power to impact so many people around you for generations to come! I have witnessed countless breakthroughs in my own personal life and in the lives of others who have intentionally put this into practice! Keep this spiritual truth in mind about the power of words regarding those closest to you, particularly about your spouse and your kids. They will often rise to the level of the words you choose to speak over their lives and directly to them. As future parents and parents especially, we all have the responsibility for our own personal relationship with God and teaching our children about how to have their own personal relationship with the Lord but how can we teach and model something to them we don't live out ourselves? Before revival looks like a massive outpouring and a move of God through supernatural wonders, signs and miracles it looks like people with a healthy personal relationship with God based on intimacy and two way communication. Real revival that is sustainable looks like your personal loving and affectionate relationship with God causing healthy family type relationships to be cultured within your own household, school, Church and workplace based on God's love, grace and power! Finally revival looks like you taking God's love, power, word and presence with you wherever you go and allowing it to overflow out of you to those you encounter every day, so they can experience God's passion and excellence through your life! The outpouring of the Holy Spirit's love and the powerful move of God starts with you!

In the Church body and in life, human beings will disappoint you, hurt you, let you down and wound you in some ways. We cannot afford to allow people who are Christians and even Church leadership to be our image of who God is. Because they are not Jesus but imperfect human beings and at some point, in some way, they will most likely let you down. Ask yourself what's my image of God based on? Your image of God should always be based on the love, grace, life and Word of Jesus Christ, anything else and it is a false image of God and will lead you to drawing false perceptions about God. So many people struggle with drawing false images of God within their minds based on their life experiences, especially how other people have treated them. Particularly people who said they were following Christ but their actions towards you did not always match up to their confession of Jesus. Then we get disappointed, offended and hurt by people but also mad at God because we have elevated what we experienced in an imperfect human as our image of who God is. I want to encourage you to intentionally guard your heart against these false perceptions of God which are often subconscious conclusions we draw about God based on other people who we somehow associate with God. Because if you do not, by way of the imperfect nature and actions of people you will leave yourself open to developing a false image of God's nature, goodness and love. I know this all too well myself. I have fallen into this trap at various points in my life so I share this with you from a place of experience cautioning you to not get caught in the same traps I myself have fallen into. As well as countless others who have had the same snare lead them into drawing false images of who God is. Don't let your life experiences and even sin that is done to you, produce sin, unforgiveness and division within you. When the enemy feeds you negativity about other people or when you find yourself getting offended by the actions of others, ask God about the situation. Ask Him for insight so you can see the situation and the people through His heart and His eyes. God will give you truth to destroy the lies of unforgiveness. Thoughts such as "that person in the Church does not like you, you don't belong here, you will never be accepted by these people, these people are all a bunch of hypocrites". The enemy loves using this word "hypocrite" to separate us from other people. I hear people throw around the word all the time and they don't even realize they are being manipulated by the enemy most of the time. The word hypocrite really means someone who is saying one thing while knowingly doing something opposite with no heart desire to be accountable or change but only to manipulate and wear a mask. If a person has any desire, motivation or heart intent to become more like Jesus they are not a hypocrite, they are just in the process of refinement to become more Christlike. So with that said, yes there are hypocrites and manipulators in the Church as well as everywhere else that we go on a daily basis, but you don't stop going to the grocery store or to your job because of hypocritical people do you? Of course not. So don't let the enemy stop you from fellowshipping with other Believers and isolate you from having a local Church family. You will never find the "perfect Church" with "perfect people" because neither one of those things exist. ***"Let us not give up the habit of meeting together, as some are doing. Instead, let us encourage one another all the more" Hebrews 10:25 Good News Translation***

Christians are not perfect people, they are people who have realized they have sin, imperfections and have a desire to be spiritually connected to God and are in desperate need of the Savior, Jesus Christ. Christians are people that have come to the realization that they cannot live their lives effectively on their own self-will, self-effort and self-desire. They need the blood of Jesus and God's Spirit living in them to be delivered from themselves! We are all a "work in progress" and in the process of becoming Christlike and allowing the Holy Spirit to guide and direct your thoughts, words and actions is a lifelong journey. We are all still "in process" of having our mind, will, emotions, personality and perceptions transformed by God's Word, Spirit, presence and love.

I hear people struggle with all kinds of negative thoughts when they are trying to connect with other Believers as well as wanting to personally walk closer with God. Thoughts such as "don't go to that Church they are all a bunch of hypocrites anyways", "you can't trust them", "they are not going to accept you". These thoughts are designed to put us personally into guilt, shame and isolation when we are trying to make changes in our lives for instance "you can't have a relationship with God, you are still sinning you don't want to be a hypocrite". These are all lies that the enemy uses to separate the Body of Christ and tries to hinder your personal relationship with God. Comparison is also a trap many people fall or have fallen into, myself included. Comparison will often make you feel inferior to others when you compare yourself to them at how "good they are or how good their life seems" and on the other side of the spectrum you may suffer at the hands of self absorption and pride by saying well I do "more good" or "less bad" than them which makes me more deserving of God's blessings. Neither of these results of comparison are positive. When you try to live by the law of works and put yourself above others because of how "good of a person" you see yourself as or when you use the "not so good or evil works of other people" that your not doing to validate you putting yourself above other people the Bible says in both cases you make God's grace and favor in your life less effective. So no matter the situation comparison can be a trap and a hinderance to your relationship with God. It's also a trap that is easy to fall into so beware of the thoughts and intents of your heart when it comes to comparing yourself to others around you. When negative thoughts about yourself and others or comparison happens go into forgiveness mode for yourself, God and others. Also ask God, "Lord what lies am I believing about myself and these other people around me? Lord how do You see me? Lord how do you see these other people?" Then listen to what you sense God is telling you and showing you. As I engage the Holy Spirit by faith, God has broken my heart wide open for so many people in numerous circumstances. God has shared His heart with me and told me how much He loves me and them. He has shown me visions of their childhoods, given me an impression of hurt they had in their heart that was influencing their behavior. He has also given me downloads about their gifts, talents, potential and created purpose. If you choose to put these spiritual tactics into practice He will do the same for you too!

The Bible says where there is envy, strife and offense there is every evil work (James 3:16) and the devil is always trying to create wedges in the Body of Christ. Attempting to keep us divided and not in unity as the Family of God that Jesus wants us to be, especially in our local Church family. Oftentimes people don't even know they are being used or manipulated in this way. Allowing past hurts, lies, fears and experiences to isolate them, which hinder the unity they can have with other people, thus hindering the lives of everyone God wanted to bring together for the building up and encouragement of His children. This also negatively affects the unity of the local Church body as a whole, because you have people not coming together bringing with them their talents, abilities, gifts, callings and resources which God put inside of them and blessed them with to be used to build up His Church. God encourages us in His Word to have fellowship, friendship and community with other Believers. While connecting with a local Church family is an important aspect of growing and developing your relationship with God, a common mistake many people make is they view attending Church services as the foundation of growing, developing and sustaining their personal relationship with God. Keep in mind it is the intimacy you will build with God relationally such as spending quality alone time with Him, hearing His voice on a daily basis, reading His Word, encountering His Holy Spirit, celebrating His activity in your daily life and talking with Him throughout your day that is truly foundational. This kind of daily relationship with God will transform your life into becoming like Jesus as well as developing and sustaining your personal companionship with the Lord. At the same time being connected with a local Church family is an important part of your Christian life and is not to be ignored or avoided. So right now I want encourage you to pray and ask the Holy Spirit if you have any false perceptions and images of God because of others and if you are holding on to hurt done by those in the Church. Then listen and allow the Holy Spirit to bring those things to your heart and mind. Lastly I want to ask you to give that hurt, pain and unforgiveness over to Jesus so you can be free. Jesus had the best reason to isolate Himself, He had great Church hurts, He was questioned, mocked, rejected and in the end killed by the Church and religious leaders of His day. However, the Bible tells us that after His resurrection He came back to empower and love the Church which He is still doing to this very day. If anyone had a reason to disconnect from the Church and people in general it's Jesus but instead He gave His life for the very people who rejected Him as well as you and I. That's what love does and that's what Jesus is calling all of us to do is to unify as His body of Believers and be His hands and feet upon this earth.

I want to encourage you to be part of a local Church congregation where you can build community and healthy relationships with other followers of Jesus! It is important to connect yourself with a local Bible believing Church in your area which welcomes God's love, voice, presence and the Holy Spirit. If you don't currently have a local Church family pray, listen and allow the Holy Spirit to lead you to a Church family that is right for you. Often as you visit potential churches there will be one which emerges and stands out. As you pray about it God will speak to you. It may be through a vision you have, an inner knowing or a peace in your spirit. However God speaks, you will know when you find the Church family God has purposed for you. If you are currently plugged into a local Church pray and ask God to show you what His purpose is for you there and how you can be a blessing to your Church.

At times, God has also used people in my life that are not necessarily walking with Christ in a relationship, to speak into my life or confirm something I have been talking to God about. They will be talking to me and say something, often unknowingly, that God has already been telling me and I will sense that God is speaking through them.

When looking at this situation in particular as a confirming word from God, it needs to match up with God's Word and His nature. There is a demonic deceiver out there called the devil who can also use people to give you false signs and lead you in the wrong way. It is important to always make sure no matter what you are sensing that it matches up with the Word of God and what the Holy Spirit tells and shows you in your personal prayer time with the Lord. I use to struggle with this issue for years in my life. I would just look for signs and circumstances but not line them up with the Bible nor would I attempt to get a personal word and guidance from the Lord on the signs I was experiencing. There are plenty of times in my life when this error in my thinking lead me down the wrong path. That is why we have the Holy Spirit and the Word of God to guide us into all truth! *"But when He, the Spirit of Truth, comes, He will guide you into all the truth [full and complete truth]."JOHN 16:13 AMP*

God also speaks through anointed preachers, teachers, and evangelists. When you feel like they are speaking right to you or to your situation, pay attention because that is indeed God speaking to you through them. Have you ever been in Church or watching a sermon online and thought to yourself, "I feel like this person is speaking right to me, they are speaking to my situation?" Pay attention to what they are saying because that is God speaking to you! When I am preaching or teaching in any capacity I always ask God what to speak on and what He wants me to say because He knows what His people need to hear. Even after He downloads ideas and a sermon into my heart, as I deliver the message, I always at some point in the message start to say things that were not in my notes and the sermon never goes exactly how it is planned. I have learned to just follow the flow of the Holy Spirit. As I have done that people will often come up to me after the sermon and say, "Hey, what you said really spoke to me. I feel like that was for me!" What's so funny is a lot of the times what I never planned to say is what ends up hitting their hearts the hardest and when that does happen I let them know, "It was for you because I had not even planned on saying that but the Spirit of God lead me in that direction."

There are so many times in my own life when I have been speaking to God about something and then, when it is time to listen to my daily dose of teaching and preaching, I will ask God, "Lord, who do I need to listen to or watch today.?" I will get a sense of a certain preacher that seems to come to my mind or I sense I am in the mood to listen to a particular topic. There are even times where I will get the flowing thought of the exact preacher and God will lead me on which sermon to pick. Other times I just open up YouTube or I am searching on the web and the sermon I need to listen to seems to jump off the screen at me or may stand out to me as if it's saying, "watch me"! A sermon may be highlighted, meaning you sense you are more drawn to a certain video or topic more than others. This is the leading of the Holy Spirit. It can be a subtle difference, but pay attention and keep your heart open to God's leadership. Then, I put the sermon on and I feel like the person is in my living room or in my car talking to me and directly speaking to my situation. This kind of encounter with God will usually leave you feeling well cared for, encouraged, and loved by your Heavenly Father. It is like He is saying, "I got you!" This is God speaking to you through other Believers. So remember if you feel like God is speaking to your heart receive it as direct revelation from God to you through anointed men and women of God.

God will also speak to you and give you the words to speak to others through anointed conversations. This happens when you invite God into your conversations with other people by praying, before and during the conversations, for the Holy Spirit to guide your words and heart. It also helps to pray that God would open up their hearts to receive the words God has given you and open your heart to receive from them in a way that honors them and God. I have seen this kind of prayer tactic blaze a trail of favor for myself and others. Anointed conversations have led to the restoration and healing of relationships between family, friends and coworkers. When you involve God in conversations He will take the anxiety, worry and fear away from talking to others. There are so many times in life that you will need to talk to someone about something and you will find yourself replaying the potential conversation within your mind over and over again. This type of thinking often causes racing and anxious thoughts about the unknown future which in turn often causes fear and worry to come.

To combat this, remind yourself that you are projecting yourself into the future without God and that He will be there to guide, direct and provide for you. When you think about the conversation, instead of mentally rehearsing all these different versions of what you are going to do and say, which I have found rarely workout anyways; begin to pray for God to give you His words of wisdom to speak, thank Him for His favor, blessings and anointing over your life. Begin praying for the person you are going to talk to. Pray that God's love surrounds them. That they are free of any fear in Jesus Name. I often will pray, "Lord I plead and apply the blood of Jesus over them and their family." It is important to note that the blood of Jesus and the name of Jesus are extremely powerful and effective weapons against any circumstances and challenges that may come at us. Next, thank God that He is opening their heart to receive the Holy Spirit guided words that He is going to give you. Also pray that God provides a time for you both to meet where your hearts will be open to talk to one another with love and understanding. This type of prayer works especially well for when you have to have a difficult conversation with someone. When I started praying this way I was astonished at the peace, favor and ease that would come over these conversations.

God would set up appointed times for the difficult and challenging conversations that I would have to have with people from time to time.

Those have the potential and the tendency to cause the most stress. Praying in this manner, anytime I thought about the conversation or meeting, totally took the stress away! I used the stress as a call to prayer instead of a cause to worry! When I did this it was like God would consistently put us together at just the right time for our hearts to be open and ready to talk some things out. The difference in your level of peace and your lack of stress before, during and after the conversations you have as you put this type of praying into action in your life will be like night and day. God will guide your tongue and your heart if you will give it over to Him and surrender it to Him in prayer as illustrated above.

God speaks through other people around you so remember to be watchful, expectant and discerning of how He uses people to speak love, guidance, correction and encouragement into your life and heart!

8

DREAMS AND VISIONS

SEEING THE UNSEEN

GOD SPEAKS THROUGH DREAMS AND VISIONS. THESE DREAMS AND visions can be any of the following: a warning, a confirmation, imparted wisdom, correction, teaching, encouragement or other forms of guidance. Sometimes dreams are just dreams, but more oftentimes they have a deeper meaning from God especially if you have surrendered your dream life over to God by praying and asking Him to guide and direct your dreams. A dream is something you will generally have while you are asleep and a vision is something you generally see in your mind while you are awake or it can come while you're asleep, visions while your asleep I would describe as very vivid dreams. It is important to talk to God about them, and in doing so there is often an inward knowing you will receive in your heart that will reveal a deeper meaning and the interpretation of the dream or vision. *"For God may speak in one way, or in another, Yet man does not perceive it. In a dream, in a vision of the night, When deep sleep falls upon men, While slumbering on their beds, Then He opens the ears of men, And seals their instruction." Job 33:14-16 NKJV*

God uses dreams and visions to culture our hearts to His love, ways and purposes in our lives. There are dreams and visions that have cultured my life and heart because I finally began to recognize God was actually communicating with me through them and I stopped dismissing them as "just random, weird or strange dreams". Instead I began to value the dreams in my heart as God communicating with me and I started writing the them down, rereading them, meditating on the significance of certain symbols and metaphorical illustrations. I also started asking the Holy Spirit what the dreams and visions meant, researched the Biblical and symbolic meaning behind certain colors, numbers, actions and images within the dream then I listened to and wrote down what I sensed God was telling me about the dream. Now I am always expecting God to talk to me and communicate to me in all kinds of amazing ways. Therefore, I stay expectant, attentive, and watchful for God speaking and His activity. Even when I don't remember my dreams or I only recall small parts of them I don't allow myself to get frustrated in performance or perfection. Instead I trust God to "seal their instruction" within my subconscious mind and use them for my good. I have experienced situations where something I did triggered a dream I had not remembered or had not fully understood which God brought back to my remembrance to give me guidance and assurance when I needed it. What happened? God had done what Job 33:16 said He would do for all of us He sealed the instruction I needed within my subconscious mind through the dream. Then at the right time He used it for my good, God is so amazing! God wants and yearns to speak to all of us through dreams and visions it's up to you and me to recognize His activity in this area of our lives and then respond to God by faith. Which can look like the personal example I shared above of how I started acknowledging and valuing my dream life.

THERE ARE 3 DIFFERENT PLACES DREAMS COME FROM:

1. God dreams; where He is communicating with us. Spiritual dreams are the main topic we will focus on developing in this chapter.

2. Dreams of our soul (mind, will and emotions) and flesh that we cause ourselves to dream. These dreams are more centered around our fleshly wants and desires. For example, a dream that revolves around self; you being popular, you getting the car you want, you doing drugs, you dating the celebrity you're infatuated with, these types of dreams are often centered around selfish desires. These will often show you strongholds, core fears, negative thinking, habits and fleshly desires that don't line up with God's will for your life. Take these to God as well and He can help you become more self aware of what is going on in the dream and what changes you may want to take a look at making.

3. Dreams from the demonic realm of the enemy. These dreams generally involve sins such as fornication and violence against others. Fear based dreams, such as nightmares, that try to create fear, uneasiness and terror in our hearts. These can be also be

sexually charged dreams of lust and sexual acts with people who are not your spouse. I would suggest taking these to God for interpretation as well. Get them into God's light and He will often show you ways in which the enemy is trying to create fear, doubt, shame and sin in your life. This way you can be aware of the enemy's tactics and where they are trying to attack you in order to cause havoc in your life. This will allow you to not only be aware of the enemy's attack, but to pray against it, talk to God about it for guidance and make any changes you need to make to your spiritual warfare life such as praying before bed, reading the Bible before you go to sleep and listening to Christian music while you sleep. God may also be leading you to confess, repent and break agreement with certain patterns of sin in your life.

God speaks through dreams all the time. Actually, about one third of the Bible was written through accounts of dreams and visions! You also spend about a third of your life sleeping. God wants to culture your heart, guide and speak to you even while you sleep. What a good Heavenly Father we have! God also used dreams several times during the Gospels to guide and protect Jesus's life before and after He was born. You may be saying *well Sterling I don't have dreams.* The fact is everyone has dreams at night, it is scientifically proven that everyone dreams, even if they do not remember their dreams they are still dreaming. If you feel like you are not dreaming or you cannot remember your dreams I would encourage you to begin to ask God before you go to bed at night for dreams from Him and for you to remember your dreams when you wake up whenever that happens to be. When I get up in the morning I often ask the Holy Spirit to bring any dreams I don't remember to my mind. Then I get still and allow Him to bring things to my mind. Sometimes I get small pieces of dreams that I write down, other times it seems like a total digital download of a dream I had in the night and sometimes I don't sense anything and I go about my day. So it is important to surrender our dream lives over to God while we sleep. How do you do that? By releasing your faith in prayer. I have written out a simple prayer for you to use as a model:

"Heavenly Father I surrender my dream life over to You while I sleep. Please guide me, direct me, correct me and speak to me as I sleep. Thank You Lord Jesus for protecting me as I sleep and guiding my dreams. Holy Spirit I thank You that I am going to remember my dreams. Thank you for the interpretation of my dreams and that You make all things known to me when I bring my dreams to You. Amen."

I still use some variation of this prayer on a weekly basis because surrendering our dream life over to God is a continual act of faith and a heart position. It is also important that we value our dreams enough to ask the Holy Spirit to give us the interpretation, to write them down, to pray over them, and to ask God questions like "Lord, what does this dream mean?" As we still our souls, listen, and write down what we sense God is telling us, there will be more revelation given. I have found an effective way to do this is to break the dream up into portions of the symbolism, activities and objects that stand out to you and ask God what they mean. Then, you listen and write down what you sense God is saying to you. As you write down and record your dreams, you will see patterns often times begin to emerge like metaphors, figurative pictures of things going on in your life, puns for instance the "sun" in a dream can oftentimes be a reference to Jesus as the "Son" of God. God uses object lessons and symbolism within your dreams to illustrate your mindsets, actions, strongholds and things He wants to guide you on, encourage you in, or correct you with love. For instance if the lighting in a dream is dark or if it is a night time scene God is often indicating to you that something He is showing you within the dream is bringing darkness, negativity or sin into your life. If it's a daytime or light scene, God is often trying to bring some enlightenment, positivity and revelation into your life in regards to what He is showing you. This is a form of contrasting where you ask yourself and God why this and not that, why was the scene dark and not light? Contrasting is a great tool to break down dreams. For example why did God use this certain symbol instead of another symbol or object why was I riding a bicycle in this dream instead of motorcycle? Bicycles in a dream generally stand for a personal calling or season of life that God is trying to show you which will take more effort on your behalf, hence the pedaling than say the effort it took to drive a motorcycle. Therefore contrasting in these examples above would give you a better framework of what God is saying to you within the dream. So many times people will think to themselves I had a weird dream and just dismiss it. What they don't realize is that dreams oftentimes are not literal but figurative truths of what is going on in your life which God wants to show you. Dreams often are symbolic although, in some cases they can be literal. God uses imagery and the nature of what you're seeing to communicate with you. For example a bathroom in a dream or vision can be symbolic of some spiritual and mental cleansing God wants to do in your life. In the natural reality of our lives, a bathroom is a place of physical cleansing and grooming. So think about the items that stand out to you within your dreams, for example a pregnancy or a newborn baby in a dream does not always mean you're having a baby in real life but it can metaphorically represent God wanting to birth something new in you or there is a new season or a new opportunity coming your way.

Another common pattern God uses in dreams is in the people that show up within your dreams. Often God is using their character traits, who they represent in your personal life or God may prompt you to look up their actual name meaning in order to convey a symbolic and metaphorical message to you. For example dreaming of an old friend from your past that was not a good influence on you may represent an old way of thinking or an old mindset that you're currently struggling with. Which God wants to highlight to you and bring to your attention, so He can help you to change that old way of thinking. Another example is dreaming of a person who's name is Isaac or Naomi, which means "joyful and cheerful" God may be using the actual meaning of their name, combined with what they are doing within your dream, as a metaphorical way of speaking to you about an aspect of joy and cheerfulness within your personal life. An illustration of this example could be dreaming of a person named Naomi and in the dream she is at work and seems very unhappy with some people at her job. In this case God may be showing you that people within your work life are robbing you of your joy and cheerfulness as well as encouraging you to forgive them and release the situation over to Him in prayer.

When writing down your dreams, if you feel lead to use certain words you normally would not use, follow the flow and use those terms. They may be clues to what the Holy Spirit is saying to you. It can be helpful to look up the definitions or to meditate and pray on why God lead you to use that word or phrase. You also want to write down what you sense God maybe addressing within your life in relation to what you have been thinking about, saying, doing and asking God about and how it relates to your dream. Dreams are often God's response to things you have been thinking, saying, doing or asking Him about which He wants to address, guide and direct you on with His wisdom, love and perspective. Dreams are like your own "God personalized daily devotionals" for your life.

I would also suggest you seek out and invest time into listening and reading good Biblical teaching on this subject. In my opinion, John Paul Jackson is one of the most gifted teachers on this subject over the last 50 years. His ministry has helped me develop a great platform for the Holy Spirit to utilize when interpreting my dreams. He has many books you can read and teachings you can listen to. I would also suggest books by Ira Milligan such as "Understanding the Dreams You Dream" as well as Dr. Barbie L. Breathitt's "A to Z Dream Symbology Dictionary" which has over 10,000 symbols God can and does use to speak to you through dreams and visions. I also use a website called "ChristianDreamSymbols.com". Although these resources are great, remember to always rely on the Holy Spirit to guide you in the interpretation.

Over the last couple of years, I have been valuing my dreams more and more. As well as investing time into studying how God uses various symbolic images and meanings within dreams and visions to communicate with us. Because of this, God has given me more revelation through dreams and visions. As we steward and celebrate the things of God within our lives, He is willing and able to give us even more! It is our choice to treasure the hidden mysteries of God's kingdom within our dreams. Often, it is the way we respond to these gifts that determines what will be given in the future. Thank God for the dreams and visions He gives you. Treat them as valuable by relationally seeking God in the process of discovering the meaning, intention and interpretation behind your dream and vision experiences.

God wants to speak to us in innumerable amounts of ways and often uses dreams and visions to enrich and mold our hearts with His love, guidance, and understanding. *"I, the LORD, reveal myself to them in visions, I speak to them in dreams." Numbers 12:6 NIV* Remember even if a dream or vision is received that has its origin from the soul or the enemy, it still has the potential to create insight and help lead us in paths of righteousness. For example, the enemies' tactics in a situation or a stronghold in the life of the dreamer may be revealed if taken to the Holy Spirit in prayer. This revelation allows for the dreamer to become more self aware of challenges they may have, cover this revealed area of attack in extra prayer and seek God for wisdom and guidance on how to proceed. I have seen so many soulish and demonic dreams as they are brought to the Holy Spirit in prayer they reveal the enemy's plan and tactics. Which is to create fear, shame and doubt about the person's value, identity and worthiness in Christ, as well as God's love and protection in the life of the person who is having these types of dreams.

So submit your dream life to God! Even when the enemy gives you a dream, pay attention, because he will expose his plan! Then, you are able to pray the opposite of what the enemy is trying to do in your life and heart. Knowing the enemy's voice comes with some kind of fear, accusation, temptation and shame with his purpose being to isolate and hinder you from having a vibrant relationship with God. However, God's voice comes with love, hope, grace and redemption bringing you into a deeper sense of your true purpose and identity in Jesus Christ. When you bring these things to God, nothing is wasted.

The interpretation of dreams and visions is the first spiritual gift I ever prayerfully asked God for and like the good Father He is, it was His pleasure to give it to me. I now have been honing that gift for a numbers of years and it continues to grow in me and God will do the same for you! The Holy Spirit has blessed me to see patterns in dreams often very clearly. Other times I have had to seek the answers out like a treasure hunt. The treasure hunt always needs to be guided by the Holy Spirit, through us prayerfully asking God to highlight and make known to you what He wants to communicate to you through the dream. Additionally, ask God what He wants you to do in response to the dream and His communication with you. For example, does He want you to be aware of something you are doing or change your mindset on a certain aspect of your life?

When you approach dream interpretation in this relational context, you will have a clearer sense of what will stand out to you and what will not. God uses a variety of confirmations. It often seems like God will highlight various things to you when you are searching for interpretations to your dreams. You will sense in your spirit a peace or an inward knowing of what is spoken to your heart. For instance, after I pray for the interpretation, God will often give me the idea to go to John Paul Jackson's Dream Dictionary on his website. Other times, God will give me the thought to Google certain things that stand out in the dream and I will just put in phrases such as "what does a car mean in a dream" then hit "search". Oftentimes, I will read a couple of articles to see which ones stand out to me. Make sure you are using Christian based sites on Biblical dream interpretations and use your discernment. Many times, there is a peace that will come over you when you read a certain interpretation of the item or circumstance you are searching out for an interpretative meaning. It is also important to write down and note what your thinking and how you are feeling during the dream and as the dream ended. This can give you a sense of what God is trying to show you and can play into getting a fuller interpretation of the dream's meaning. The time you had the dream is something that I often record as well if I can, because the time can have significance. I have seen times and numbers in dreams correlate with scriptures in the Bible or have some type of symbolic meaning to them. Again, there will be a thought or a sense you will get that the time you had the dream was significant. Ask God questions such as, "What book in the Bible does this relate to, God?" Then listen and go check out what you sense God is telling you. During the listening process you will often have thoughts about a particular book in the Bible or you may see a mental picture of the name of the book and chapter in your mind. I have found that sometimes you go to a couple of different books in the Bible and then one will seem to stand out for you it will become highlighted, or you will sense that's the one! It truly is a Holy Ghost treasure hunt!

Many times, there will be a peace once God has led you to the interpretation of the dream. You will experience a release and satisfaction in your spirit in which you come to a sense of understanding what God is communicating through the dream and vision. The important thing is to prayerfully consider the dream, thank God that He is leading you to the interpretation and have fun with God in the process. Have confidence and expect Him to reveal the interpretation to you. I want to caution you not to get crippled by performance or trying to get the interpretation to every detail of the dream. Our God is a relational God. Sometimes, the revelation and understanding of dreams and visions happen over time as you experience life in a loving relationship with God. Relax and know that you are not always going to understand the full context and extent of all of your dreams. There are dreams I had years ago which I am still coming to a greater understanding of, even still today as you read this book. God also will use dreams you have had in the past to guide and direct you where He will bring the dream back to your remembrance conveying the overall message to you of, "Hey this dream you had is in relation to or applies to this situation" and in-turn you receive God's wisdom, direction and guidance for the current circumstances your experiencing.

Some ways in which you can practically value dreams are: to write them down, capture them on the voice recorder on your phone, pray about them, ask God to tell you and show you the meaning of the dream, research and study Biblical dream symbols and meanings to develop your understanding of dreams, ask God what He wants to communicate to your heart through this dream. God is not trying to make this process hard. Oftentimes, people complicate things God made to be simple. At the same time God does enjoy watching you come to Him with these mysteries and seek out the answers and interpretations with Him which builds relationship, trust, faith and heart level experiential knowledge of God.

If you have not written your dreams down or used a voice recorder to record your dreams, I encourage you to begin to write them down on the notes section of your phone or use any free app voice recorder to record them audibly. This is what I do as I have dreams and visions. I try my best to write them down or record them as soon as I wake up from the dream. I have told myself so many times during the night, "this was an amazing dream, there is no way I will forget it" then I go back to sleep. Most of the time when I don't write them down, by the time I wake up to start my day I have often forgotten the dream or forgotten important details which may have been keys when interpreting the dream.

I may sleep a little less, but I have started to value them enough to grab my phone in the middle of the night and write them down in the notes section of my smartphone, often with one eye open! Sometimes I use my voice recorder, but I personally prefer to write them down on my phone. This helps me to organize my thoughts more effectively and even more importantly I don't wake up my wife. The important thing is that you capture the essence of what the dream is about, even if it is only a line or two about the main points of the dream. I have found these simple notes will help jog your memory enough so later on you can write out the dream in its fullness and receive an interpretation from the Holy Spirit. If later you do not remember all of the dream or you miss something, pray "Holy Spirit, help me with this because You know all things and bring to my remembrance this dream." Then write down what you can remember and, oftentimes, other parts will come back to you as you write down or record the dream. As I have valued and cherished my dream life with God He has been good to speak to me even more through wonderful and powerful dreams. Sometimes they are dreams of correction, guidance, encouragement, warning, and various other types. It depends on what God is trying to show you, which is another reason why it is so important to seek Him out in this.

Here are some dream questions for interpretation you can use that have really helped me. Ask the Lord these questions, then listen and write down what you spiritually hear, see and sense God is saying to you about the dream you are trying to get an understanding on.

1. Lord what does this part of my dream mean?
2. Jesus what are you saying to me in this dream?
3. Holy Spirit what do You want me to do in response to this dream?

As we stated, when dreaming it is important to capture the dream as soon as you can either by writing it down or voice recording it on your phone. If you are married, it is wise to let your spouse know what you are doing and encourage them to do the same thing with their dreams. You want to make sure they are on the same page with you on this so there are no issues with you using your phone in the middle of the night and them doing the same thing. It has been such a blessing for my wife and I to share some of our dreams with one another as part of our quality time together or daily conversations. It has added an amazing insight and intimacy to our relationship with each other and with the Lord. God will oftentimes give us unique interpretations that will fit together like a puzzle with each of us having a little bit different perspective on the dream and at the same time it often brings a fuller understanding of what God is saying to us within our dreams.

It's important not to get legalistic or frustrated in this process of growing in your dream life. The voice of the enemy or self doubt will come in with thoughts such as: "You didn't even get up and write the dream down so you lost it", "God is not really speaking to you in your dreams", "You didn't get up right away to write your dream down so you don't really love God", "You missed God", "God is not going to give you any more dreams", "These dreams don't really mean anything so don't waste your time", "Your dreams are not going to change your life anyways". Understand those kinds of thoughts are all lies! God loves you so much and He is so patient and He loves your effort! He knows it takes a lot of effort to value your dreams and record them especially when your body is screaming at you, "I am tired, go back to SLEEP!"

There are times I literally do not wake up from the dream to write it down or I do wake up momentarily but the tiredness wins out and I don't write down anything. So I just write down what I can remember later in the morning when I wake up. When this happens, because it will, forgive yourself, give yourself some grace, let yourself off the hook and know God's love is always for you. During these times I often will write down what I can remember and so many times as I am faithful to write down the little I do remember God gives me more. As you ask the Holy Spirit to help you remember what He was trying to show you in the dream you frequently will get more detail and sometimes other dreams you didn't even remember having at all will come to your mind. As you are faithful to write down what are sometimes very small fragmented pieces of the dreams you remember at first, God is faithful to bring more revelation to your heart. Other times you can use your quiet time with God to record and talk about your dreams with Him. Perhaps on your drive to work you can talk the dream over with God or use a voice recorder app on your phone to capture the dream. You could utilize your coffee or lunch break at work. Practically it can be whatever time you can make to at least talk the dream over with God and if you can, to record the dream. Then, as time permits, you can; even if it's days later, sit with God and discover with Him the fuller interpretation and meaning of the dreams. There is no performance and no pressure in God's love. He already, and always will, love you because you are His child. However, developing your faith and a close relationship with God does take effort, intentionality and there is resistance from your flesh and the enemy. Even with that understanding I want to encourage you to rest in God's love, understanding and grace for you! Like a good *good* Daddy, God sees the best in you!

As you invest time, attention and effort into your personal dream life, get comfortable with talking to God about your dreams and become familiar with the way God uses symbols, patterns and metaphors within dreams, you can eventually begin to help other people with the interpretation of their dreams as well. It is an amazing feeling to have someone tell you a dream they have had which they think makes little to no sense, then as you pray to God and listen, the Holy Spirit begins to open up to you what their dream means. Then you share what you sense God is saying to you and the interpretation God gave you resonates with them and gives them encouragement and guidance. I experience and hear about these types of things happening all the time, with people of various ages and backgrounds. Dream interpretation is a powerful way to hear God for yourself and for others.

Deja vu can often be something you have seen in a dream previously or a vision God has shown you. It literally means to have "already seen" or "already lived through" something previously. God often brings these things back to you to let you know you are on the right track or to lead you to make a certain decision you have seen yourself make in a dream or vision. I had a very powerful experience of deja vu when I was in a ministry time with a young lady who was looking to start and develop a relationship with Jesus Christ. She and I were sitting in a cafe when I had the sense, during the latter part of our meeting, I had seen this happening in a dream previously. The dream happened months ahead of ever knowing her. As I told her what I was experiencing, the manifest presence of God fell on us both and a wave of peace and love washed over us to where we were both in awe of what had just happened. The whole atmosphere of the room and the meeting radically shifted and both of us could tangibly sense it. The power of God was so strong that the young lady gave her life to Jesus and was born again two days later! She shared with me the shift in her heart was caused by the manifest presence of God she had experienced that day in the cafe. She has continued to develop her relationship with Jesus since then, and even after talking to her later in her walk with the Lord, she still sees that day as a day which marked her belief in Jesus!

I want to share two examples of life-changing dreams and visions God gave me in order to illustrate to you this point of how amazing and encouraging dreams and visions can be.

The first dream I want to share with you is a correction dream God gave to me to help guide me away from being angry, unforgiving, and easily irritated. In the dream, I was in an ancient Inca or Mayan type temple. I was there in a great hallway with Jesus right beside me and I felt very peaceful and calm. Then all of these beings with Inca masks on started coming at me. I sensed in the dream they were demons. Jesus just calmly moved His right hand in their direction and they all disappeared and were destroyed. Then, more came and He said to me "You do it" so I did the same thing with the same results as He had! As one got close to me after that, I started fighting him with my fists instead of doing like Jesus had shown me.

The more I fought in anger, the more demons came. Before I knew it, I was fighting like 30 of them and I could not see Jesus. Then they all began to pile on top of me. I thought to myself in the dream *I am going to die*, I cried out for Jesus and instantly they all flew off of me in what seemed to be in slow motion, like I was in a movie. It was as if the hand of God had lifted me up! I went flying through the roof, which I amazingly passed right through as if it were not even there. As I was flying up into the air above the temple I looked down at the roof which seemed to fold back together, like a puzzle coming back into its place it spelled the word "WRATH" in big block letters which had a tan color that looked like human flesh. The word had the texture of steel with these huge bolts on the border of the letters. As I was flying through the air looking down at this word, I woke up with tears in my eyes.

I wrote down the dream and then I asked God what it meant. This phrase came to my mind in the form of a flowing thought I will never forget: "You cannot be a child of God and a child of wrath at the same time". Meaning, it was impossible for me to manifest my true identity as child of God when I was acting out as a child of wrath through my anger, frustration and ungodly aggression. Those words jolted me as if a bolt of lightning had hit my heart! Then, I began to review the dream and I realized that Jesus was with me the whole time, but the more I fought in anger and hate against these demons the less I could sense the presence of Jesus. This was also true in the reality of my own life; as I had been trying to fight battles in my own self-will and anger, as I did that, I would sense God's presence less. God used this dream to culture my heart to start living a lifestyle of forgiveness on a daily basis and be quick to forgive myself, God, and others. Today I am a totally different person when it comes to getting angry, mad or irritated with other people. Now I am quick to release those types of feelings over to God in prayer which allows me to be quick to forgive and walk in God's love and Spirit. I no longer have the anger problems I use to have and God used this dream to change my heart and life. God still uses this dream years later to guide and correct me at times because like all of us I am still in the refinement process. So when I am struggling with being angry or upset He often will bring this dream to my heart and parts of it will replay in my mind and almost immediately the anger or irritation will begin to melt away as He lovingly reminds me you cannot be a child of God and a child of wrath at the same time.

The other dream I want to share with you is actually a series of two dreams and a vision God gave me which called me and lead me into the ministry and ultimately to write this book. It is something I have leaned on so many times when I feel like giving up on ministry personally and the calling of Sterling Harris Ministries to the world. God has used these to culture and mold my heart to love and to believe in my purpose and calling.

In the first dream, I was at the bottom of a huge mountain in a grassy valley type area. Then, I flew up to the top of this mountain. At the top, there was this beautiful, mature oak tree that was green and flourishing. I woke up and wrote this simple, but powerful dream down. Then I prayed and asked God what it meant. I wrote down what I sensed He was telling me. He said, "I am going to lift you high above your circumstances so you can preach truth to My people." He put on my heart (meaning I got a flowing thought that seemed wise and peaceful) to look up Oaks in the Bible. This search led me to Isaiah 61 where God called us as Believers in Christ, "Oaks of Righteousness." While reading this chapter, I realized this was also the prophetic calling card of Jesus Christ and was the specific section in the scroll of Isaiah He read aloud in Luke 4:18; proclaiming and announcing His ministry to the world. So, as I read this, I sensed God telling me and encouraging me, "I have called you to the ministry and will provide for you" which matched up with other ways I sensed He had been communicating this truth to me, this dream was a confirmation of God's other activity in this area of my life. In reality I had been wrestling with preaching the Word of God and if God was in fact calling me into a ministry position in the future. God loves to use confirmations so you know you are on the right track. They are like a flowing river of God's activity that He wants you to experience Him through. The Bible says in *2 Corinthians 13:1 "that out of the mouth of two or three witness a thing will be established."* I experience God using this principle all the time in the lives of His children. This is also a pattern throughout scripture. We see this principle of God using various confirmations as witnesses to guide and direct His people throughout the Old and the New Testament.

In my second dream months later, I saw the same beautiful mature Oak tree from my first dream rise slowly out of a vast sea of blue water, until it rested above the sea, and then I woke up with an inward sense of peace and confidence. I prayed about the dream. I knew from the Book of Revelation a sea stood for a body of Believers and groups of people. I sensed God was telling me, "I am calling you out of a nation of people and I am going to have you preach to seas of people, both large and small". Once I wrote all of this down, I felt a release and a peace in my spirit (the gut feeling we referred to earlier). This also was a further confirmation of what God had been telling me through His other activity in my daily life. This dream was encouraging me to step out into the ministry and have the courage to preach to groups of people both small and large. In my life at this time I had just started to step out by faith to preach the Word of God. I was also starting to see great increase in my ministry life and was starting to become convinced that God did in fact having a calling on my life to preach and teach the Word of God on a larger scale.

The third encounter was a vision I had while I was in a Church service singing, praising and worshipping the Lord. I saw this vision with my eyes open in what is referred to as an open vision. An open vision simply means your eyes are open when God uses your mind, imagination and your optical eyes to show you spiritual realities while you are awake and with your physical eyes open. It can be like seeing a hologram projected over what you see in the physical world around you. I saw myself at the bottom of this huge mountain in a valley type area; the same scene I had experienced in my previous dream which was now several years in the past. Then, these giant white dove wings came and picked me up and flew me to the top of this mountain. As I stood there, I sensed I was in the presence of God. Then, in the natural, my eyes started burning and tears began to come down my face. I felt prompted to write down what God wanted to tell me through this vision. I grabbed a piece of paper and this is what God told me about the vision through a series of flowing thoughts and words I saw in my mind. He told me the Holy Spirit was the dove wings and He was going to provide all of the provision I needed to perform the vision and calling He had on my life and ministry. At this time, I was newly out of federal prison (you can check out that part of my testimony on our website and YouTube Channel) and God had given me a big vision for this ministry. I was concerned about how this was going to happen and where the resources were going to come from. This was God answering that prayer of my heart and encouraging me that as I followed Him, He would provide and He had already provided everything I would need to achieve my purpose. You see, when God planted your calling, purpose and destiny into your heart, He had already provided the provision for it to come to pass. Your job is to have a relationship with God and follow the Holy Spirit so He can reveal these things to you and so you can become like Jesus upon this earth in your own special way. It may not come like you think it should and rarely does God do it all at once because it takes time, trust and faith to build the character of Jesus within you. As you take daily steps of faith and obedience, He blesses you with more provision and divine connections.

Now, some of you are thinking to yourself, "That is good for you, Sterling, you are a preacher and I am just a regular person". God has a purpose for all of us and just because I have a calling on my life to preach and teach the Word of God does not make me any better than any other Believer. What makes me special is that *I am just like you*! I am a beloved child of the Good *Good* Heavenly Father! You may already know what your purpose is and may wonder how God can bring it about. Let me encourage you that I was in federal prison and had pretty much lost everything material in my life, including my physical freedom, when those first two dreams came to me. Now we have a far reaching and ever growing worldwide ministry! These dreams and visions have helped me believe, even when I didn't see a way that God could actually use me and bring this to pass! He can and He will do the same for you and even more than you can imagine as you follow Him!

God has a plan, purpose and destiny for your life, along with that God has already set aside all of the provision, resources and divine connections you will need and He wants it for you more than you do! So begin to value the dreams you dream, take them to God and allow Him to culture your heart with His guidance, correction, encouragement and love.

9

CHRISTIAN MUSIC AND WORSHIP

LISTENING BEYOND THE SONG

GOD SPEAKS TO PEOPLE THROUGH CHRISTIAN MUSIC AND WOR-
ship. You know those times when the words of the songs seem to
speak to your heart and take on a life of their very own for you in a real and
personal way? That is God speaking to our hearts through praise and
worship music! God wants us to sing songs of praise to Him. God actually
commands us to sing and give shouts of praise to Him throughout the Bible
because He knows praise and worship is a powerful spiritual force that
causes transformation in our hearts and thus our lives! Listening to Christian music and singing to God is one of the greatest ways that we can allow
the Word of God to dwell within us richly. As we answer the command to
continually sing and listen to psalms, hymns, and spiritual songs with gratitude in our hearts; both individually in our personal lives and together with
other Believers, we are promised that the Word of Christ and the Holy
Spirit will dwell in us richly (Colossians 3:16, Ephesians 5:19).

This can happen in our daily lives as we take time to listen to Christian
music of all types and kinds. The thing that qualifies music as Christian
music are the lyrics and the intent of the artist that is creating the music.
Most of the Christian songs you listen to will have words to them. However,
there are certain Christian music artists who have worship music that is
instrumental only and they created it with the heart intent of glorifying
Jesus, for your listening enjoyment and for you to encounter God's presence through the music. In my quiet time with God and when I read the
Bible I often listen to instrumental Christian music. For me it creates an
atmosphere for encountering God's love and presence. Generally Christian

song lyrics will be inspired by the love of God the Father, by the faith, hope and message of Jesus Christ, and the empowerment of the Holy Spirit. This kind of creative intent personifies Christian music. As we listen to Christian songs, God will often speak to us through the lyrics and the musical instruments. For example, there are times when I am praying, that I will turn on some music and as I am asking God a question or as I am talking to Him, my ear seems to tune into the song at just the right moment where it seems as if God is speaking directly to my heart through the song lyrics. After sharing that experience with others, I have heard countless people share the same experience. Other times, I will be listening to a Christian radio station and some of the songs that are played seem to speak directly to my circumstances at the time. I have learned that God is using these songs to uplift me, love on me and guide me through the music. There have been songs I have heard numerous times before, but when they are played at certain times I am moved within my heart by the Holy Spirit in a powerful way, often even tearing up and crying as the song seems to take on new meaning at that moment in time. This is God speaking to and touching us with His tangible presence. There are times when I wake up in the morning with a phrase to a worship song that seems to be playing on repeat in my head, oftentimes it will not even be a song that I had listened to recently. Then I look up that song or the phrase of the song and as I begin listening it seems to speak straight to my heart and current life circumstances. These are all practical ways and patterns God will use music to speak directly into your life, heart and present situation.

Music is a huge part of our society and some of us spend hours a day listening to music. It is important to realize that what you continually allow to come into your heart will eventually affect your thoughts, words and actions. Thus it comes out of your heart and manifests itself in your life. The more words filled with faith, hope, love and righteousness that you put into your heart on a daily basis, the more of those same things will come out in the thoughts you think, in the things you say and the daily choices and actions you make. Allowing Christian music to be a daily part of your life gives the Word of Christ authorization to dwell richly in your heart! Also playing worship music in whatever room you're in or throughout your home will change the spiritual atmosphere of where you live. It brings a spiritual lightness and peace into your home. Carefully consider and be aware of what you listen to and what you watch, make sure it matches up with who you are in Christ, who you want to be in life and with the purpose and destiny that God has for you in your future.

The other times that Christian music can really speak to you is during the praise and worship time at Church services and worship experiences that we attend with other Believers in Christ. We, as Believers and worshippers, are to live a lifestyle on a daily basis that ministers to God and brings forth His presence into our personal lives and to all of the world around us. *"Worship the Lord with gladness; come before Him with joyful songs. Enter His gates with thanksgiving and His courts with praise; give thanks to Him and praise His name. For the Lord is good and His love endures forever." Psalm 100:2, 4-5 NIV* This part of the Church service is meant to be a time of praising, thanking, and celebrating God as we posture our hearts in praise and minister to God's Heart with love and gratitude for His greatness and goodness. This worship also gets us in the right frame of heart to receive God's Word in the teaching and preaching that generally follows. After singing songs of praise and worship, people often have a sense of being renewed, uplifted and lighter spiritually. This is God's activity in your life, and thus, Him speaking. *"Let the Word of Christ dwell in you richly in all wisdom, teaching and admonishing one another in psalms, hymns and spiritual songs, singing with grace in your hearts to the Lord." Col 3:16 NKJV*

Expressing our love to God through music; whether it is singing along with a song in our car, listening to worship music while focusing our hearts on Him, playing an instrument and even dancing around our living room with Him as our audience of One, music is such an intimate way to connect with our Heavenly Father. God enjoys hearing our hearts for Him through singing shouts of praise and thankfulness. Think about how good it feels when someone you love tells you in words of gratitude; how thankful they are for you and how much you mean to them. Worship is you ministering to and caring for God's heart, which in-turn actually transforms and blesses your heart in the process. You do not have to be a good singer to sing to God. You do not have to be the best guitar player to write music and play for Him either. The Bible says to worship God in spirit and in truth (John 4:24). It does not say that the best vocalist is at the front of the line or more appreciated in Heaven! The point is, to God it is all about the heart intent. 1 Samuel 16:7 says, *"The LORD does not look at the things people look at. People look at the outward appearance, but the LORD looks at the heart." ESV* What a comfort! For me especially, because singing in tune is the least of the strengths that God has given me! However, it does not stop me from singing and praising God in song, both in my daily personal life and when I gather with other Believers. God loves my voice, He loves for me to sing to Him and He loves when you do the same thing in your own way! The Bible says to *"Make a joyful noise unto the Lord, all the earth: make a loud noise, and rejoice, and sing praise." Psalms 98:4 KJV* For me joyful "noise" is the saving grace of this verse the Bible does not say I have to sing on key or sing well; it says I can make a noise as long as it is joyful and praising God! It is all about your heart intent towards God and seeking after Him and knowing Him intimately! So let loose and have fun with God!

In addition to being a vital and integral part of having a vibrant relationship with God, worshipping through music, singing and dancing is also a spiritual warfare tactic. It is a very powerful and effective weapon! There are many accounts in the Bible where the Israelites were being attacked and God instructed His people to sing, dance and worship Him. Then through their act of faith and devotion God helped them to defeat their enemies plans to bring destruction upon them. God, oftentimes, throwing the enemy armies into such a confusion that they turned on each other and destroyed themselves without Israel even having to physically fight anyone (see 2 Chronicles 20:1-30). That same promise of victory is still alive and active today for us as God's people! When we choose to live a lifestyle of praising, thanking and worshiping God; even in the midst of challenging situations that we might not understand; God honors those acts of faith in Him and fights our battles with us and for us! When the enemy is attacking us hard, in our flesh and carnal mind, we can easily get caught up in the bombardment of anxious thoughts and feelings that the enemy is using to manipulate our emotions. It would be easy to allow the enemy, our circumstances and negative emotions to drag us down and to get caught in the web of lies that those kinds of things bring into our minds. Remember that the enemy's voice and activity come to bring fear, shame, anxiety, stress and anything else that causes distractions, discouragements and disconnection that get you off track in your relationship with God in order to hinder your transformation in becoming more like Jesus. This is when our choice to worship God in song can be the most powerful! As we choose to worship and praise God despite our circumstances or the way that we feel, we triumph over evil and over life's challenges with the spiritual force of our praise, thanksgiving and worship! I have seen praise and worship cause all kinds of breakthroughs in my life by shifting the way I think and feel, from feeling emotionally heavy and worn down to a place encouragement and joy. I have even experienced financial breakthrough within my personal life and the lives of others through worshiping God in the midst of financial challenges! Worship is a powerful spiritual warfare tactic that throughout the Bible brings God's presence and power into seemingly impossible situations causing victory and breakthroughs in the lives of God's people! The good news is He is still the same God of victory and breakthrough today in the lives of those people who will choose to live as worshippers despite their life circumstances and challenges!

Halal is a primary root word for praise, our English word "hallelujah" comes from this base word. It means "to be clear, to praise, to shine, to boast, to show, to rave, to celebrate", and now my personal favorite "to be clamorously foolish" (Strong's #1984)! I want to share a short testimony of how I became a worshiper that I pray will inspire you to step out and be bold for God in worship through music, praise, singing, dancing and ministering to God's heart through vibrant and extravagant worship. I was raised in a Church where praising God vibrantly, loudly and raising holy hands was looked upon as being prideful, trying to draw attention to yourself, embarrassing and almost considered shameful; especially for a male to act that way. Even in churches I still go to today, all the time I see people bound up, just standing there not engaging the Holy Spirit and being free in their worship of God to even raise their hands or sing along with the song with passion and joy. I have found most often when I minister and talk to people that struggle with passionately worshiping God in a Church setting that their private praise and worship time with God often lacks the same vibrant passion. Now you put those same people at a big sports event or their child's basketball, soccer, football, volleyball or baseball game, or even watching a sporting event on TV and they come alive! They will be throwing their hands up, yelling at referees, players and coaches, jumping up and down and even at home they will be talking to a TV that they know fully well cannot hear them! Yet when you get these same people in Church, men and women alike, they are reserved and somewhat quiet compared to their favorite sporting event or social gathering with friends. Sadly this passive behavior in the worship of God has been passed off as a false sense of respect and reverence for God. No, God wants you to be vibrant, passionate and even extravagant in your worship of Him through music no matter if you are in the comfort of your home, driving in your car or singing and worshiping at Church!

If you demonstrate more passion, joy and energy for sports or your favorite secular song than you do Jesus you might want to take a look at what is going on in your heart. I too use to suffer from this same reserved behavior when it came to Church and praising the Lord in my private worship time. It took me a lot of courage to just raise both of my hands and sway back and forth. I would get these thoughts of embarrassment; fear of being judged by others; fear of bringing undue attention to myself instead of God; being looked at as prideful and looking like a fool to others around me. For years this type of thinking and seeing others not really worship with any type of intensity and vigor left me feeling comfortable in my complacency to just come to Church and stand there during worship and even when I was at home listening to Christian music or in my car, by habit I stayed somewhat reserved in what I now know was a false sense of dignity really rooted in unBiblical religious traditions, lies of the enemy, fear of being judged, shame and pride. When I began to read the Bible for myself through the guidance of the Holy Spirit, I developed a personal relationship with God and as I came to know Him by experiencing His presence and listening to His voice God convicted me of this type of thinking when it comes to worshiping Him.

I remember the very moment He began to shift my thinking in this. I was standing in Church one day and I wanted to raise both of my hands but I was struggling in my inner dialogue, "What would others think? Am I just drawing attention to myself? Am I going to look foolish to others around me? Am I really feeling the song that much?" Even thoughts such as, "God would be unhappy with me. I am not that holy so I have no right to worship God like that, I would be a hypocrite if I do that." Right then the Spirit of God spoke to me in the form of a flowing thought. God said, "Sterling you were the hype guy for your football team, you were the person always dancing in the club and wanted to be the life of the party, you get so into football and the things of the world but you want to hold back when it comes to worshipping and loving Me?" Right then these video clips began to play in my mind over my life of how I use to hold back in my worship of God in Church and when I listened to Christian music, then at the same time I saw myself getting all pumped up on secular rap, country and rock. I saw myself jumping around before football practice and the game getting other people hyped up for the day and how I would literally go wild during a game emotionally. He showed me yelling and jumping around watching the playoffs in football and basketball on TV. The last set of visions were me in these nightclub hot spots singing along with the songs and dancing in the VIP like I was on the latest rap video. At that point the Holy Spirit rose up in me and a boldness came over me and I declared, "No more!" I am going to dance, sing, praise and worship God with a boldness of joy more than I did for any sporting event or nightclub or the latest hit secular non-Christian song! Right then I raised both of my hands and began to jump up and down and I decided to be a joyous child before the Lord worshiping Him with all that I am in childlike faith! That day marked my life forever and I pray that hearing my testimony has been a marked day for you when you say, "No more holding back I am going to worship God with all that I am! No matter what!" Now I worship with a vibrant and passionate childlike faith all the time whether at Church, in my car or dancing around in my house with praise and worship music on. Do I still get those thoughts of negativity, do they still come? Of course! The enemy and my old ways of thinking still try to come up, but now I refuse them and I raise my hands higher, shout louder, dance harder and praise God even more because now I am not scared to look like a fool for Jesus! Because in His eyes He loves it!

When I am struggling with those types of negative thoughts during worship sometimes God will bring a vision to my mind of King David dancing in 2 Samuel Chapter 6 as he was bringing the Ark of God, which in those days stood for the Presence of God, into the City of David with "rejoicing" the Bible says. I pray as you read these scriptures God will give you your own personal vision of you dancing and praising God like King David did! That way when you're struggling in your praising and worshiping of God you can draw encouragement from this like I have!

"And David danced before the Lord with all his might, clad in a linen ephod [a priest's upper garment]. So David and all the house of Israel brought up the ark of the Lord with shouting and with the sound of the trumpet. As the ark of the Lord came into the City of David, Michal, Saul's daughter [David's wife], looked out of the window and saw King David leaping and dancing before the Lord, and she despised him in her heart. Then David returned to bless his household. And [his wife] Michal daughter of Saul came out to meet David and said, How glorious was the king of Israel today, who stripped himself of his kingly robes and uncovered himself in the eyes of his servants' maids as one of the worthless fellows shamelessly uncovers himself! David said to Michal, It was before the Lord, Who chose me above your father and all his house to appoint me as prince over Israel, the people of the Lord. Therefore will I make merry [in pure enjoyment] before the Lord. I will be still more lightly esteemed than this, and will humble and lower myself in my own sight [and yours]. But by the maids you mentioned, I will be held in honor." 2 Samuel 6:14-16, 20-22 AMPC

I love some of the other translations of David's response to his wife Michal in 2 Samuel 6:22, she clearly suffered from the same false thinking I use to have about the vibrant and passionate worship of God. *"I will become even more undignified than this" NIV; "Yes, and I am willing to look even more foolish than this" NLT; "I'm going to act more shamelessly than this" ISV.* To give context to what was going on with David's wife; a king was supposed to be reserved and wear his kingly garments, especially in front of people in public. However, David was so passionate about praising God for His goodness and His presence that he broke out of the image of kingly etiquette by shamelessly and humbly worshiping the Lord! This is one of the reasons I believe that God refers to David as a man after His own heart (Acts 13:22)! The question to ask yourself is, what image do you need set aside and break out of like king David did in how you personally worship God?

This vision of King David dancing always reminds me that I am dancing before the Lord. It is all about Him and bringing Him the sacrifice of praise! I will not be ashamed and allow the fear of what others might think, some false religious beliefs from my past, or even my current circumstances of how I feel emotionally to compromise my worship and my praise to God like I did for so many years. It also changed the way I approach going to Church. I use to come to Church just to worship and try to get filled up and connect with God. I didn't have an intimate daily relationship with God, so I tried to sustain and grow my relationship with Him mostly through attending Church, which is a common mistake I have seen many people make. Now I live as a worshiper of God and I am constantly being filled up through my fellowship and companionship with Him on a daily basis. So now I come to Church worshipping. Meaning, I am filled up through my daily interactions with God and I am able to be encouraged, strengthened and built up when I am at a Church meeting. At the same time now, even when I come in facing some difficult life situations, I am able to also bring and deposit something when I come to church as an offering to God, which benefits others in the Church as well. There have been so many people over the years who have come up to me since I chose to praise and worship God like this and say, "I love the way you worship God, it is so amazing, it is like you're a little kid before Him or like you're at a sporting event and your favorite team is winning. Your worship inspired me to raise my hands and get out of my comfort zone before the Lord, thank you." I often will tell them my quick testimony of how I broke free of being hindered in my worship of the Lord and how they can too! I also remind them that it is a choice and I don't always "feel like worshipping God" but that's when I know I need to worship Him the most and not be moved by how I feel! You too can be the relentless love and passion of Jesus that your heart longs to become and that others so desperately need to experience. I pray my testimony will challenge you to worship with passion and inspire you to lift your hands to the Lord, sing, shout and dance for Him for He is worthy to be praised! Everyone's worship of God is different so be free to be the best version of you when you praise and worship God. No matter what that worship looks like do it with passion, joy and love towards God. You can be assured of this, that whatever your offering of worship manifests as or looks like, it is awesome before God!

Your vibrant and passionate worship of God can express itself in a lot of different ways: on your knees with your hands raised, just standing in His Presence in a place of surrender, lying on the floor of your room in total submission to God or jumping for joy for His goodness, raising your hands in the air or waving them back in fourth in total thanksgiving, singing loudly with all you have or just singing under your breath, sometimes just sitting still listening to worship music and trusting God with your heart has been such a powerful place of praise for me! The key is to engage God and worship in freedom before your Heavenly Father and be transformed into His love! God adores you! Open your heart and be surrendered in your worship to God in whatever way, heart posture and body position that the Holy Spirit moves on you to worship in. God loves it all! He wants you to know Him and have your heart completely opened wide to worship Him. You will be transformed by His presence through music and worship!

So next time your in a Church worship service sensing you are holding back, or in your everyday life feeling down or stressed and hearing what you now recognize as lies from the enemy and self doubt, you can make a point to not allow the pressures of life to overcome you by singing, dancing and worshiping God with even more passion and energy than ever before! Knowing that listening to Christian music combined with living a lifestyle of praise and worship is a powerful spiritual force that will cause you to live a victorious life! Break out in song and lift your hands during your Church worship service. While you're driving put on a Christian radio station and jam out with Jesus. When you're at home in your private worship time put on some of your favorite praise and worship songs: listen, sing along, dance around the room before God or just sit and soak in the music enjoying God's presence. You can even break out into your own song, dancing and making music to the Lord! Start thanking God for all that He has done for you! Watch Him work! The power of worship and song is amazing to experience. Even as the pressures and busyness of the world come at us and the enemy tries to attack us and even when our life circumstances try to speak louder than God's Truth, God speaks to us in these places of praise and worship! He comes in to rescue us and fights on our behalf as we cry out to Him in praise, thanksgiving and worship for what He has already done for us by His grace through Jesus Christ! Remember, worship is a lifestyle and is truly a personal expression of a human heart that is full of praises and thankfulness towards God! As we speak to Him and call upon Him, He will answer! It says so in His Word! So listen to Christian music with a heart posture of worship. Allow the Word of Christ to live abundantly in your heart through singing, lifting holy hands, dancing, shouting thanksgiving and praises to the Lord and watch the walls of your heart come down, battles be won, mountains in your life be moved, your life radically transformed and overflowing with God's loving and joyful presence!

10

CREATION

CREATION DECLARES HIS GLORY

G OD SPEAKS TO US THROUGH CREATION IN THE ORDER, ART AND design of the earth and the universe at large in such magnificent and powerful ways. However, many of us do not recognize the phenomena for what creation truly means for God's people. It seems too obvious to mention, but because we see it all the time, many of us do not recognize the conversation God is having with each and every one of us all of the time. God is speaking to you through the splendor of HIS CREATION! Take a look around you and treat yourself to a deeper look at what lies before you as far as your eyes can see. God, in His mighty and powerful way, spoke into existence ALL life on this Earth, all except you and I of course. Because unlike the rest of creation God intimately chose to breathe His very own life breath into mankind when we were created. The Bible says we were created in His very own image and likeness! He gave color, texture, and depth to all living things that we can see, hear, smell, touch, taste, and experience for the sole purpose of our use and delight. From the very beginning of His Word in Genesis, the whole first chapter tells us of the wonder and the ways in which God created every living thing that even today we are blessed to witness.

"So God created man in His own image; in the image of God He created Him; male and female He created them. Then God blessed them, and God said to them, 'Be fruitful and multiply; fill the earth and subdue it; have dominion over the fish of the sea, over the birds of the air, and over

every living thing that moves on the earth.'" **Genesis 1:27-31 NKJV**

God, in His generosity and provision, knew not only what we would need for food but He loved us so much that He gave us things simply for our delight. This makes me think of creation as a love language. God expresses His love to us through the beautiful ways in which He interacts with us through creation everyday! How many times have you been in your own thoughts or troubled by something that seemed to take up all your energy? And in that moment, perhaps in the depth of your despair, you suddenly noticed a colorful tree of fall leaves, or smelled the fragrant aroma of a flower in bloom, or felt the flutter of a butterfly on your skin, or heard the song of a perched bird, or been delighted to see a whale breach the surface of the ocean, or caught the glimpse of a brilliant rainbow, or witnessed water so pristine and still that you were twice shown the scene in both real time and in reflection off of the still water, or a sunset so breathtaking that it erased the troubles of your day!

God constantly communicates with us through creation! Just like God uses signs and symbols through dreams, visions, numbers and circumstances God also uses creation to speak to us! In the Bible, God communicated with Noah in the days of the great flood by placing a rainbow in the sky after the rain had stopped. He said that the rainbow would be a sign of His promise to never again destroy the whole earth by flood water. Now when we see the rainbow, we are reminded of that promise and His eternal covenant with us!

God may use a plant such as a flourishing tree or a colorful flower or an animal like a loyal dog, a soaring bird or beautiful butterfly to communicate certain themes, illustrations, characteristics, or to lead you to a scripture that He wants to show you! As I mentioned earlier, God used a dream of a large flourishing Oak tree to explain, encourage and guide me into a huge part of my purpose, destiny and calling in life. As I went looking for more detail about what God was saying in this particular dream, it was helpful to research and lookup scriptures that talked about trees in the Bible. For example, In **Psalm 1:3 it says, "He will be like a tree firmly planted by streams of water, which yields its fruit in its season. And its leaf does not wither; And in whatever he does, he prospers. ESV"** As I read it, this scripture agreed with my spirit, meaning I felt a peace in my innermost being that this is part of what God was saying by showing me a tree in my dream. The interpretation God spoke to my heart is that: I am a tree (a person) that is firmly planted by streams of water (water is symbolic of the Word of God and the Holy Spirit) and I will yield fruit (the fruit of the Holy Spirit and blessings Galatians 5:22) through this ministry as He prospers me by His hand. I will not grow weary because my strength comes from knowing God through intimate experiential knowledge! The Holy Spirit is the living water that sustains us! See how much fun God's Holy Spirit treasure hunts are! God eventually lead us to use the tree from my dreams and visions as part of our Ministry's logo. Sometimes now when I see a tree near streams of water or I see a large mountain with trees near the top of it I will sense God using nature to speak to my heart encouraging me to stay the course in my calling to manifest Jesus to the world, keep pressing into my faith and keep my relationship with Him and His Word first place in my life. The good news is that God wants to use nature to speak into your life too! It's a love language God wants to develop with you. As you begin to realize and acknowledge God's activity and that He wants to speak to you through nature, you will begin to notice certain patterns where God will use things within creation to encourage, guide and speak to your heart. For my wife it's red robins, doves, falcons and butterflies for you it maybe something totally different. The key is being open and aware of God's activity.

In Psalm 19:4-7 God's Word tells us *"Their line has gone out through all the earth, And their words to the end of the world. In them He has set a tabernacle for the sun, which is like a bridegroom coming out of his chamber and rejoices like a strong man to run its race. Its rising is from one end of Heaven, and its circuit to the other end; And there is nothing hidden from its heat."* Notice in the Scripture above it says the solar system and the sun speak, meaning just their existence demonstrates God's power, wisdom and glory! It's as if God in this Scripture is imploring you to experience the vibrant colors of a glorious sunrise, assuring you that He holds you in the palm of His hand.

All of these examples and thousands of others that are too numerous to mention, are ways that God is speaking to you through all He has created. He is showing you His works in a tangible way that enables you to experience Him; His love, His power, His generosity, His gifts, His promises, His voice, and His creation all because He loves you! He wants you to know He's speaking to you and showing you His great and mighty LOVE! I was jogging along one day and God spoke to me in my spirit, meaning I had this flowing thought from the Holy Spirit within me, "Stop for second I want to talk to you." It was my Heavenly Father! He said, "Do you see these birds, these trees, you see all the different plant life, wildlife and insects?" I said "Yes, Lord I do." He said, "Everything you see glorifies Me. It does exactly what I created it to do. Everything on this earth glorifies Me by its God given instinct except you, Sterling." I was convicted and felt a godly sorrow because I knew it was true. He went on to lovingly say, "Humans are the only beings on earth with the power to speak words, the power of freewill and the ability to choose to have a relationship with Me and glorify Me or not to." After that conversation, I was so humbled and, like David did here in this Psalm above, I began to see God in every part of creation and how He uses it to speak to us all, about the depths of His glory, power and presence. A simple jog around this beautiful wooded area marked me and changed my heart as I stopped and took in God's creation and the great honor He gives us as humans to choose to love Him and have a personal relationship where the God of the Universe comes to live inside of you and me. How amazing!

God has used Psalms 19:4-7 to encourage me literally hundreds of times over the past years of my life. God spoke to me one morning as I was watching an amazingly beautiful sunrise. He had been showing me that He had called me to a worldwide ministry to reach people with the Gospel message of Jesus Christ, helping them start and develop a vibrant personal relationship with the Lord through knowing Him intimately. You might be saying, "well, that's awesome for you Sterling" and it was. The problem was I watching that sunrise from federal prison and I had lost all the financial resources that would have made something like that possible. I had been talking to God; asking him how He could use me, a man who had drank what the world had to offer on both the positive and negative spectrums and everywhere in-between? Yet, until I found a daily spiritual love relationship based on knowing God on an intimate heart level I was still thirsty and unfulfilled. How could God use a person who had fallen so far financially and in social status; from a former NFL Player, successful business owner, motivational speaker and youth mentor to a now federal prisoner who by all accounts in the physical realm and from a worldly standpoint I was at the worst place I had ever been in my life. As I looked out at the sunrise, the Lord spoke to me in my spirit. For me it was a flowing thought that came with such wisdom and peace I perceived it was not my thought. He said, "Sterling, do you see that sun?" I said, "Yes, Lord." He brought to my mind the fact that I just had learned that if you hollowed out the sun you could fit almost one million earths inside of the sun and a video type memory of me learning about that played in my mind. He said, "The same power that spoke that sun into existence is the same power that lives inside of you and every other Believer. It is also the same power that powers your life and the ministry I have called you to."

Right then, a sense of peace came over me and tears began to stream down my face as God's loving presence seemed to wash over me in warm waves of His peace. I could sense God saying to me, "Son, I got you." Then, God brought Psalms 19 to my heart by replaying in my mind a short segment of a sermon I had heard a preacher speaking about Psalms 19 and how creation demonstrates to us the glory and power of God. I got my Bible out and began to read it and the words seemed to jump off of the page into my heart. God uses this spiritual marker and my personal "Gospel Experiences" with Him to encourage me all the time. When I am getting up in the morning and I see the sun through my window, I will get the flowing thought, "Psalms 19". This is what I call a Holy Spirit flashback of a spiritual marker. It's when God brings back to you a prior experience with Him that encourages, empowers, and guides you. When I look at the sun, oftentimes God will speak to me of Psalm 19 to remind me that the same power that spoke the sun into existence is the same power that lives in me and is empowering my life! I cannot tell you how many times looking at the sun in all of its power and glory has encouraged me in whatever daily circumstances, trials, situations, problems or blessings I am experiencing. It reminds me that God's got me and to put my faith into action like my Heavenly Father did when He spoke the sun into existence. I hope and pray that my encounter with God has blessed your heart and that you will allow it to become a personal word for you. When you look up and see the sun, remember that God's got you!

God wants to do more in your life than you can ever imagine! He is the God of Creation and loves to use His very own creation to speak, encourage and guide you within your daily relationship with Him! You have the same faith, power and Holy Spirit living on the inside of you that created the Earth and every living thing upon it as well as the vast Universe! Our God is a huge God! He is so vast and powerful yet He longs for personal relationship with you where you experience intimate heart level knowledge of Him. God speaks through creation everyday! I want to encourage you to tune your heart into the frequency of God's voice and love language as He communicates to you through all of His vast Creation!

11

THE DEMONSTRATION OF GOD'S LOVE AND POWER

BY LOVING OTHERS THROUGH ENCOURAGEMENT,
WITNESSING, HEALING, AND FLOWING IN THE GIFTS OF THE
HOLY SPIRIT

WHILE A WHOLE BOOK COULD BE WRITTEN ON EACH OF THESE subjects and has, our goal of this book has been to give you practical and foundational truths, as well as examples, that will empower you to hear God's active voice, sense His activity and tune your heart to His frequency in your daily lives. With that understood, we are going to give you some brief overviews and examples of how God speaks through these demonstrations of His love and power as well as how you can be personally empowered to manifest Jesus to the world around you. *"And my message and my preaching were not in persuasive words of wisdom [using clever rhetoric], but [they were delivered] in demonstration of the [Holy] Spirit [operating through me] and of [His] power [stirring the minds of the listeners and persuading them], so that your faith would not rest on the wisdom and rhetoric of men, but on the Power of God." 1 CORINTHIANS 2:4-5 AMP*

LOVING OTHERS

Our purpose and great commission as Believers is to live a lifestyle of manifesting God's love to other people around us as defined in 1 Corinthians Chapter 13 in the Amplified Bible and by the supernatural lifestyle of love that Jesus lived, modeled and walked out for us while upon this earth through knowing God personally and intimately. We are called to live in a daily love relationship with God, allowing God to love us by opening our hearts to receive His unconditional love consistently and constantly, finding our identity in knowing Him as we love and value ourselves as His sons and daughters. Out of that intimate love exchange and overflow, we are then empowered to love those around us. We want to live our lives from a place of the overflowing love of knowing Jesus because it is hard to pour out of an empty cup. We want our cup of God's love, Word and Spirit to be overflowing! We are to be lovers of God more than anything else, and out of that love, God has called ALL of us to love others and to manifest the love and the image of Jesus to the world! Starting with loving ourselves, by receiving God's love into our lives and then spreading that love to our own households and moving outward like a ripple effect to those in our daily life path, leaving behind a legacy of love. We are called by God to be the LIVING Word of God upon this earth and the hands, feet and body of Christ! If Jesus is the Word, and we are IN Christ, then we are called to BECOME the Word of God as well. That's why we are called to not only read the Bible and love others, but to become the Word and become our Heavenly Father's love to others. It is a state of becoming like Jesus and being like Him. It is who we are as sons and daughters of God and followers of Jesus Christ. It is out of this place of identity and knowing God through fellowship and relationship with the Holy Spirit that we become like Jesus which overflows in our actions and our doing. Because for us to broadcast the love of God wherever we go we have to first tune our hearts into the frequency of His voice, love, presence and Spirit.

We are called to live a life of excellence in all that we do, to value, honor and love people so well that they feel like the best versions of themselves when they are around us. This is how Jesus was able to transform the lives of people around Him. He transformed the people that others, especially the religious people of that time, deemed as unreachable and not valuable. Jesus always kept His love on, shining it towards people. He molded and shaped people's hearts with the love, power, and goodness of God the Father! *"The only thing that matters is Faith working through Love." Galatians 5:6 NET Bible*

How did Jesus love other people? To answer this question we look at His actions while on the earth. First and foremost Jesus always kept in constant communication and close relationship with His Heavenly Father empowered by the Holy Spirit. Through this, Jesus valued people, listened to them, spoke God's truth to them, challenged them, encouraged them and modeled for them how to live life in victory by having a personal relationship with the Father. He operated in the gifts of the Holy Spirit, He healed the sick, cast out demons, performed miracles, prophesied over people, operated in words of knowledge, cleansed those with leprosy, raised the dead and preached the truth of the Gospel to all who would listen. He lived a life of radical forgiveness, generosity and giving. He walked in the power of the Holy Spirit through living a life of intimacy with the Father producing moral purity, excellence and the fruit of the Spirit for all to experience love, joy, peace, patience, kindness, goodness, faithfulness, and self-control. People experienced the Heavenly Father and the Holy Spirit through Jesus and God is calling us to do the same things Jesus did and even greater things (John 14:12)!

As you live this kind of lifestyle, you become a place where the favor of God can rest upon you and dwell within you in powerful ways. God can begin to trust you to be a great love ambassador of His. As you do this, you will experience the favor of God upon your life in the form of a healthy love for yourself, God, and others. Out of this overflow of love, there can and will be signs, wonders, healings and gifts of the Holy Spirit that will follow you and materialize in your life!

"And Jesus said to them, "Go into all the world and preach the Gospel to all creation. These signs will accompany those who have believed: in My name they will cast out demons, they will speak in new tongues; they will pick up serpents, and if they drink anything deadly, it will not hurt them; they will lay hands on the sick, and they will get well"
MARK 16:15,17-18 AMP

"Behold, I give you the authority to trample on serpents and scorpions, and over all the power of the enemy, and nothing shall by any means hurt you." Luke 10:19 NKJV

And they went out and preached everywhere, while the Lord was working with them and confirming the Word by the signs that followed." Mark 16:20 AMP

Notice in the Scriptures above we don't follow these signs. These signs follow them who believe in Jesus' name and choose to put their faith into action! Those who become and do the love and the sayings of Jesus! Purity, excellence, humility, signs, wonders, healings, a transformed life and gifts of the Holy Spirit will be evidenced and manifested in the life of every Believer who chooses to be a lover of Jesus and a doer of the Word of God! Because through what Jesus did for us we are all qualified by God to do the works that Jesus did! So you are already called and qualified to walk as Jesus walked! Your "Full Christian Benefit Package" is available as soon as you make Jesus Christ the Lord of your life, you can immediately operate by faith in the Word of God and in gifts of the Holy Spirit you don't have wait! Wherever you are in your relationship with God you can choose to begin to step out in an increased measure of faith right now! Because with God there is always more!

Everything we will talk about and teach in this chapter can, will, and does flow out of a daily spiritual love relationship with God the Father, Jesus Christ, and the Holy Spirit! That relationship is real, intimate, personal, and powerful without it you will lack the effectiveness in putting the Word of God into action in your life and making any real changes in your life and in the lives of others. I want us to understand that everything we are covering in this section as we discuss flowing in the powerful gifts of the Holy Spirit and putting the Word of God into action in everything we do, all happens based on developing a deeper relationship with the Lord and as the Book of Ephesians puts it, so we may "Know Him Better" thus being changed into the likeness and image of Christ (Ephesians 1:17).

Having a relationship and intimacy with God, combined with knowing our identity and value as His sons and daughters allows and empowers us to live out His promises and His Word. This means becoming God's love, power and peace upon this earth in our lives and in the lives of others around us.

Saying I Believe in God is not enough to live in victory in this life! Belief denotes ACTION; being a doer of the Word of God. Saying I believe in hamburgers is not going to get one into your hands without some action. Saying I believe in TV won't help it turn on without the action of you grabbing hold of the remote and pushing the power button that releases and communicates to your TV a signal that you can't see and causes what you believe in to turn on so you can benefit from what you believe in which is the TV working. That's like prayer grabbing hold of the Word of God, speaking it by faith, sending a power and signal out that you can't see, and turning on the POWER of God's Word and Spirit in your life and in the lives of others. So you can benefit from what you believe in which is GOD'S LOVE AND POWER! The Amplified Bible describes belief in some very powerful ways. It defines belief as trusting in, to confidently rely on, remain steadfast to, lean on, and adhere to. Notice that these definitions are all consistent and constant perpetual actions. Grace makes all the finished works of Jesus Christ and all the promises of God available to you as a Believer in Jesus Christ. This includes the powerful indwelling of the Holy Spirit to walk out and live out what the truth of God's Word calls us to in our lives and in the lives of others, even though we did nothing to earn it, that is God's grace. Faith takes what Grace makes available to us and causes the Word and promises of God to become a reality in our lives because the Bible says *"for it is by grace you have been saved, through faith" Ephesians 2:8 NIV*. Lastly love wraps it all together because faith works through love (Galatians 5:6). It is all about living out and becoming God's grace, faith and love in our lives and in the lives of others!

Jesus in the Gospel of John explains to us how He did this and gives us a model of how we are to live like He did and get results like He did. ***"I tell you the truth, the Son can do nothing by Himself. He does only what he sees the Father doing. Whatever the Father does, the Son also does. John 15:19 NIV***

For I have not spoken on My own authority, but the Father who sent Me has Himself given Me a commandment—what to say and what to speak. (What to say and how to say it) John 12:49 NIV

Jesus only thought like His Father, spoke like His Father, and only moved and did what He spiritually heard, saw and sensed His Heavenly Father was saying and doing. If we are to mimic and imitate Jesus Christ, we need to be doing the same things He did. You may be saying to yourself, "well, that is all fine and good, but that is Jesus not me!" Jesus also promises us in His Word ***"Truly, truly, I say to you, whoever believes in Me will also do the works that I do; and greater works than these will he do, because I am going to the Father. Whatever you ask in My name, this I will do, that the Father may be glorified in the Son." John 14:12***

So let's at least start doing what Jesus did and then we can move on to the greater works! What does this look like? It looks like doing the sayings of Jesus and doing what Jesus did; having an intimate fellowship, friendship and relationship with God, through hearing His voice and sensing His activity in your daily lives which is what this whole book has focused on. Being established in a healthy self esteem and self love based on God's Word. Loving other people and living a life of moral integrity, purity, excellence and radical generosity. Speaking faith and life giving words over people, praying for the sick, and operating through the gifts of the Holy Spirit on a daily basis. We are called to become a standard of excellence to this world wherever we go, Christlike shining lights for all to see! ***"Those who say they live in God should live their lives as Jesus did." 1 John 2:6 NLT***

If you are a Believer, draw a circle around where your standing. Revival starts within that circle; within your own heart, then your home, and then it spreads to the world around you. Our job is to become the move of God that we hope to see. That we would become the revival this world so desperately needs! *Becoming the move of God* starts within you, living out the Gospel on an everyday basis; first in your own heart, mind and life. As you do that, it will be spread to others out of the overflow of your relationship with God.

The Hebrew word for "revive" is "chayah" and means "to be quickened, to be made alive, to have life" and "to be restored" (Strong's 2421). You have been made alive by the Holy Spirit living and dwelling in you and you have eternal life in Jesus Christ. The Hebrew Word for revive is also "shuwb" and it means "to return, to turn back" so revival, means to be made alive and is a turning away from sin and a turning towards God and the teachings and instruction of God through His Word and the Holy Spirit (Strong's 7725). So THEY do the converting, transforming, and the reviving of your spirit, soul and body as you put THEM first place in your life and become a doer of the Word and a follower of God's Spirit within you on a daily basis!

This world needs a revival and it is up to us as Believers to live in a place of revival everyday in our hearts and in the lives of those God puts into our path. This is especially true of those closest to you like your spouse, children, family, friends, classmates and coworkers. We are to be influencing and changing the atmosphere wherever we go. For instance in your household and on your job you are the thermostat; you set the spiritual temperature of your household and workplace because of the Jesus that lives within you.

This is because *you plus Jesus* changes the temperature of the atmosphere wherever you go, just like the thermostat in your house! You're not the thermometer that only takes the temperature. You have the Holy Spirit living inside of you! God empowers you to change the spiritual temperature of every place you are, by walking in the love, power and the Spirit of Jesus! There are practical actions you can take to become the love of Jesus in your daily life; such as living a life of moral purity, spending quality time with your spouse and kids, being an active listener. Living a life full of passion, excellence, joy and praise that people can experience, even in the midst of stresses and challenges. Living a lifestyle of generosity, bringing food or some type of blessing to people you work with, giving to those in need and the less fortunate, living as a forgiver, working with excellence unto God and not to people please, praying for people at work and in your daily life. Practice having a positive attitude, being thankful and joyful. Refuse to take part in gossip at work, choose not to participate in sinful conversations. Being a loving and supportive spouse and parent, playing with your children, attending their events at school, when you do mess up, which we all do at times, be quick to take accountability, humble yourself and apologize, living a life of transparency when you do fall short letting people know, *"Hey I was not acting like Jesus in this situation I apologize for that, I am working with Him to refine that out of me."* Being emotionally present and actively listening to your spouse, kids, family, friends and others is vitally important and needed especially in the age we live in with so much stimulation from our phones, tablets and various kinds of media. Listening with your heart is all part of walking in God's love, integrity and moral excellence where people in your sphere of influence feel valued, accepted and loved. In order to live out these practical actions effectively and have them become part of your character you have to spend time with God where you're experiencing His unlimited love, grace and presence so you can give out of the overflow of what you experience through your intimate fellowship with Him.

"Keep asking, and it will be given to you. Keep searching, and you will find. Keep knocking, and the door will be opened to you. For everyone who asks receives, and the one who searches finds, and to the one who knocks, the door will be opened." Matthew 7:7-8 HCSB The Kingdom of God advances in our lives by us asking, seeking, knocking, and receiving God's love, power and grace; then out of the overflow of your life pouring out on other people what you received by asking, seeking, knocking and receiving from God. This is foundational in living a healthy Christ centered life. You give away the Kingdom of God because it's within you, and it comes out of you by the overflow of what's in your heart through experiencing and knowing God through your daily relationship with Him. The Kingdom of God is built on this lifestyle of asking, seeking, knocking and receiving God's presence, Word and love. You cannot give out what you don't possess and if you are possessed by the love of the Father, the grace of Jesus and the power of the Holy Spirit then what is within you will come out of you on a daily basis. As you live a lifestyle as a lover of God, yourself and other people, you will join God in His activity and see Him do amazing things, first in you, and then through you! Jesus said: *"If you love Me you will keep My commandments (My Word)." John 14:15 NASB*

"Which commandment is the most important of all?" Jesus answered, "The most important is, 'Hear, O Israel: The Lord our God, the Lord is one. And you shall love the Lord your God with all your heart and with all your soul and with all your mind and with all your strength.' The second is this: 'You shall love your neighbor as yourself.' There is no other commandment greater than these." Mark 12:28-31 ESV

"I give you a new command: Love one another. Just as I have loved you, you must also love one another. By this all people will know that you are My disciples, if you have love for one another." John 13:34 HCSB

Suicide, self-harm, cutting, depression and anxiety are real and critical issues within this world. This is why speaking and acting through the love of Jesus, which is imparting life to the people God puts into your daily path, is so vital and fundamental. You never know what people are going through but you do know everyone is in the need of more of Jesus' love and power!

A LATE NIGHT SUGAR RUSH AND SHARING THE GOSPEL

I want to share one such God story to encourage you and show you how loving others will cause you to hear God's voice, sense His activity and experience Him work in miraculous ways. I was driving to the grocery store one night at about 11:00 p.m. to get some ice cream because I was about to go on a 40 day and 40 night fast called the promised land fast. It is an all liquid fast consisting of milk, honey, water, and broth. I was trying to get my last minute sugar rush in before 12 a.m.!

As I walked up to the front door, I saw two young men sitting outside and they seemed almost highlighted; meaning they seemed to stand out to me as I walked up. God gave me an inward knowing and impression which came with a flowing thought that He wanted me to help them in some way. One of the young men came up to me and asked me for money. I said "Here, you can have the cash I have. It is not much, just a couple of dollars." He said, "Truthfully man, we are just hungry and want something to eat." I always try and keep my love on and use guidance and good wisdom from God by praying about decisions I make. In this case, I felt compelled to help these young men. Based on an inward intuition and a peace I had about it, I said, "Well, come on into to the store with me and I will buy you both some food." I made the decision years ago to live a lifestyle of Holy Spirit lead radical generosity and extravagant giving in everything I do. ***"You must each decide in your heart how much to give. And don't give reluctantly or in response to pressure. For God loves a person who gives cheerfully." 2 Corinthians 9:7 NLT*** Giving myself first to God in my focus, praise and worship of Him, then out of the overflow of knowing Him I give to others through: living as a radical forgiver, giving grace to myself and others, generously praying for and loving on others, cheerful financial giving and making it my goal to always speak from a place of godly wisdom.

I walked through the store asking them what kind of food they liked and then grabbing food off the shelves for them we even found some fried chicken in the deli. I don't know about you but to me nothing says Jesus loves you like fried chicken! As we walked I asked them to tell me about their situation. As they talked, I listened and valued what they were telling me, in love. After they told me a little about their situation, I knew they were in desperate need of the love of Jesus and a life change. Which in truth the same can be said about all of us. I am still in desperate need of God's loving presence everyday in my life and I am always pressing into God's continual promise of making me more like Jesus as I follow Him! So I asked them, "Do you have a relationship with Jesus Christ?" They both stated "No, I am not religious, but I respect all religions." I said, "Good, I am not religious either. I have a spiritual love relationship with Jesus Christ." They seemed puzzled at my answer. I said, "I am in love with Jesus, meaning I have a daily relationship with God where I experience His love and I know Him personally and He loves you and wants to have an intimate relationship with you too. God through Jesus Christ wants to give you His love, acceptance, understanding, joy, peace and righteousness. Would you like to have more of those things in your life?" Of course this is a great witnessing tool because the answer to that question for everyone is "yeah of course"! Who truly says in their heart, "Oh no, I can't use any more love, joy and peace in my life", if we are being honest within ourselves we all yearn for more of those things within our lives! The good news is we can find all of those things and more through our daily connection with God!

At that point, I insisted that they get some Double Stuf Oreos and join me in my sugar rush! Then, I began to share my testimony, in love, with them about what Jesus had done for me personally. I was not talking or preaching "at them" but sharing God's love "with them" through my own personal Gospel Story of what Jesus had done in my life and what He wanted to do in theirs. Of course the enemy was telling me "they don't want to hear it", "they don't care what you're saying", "you are boring them" but now I know when I get those types of thoughts I am on the right track because I have the answer every person needs; a loving relationship with Jesus! So if you hear negative thoughts such as those trying to get you to shrink back from sharing the love of Jesus with someone; go against them and share what God is putting on your heart! I often tell people *you don't have to be able to quote a whole bunch of scriptures or have a vast Bible knowledge to lead someone to Christ.* That is often a huge roadblock and a common misconception people have that leads to them being uncomfortable with sharing their faith with others. You need a basic understanding of God's "grace gift" of salvation through Jesus Christ coupled with your testimony of how you have personally experienced God.

When I witness to people, I generally share with them some simple and profound truths. Such as Jesus loves you, He died for you so that your sins can be forgiven and removed from you forever, and so that God's Holy Spirit can come and make His home inside of you! Jesus wants to help and guide you in your life right now. He wants to show you and lead you in the plan, purpose and destiny He has for your life, empowering you to prosper. Jesus wants to cause you to have right standing with God (righteousness) peace and joy in the Holy Spirit (Romans 14:17). Then, when you leave this earth, you have eternal life with Him in Heaven forever! Salvation is a free gift, but you have to receive it to benefit from it. It's like having a bank account; you have to withdraw from your account for it to benefit you. Just knowing you have it does not benefit you until you make the decision to withdraw from it. It is the same with salvation in Jesus; it is a free gift from God, but you have to make the choice to receive it.

"For God loved the world in this way that He gave His One and Only Son, so that everyone who believes in Him will not perish but have eternal life. For God did not send His Son into the world that He might condemn the world, but that the world might be saved through Him." John 3:16-17 HCSB

"If you confess with your mouth that Jesus is Lord and believe in your heart that God raised him from the dead, you will be saved. For everyone who calls on the name of the Lord will be saved." Romans 10:10,13 ESV

I use my testimony and tell people how much Jesus loves them and wants a relationship with them. Mainly because people can argue with the Scriptures and debate them with you, but they can't argue with what you have personally experienced God do and your "changed life in Christ". When you share how you have personally encountered God's love it resonates with people, because in reality everyone wants to be loved and cared for.

For your basic testimony choose 3 to 5 words that describe your life before you had a relationship with Jesus and then 3 to 5 words that describe your life after having a relationship with Jesus. Try to keep them emotionally relevant where they are short and ordered. For example the testimony I use is; "Before I had a relationship with Jesus I felt lonely, worried and stressed all the time even when my life from a worldly perspective was successful and good things were happening. I still felt there was something missing, like a void in my heart that could not be filled. Then I came to know Jesus through an intimate relationship with the Holy Spirit and now I am fulfilled, joyful and peaceful all the time even when challenging things happen to me I am able to handle them in a totally different way because of my relationship with Jesus and that void in my heart is now totally filled!"

This becomes your basic testimony and then you can add from there as the conversation flows but this gives them the immediate contrast of what Jesus has personally done in your life. As I did this, they exchanged some of their personal stories with me outside of the grocery store in the parking lot. As I ate my ice cream and Double Stuf Oreos, sitting there on a turned over shopping cart, I was faithful to listen to them and share my own personal love story with Jesus. Thirty minutes later, they realized that they had been trying to fight a spiritual battle with their own self-will, self-effort and in their own flesh which is like bringing a knife to a gunfight! They realized they needed God's help. They had tried life on their own terms but they needed help. They realized that Jesus had died for them and that their sins could be taken away. Their spirits could be born again and their minds and lives completely transformed. I explained to them that "The Cross"; meaning and referring to the death, burial, and resurrection of Jesus is not just the revealing of our need for a savior to save us from our sin, though this is something we all desperately need and receive when we make Jesus Christ the Lord of our lives. The Cross is also just as much the revealing of our true value and identity in Christ, because it defines our value and what we are worth in God's eyes; the very life and blood of Jesus Christ Himself. This is the highest price God could pay and it is the most expensive thing in Heaven and on Earth. Jesus is God's very life and blood being shed on the cross for us through Jesus. So you are worth the very life and blood of Jesus! That's your true value and worth! As highly valued and divinely treasured sons and daughters being your true identity!

I lead them both in a prayer of salvation, much like the prayer in the salvation section of this book and to surrender their hearts and lives over to God through the precious blood of Jesus Christ. They repented of their sins; asking for God's mercy and forgiveness to be upon them. I usually ask people if they want to pray a prayer themselves to make Jesus Christ the Lord and Savior of their lives, or do they want me to lead them in a prayer by repeating after me as I pray for them to give their lives to Jesus? Most of the time, as in this case, they chose to repeat after me. I would suggest reading over the scriptures above and the "Salvation and Hearing God" section of this book. Then just allow the Holy Spirit to lead you in a prayer to pray with them, there is no specific formula. However, I do find it helpful to use Romans 10:8-11 as a guide because then they can go back and read something similar to what they prayed when the devil comes to try to convince them at a later time that what they prayed somehow didn't work. Which is a tactic I have seen him do, often using peoples missteps and actions to create shame and doubt. That's why it's good to remind yourself and others that transformation and renewing your mind to become more like Jesus is a relational and an on-going process with God. This is also why I often suggest this scripture as one they look at and re-read several times within the first couple of weeks of their salvation experience. I also encourage people that it is their heart intent behind the words they are speaking which are in agreement with God's will for them to be saved, that actually authorizes and invites God's Holy Spirit to come live within them. God knows their hearts and He wants a relationship with them more than they do. God is not looking for reasons to hold out on anyone He paid the very life and blood of Jesus to ensure our salvation!

As we prayed together right there in that moment in a grocery store parking lot, miracles of salvation and healing happened! I saw two people go from death to life; meaning from being spiritually disconnected from God (death) to being spiritually connected to God through the Holy Spirit (life) now living inside of them. Their lives would be forever marked and changed by the love of God! Then, as they opened their eyes, I learned of another miracle. One of the young men shared that he was shocked that when he opened his eyes something physically had changed. He was amazed and looked over at his friend and said, "Bro, do you know how I have been complaining the last couple of days about my eyes being foggy because my contacts scratched my corneas?" His friend responded inquisitively, "Yeah, what's up?" He continued, "Bro, I can see clearly now, my eyes are totally healed!" I began to laugh at the goodness of God and the phrase of a song joyfully rose out of my heart and I began to sing the song, "I can see clearly now the rain is gone!" (Johnny Nash) We all celebrated together and we got to intimately experience the healing power of Jesus Christ in several different ways! They also both said they felt lighter like the world got lifted off of their shoulders and felt a sense a peace upon them which is a common feeling when people experience the presence of the Holy Spirit. Later through doing some medical research I found out that God had instantly healed the young man of what is medically referred to as a "corneal abrasion". Then we prayed together about a place for them to stay and within about 15 minutes God provided them with a place to stay for the night, they got back on their feet and are now in the process of being transformed by the power of God's love and Word on a daily basis! Why? Because someone dared to share the love of Jesus with them! God is calling you to be a witness to others around you of His goodness, love, truth and power.

I ask people all the time in conversations, "Do you have a relationship with Jesus Christ?" That is the most important question in life. I have come to realize if I truly say I love and care for people, why would I not tell them about Jesus and ask them about having more peace, joy and freedom here on earth and eternal life in Heaven? If I do really care and love people then I will ask the most important question on earth and share with them the ultimate life transformer, game-changer and peace giver, Jesus Christ! We just covered loving on and witnessing to people who are not saved in the section above, but what about encouraging and loving on the people who have already made Jesus Christ their Lord and Savior? I am glad you asked! When I encounter people who have already been saved and born again I encourage them in love about the amazing and awesome decision they have made, how good God's love is and how He wants a deep intimate relationship with them! Sometimes I don't have time for a long conversation, like if I am in a store or at a restaurant, so I usually tell them "Jesus loves you so much, you are amazing and you are His favorite" because He does love them, they are amazing and they are His favorite, we all are! That is some simple but profound encouragement that we all can easily give to people in our daily lives. As we move throughout the day we can look for opportunities to be a blessing to other people, encouraging them and building others up with the love and power of Jesus! God makes it very clear to us in the Book of Proverbs what living a lifestyle of radical generosity will do for our lives as we impact those around us by being a blessing. ***"Generosity brings prosperity but withholding from charity brings poverty. Those who live to bless others will have blessings heaped upon them, and the one who pours out his life to pour out blessings will be saturated with favor." Proverbs 11:24-25 TPT*** It can be smiling and saying Jesus loves you to someone, giving a kind word of encouragement to a coworker, opening a door for someone, being kind to the waitstaff at a restaurant and tipping them generously, financially giving to your local Church, a ministry or social cause on a consistent basis that God places on your heart and living your life with a sense of joyful excellence that others can see and experience what Jesus is actively doing in your heart. Then even as challenges and stresses come your way you choose faith, joy and love within the thoughts you think, the words you speak and the actions you take. How we live our lives everyday is the greatest witnessing tool we have to manifest the fruit of our relationship with Jesus to others around us.

Other times when the opportunity is there for a little more conversation I will often ask people, "How is your relationship with Jesus?" Usually people look at me for a moment and then they tell me "Oh, I go to this Church or that Church" or "I belong to this denomination" and they often will give me a run down on their Church attendance for better or for worse. I get those kinds of answers I would say 80%-90% of the time. You might be saying, well what is wrong with that, Sterling? The issue is that I asked them how their relationship with Jesus is, not their Church history and attendance record. That would be like if you asked me how my relationship with my wife is and I tell you that we go out on dates once a week and I tell you about the places we go, how good the food is at the places we eat together and that we should try to go out on more date nights. You would probably look at me kind of funny and think to yourself this guy does not know what a healthy relationship with his wife even smells like because he can't even tell me anything that he likes about her character, what she means to him and who she is as a person. No, if you ask me about my relationship with my wife I am going to tell you how much I love, adore, value, and cherish her. I would also share with you about her character because I know her intimately and about our relational connection with one another that is rooted and grounded in Christ. So when people ask me about my relationship with Jesus I don't talk about what Church I go to. I talk about how amazing He is, how much I love Him, how much He loves me, and how He has radically changed my life through my experiences of knowing Him in a loving daily relationship. You see the difference in focus? So many Believers place going to Church and doing things for God in the place of a loving, intimate, healthy and daily relationship with God. That is the difference in having religious principles and practices versus having an intimate relationship, friendship, fellowship and sonship with God. Trying to live a life based solely on religious practices and Church attendance will leave that void in your heart empty because that place in your heart was not designed to be filled with anything other than a daily spiritual love relationship with God the Father, God the Son, and God the Holy Spirit, you in Them and They in you!

I often ask a more pointed question to get people to think a little more about the most important relationship that they have on this earth and in Heaven. I say on a scale of 1 to 10, with 10 being *on fire for Jesus*, meaning you know His voice and you talk to Him on a daily basis in a two way communication where you talk to Him as well as listen and hear His voice. That the Word of God is coming alive in your life and you are being led by the Holy Spirit in you. Then with a 1 being well, I know Him as my Lord and Savior but my relationship with Him is not thriving. You may be saying to yourself that seems like too personal of a line of questioning and can be taken as condemning or calling someone out. Can I share with you, this line of questioning has been a revelation to so many people and blessed them because when you put it in relationship type terms it allows so many people to recognize where they are. Whatever number they give me, I love on them and I always keep it light and positive. I encourage them that God wants a deeper relationship with all of us. That I too am trying to grow in my relationship with Him everyday. Not to be discouraged or condemned no matter where your relationship is because "God loves you and you can start to go deeper with Him today, it is never too late!" Two great follow up questions are: "What would a deeper relationship with God look like for you?" and "What would you like to have in your relationship with God in the future which you do not have now?" These questions get them to start thinking about what they want from their own personal relationship with Jesus. Then I say, "Can I pray for you?" and then I pray things like "Lord, I thank You they hear Your voice more clearly, that You visit them with dreams and visions, I thank You Lord they experience an increase of intimacy with You, Jesus. Touch them with Your presence in a new way where they will know it is You! Holy Spirit, light them on fire for You, Lord!"

Let God lead you on what to pray and allow your heart to bless their heart. Pray for more peace, joy, blessings, healing, freedom and harmony in their life I have never met a person who says, "No, I have too much peace and joy I can't stand to have any more of that." Sometimes if God leads me I will share a video, book, preacher or a sermon I think would bless them in their relationship with God and where they currently are in their life. You can share this book with them and what you have learned about hearing God's active voice and how He communicates with you. You can ask them how they have experienced God working and speaking in their own lives. I cannot tell you how many people have shared with me they were touched and blessed by me just caring enough to ask them about what really matters in all of our lives the most, our personal relationship with Jesus Christ.

Don't let the fear of rejection, the fear of people and fear of judgment stop you from being the Jesus people need to see and experience in this world on a daily basis! When I talk to people about living a lifestyle like this, they often share with me that they frequently have thoughts such as, "Yeah, that works for Sterling, but I am not like that, that is not my personality or that is not my calling." Hear me on this, do not allow yourself to be disqualified because Jesus has called you, qualified you, and empowered you to become His love, His power, and His Word in this world! Keep in mind we are all sowing seeds, preaching and ministering everyday of our lives to someone, at the very least ourselves, through the thoughts we think, by the words we choose to speak or withhold and by the actions we take. The real question is what kinds of seeds are you sowing? Seeds of love, kindness, faith and passion or fear and worry. What kind of sermons are you preaching and acting out? The love of Jesus and living with an attitude of gratitude, or being negative and unthankful? What are you ministering and transferring to yourself and others around you? The truth and assurance of God's promises of life and blessings being active and true or creating doubt and fear about God's goodness and His love for you and others? We influence ourselves and the world around us positively and negatively, directly and indirectly by the way we choose to live our lives on a daily basis.

If you struggle with those same types of hesitant thoughts of not wanting to step out on faith and manifest Jesus to others around you in your daily life, it's ok and actually it's perfectly normal to have those types of thoughts. I still struggle with them too at times, but do not be disempowered! Instead, start taking action against that negative thinking! As you do this, your mind and life will be transformed and it will get easier and easier to share the love of Jesus in various ways. Start out by encouraging people! How hard is it to say, "Jesus loves you" to someone you meet instead of "thank you" or "have a nice day?" When people ask you "how are you today?" saying "I am blessed and highly favored, how about you?" Then after they answer you, saying "I want you to know that Jesus loves you" then after that settles in their heart for a moment say, "and you are His favorite" (the last part usually gets a smile). Both of those are simple truths Jesus does love them and they are His favorite! You can use these simple tools to encourage people and spread the love of Jesus in your life everyday! Just imagine what the world would be like if just the estimated 2.3 billion people that already claim to be Christians across the world began to live a lifestyle of being God's love in their everyday lives that overflows out of their intimate relationship of knowing God, it would begin to transform their hearts, families, schools, workplaces and the people they encounter! Imagine how many times people all over the world would hear *Jesus loves them* in a day, and experience the peace and joy of the Lord radiating towards them from Christians! How amazing and awesome would that be? As you live a lifestyle of Christlike love that overflows out of your connectedness with God you will see God bless your life and the lives of others!

I want to invite you to encourage others around you with the love of Jesus. Offer to pray for them and remember, that Jesus gives us all the same Holy Spirit! It is just a matter of moving past the fear and stepping out of your comfort zone into faith! To be transparent, I often still have to fight the initial thoughts of what will that person think of me, what if they reject me, what if they think I am crazy or weird? I remind myself that people don't define my value and identity, but that my Heavenly Father does and He loves it when His children share Jesus and His love with others! God has accepted you and He loves you!

When witnessing and praying for people I told you a God story that worked out, but know that there are a lot of people that have rejected hearing the truth of the Gospel from me in some way, shape or form, so know that rejection does and will happen. People have even rejected receiving prayer when I have asked them "can I pray for you?". Their rejection, at whatever level, still does not stop me from at least letting them know that Jesus loves them. Always remember this, you planted a seed and you watered their heart; even if it does not seem like that in the natural. The Bible says if you're rejected for the Gospel and persecuted then you are blessed. You don't know their whole life story or the pain of why they might seemingly reject you but Jesus does and He wants to love them no matter what they think or how they feel. The truth is they are not rejecting you personally, they are rejecting and battling against God's love for whatever reason, so try not to take it personally because it's not about you. It is our job to sow seeds and water their lives with the love of Jesus remembering it is God who gives the increase. The Apostle Paul reminds us of this truth which is, we are to be continually planting seeds and watering people's lives. ***"The one who plants and the one who waters work together with the same purpose. And both will be rewarded for their own hard work." 1 Corinthians 3:8 NLT*** Notice the work of sowing seeds and watering will be rewarded by God Himself! So don't let being rejected or the fear of rejection hold you back from stepping out and sharing God's love with the world around you! No matter what, when you live and share a life of passion, joy, excellence and God's love, you win!

Remember this is not a competition to see who can do the most for the Kingdom of God and letting the enemy try and condemn you saying things like "You're not doing enough, this other person does way more for God than you", or tell you, "Oh, you should have witnessed to that person, or you should have loved on more people today, God is disappointed in you, He doesn't love you."

The enemy tries those lies on me from time to time. There is no competition and no comparison in the Kingdom of Heaven, only collaboration with God and other followers of Christ. That revelation set me free as a person who comes from a competitive background in sports. The enemy would use that to create unworthiness, envy, comparison, jealousy, and offense in my heart for myself and others. We are on the same team with God and other Believers! There is plenty of God's love, favor, and blessings to go around, in Jesus they are limitless! A kingdom divided against itself cannot stand! In that, also know that your value is not based on what you do or who you help. Your value is based on God's love for you and what He sacrificed for you to be free from sin and alive in Him which is the very life of Jesus Christ. Your value and identity are also based on who God says you are in Christ as His son or daughter. At the same time, God does want you to share His love, His Son, and the power of His Holy Spirit with others around you! God wants everyone to come to know Him! God's will is that all people be saved and come to the knowledge of the truth (1 Timothy 2:4). He desires and commands us to share His love with others! Love is not just a suggestion, Jesus called loving God, yourself and others the greatest commandment in the Bible. When you keep your love on and your heart sensitive to God's voice and prompting by the Holy Spirit, you can see miracles happen even on a late night sugar rush to the grocery store like I did!

DIVINE HEALING

Through divine healing you can hear God's active voice, sense His activity, as well as experience His supernatural power at work in a tangible way. Healing is God's will. Healing is also God's nature. As we look at our own bodies, they all have a God given and God designed "natural healing process" when functioning properly. So with that understanding we know being in good health is the natural state of the human body, on the other hand sickness and disease is when that natural God given state of health is some how being compromised and attacked however, it is God's nature and will that we be healed. Healing is also a Biblical subject that I have struggled with and one that has challenged my faith at various times in my life. I have experiences where I see immediate healing breakthroughs and results. Then in other situations, healing might not happen where I can see it and experience it for days, weeks, months or in some cases years of speaking, believing and thanking God for His will and His nature to heal. Then at times it seems like nothing is happening and nothing changes in the natural. But I know it's God's will and nature to heal in this life as well as our permanent healing that happens when as Believers we get to Heaven. I also recognize, as we talked about earlier in the book, that God's Word is a seed. When you read, meditate and hear the Word of God on divine healing, faith in that area comes, so in essence you plant it into your heart. When you speak the Word of God in faith it has the ability and power to bring to pass the promise attached with the Word spoken, in this case healing for your body and your mind.

We have this direct commentary about healing being God's Will for His children meaning we have a verse in the New Testament that directly confirms and interprets a passage from the Old Testament.

And when Jesus went into Peter's house, He saw his mother-in-law lying ill with a fever. He touched her hand and the fever left her; and she got up and began waiting on Him. When evening came, they brought to Him many who were under the power of demons, and He drove out the spirits with a Word and restored to health ALL who were sick. And thus He fulfilled what was spoken by the prophet Isaiah, He Himself took [in order to carry away] our weaknesses and infirmities and bore away our diseases. [Isa. 53:4.] Matthew 8:14-17 AMPC

We see here that Jesus destroyed all sickness and disease that He came across and He came to do the will of His Heavenly Father. He said I can only do what I spiritually see the Father doing and I can only say what I spiritually hear the Father saying (John 5:19-20). The Bible also says Jesus came to the earth to destroy the works of the devil and the demonic realm. So by these truths in the Word of God we understand that all sickness, disease and illness of any kind is a demonic attack on our bodies, which are the Temple of God. Therefore we have the authority to come against all sickness and illnesses with the Word of God, the Blood of Jesus and the power of the Holy Spirit in us as Believers in Jesus Christ. *The Son of God appeared for this purpose, to destroy the works of the devil. 1 John 3:8 AMP*

So if Jesus prayed for people to be healed and destroyed the works of the devil while He was here on this earth, then our job as His followers is to do the same. So one of your purposes is to manifest Jesus and destroy evil on this earth on a daily basis through the way in which you choose to you live your life.

When praying for others and yourself for healing, there is also the fear of disappointment and the fear being judged by others as weird or fanatical. As a Believer if you want to see God's power, you have to get over the fear of disappointment and the fear of people rejecting you. At the end of the day when you offer to pray for people, most of the time they are not going to turn you down and most of them don't know what to expect as far as experiencing breakthrough immediately. The worst thing that can happen is they get blessed, loved on, prayed for, the healing power of God's Word as a seed got implanted into their hearts and is now working inside of them healing their bodies from the inside out and the love of God in you was demonstrated! All of these are truths and extremely powerful. On the other hand you can see radical breakthroughs, healings, miracles and mind-blowing experiences for yourself and others. I have prayed for a lot of people for their healing and over the years I have seen some amazing healing testimonies and experienced a lot in my own body. Jesus said to him, *"[You say to Me,] 'If You can?' All things are possible for the one who believes and trusts [in Me]!"Immediately the father of the boy cried out [with a desperate, piercing cry], saying, "I do believe; help [me overcome] my unbelief." Mark 9:22-24*

PRACTICAL TIPS WHEN PRAYING FOR HEALING

I want to share some practical tips with you when praying for others to be divinely healed. When you hear of anyone being sick around you or you see someone hurting physically I want to encourage you to start asking them if you can pray for them. Especially those in your daily life's path and people in your sphere of influence such as; your family, friends, classmates and coworkers. That is part of being God's love wherever you go and manifesting Jesus to others. You can open up the conversation by saying something like "Jesus is a healer and He said these signs will follow them that believe, that we will lay our hands on the sick in Jesus Name and they will get well, can I pray for you? Jesus loves you so much." (Mark 16;17) Another one you can use is "The Bible says the prayer of faith will heal the sick and God will raise them up, can I pray for you? Jesus loves you so much." (James 5:15) I would suggest saying a healing Scripture like in the examples above within your request to pray for them. Because God's Word is the foundation of what you are basing your faith in God's will and power to heal them upon. This helps build your faith in praying for them and build their faith in receiving their healing based on God's Word. Also in praying for healing it's helpful for you take the time to personally read and meditate in healing scriptures to build your own faith in divine healing, when you pray for healing in your own body and in praying for people who need healing.

Before you begin to pray for a person for their healing you want to ask them on a scale of 1 to 10 with 10 being the highest pain level and 1 being the lowest, where they are on that pain scale. You can also use the same type of scale for measuring mobility and increase in bodily function such as, breathing, hearing, sight and an overall sense of how their body has in some way shifted. Because when we pray we are expecting things to shift and happen! This way when there is a decrease in pain or an increase in mobility they will be able to quantify it, which I have seen build so many people's faith in healing, including my own. Since I started having people rate their pain it seems the number of healings I have experienced have increased. It also gives you something to build on and celebrate as their pain level goes down or their mobility increases as you pray for them, sometimes several times, depending upon the person, circumstances and situation. You also want to ask them, "How would you know Jesus healed you today? Would you have more mobility, less pain? What would healing look like for your personally?"

After they rate their pain you generally want to ask for permission to place your hands on the area that hurts or needs healing, so long as it's an appropriately safe place on their body like a knee or an ankle. As a safety and comfort issue especially with the opposite gender you want to ask for permission to place your hand on their shoulder as a point of contact. If they say no or they seem uncomfortable with that, it is not a big deal you can just hold their hand or not touch them at all. The power is in using and applying the Word of God, the Name and Blood of Jesus, through the empowerment of the Holy Spirit, to their bodies, through prayer. Then you begin to pray and speak to the body part, pain and sickness directly and command it to be healed in Jesus Name. Keep in mind the voice volume at which you pray can be your normal voice tone, just because the prayer is louder does not mean it will be more powerful or effective. Praying loudly will most likely just make the person feel uncomfortable and draw unneces- sary attention to them and to you. I suggest praying with passion and faith- filled energy in your normal voice tone unless the Holy Spirit directs you to pray in another way. For example if a person's back is hurting you can say "Jesus I thank You that You are a healer, back I speak to you in Jesus Name and I command you to be healed by the Blood of Jesus, pain be gone and back be healed in Jesus Name. Amen." Then ask the person to put their faith into action and try to do something they could not do before and check their pain level to see if there was any decrease in pain and increase in mobility. Many times it's as they take this small step of faith that I see people receive their healing and breakthrough. Notice we are using affirmative thankful prayer and we did not beg God to heal the person. We know in His eyes, through Jesus, He already has healed them and it is His will to heal them, the Word of God says so. So what you are doing is thanking God that He is a healer and you are applying that truth and releasing God's peace and power into their bodies and commanding it in Jesus Name to get in line with the Word and the Will of God. For their body to be healed and made whole by the power of God. You are calling their body back to its original design and proper working order. As you pray for them visualize Jesus touching them with His loving hands and envision the Word of God working on the body part you are praying for. Because in the spiritual realm it's you and Jesus praying for them, not just you. Because Jesus gave you His Holy Spirit and His authority to heal the sick. The visualization of this truth will help you to focus while you are praying. After they tell you how much the pain has either went down or stayed the same you want to celebrate and thank God for anything happening within them that they can sense is different no matter how small it may seem, then pray again, maybe one or two more times depending on the situation or until their mobility has increased and their pain has gone down completely, or you sense you have taken them as far as the Lord is leading you to take them at that time. During this time you can also ask them if they sense anything happening that's different within them than before you prayed for them. So often people will also experience peace or another manifestation of God's Presence.

Let's go with a back pain testimony that I personally experienced with a coworker of mine as an example. I saw him walking stiffly one day at work. I asked him what was going on. He tells me that he has been experiencing severe back pain and a lack of mobility. I asked him about his pain level and he told me it was at an 8 out of 10 and that he could not currently bend over and touch his toes. I said, "Jesus said these signs will follow them that believe, that we will lay our hands on the sick in Jesus name and they will get well. Jesus is a healer, can I pray for Him to heal your back?" He said, "Yes you may." Then I asked him, "What would it look like for you to be healed?" He said if his pain level went down and he could touch his toes without pain then he would know Jesus healed him. I said, "Can I place my hand on the middle of your back and on shoulder?" Again he agreed. After we prayed the first time using a prayer similar to the example I gave in the paragraph above "Jesus I thank You that You are a healer, back I speak to you in Jesus Name and I command you to be healed by the Blood of Jesus, pain be gone and back be healed in Jesus Name. Amen." Then I asked him to check his pain level and rage of motion. His pain level went from an 8 to

a 4 and he could bend over farther than before. We praised God and celebrated the victory! Then I asked, "Can I pray for you again real quick for all
the pain to go away?" He nodded yes. I then prayed "Jesus thank You for
Your healing power and for totally healing their back, now all pain go away
and back be totally healed in Jesus Name. Amen." Then I asked him to
check his back again, it had gone from a pain level of 8 to a 4 to a 1! The
Word of God is like a hammer it just keeps hammering away at sickness,
illness and disease the more you use it, until the healing is totally received
by their bodies. There are times I have prayed two times or as much as four
times for a certain person depending on the circumstances. In this case after
the third time we prayed together all of his pain went away and he could
touch his toes for the first time in several months! We thanked God together
and we both got to personally experience Jesus Christ the healer! The other
amazing part is it took less than three minutes! In situations where it is
something like a cold, tumor, cancer, or something that you cannot just rate
pain or mobility, in cases like these you want to pray for them and
encourage them that the Word of God is working in their bodies and by
faith they are healed and to keep speaking to the sickness and command it
to go away and be destroyed in Jesus Name and keep thanking God that
they are healed because His Word says you already are. For them to keep
applying the Word, Blood and the Name of Jesus to their bodies just like
you would take medicine several times in a day if you were not feeling well.
I have had so many people come back to me with amazing medical reports
and say thank you for taking the time and having the courage to pray for me
and share God's Word on healing with me. Some people I never see again
but I know that I loved them enough to pray for them and encourage them
in their healing and circumstances. We are all called to live a lifestyle of
loving on and praying for people with sicknesses of all kinds both physical
and mental. As a Beliver in Jesus you have the power of God's Spirit within
you to heal! It's just a matter of stepping out on faith and releasing the Holy
Spirit's power through prayer and encouragement. Variations of this same
process can be used in praying over yourself, your children, family, friends,
classmates and coworkers, in person, over the phone, video chat, text
messages, emails and even social media. I have experienced people radically
healed through the power of prayer using all kinds of means of communication. Be generous in your giving when it comes to praying over those that
are sick and in need of healing especially those closest to you. A lot of times
it can be uncomfortable to pray for those closest to us because of thoughts
we have such as "What if nothing happens? What if they don't get better?
What if they feel worse? What if they are disappointed? What if they don't
believe how I believe? What if I look foolish?" and since they are so close to
us we feel we have more to lose. I know sometimes with my own family and

friends I still fight these types of thoughts. It is a matter of realizing that all your prayers can do is help them and aid in their healing. Then choosing to go against those fears and step out on faith in God's Word and release God's healing power anyways through prayer and encouraging people to put their personal faith into action when it comes to them partnering with God in receiving their healing and breakthrough.

What happens when you don't see any immediate breakthroughs such as decrease in their pain level and increase in mobility? Be humble and lovingly tell them *it's ok Jesus loves you and it is His nature and His will for you to walk and live in complete healing and divine health.* Encourage them that even with Jesus some of the healings were progressive like in Luke 17:12-19 when the 10 Lepers were cleansed as they obeyed Jesus by faith and went to show themselves to the priests as Jesus had commanded them to do. The Bible says as they went they were cleansed by their faith in what Jesus had said to them. So healing is sometimes a process over a period of time. In the Gospels in one instance Jesus prayed for a blind man twice before he received his total healing and complete vision back (Mark 8:22-26). Remember your value, identity and how much God loves you is not based on you getting healed or seeing people healed it is based on who God says you are as His child and your value in Jesus Christ.

You also explain to them that the Word of God is like a seed. You plant it, water it and it will grow and produce after its kind. So advise them to look up and read healing scriptures in God's Word in order to plant more seeds of healing within them and water those seeds by continuing to confess those scriptures over their body in faith on a daily basis until they fully receive their breakthrough. Encourage the people that you pray for that the prayers are working, the Word of God is working in them and that they are going to feel better as it works and that by faith they are healed! I have seen plenty of instances where we did not see breakthrough right away, or even after praying a couple of times. However, I do not let what I experience, whether it be an amazing healing miracle or if it seems in the natural that I don't experience anything happen, be my truth and my authority. I let the Word of God be my total and final authority and Jesus is our model and our standard, I know if Jesus walked in the room and prayed for them they would be healed and I know He said if we pray for the sick they will get well and be healed. So you always want to base your faith on Jesus and the Word of God being your truth and your final authority knowing that all of us are forever growing and pressing into supernatural healing. We know when you pray that the healing power of God always comes because Jesus said it would, it boils down to the person's body receiving the healing power Jesus has already provided. It is our job to do the works of Jesus and allow His healing power to be released through us, in our own lives and the people's lives around us so we all can experience His love and power. I have prayed for a lot of people over the years. In some cases I have seen healing manifest right in front of my eyes in amazing ways. Other times I have seen it manifest a day, week or months later. And with others I did not see any manifestation in the natural realm. So I have seen some of the people I have prayed for in the natural sense not seem to get anything. However, I know from the supernatural stand point that the supernatural healing power of God was released into their bodies and it is working even if I can't see it. Before you get frustrated with the divine healing process keep in mind that in the natural world no medication on earth works instantly. Even with all of our technology and health breakthroughs we still don't have medications where the moment you take them you are healed instantly. No, they work over time and it can take your body a short time or a long time to process them to where your totally healed. It has to get "into your system" for the medication to start working some medications work faster than others but all of them have to get into your body and take some time frame to start taking effect. Divine healing works in a different way where the decreases in pain, increases in mobility and recovery of bodily functions like increases in sight, hearing and breathing can happen in an instant and they can also happen over a period of time.

The reason why this happens no one really knows. There are many speculations but the most important thing to remember is the Word of God, the Blood of Jesus, the Name of Jesus and the power of the Holy Spirit always work, it's just a matter of time until what we confess in prayer based on God's Word becomes a reality within our lives in this case healing for your physical body. Because what you confess you will eventually possess. Meaning what you confess, think and believe by faith will eventually become a reality in your life if you hold steadfast to your faith and choose not to give up. It sounds simple and it is simple. However, it's not easy especially when your praying, confessing the Word of God and believing God for divine healing to the best of your ability and in the natural realm your circumstances don't seem to be changing. It's easy to get frustrated, disappointed and discouraged and say to yourself well this healing stuff must not work, I guess it's not God's will to heal, I know God can but I guess this time He doesn't want to heal or maybe He wants to build my faith through all of this. No, those are all lies of your own self doubt, lies of religion and well meaning people and lies of the enemy. It's always God's will to heal and the Bible says He does not change, that Jesus is the same forever and Jesus healed everyone who came to Him for healing. Jesus is our standard and He is our model that we base our prayers, faith and life upon.

Like a mixed martial arts fighter or a boxer fights and contends to defend his title so must we contend for our healing and the healing of others we pray for until we take possession of it in the natural. As that fighter diets, exercises and trains in order to hold up his championship belt once again after he successfully defends his title so must we do the same, through a continual diet of the Word of God, exercising our faith in prayer and training on a daily basis in the things of God in defense against sickness and disease! Your not the sick trying to get well. Your the healed, your the champion in Jesus Christ fighting off and contending against sickness's attack on your body which is the temple of the Holy Spirit! The point is, divine healing is a wonderful power that all Believers possess through the blood of Jesus, the Word of God and the power of the Holy Spirit that can destroy evil and radically change people's lives. Even if you prayed for a hundred people and you only experienced in the natural one person get healed by the power of God would that not be worth it? I can tell you from experience to that one person it is! Keep in mind most of the people you meet will just be moved that you cared enough to pray for their healing so just stepping out on your faith you always win and you bring blessings to others. Even those people that may decline your offer to pray for them, I would encourage you to generally pray for them anyways but just do it under your normal voice tone between you and God instead of with them.

Divine healing is like having a bank account with money already in it because the Bible says **"by His stripes (wounds) we are healed"** **Isaiah 53:5 AMP** notice "we are healed" is in the past tense therefore in God's eyes healing is already a finished work, meaning the provision of money for divine healing is already in your heavenly bank account. So what you do through prayer is you apply the provision in your bank or the person's bank account you are praying for, to their bodies. Thus you are making a withdrawal from the provision already provided for by Jesus dying on the Cross for our sin and sickness. It is kind of like having a bank account with a million dollars in it that you don't know about. If you don't know about the money that has already been put in your name than you cannot benefit from it. In the same manner you can know about that million dollars but if you never debit the account or withdraw money from it you can have a million dollars sitting there and live poor and broke. The same is said for divine healing. What you are doing is making people aware of their inheritance in Jesus and applying that healing provision to their bodies. In essence you are putting the Word, Blood and Name of Jesus to work for them and you.

I want to share a couple of *God stories* with you to demonstrate how God speaks through healing, the power of prayer and the will and nature of God to heal through His amazing grace! Grace is defined as unmerited and unearned favor and that it is. Grace actually is so much deeper than we could ever define on this side of life, but I asked the Lord for a working definition of grace and this is what He shared with me, I pray it blesses you. **Grace is God's Willingness to give us unlimited, unrestricted and unprecedented access to Him as well as access into all of the finished works of Jesus Christ, His power, love, forgiveness, bodily healing, Holy Spirit and all the Bible promises even though we did not do anything specifically to earn it. Grace is a free gift from God, yet at the same time we have to receive it. When we enter into Grace we enter into all of the finished works of Jesus Christ which includes healing for our spirit, soul and body.**

THE FIREFIGHTER

One day I was at a coffee shop for a ministry appointment that I had with a woman who had come to me for some spiritual counsel. I was sitting there with my drink and everywhere I go as I pass by people I will often pray for them without their knowledge. I began to do this years ago to combat being judgmental. When I would find myself judging someone's appearance I would begin to pray for them to get my focus back on how much God loves them and how He sees them. I would often start out praying opposite of the negative thoughts to make it simple so if I thought the person looked mean I would pray for their heart to be softened and God's love to shine into their hearts. If a person was overweight I would pray for them to be delivered from whatever was keeping them bound to food or by a health issue that is causing or contributing to them being over-weight. I know what that is like, I use to be overweight and an emotional eater. I would eat to fill a void in my heart, to feel better in the moment not really knowing I really had a longing for the emptiness I felt to be filled with God's Spirit and Presence. Later I would feel guilty about what I ate as well as shame about the way my body looked. So I pray for them to be filled with God's Spirit, to love themselves, to be healthy, healed and whole, to have self-control and have the ability and motivation to exercise. I also prayed for myself, for God to give me His eyes to see people as He sees them. As I practiced this I found myself being led to pray for more and more people. It was like God began to highlight people to me and I would get a thought of, "You should pray for that person". So praying for people became a habit and helped me have a greater love for what God loves, which is people.

So I am sitting there in the coffee shop looking around and praying for people under my breath as God puts them on my heart, it is like interactive people watching. As I do this I say "God what do they need prayer for?"

and I practice listening and praying by faith in what I sense God is telling me. Through this practice I began to get clear words from God about people at times and He began to share with me what the Bible calls a "Word of Knowledge" which is information that you know about a person or situation that you do not know by natural means but through God's communication with you (1 Corinthians 12:8). As I am people watching, listening to God, reading my Bible and occasionally scrolling through my social media, this gentlemen next to me asked me a question about a test he was studying for. I found out while talking and listening to him that he was studying for his captain's exam for the fire department. I thanked him for his service and let him know how much his job and life was valued and appreciated by me and by Jesus!

I helped him with his question and as usual, I asked him if I could pray for him and what he would like prayer for? At this point I also usually ask if they need prayer for any healing in their bodies and if they have any pain? Because God is a healer and healing is a very powerful confirmation of God's love and power. He said, "You can pray for wisdom for my test." I said, "Ok great!" I then asked him, "Are you a follower of Jesus?" He hesitated and then he said, "Kind of". I usually ask people if they have a relationship with Jesus, this question gives you a better idea if they are saved or maybe in need of some encouragement in their relationship with God. If you ask people do you know Jesus a lot of times they will say yes because they know about Him. You can also ask them if they know Him as their Lord and Savior. I have found the relationship question works the best, and then I ask them when they started their relationship with Jesus. This is not only a conversation starter but it lets you know if they are really in fact saved. There are many people I meet that think because they attended Church or grew up in the Church they are saved, but Church won't give you eternal life, only receiving Jesus Christ as your personal Lord and Savior will do that. I then let God lead us from there. Think about it this way, if you say you love your family and the people around you, but then you are not sure where they are going to spend eternity and not sure if they have the peace and joy in their hearts that only Jesus can give then do you really care about them?

I prayed out loud in my normal voice tone for his mind to be sharp and that God would guide him and give him wisdom and favor on his test. I have found short powerful prayers work just as well as long ones, so when praying for others especially in a public setting like this, try to keep it short, powerful, to the point and always out of a place of love and encouragement! Allow God's voice to flow through you by praying what you sense God is putting on your heart. He thanked me and went back to studying for his test. At this point I did what I usually do I asked God, "Lord is there anything you want to say to this man?" As I listened I felt like God was telling me, "You told him about My love" this came as a flowing thought. Then I asked the next question, "Lord is there anything in his life that You want to heal?" As I did that my left knee began to tingle and burn a little bit. What I was experiencing was what the Bible refers to as a Word of Knowledge (1 Corinthians 12:8) which is when the Holy Spirit gives you specific knowledge about someone or something that you do not gain by natural means which Jesus demonstrated throughout His ministry. I began to get Words of Knowledge as senses within my own body as well as flowing thoughts about things people needed to be healed of several years ago when I began to have intimate fellowship with the Holy Spirit. They started out as flowing thoughts, mental pictures within my imagination and an inward sense that I knew something in my heart but I was not really sure why I knew it. Then as I began to step out and share what I sensed God was telling me sometimes I was hearing right and sometimes I was off, and if I was off I would just tell them "I am learning how to hear God and I sensed you needed healing for something and I thought it was this". Sometimes it would lead them to tell me about something else that needed to be healed and there were instances where they experienced breakthrough right away on a wrong Word of Knowledge but even at the least bit you can still share God's love with them, encourage them and pray a blessing over them and their family. I also got to personally experience what it felt like when I heard God correctly on a Word of Knowledge and when I was hearing myself talking. So as my knee began to tingle and burn I asked God, "Does he have pain in his knee?" and I began to pray in my supernatural prayer language, also known as praying in tongues, and as I did that the feeling would get more intense. I knew this was a confirmation of "yes" to my question. Then as I thanked God for showing me this I looked over at the firefighter and I saw the word "shoulder" in my mind and I sensed God was telling me his shoulder was hurt too. Words of Knowledge for healing can come with physical impressions such as senses of tingling, burning, slight pain, heat or pressure within your own body in relation to the body part God is showing you He wants you to pray over so He can heal them. Also parts of the body can seem highlighted, meaning they seem to stand out or you sense God keeps drawing your attention to it. Another way is maybe you ask God what needs to be healed and you see in your mind picture of a knee, shoulder or neck or like in this case I saw the word "shoulder" as a mental picture within my imagination and got some flowing thoughts about his knee and shoulder pain.

I have realized over the years that timing sometimes is important, so I often will ask God in a situation like this where I have some time before we part ways, when I should approach the person about this. When I asked

God when to do it I got the flowing thought, "Be patient you will know the time, I will show you". So I went back to what I was doing and my appointment got there and I began to talk to them. I introduced the firefighter to the woman I was meeting with and made small talk for a second. I still did not sense it was time. Then a couple of minutes later the firefighter got up to go and thanked me for helping him with his question. At that point I felt a prompting in my spirit as if God was saying, "Go ahead ask him" so I did. I said, "Hey bro this may sound a little strange but do you have pain in your left knee?" Looking puzzled he said, "Yeah what is this?" I said, "Bro this is Jesus He loves you so much and He showed me you had left knee pain." I explained to him how God had shown this to me. I often explain to people my process of hearing God to demystify hearing God and how He speaks in the hope that others will be empowered and motivated to hear God for themselves. I said, "I believe God wants to heal you right now, can I pray for you?" He shrugged his shoulders still in a state of shock. I said, "Do you also have pain in your right shoulder?" He said, "Yeah what is going on here?" He looked around like someone with a camera on a reality TV show was going to jump out any second. He told me later that he thought some of his firefighter buddies where playing a trick on him! I said, "Brother this is Jesus!" He sat down and I asked him if he had pain in his knee right now he said, "Yes my knee always hurts, it has for a while".

If they do have pain I ask them to rate it on a scale of 1 to 10 with 10 being the worst and after that I pray for them, then I ask them to try to do something they could not do before, then I ask them to rate the pain again. As I began to pray for him I thanked God that He is a healer, that He loves His son and then I commanded the knee and shoulder to be made all new in Jesus Name! As I was praying he began to sweat and he told me that his knee and shoulder were getting hot and tingling. This can happen sometimes when we pray and lay hands on someone for healing and every situation is different. People can experience sensations of tingling, warmness, heat, low level feeling of electricity, a sense of peace coming upon them, feelings of things popping within their body as they are healed and pulsating senses of energy through their body are some of the physical manifestations I have experienced when praying for others. It is important to understand that we are not going off of feelings, sensations and physical manifestations of God's healing power flowing through them. It is amazing and awesome when it happens but it is not a necessary part of them receiving their healing. We are basing our prayers and their healing off of God's Word, His love and the will and nature of God to heal them. There are plenty of times where the person being prayed for did not feel or sense anything happening and still received a total miracle healing from God. So the people seemingly felt nothing but they were still radically healed of a serious illness. It's about releasing the Word of God by faith and God's healing power into them. So while physical manifestations of God's healing power working within them are amazing to experience, it's the faith in the Word of God and their bodies receiving the healing power of the Holy Spirit that's important.

As I finished praying for him I asked him to check to see if he can sense any difference in the pain level and the mobility in his knee and shoulder. As he began to move his knee a look of shock and surprise came over his face. He exclaimed, "What is this! The pain is completely gone!" Then he checked his shoulder and all his pain was gone and he had complete mobility! Praise God! Healed in Jesus Name! Right there in a coffee shop in Dallas, Texas we all three experienced God's healing power and a miracle in action! All because I made the commitment and decision to live a lifestyle of sharing the love and power of Jesus with those around me and you can do the same thing! The truth of the Gospel of Jesus Christ is we are all commanded and empowered to be radically generous with the love, power, grace and blessings of Jesus!

The story actually gets way better the gentlemen leaves, finds me on social media and sends me a message. He told me that he had really given up on God and on prayer. That what had happened to him had restored his faith in God where, according to him, there was no faith in God left! You never know who needs to see Jesus in you to change the course of their lives! What did I do and what is God calling you to do? It is the same thing the Apostle Paul reminded Timothy of in 2 Timothy 1:6: ***"I'm writing to encourage you to fan into a flame and rekindle the fire of the spiritual gift God imparted to you....For God will never give you the spirit of fear, but the Holy Spirit who gives you mighty power, love, and self-control." 2 Timothy 1:6-7 TPT*** God is calling you to stir up the gift and fan the flame of love, power and grace inside of you through the Holy Spirit! As you love and follow Jesus in companionship you become like Him and you allow His nature to flow through you to love others in and around your life. You become like a shaken up soda bottle that is opened and then the soda gets on everything in its area! When you become like Jesus through knowing Him by spending time intimately experiencing God through a daily relationship, just like the shaken up soda you become explosive and amazing acts of love will happen in your daily life.

So he goes to work at the fire station the next day and did squats and tested his new shoulder and new knee out in the gym there and to his surprise they were totally healed and without any pain! I came to find out that he had pain in his knee for almost two years and it had gotten so bad that he knew he needed surgery. Jesus is so good! God lead me to counsel with him over the next couple of months as a spiritual mentor. He got on our 21 day spiritual fitness program which is a combination of speaking to and listening to God in prayer, reading the Word and listening to inspired teaching and preaching and his relationship with God has not only been restored but it has grown to new heights he never thought were possible! He has even begun to spread God's love to his family, friends and those around him!

The FACT is I do not always see this kind of activity and breakthrough but the TRUTH of God's Word is there is always activity and break-throughs in the spiritual realm, when we release our faith in prayer and love one another as Jesus modeled for us to do! People will often tell me, "Ster-ling you are not dealing with the facts, you're just being spiritual and naive. You need to face reality, these are real issues and challenging problems." I explain to them that I am actually dealing with something that is higher than facts, reality and any issue you can face in life which is God's truth. You see God's truth takes into account something that people who deal in only facts and logic don't take into account and that's the supernatural power of God and the spiritual realm. So I am actually taking into account the facts, reality, and issues as well as the whole spiritual realm of God as well as the demonic realm of the devil. I know as I communicate with God, speak God's truth in faith empowered by the Holy Spirit and say what God says about the situation in the unseen spiritual realm God is listening, speaking and working on my behalf. His angels are also moving, working and ministering on my behalf as well, to bring about God's Word, purpose and destiny for my life and in the lives of others that I pray for and with. You see God's truth has the supernatural ability to change facts, human realities and life's issues. For instance when I have experienced supernat-ural healing the medical facts said the person could not be healed but in truth we prayed and I saw them healed which shocked the doctors and others who knew the medical facts. Have you ever responded to a chal-lenging situation in life by saying to yourself or someone else in a helpless or defeated type of tone, "Well all I can do is pray about it" or heard another person respond to a difficult situation by saying, "Well you know all we can do is pray about it"? I have made those statements personally and heard some form of them time and time again. Then God corrected me one day and showed me that I was discounting the power of prayer that I said I faithfully believed in. I saw how those statements and mindsets were like a slap in the face to God. I realized that when I discount the power of prayer in my life I am discounting what Jesus did on the Cross by giving us bold and unrestricted access to God's Presence, Power, Spirit as well as all the blessings in the heavenly realms through Christ Jesus! So realize your words and your prayers change things in the spiritual realm and eventually the physical realms as well!

There are many accounts, throughout the Bible as well as in my own personal life, that faithfully acting on God's truth in love caused seemingly unwinnable battles to be won by God's people. Deliverance from captivity, demonstrations of God's power through supernatural miracles, financial breakthrough and provision, God's joy and peace in the hearts of His people even during the midst of very challenging life circumstances, supernatural healing of people's bodies and minds, and various kinds of blessings that happened but in the natural logical realm it did not make sense how it came to pass. However, living a life of faith in God's truth takes into account the supernatural unseen spiritual realm which can and does change and supersede facts! So go out and become the love and power of Jesus in this world! Let your daily prayer be, *"Lord use me to be a miracle in someone's life today,"* you will be amazed by how many ways God answers that heart position of love!

CRUTCHES NO MORE!

Wherever I go when I run across people struggling with sickness or people in pain both emotional and physical I make it a point to pray for them and as I have done that more and more and taken risks I have seen God do some amazing things. Some are instant, some take time and some you are believing by faith in what you can't see knowing God is good to His Word and His Nature as a Healer. The point is for you to manifest the Father's love, power and grace found in Jesus to the world around you by living your life through the overflowing knowledge of your daily relationship with God. Then through that overflow, to be a light that others can see God through by the way you live a life of excellence, joy and faith. Make the daily choices to step out of your comfort zone being generous with God's love, forgiveness, joy, peace, power and the gifts He has given you to bless others. Start praying for people and putting what Jesus did into action, *"And you know that God anointed Jesus of Nazareth with the Holy Spirit and with power. Then Jesus went around doing good and healing all who were oppressed by the devil, for God was with Him." Acts of the Apostles 10:38 NLT* You might be saying, "Well Sterling what if the healing and breakthroughs do not happen where I can see or experience them? What if they do not get healed?"

The answer is simple, you keep praying for yourself and others, being encouraged by reading, hearing and meditating in God's Word on the subject of healing and the power of faith-filled words taught and demonstrated throughout the Bible. Continue laying your hands on the sick and those in emotional and physical pain praying for them in faith releasing God's healing power over them. Do not let what you see and experience be your measuring stick, let the life of Jesus Christ and the Word of God be the truth you measure things by. I am not saying it's easy I am saying that it's what we as Believers in Jesus must make the daily decision and relentless commitment to do! This is what I did when I had a job as an assistant counselor at a drug rehab facility for teenagers and young adults. Where I prayed for a young man that was on crutches with a broken ankle. His ankle looked so swollen and he had such a bad limp I contemplated not even praying for him. I got thoughts such as, "His ankle is broken what's prayer going to help? Nothing is going to happen, you're wasting your time. He is just going to think you're weird. What if nothing happens, then you are going to hurt his faith in God?" However, I know those are lies from the enemy coupled with my own self doubt and the fear of disappointment just trying to get me off my faith and into fear so that I would not put my faith into action. So what did I do? I refused those thoughts of fear and stepped out on my faith and told myself *God is a healer no matter what I think or how I feel it's who He is!* Keep in mind when your praying for others it's normal to feel nervous, uncomfortable and even embarrassed at times, that's all part of stepping out on your faith. When you get thoughts of doubt, fear and nervousness when it comes to stepping out in faith on the Word of God in prayer make it a habit to pray and do the opposite of those types of thoughts and feelings which is what I did in this case. He had a diagnosed hairline fracture in his ankle he was limping really bad that morning and I asked him, "Hey can I pray for your ankle to be healed and for a speedy recovery in Jesus Name?" He said, "Yes, sure." I had several negative thoughts of doubt rolling around in my mind but in my heart I know God's Word is true! So I prayed for him and asked him if he sensed any less pain and any additional range of motion, he said he did a little bit. Then I told him *lets both continue to thank God for your healing* and I asked him to say, "Thank You Jesus that I am Healed" anytime he thought about his ankle or if it started hurting, I told him to command the pain to go away in Jesus Name. He agreed.

I have seen many cases where this tactic of affirmative thankful prayer was what brought healing breakthrough and people were able to learn how to put their own faith into action. An hour later the young man is in school and he gets up to get something from across the room he gets about halfway across the room when he realizes that he forgot his crutches and to his surprise he was not limping either and he had no pain, totally healed and restored by the love and power of Jesus! He began to jump up and down screaming, "I am healed! I am healed!" The teacher approached him asking him, "What is the matter with you? Why are you yelling?" He tells him about how we prayed and Jesus within a matter of a couple of hours or so completely healed his broken and severely sprained ankle! I see him as he comes out of school carrying his crutches with no limp jumping up and down screaming, "Look Sterling, Jesus healed me!" I am in shock even though I had seen Jesus heal before it was just amazing the turnaround! I spent the rest of the day with him on and off he was playing basketball and football running around like he had a new ankle, which he did! At one point in the day as I watched him jump for footballs and run around with no limp I found myself with my jaw just dropped with amazement at the love and power of God! That is one of the most amazing healings I have ever seen and the glory and power of Jesus was on display for everyone to see. God spoke loud and clear through divine healing that day! There were many young people there that came to have a relationship with Jesus because of what they witnessed that day, the love and power of Jesus demonstrated! The nurses could not explain it and when he and I told them that Jesus healed him they just looked at me in unbelief even though they knew Jesus could do it and they were Believers they just had not experienced God's healing power first hand in that way before. Remember what we said about the Word of God it is a seed and it has the ability and power to bring about the promises of God and that is what we saw happen here. The seed of Mark 16:17, James 5:15, Isaiah 53:5 was planted and it was watered with thanksgiving by him and me as we thanked God by faith for his healing before we experienced it in the natural. As that happened the Word, our faith and the healing power of God was working and healing his ankle from the inside out, then breakthrough came with his ankle being totally healed!

I praise God for His will and His nature to heal and for this healing miracle that so many of us got to experience, but it almost didn't happen because I almost shrank back because of negative thoughts, doubt and the fear of disappointment. Accepting that kind of thinking would have caused him and everyone else to have missed out on seeing a miracle in action! Miracles, signs, wonders and healings are all expressions of God's goodness and love which is exactly what everyone experienced that day.

The Bible says the whole creation and world moans and groans waiting for the sons and daughters of God to stand up and be revealed (Romans 8:18-22)! Meaning that no matter what is happening in our lives we are to be uncovered coming out of and putting off fear, pride, shame, unforgiveness and our old self will. Instead we are to reveal the Jesus within us and demonstrate a supernatural lifestyle of compassion, integrity, power, purity, forgiveness and faith that our Heavenly Father gives us through our relationship with Jesus Christ. God empowers us to walk out this supernatural lifestyle through our union with the Holy Spirit! We as Believers in Jesus

THE DEMONSTRATION OF GOD'S LOVE AND POWER | 279

Christ are to be living examples of God's freedom, joy and glory to the world even as they moan, groan, complain, reject and even attack us, God is looking to us to manifest Christlikeness to them! We are to be God's light to the world around us!

I wanted to include this Word from God that I received from Him as a series of flowing thoughts which also came with my eyes burning and the top of my head itching, these are often spiritual confirmations for me when God is speaking to me. These came while I was documenting this healing in my spiritual journal. These words have given me great encouragement and wisdom. I hope and pray that this blesses your heart as it has mine! These words are straight from the Father's Heart to mine and now to yours enjoy: ***"Know and Believe the more you step out on My Word, the more I perform it, the more I bless you to see Increase, always focus on My Power, Will and Nature to heal! Never on who does not seem to receive! I AM THE HEALER!"***

BOATING AND BACK ISSUES

I wanted to share this God story with you because it is very personal to me because it was within my own body and something I labored in faith and patience with for almost two months. I was tubing on a nearby lake early on in the summer. For the people that don't know what I am talking about tubing is when you drag a large inflated tube or air mat behind a boat and the point for the tuber is to hang on for dear life while the driver goes really fast and swings the boat around thus whipping the tube at speeds that can be in excess of 15 to 20 miles per hour. I consider myself a pretty good tuber because I have a strong grip so it is usually very hard for me to get thrown off of a tube even going at high speeds. This day though I had met a driver who knew a lot about how to go fast and whip the boat around just at the right time to send most tubers hurling into the air. So there I was, one on one with him, well to make a long story short he won! Before I got on the tube I heard the Holy Spirit say "Don't do it, it's a trap" meaning I had that flowing thought come to my mind. I also had an uneasy sense in my stomach which is in the area of your spirit but I ignored both warnings. Thinking to myself "What a strange thought and feeling to have". To be transparent my pride got the best of me and I listened to my pride and competitive nature instead of the Spirit of God in me. A lot of us, if we think back to where we made decisions that had negative consequences in our lives we either didn't ask God what He thought, disregarded the unpeaceful feeling we got or we just plain knew it was not a good choice but out of self will and pride we did it anyways. Not to say if you follow God closely and do try to live your life being guided by the Holy Spirit that your life will be without challenges, storms and tribulation that is unrealistic. Because we know those types of things do happen, no one is immune to the trials and tribulations of living in a fallen world, the point is if you follow God you can eliminate a lot of the negative consequences we tend to bring upon ourselves. Well after a couple of rounds of me hanging on with all I had he whipped the boat around and sent me hurling in the air end over end. I landed on the water in such a way that it folded my back in half, initially I thought I had literally broken my back in two. I was praying as I was in the air for God to save my life and to my thankfulness He did.

However, when I came down I could feel my back violently popping and cracking and the middle part of my back suffered the most trauma. At the moment I hit the water the hardest I remember praying to God "Lord please don't let me be paralyzed from this for the rest of my life". That is how serious this accident was. When I realized I could kick my feet I praised God that He had spared my life and preserved the movement of my legs! I got back into the boat and right away began to repent asking and thanking God for His forgiveness for not listening to Him, then I started to confess God's Word over my back for it to be healed. The next day I was in so much pain walking was difficult.

The whole day I confessed God's Word over my back and thanked God for my healing, rested, stretched out, put ice on my back and took the necessary medication. People often have this misunderstanding when it comes to divine healing about acting on what medical wisdom says and acting on what faith in the Word of God says that you cannot combine the two. When in truth you absolutely can and you should do both! In my case I stretched, rested, iced and took an anti-inflammatory medication. Those were the wise medical actions to take in my situation and I felt peace in my spirit about doing it. At the same time I did what faith says which is to do things like pray, read and listen to healing scriptures and confess the Word of God over my body, commanding my body to receive God's healing power. So I encourage people when it comes to healing do both. Use medical wisdom and the spiritual power you have in Jesus! Get healed by any and all means necessary! The devil is not in the healing business he is not creating ways to heal you, God is the author of healing. So I would encourage you to use medical wisdom. As well as pray about what medications to take and allow the Holy Spirit to guide you in all of your medical decisions. Even before I take a medication of any kind I pray over it for God to use it to heal my body. That it would have no adverse side effects on me and I thank Him that His supernatural healing power is upon the medication. God put Doctors here on Earth to help you so utilize the great medical advances He has blessed us with at the same time releasing your faith and allow the Holy Spirit to guide you!

I also spent part of the day listening to healing messages online by various preachers like Charles Capps, Kenneth Copeland and Kenneth Hagin. Men I knew preached the healing power of Jesus Christ for your body! As I prayed the pain would go away for a time, then return and then I would command it to go away again in Jesus name and thank God that I am healed. After a couple of days I realized I had a bulging disc in my back and there was a sizable lump in the middle of my back where the bulk of the trauma had happened. I had all kinds of thoughts running through my mind of, "God is not going to heal you because you disobeyed Him. Your back is going to be messed up forever. You're going to have to have back surgery. You are just speaking words into the air, your prayers don't matter. You know just speaking some words is not going to change anything." I knew these were the lies of the enemy so I would refuse those thoughts in Jesus Name and then I would release those thoughts over to God and then claim my healing by speaking God's Word on healing and thanking God and praising Him that He is a healer, that He loves me and that my back is healed in Jesus name. This battle went on for almost two months. The pain would come, I would pray, then oftentimes it would go away or reduce. Sometimes the pain went away immediately and sometimes the pain persisted and then it would come back at another time. The bulging disc never got smaller even though I had commanded it to be healed in Jesus name several hundred times. I had several people lay hands on my back and pray for me. I listened to healing messages and read healing scriptures over myself. Yet, I did not see in the natural any major breakthroughs. Meaning the healing God promised me in His Word had not yet become a reality in the natural seen realm at least from what I could sense besides the pain management through prayer which I was very thankful for.

However, I had made a decision that I am going to ask you to make right now. I made the decision and commitment that I would not be moved by my feelings, emotions, circumstances or what is visible I would only be moved by God's Word and that no matter what God's Word is TRUTH and cannot return to Him or to me void of power! So even though I did not feel healed I claimed my healing anyway, cast down negative thoughts, forgave God when I got frustrated at not seeing breakthrough, listened to healing videos, and praised and thanked God that He loves me, by His Stripes I am already healed in Jesus Name and that it is always His will and nature to heal and healing is a finished work of the cross! I did those things over a 2 month period probably hundreds of times knowing that if I continue to think, speak and act in faith that I would be healed because Jesus said that I am already healed and I believe He told the truth! That means healing will become a reality in my life and in my body if I continue to believe, which means to take God at His Word, which is an active, ongoing process of thinking, speaking and acting as if the Word of God is true which it is! You see faith, patience, trust and resting in God's promises is not inactivity it takes action and labor to stay in a place of trusting and resting in God's promises. That is what I was doing is laboring to enter into the rest of God. *Let us therefore make every effort to enter that rest [of God, to know and experience it for ourselves], so that no one will fall by following the same example of disobedience [as those who died in the wilderness]. For the Word of God is living and active and full of power [making it operative, energizing, and effective]. Hebrews 4:11-12 AMP*

During these two months I continued to pray for others and I am seeing others get healed by the love and power of Jesus! On one hand I am really joyful, on the other the enemy is handing me thoughts such as "Oh God cares about them but because you are a preacher He is having you suffer." I also know those are lies as well straight out of the pits of hell, my Daddy loves me and I know He is a healer so I refused those thoughts, released them over to God, forgave God and myself for those thoughts and then I thanked and praised God that according to Isaiah 53:4-5 *"by His stripes I have been healed!"* What was I doing? I was standing on my faith and trusting in God's Word, being patient and laboring to enter into the rest of God's promises.

The Word of God was always working in my body and it was working on my back the whole time whether I could see it or not. Notice in the scripture below Jesus tells us how breakthroughs happen. The Word gets in a person's heart and then it comes to pass meaning, what the Bible says becomes a reality in our lives. *"The upright (honorable, intrinsically good) man out of the good treasure [stored] in his heart produces what is upright (honorable and intrinsically good), ...for out of the abundance (overflow) of the heart his mouth speaks." Luke 6:45 AMPC*

So two months after my accident I am laying in my bed late one night and my back is still hurting, the enemy is still handing me negative thoughts and the bulging disc is still there. So I begin to do what I usually did any time those things began to happen to me, I worshipped God by praising and thanking Him that I am healed and I commanded my body to get in line with God's Word. Right then as I am praising and thanking God for my healing I closed my eyes and in my mind I could see an image of my back and all of a sudden I saw this horizontal beam of white light go across the mental image of my back in the exact same place where the bulging disc was, then I hear as a flowing thought from God in my heart saying "Check your back, you are healed!". My eyes popped open and I rolled over to check my back. The pain was gone and I felt for the bulging disc and my back for the first time since before my accident was smooth and without any pain! I praised God that my breakthrough had finally come! What did I do? I claimed God's Word as my truth and authority until it manifested meaning, God's Word showed up in the natural seen realm, in essence I was now living in the reality of my healing that Jesus said I already had!

God shared something with me one morning in the middle of my two month battle that has helped me to overcome this and other health issues I have had that I want to impart to you. I was asking Him, "Lord why am I not receiving my healing and breakthrough?" Notice I did not ask Him, "God why have You not healed me?" Because you see that would be a subtle statement of unbelief. God showed me in His Word that He has already healed us. Therefore our healing has already been provided it's a matter applying and appropriating that healing provision and receiving it into your body and it becoming a reality in your mind and body. Hopefully you can now see the subtle yet distinct difference in those two questions and the mindsets behind both. I went on to ask God, "Lord have I done something wrong? Is there some sin in my life I need to confess that is blocking me from receiving my healing? Am I not praying effectively? What are You saying about this Lord?" When I finally stopped to listen after the rapid fire of all of my questions the first thing He said came to me as a flowing thought and I saw this phrase in my mind in red block letters on a white background "Son I love you" as that happened a peace came into the room and over me, He is such a good Dad!

Then God gave me three things that lead me to victory and breakthrough. These three things came as a combination of flowing thoughts, words of text I saw as mental pictures within my mind and Bible verses He brought to my remembrance. I felt Him prompt me to open my spiritual journal in that moment, wait on Him to speak and I wrote down what I sensed He was telling me. I pray that they cause the same breakthroughs and victories for you that they have in my life! He said, ***"One, stay in right relationship with Me and don't allow yourself to get frustrated or upset with Me and when those thoughts come repent, release them to Me and forgive Me and forgive yourself. Two, speak the Word only; meaning speak My Word over the situation only say what I say about your healing thus standing on the Truth of My Word. Three, know it is always My will and nature to heal and that healing always comes in this life and the next and always thank Me and praise Me for that truth even when you don't see it in the natural reality of your life yet, because it is already a*** *finished work. Offer to Me praise and thanksgiving for what you don't see in the natural yet, for that it is one of the highest forms of believing and faith."* I followed His advice and I praised, thanked and worshiped God for my back being healed probably hundreds of times in the two months before that night even when I didn't feel like it and at times seemed meaningless, but I refused to let go of my faith concerning my situation. You see, the time between when you claim, confess, believe and thank God for your healing and the actual materialization and manifestation of God's promises becoming a personal reality within your life is the "faith realm". Faith is what you believe and act upon between the time you start believing in the promises of God to manifest and the time you take possession of what you believed for and it becomes a reality in your life.

Since that night of the manifestation of God's healing promises becoming reality in my life I have not had any pain and my back is totally healed! All because I made a commitment and decision to believe, confess and put the Word of God into action! I want to challenge you to make this same commitment in all the areas of your life to say what God says about your situations like finances, relationships, marriage, children, family, health, career, school and no matter what you're facing remember that you can overcome through Jesus Christ who has made you more than a conqueror (Romans 8:37)! Remember the Word of God gets into a person's heart and then out of the treasure that is stored up, then it comes to pass and becomes a reality in your life, don't let go of your victory! Step out and pray for yourself and other people around you and allow the God in you, to heal you and others through you!

This is living a regular Christian lifestyle. Practice and train daily in living a life of divine health and favor through intimate fellowship with God and confessing God's Word over your body. As things come at you practice and train praying over yourself for headaches to go away, praying for cuts to be healed speedily, pimples to be cut off at the root system and any other pain, sickness, injury, impurity or disease that may try to attack your body. Remember, we are not the sick trying to get well we are the healed fighting off sickness and disease and refusing its authority to live in our bodies which is now in the New Covenant the Temple of the Holy Spirit! *Or do you not know that your body is a temple of the Holy Spirit within you, whom you have from God? You are not your own, 1 Corinthians 6:19 NIV*

I want to encourage you to practice on the little things so when the big things try to come and attack your body or your family you already have been training, practicing and walking in divine healing. Pray for and with your spouse, children, family, friends, coworkers, classmates and people you meet in your daily life, making it your goal of living a life of NO FEAR! Always be training and growing in glory.

"And we all, with unveiled face, beholding the glory of the Lord, are being transformed into the same image from one degree of glory to another. For this comes from the Lord who is the Spirit." 2 Corinthians 3:18 ESV

"For therein is the righteousness of God revealed from faith to faith: as it is written, The just shall live by faith." Romans 1:17 KJV

These scriptures tell us as we behold and focus on the glory of God by spending time in His presence and His Word, hearing His voice, experiencing Him in various ways, practicing and growing in our faith daily, we become like Jesus. Through our close union with God we are being transformed into the same image of God's glory which the Bible tells us is Jesus, thus becoming Christlike and the essence of God's love upon this Earth. I am ever increasing in faith, intimacy and glory with God because I make it a lifestyle. So the Sterling you meet this month won't be the Sterling you meet next month I will have grown to a greater level of faith and glory by then because I am intentionally and constantly growing in my personal relationship with God. Remember this, that healings, giftings, callings, ministry and miracles begin with value, identity and intimacy within a healthy family type relationship with God and will always follow radically generous love which will give you the authority to impact lives and culture. I want to challenge and encourage you to make this your Christian lifestyle and mindset one that is driven by your love for Jesus and His love for you! If you have a personal testimony about God's healing power while or after reading this book please share it with us by emailing us at info@sterlingharris.org we love to hear God stories!

LIVING A PROPHETIC LIFESTYLE AND LOVING PEOPLE INTO TRANS-FORMATION

The words prophetic and prophesying tend to get a wide variety of responses and ideas. From some scary person yelling at you that the end of the world is coming soon; to thinking hearing God's voice and sharing with others what God shared with you is only for "the spiritual elite" or for those "chosen few super Christians" or Old Testament Prophets in the Bible and every idea in-between. So I want to demystify and simplify those terms. Being prophetic is hearing the heartbeat of God for yourself and others, it's living a lifestyle of Godly love and power. For example, hopefully through the process of reading this book and doing the exercises you have heard God's active voice numerous times, as well as beginning to realize that God speaks in a wide variety of ways. If you did, congratulations you are prophetic! You are in a two way communication and dialogue with God which is what being prophetic is all about! Prophesying is simply sharing with others what you are spiritually hearing, seeing and sensing from God. When you prophesy you are engaging the active voice of the Holy Spirit through prayer and listening to the Holy Spirit within you, then communicating with others what you sense God is saying to you. Often when people hear the word prophesying they think of someone being able to foretell and give insight about future events by divine revelation from God which can and still does happen. However, prophesying can also be a divine revelation and spiritual insight from God about the past and present things as well. The Bible says prophesying is something all Christians can do (1 Corinthians 14:5). Meaning we can all hear God's voice and heart for others and then in response to what we are hearing, seeing and sensing we communicate that message to them and over their lives.

The Word tells us in 1 Corinthians 14:3 what prophecy should sound like when we hear it from God and how we should deliver it, in love to the person we are speaking to. ***"But the person who prophesies speaks to people for their upbuilding, encouragement, and comfort."*** So if what you're hearing, seeing and sensing for someone sounds like love, upbuilding, encouragement and comfort then be bold and share it with the person you're interacting with. Then ask them if what you shared resonates with them and so often it will! It can be as simple as God putting on your heart to say things such as: "I sense God is telling me that He loves you so much and that He is proud of you"; "God loves you so much as His child, you are so valuable and worthy, He is going to provide for you and He has an amazing plan and purpose for your life"; "I sense you have a deep heart of compassion for others and God wants you to give yourself the same compassion and love because you are worth it"; "I feel like God is saying you're moving out of an old season, which has been hard for you, into a new one". In other cases you may sense God is putting an upbuilding Bible truth on your heart, like how valuable the person is in God's sight as a son or daughter. God could bring a scripture to your mind to share with this person which you sense would provide some encouragement and comfort to them. It could also be as detailed as God sharing intimate insight with you about their past, present and future. As God gives you this information. He will often instill within you a certain perspective of His heart and love for you to share with them, which often sounds similar to loving encouraging thoughts you're having about the person. As you have been learning throughout this book when those thoughts and communication are from God they will often come with a peace, wisdom and flow to them which is not your own. These insights can come to your heart in a variety of ways: in a conversation with someone in person or over the phone, it may be someone you're close to, like a friend, or maybe it's a stranger, or you may be in a group of people where you sense God is putting something on your heart to share with a certain person in the group. It could be someone God brings to your mind "randomly" during the day. You may not have thought about them in awhile, but you sense you need to call them and catch up with them. These things can seem so subtle but they are often opportunities where God wants to use you to speak His love into someone's life. This is why it is so important to keep your heart sensitive to promptings and nudges by the Holy Spirit because they can be so faint and gentle at times. What you're hearing, seeing and sensing from the Holy Spirit about them can be literal, factual and detailed or it can also be figurative, metaphorical and symbolic. For a literal, factual and detailed example; sometimes when I meet people I will get a sense about them that they need some encouragement because they have been going through a rough season of life and they have been worrying a lot. In these cases I have experienced mental pictures of people not being able to sleep at night, people sitting in their rooms worrying and stressing, or I see some sort of picture of them in my minds eye which leads me to believe they have been really worried and stressed out. In these cases I may share with them what I sense and ask them if it resonates with them, or instead I may just begin to encourage, uplift and comfort them based on what I am sensing. A key is you want to allow yourself to be led by God in what you say. On the positive side, instead I may get a sense they are going through a time of transition, growth and promotion in life.

In these cases I may see a vision of them in my mind getting a new job, get the flowing thought of them changing seasons or see the word "promotion" in my mind. Then I share what I am sensing asking if it makes sense to them or I may just begin to encourage them in what God is showing me, allowing myself to be led by the Holy Spirit by asking God to guide me as I share with the person. As you step out on faith and share what you sense God is saying there will often be a flow of thoughts, impressions and senses which will provide the person with encouragement, upbuilding and comfort. Prophecy can also be figurative, metaphorical and symbolic, giving you prophetic pictures of what God is saying about them and how He sees them. A vision of a child playing may symbolize the person having childlike faith, a waterfall may speak of the person being a blessing and refreshing to others, a light can refer to the person being a light for Jesus to others and seeing a red heart may speak of God's love and compassion being an attribute within a person which God loves about them. If you're unsure about what you are getting from God, you can always pray for more clarification. So often, as you step out in faith, more revelation will come or the feedback they give you may clarify what God is showing you.

I want to encourage you to pray to the Lord and begin to hear His heart; especially for those closest to you such as your spouse, kids, family members, coworkers and classmates. Then step out and share with them what you are spiritually hearing, seeing and sensing from God about them and their lives. My wife and I prophesy over one another all the time by asking God, "Lord what are you saying about our marriage, about the season of life we are in, about a particular decision or opportunity we have been presented with, about how to handle this situation with our child?" Whatever we want God's insight on, we will pray, listen, and then share with one another what we sense God is saying to us and showing us. We have received some amazing prophetic words for one another and our family from the Holy Spirit. This also helps us to partner with God in our prayer lives based on what God is saying to us. God is really much more practical than people give Him credit for. I have experienced God giving me and others prophecy concerning starting a new job or business, a family member turning their lives around, insight into what life season you are in and how to effectively partner with God in that season, financial guidance, business advice and important life decisions. For example a while back my brother had some critical business decisions to make and he did not know what to do so I said "Hey bro lets pray and listen to what the Holy Spirit is saying about your business." In the natural it did not seem like it would matter. However, as we were praying he and I both received some strategic insight from God which we shared with one another. Then we began praying blessings and prophesying over his business based on what God showed us and as we did that by faith, led by the Holy Spirit, a comfort, encouragement and an inner confidence came. He began to put some of the strategic insight that God had given us into action and less than three weeks later his business had a huge turn around and his revenues increased dramatically. You might be saying to yourself "That does not make sense Sterling". Yes, it may not make sense in the natural, but in my brothers' case it made tens of thousands of dollars difference! Now he calls me frequently and we pray and prophesy over his business which has continued to prosper, as well as other aspects of his life. Living a prophetic lifestyle is not only supernatural it is also very practical. God wants to empower you to prosper in every aspect of your life by giving you His perspective, wisdom and resources. It is up to us to choose to invite God into every area of our lives and partner with Him through a daily intimate relationship. We want to seek to spiritually hear, see and sense God's active voice and His activity embedded throughout our daily lives!

You also want to follow the same pattern of measurement as you receive prophetic words from others which is something someone is sharing with you about what they spiritually sense the Lord is saying to them about you. It should be somewhat uplifting, encouraging and comforting to you. Be discerning and always take any prophetic word you get from someone to God for further revelation and confirmation. Most of the time what you receive will be a confirmation of something God has already been showing you or speaking to you about. There is often a peace you will sense in your spirit that what they are sharing with you is from God. If it does not sit well with you or you don't agree with it, there is no reason to argue with the person who is speaking to you and get offended. Choose to be humble about it and say, "Thank you I will pray about that and take it to the Lord" and if God shows you that it was not from Him it is ok, we are all still learning how to hear God. What you and others hear from God can be affected by your soul because what you sense God saying is often filtered through your mind, will, emotions and personality. The more you're transformed and become like Jesus the clearer your filter will be. It's a process but God chooses to flow out of us and out of our personality even from the very beginning of our transformation process of becoming Christlike. I have had the honor of leading a lot of young people to Christ over the years that were a couple of days or even minutes saved, that were brand new in their relationship with Jesus, that have heard God's active voice. Sometimes as I was leading them in an exercise in hearing God, like the ones in this book, the Holy Spirit told them and showed them things about me and gave them prophetic words of encouragement for me that were so clear it amazed me! It demonstrated to me the Bible truth that anyone that has a relationship with Jesus has the opportunity to be prophetic and share what they sense they are hearing from God with others, which is prophesying (1 Corinthians 14:31).

Realize that you and other people can misinterpret or mishear what God is saying at times. Hearing God's voice is not an exact science or a formula, it's a relational journey with God. Be mindful that it can be easy to overpower God's still small voice within your own thoughts and consciousness so be intentional about realigning your focus back to what you spiritually hear, see and sense God is saying. This is a continual realignment process for all of us. Keep in mind God created each one of us so He knows all the distractions we face within our minds and lives so there is plenty of grace and love for all of us within this life long process of hearing from God. The Holy Spirit will also speak to you in any context in which you are willing and have expectations to hear Him so stay watchful for His voice and activity in and around your heart and daily life. When we do mishear God, be humble and be accountable and admit to yourself and others if you need to, "I misheard what God was saying on that, I acknowledge this is a learning process and I am still learning", personally I have done that in several situations and it still happens to me today sometimes. Use it as a learning experience! You are on a journey in your relationship with God, hearing His voice, sensing His activity and cultivating your own personal love language with Him. Through the epic misses I have had where I missed God on what I sensed He was saying to me, I have become more discerning and in tune to when I am hearing God speak to me and what is my own mind, will and emotions talking. Once you begin to sense the difference, it provides a clarity you did not have before and like anything, it takes continual repetition and practice. God is more interested in the relationship aspect with Him and your heart intent to connect with Him, than He is in your accuracy. There is plenty of God's grace in this area so just make sure you receive it and apply it to yourself and others. Don't let the fear of being wrong about what you sense God is saying to you keep you from living a prophetic lifestyle of hearing God's voice for yourself and others, as well as stepping out on your faith and sharing it. So take risks, step out on faith and share what you sense God is saying to you! God is honored by your faith and your effort! He loves it! *"Let love be your highest goal! But you should also desire the special abilities the Spirit gives especially the ability to prophesy." 1 Corinthians 14:1 NLT*

Encouragement is a great way to flow in a prophetic lifestyle. I often will comment on a person's physical appearance the Lord highlights for me or maybe it's a sense I get about them. I like your shoes, cool shirt, I love your necklace, whatever God highlights to you. As you do this the prophetic Holy Spirit in you will often open up and begin to flow out of you. It is as simple as saying "I sense God is putting on my heart to share with you that Jesus loves you so much and that you are an amazing person" that is one of the easiest ways to encourage people on a daily basis and you will always be 100% accurate! Because Jesus does love them, they are amazing in His eyes, He does have a purpose for their lives and He gave His life for them so that they could have an intimate relationship with God through the indwelling of the Holy Spirit! I get this type of prompting from God the most, which usually comes as Him reminding me to let people know every day and everywhere that Jesus loves them.

Being compassionate towards others by trying to see others in a loving and caring way as God sees them, is also a big key to flowing in the prophetic. Which is simply living a lifestyle of love and seeking to share God's heart with the people He puts in your daily path. As I encounter people I generally ask God: "Lord show me how You see this person?", "Father, tell me what do You love about them?", "God is there anything You want to say to this person through me?" Then, after each question I listen.

Oftentimes I will pray in my mind or under my breath for them and some-times I get an impression about what God wants me to share and what He is saying to me about them. The ways He communicates in this area are the same examples we shared earlier in the book about hearing God's active voice such as flowing thoughts, mental images, video type scenes that God plays on the screen of your mind and inward impressions you may get. Even if you don't sense anything directly from God you can always say to anyone "Jesus loves you". I use this on a regular daily basis with almost everyone I meet or interact with. Think about this; how much different would the world be if people heard 10 to 20 times a day how much Jesus loves them and how awesome they are? You can become a part of the revolution of God's love here on the earth just by being intentional and committed to saying three words to the majority of people you meet every day "Jesus loves you".

It is also important to read or listen to the Bible as much as possible so the Word of God gets into your heart. If you don't know what God says in His Word about you and His other kids it is more challenging to know what He is saying to you and about other people. The more you step out in faith and speak out what you're hearing and sensing for other people the easier living this powerful lifestyle of love will become.

At times I still feel uncomfortable, unmotivated and even resistant to seeking and sharing God's heart with people and sometimes I still shrink back. I don't seek to see them how God sees them, I don't ask God how He sees them or for any direction concerning them and I don't even share with them that Jesus loves them for whatever reason. However, the more I go against this resistance by instead choosing to step out on my faith and take risks, the greater my faith grows and the more God's love and power can flow through me. During the times you're having trouble getting up the motivation and courage to talk to someone it helps me if I give myself a spir-itual pep talk, reminding myself that God lives in me, He speaks to me and there is no failure in His love; only learning experiences! If you lack bold-ness in any part of your life you can always pray for God to give you His boldness to be a witness and a light for Him. Many people did this throughout the New Testament and God worked boldness in them as they prayed and took steps of faith they experienced God's empowerment and you will too (Acts 4:29-31)! We all have times where we say, "I don't really feel like it", "I don't really want to" in times like those no matter what the situation, going to school or work, reading the Bible, working out, walking in love with other people, it can be a variety of things; you can pray and ask God to give you His motivation, His willingness and His want to's. As you keep thanking Him and receiving by faith what you pray for, before you know it a little bit more motivation, willingness and energy will begin to rise up within you!

The smiles you see, the seeds you know you planted, the responses you sometimes get such as "Thank you so much", "Jesus loves you too", "I can't believe you see that in me", and my favorite "I really needed to hear that today". Those types of responses and knowing that it makes God smile when we spread His love despite how we feel makes overcoming those uncomfortable and unmotivated feelings all the more worth it! The times you do shrink back or feel unmotivated instead of getting all down on yourself, forgive yourself and recognize you will still have other opportunities in the future. Also remember, that your value and identity is based on how much God loves you and what Jesus did for you, not how much or how little you do. You can also pray for people privately between God and you by faith and just pray whatever God lays on your heart for them. This usually takes just 20 to 30 seconds. At the very least you prayed for them and by faith you know your prayers over them are working things for their good in the spiritual realm. Living a prophetic lifestyle is such an impactful and powerful way to live! It transforms lives and hearts all around you; most importantly your own. God absolutely loves it when we seek His heart, His compassion and His perspective for others and choose to generously lavish His love upon them. So always keep in mind that hearing and sharing God's heart in love is what prophecy and living a prophetic lifestyle is all about!

WORDS OF KNOWLEDGE

Words of knowledge are a great way to flow in a prophetic lifestyle that cause you and others to hear God's voice and experience His activity in amazingly profound ways. A word of knowledge can be described as details, information and knowledge about someone or something that the Holy Spirit communicates to you through supernatural means. You do not gain this specific knowledge by logical means but through God imparting the information to you through His communication with you through the active voice of the Holy Spirit. Jesus demonstrated this gift of the Holy Spirit in His life and ministry. He knew information about people that God told Him and showed Him through His communication with the Holy Spirit. The Apostle Paul writing to the Church of Corinth states that ***"To one is given through the [Holy] Spirit..[the power to express] the word of knowledge and understanding according to the same Spirit;" 1 CORINTHIANS 12:8 AMP***

Notice Paul wrote this to the entire Church of Corinth saying that as followers of Jesus we can all receive words of knowledge from the Holy Spirit it is not just for a select few. Throughout the Bible you see followers of God operating in supernatural words of knowledge given by the Holy Spirit. You can see this gift in operation throughout the Gospels where Jesus knew what people were thinking in their hearts, detailed information about their past, people's names Jesus had never met before and what people needed healing for. He also knew where certain things and items would be located, such as the donkey that He told His disciples to untie and bring to Him. He even told them what to say to the owners when they asked them where they were taking it (Luke 19:30-32). All of this was God revealed knowledge which came through supernatural means of communication with His Heavenly Father's active voice. We can see an example of this in the Gospel of John where Jesus knew information about Nathanael being a man with "no deceit" in his heart, meaning he lived with a great amount of integrity. Jesus said "He saw" him sitting under a fig tree, but in reality He had ever met Nathanael. In essence Jesus was saying He heard with His spiritual ears from God about Nathanael's integrity and saw Nathanael sitting under a fig tree with His spiritual eyes. Jesus did this through hearing the active voice of God, such as the flowing thoughts and mental pictures we describe throughout this book. ***"When Jesus saw Nathanael approaching, He said of him, Here truly is an Israelite in whom there is no deceit. How do you know me? Nathanael asked. Jesus answered, I saw you while you were still under the fig tree before Philip called you. Then Nathanael declared, "Rabbi, you are the Son of God; you are the King of Israel."*** You see how simple and straightforward the information that Jesus gave was, yet Nathanael experienced words of knowledge and being known by God in such a powerful and profound way that he immediately recognized and declared that Jesus was the Son of God and the King of Israel! When I engage the Holy Spirit for words of knowledge through prayer, sometimes the things God shows me and tells me about people seem so insignificant or don't make sense to me. However, I have found out that oftentimes those things I think are unimportant or won't make much sense to them are exactly the opposite and they truly feel known and loved by God. Through these experiences I have learned to take risks, be obedient and share what I sense God is showing me and telling me. Many times what I am sensing is from God, and it is amazing to know what you're hearing from God is correct and meaningful to another person. Then there are those times I totally miss it and the people say, "No that does not really resonate with me or mean anything to me", it is the risk you take. However, there are those times you do hear God correctly and the words of knowledge do connect and witness to the person's heart you are sharing with. The person does truly feel known and touched by God to where it makes all the times you seemingly missed it totally worth it! I want to encourage you to treasure those moments and store them in your heart so you can draw on those experiences for motivation and courage in the future, knowing that you do in fact hear from God. As you connect relationally with God and you store up these God moments you are actually building history with God like you build history with a friend. Words of knowledge are such an amazingly powerful gift of the Holy Spirit because it brings people to a place where they have to wrestle with the supernatural information that God shows you and tells you about them. It is the realization that God knows everything about you, every detail of your life and He still loves you and wants an intimate relationship with you. The people receiving the words of knowledge have to come to terms with the God revealed information you know about them which you received through praying and listening to the Holy Spirit. It really is a *come to Jesus* meeting for you and for them, just like Nathanael had!

Later in the Gospel of John in chapter 4:16-42 we see Jesus demonstrating words of knowledge where Jesus knew personal information about a Samaritan woman whom He met at the local town water well. Even though it was culturally unacceptable for Jesus to even be speaking to a Samaritan person, especially a Samaritan woman, Jesus had compassion and care for her based on how His Heavenly Father saw her. If we want to effectively receive words of knowledge we have to care about and have compassion for what Jesus cares about. Jesus cares about people; no matter their age, race, social status, skin color, economic position and lifestyle choices. The truth is we all need more of Jesus and He wants to use each one of us in powerful and profound ways to touch the world around us. The words of knowledge Jesus shared were so impactful the woman believed that He was the Savior of the world. Then she went and told everyone in her town about her encounter with Jesus and the words of knowledge He shared with her. The Bible says she led many people in the area of Samaria where she lived to immediately believe in Jesus, and many more came out to meet Jesus. They urged Him to stay in their town and He stayed for two days and the scriptures tell us many more came to believe in Jesus as the Savior of the world, the Christ, the Anointed One, who the Scriptures and Prophets in the Old Testament said would one day come, suffer and die for the liberation and freedom of God's people and to restore intimate fellowship between them and God. So because of some seemingly simple words of knowledge a vast number of people in the city were saved and a region was transformed by the love and power of God. This is just one powerful demonstration of what words of knowledge can do. We as followers of Christ can also operate in words of knowledge and sharing God's heart for others through prophetic words which can be what God is saying to you right now, currently, about the person's talents, gifts, calling, destiny and purpose as well as their life experiences past, present and future.

God uses all kinds of creative ways to communicate with us. I am going to give some examples throughout this section of practical ways God can communicate with you in your own personal creative process with Him in receiving words of knowledge. As you engage your faith in prayer for words of knowledge God generally speaks through the 3 main categories of His active voice that we have covered throughout this book; visual, inner auditory and kinetic. Visually God uses our imagination, the digital screen in our minds to speak through mental images, a series of images and seeing scenes and mental video type clips that play out within our mind's eye. Seeing in the spirit is a way God communicates words of knowledge as well. In this type of communication your physical eyes are generally open, when you experience seeing faint hologram like pictures or images over the reality of what you're physically looking at. It's as if God uses your imagination to superimpose faint images over what you're physically seeing. These experiences can last for a split second flash or several seconds and even several minutes at times. God uses this to communicate images that associate with information that He is trying to convey to you about the person. For example when I am talking to people or praying for people as I look at them with my eyes open sometimes I see various faint images over their heads or on their bodies which correspond to gifts, talents, character attributes and abilities they have that God is wanting to show me. This maybe as simple as a flash of a mental projection or a mental image you experience within your imagination, no matter how quick or subtle; it is still God speaking. As you pray and ask God what these visual experiences mean you will often get a sense, an inward knowing and impressions of what God is saying to you which can be simple, profound and amazing. As I see these superimposed images over their heads I ask God what they mean. Often I will get flowing thoughts and impressions with them such as: a red cross for healing means they have some type of healing calling on their life like a nurse, doctor or counselor, a money symbol means God has some type of business favor on their lives, a golden pen means that they have a creative writing talent God is showing me, a microphone means God has given them a gift of influencing people through speaking, a computer means they have a talent when it comes to computers and technology, a crown on their head generally means God has given them a certain type of authority or favor in a particular area and a music note means God has given them the ability to sing or produce music. When you share these types of images with people it often resonates with them as something they are already interested in or pursuing, so it touches their heart that you know those things about them through what God is showing you. I will often say to people "I was praying for you

296 | HOW TO HEAR GOD

and I asked God to show me images that relate to you and I saw a faint image of a red cross over your head for healing and I felt like you were in the medical field does that make sense to you?" or you can soften it up by saying "Hey I sense you are interested in the medical field and you have a compassion on your life to see people healed, does that resonate with you or make sense to you?" or sometimes when I am unsure about what I am getting from God I will be even more soft in my approach by saying "Hey do you want to do something in the medical field?" So many times the people look at me somewhat puzzled and confirm yes they are in the medical field or have a desire to do that type of work. They will often respond, "That is so weird how did you know that?" to which I respond by telling them how Jesus communicated the information to me through the Holy Spirit. I will often ask if they need any prayer and provision for what I am seeing because so often God is showing you that to confirm and encourage something within them and He wants to partner with you in prayer for them as well.

One evening I was spending some time with a young man and I saw an exclamation mark and a golden pen above this young man's head for just a split second and I got the impression that he was a writer and did some form of creative writing. When I shared what I was seeing and sensing from God he was a bit taken back and at first said, "No that does not make sense to me, I don't like to write and I don't really like English". I sometimes get a little let down when a word of knowledge does not land but I have learned not to allow myself to get discouraged. I said, "Well I am still learning to hear from God and I wanted to share with you what I was getting through praying for you. Do you need prayer for anything in your life?" He told me some things he needed prayer for and so we prayed together. Even when we mishear God we can still be a witness to others of His loving kindness. Even what seems like a failure can actually be a learning experience for us and an opportunity to value and love someone God cares so much about. Words of knowledge are not just about giving someone correct information from God and "getting it right", it is about longing to see peoples created value as God sees them and imparting the love and life of God to other people. In this case the young man came back to me a little later and said, "Hey it just dawned on me, I write spoken words which are similar to raps, those are creative writings, I just never thought of them in that way until I was thinking about what you said God showed you!" I laughed and said, "Well God loves your writings and evidently has given you a golden pen to write them with!" We prayed together for God to give him amazing lyrics that would mark and change a generation for God! I also encouraged him to record them and make his own Youtube Channel and keep developing the gift God has placed within him. After we spoke he even sent me a couple he had written! God is so good!

In visually receiving words of knowledge for physical healing God may give us a mental picture of a body part He wants to heal. A good visualization technique I have used is imagining a picture of a human body, like you would see in a biology or science class, and asking the Holy Spirit to show you on the picture anything their body may need healing for. Another way is asking God what needs to be healed and seeing in your minds eye a picture of the word, in text form, of the body part that needs healing. For example the word "shoulder" may appear in your mind and then you may also get some flowing thoughts about them having shoulder pain. Also parts of the body can seem highlighted meaning they seem to stand out to you or you sense God keeps drawing your attention to it such as you keep looking at their shoulder or wrist sensing something is wrong with it.

Words of knowledge also come as inner auditory communication, such as impressions and flowing thoughts from the Holy Spirit. Also an inner knowing, that comes with peace and wisdom, about what you're hearing from God. There are times where these flowing thoughts can almost seem like "random thoughts" you're having. For instance you may be talking to someone and then all of a sudden you have a sense that God is saying something to you about them that lines up with His nature of love, encouragement and comfort. Instead of dismissing these as your own thoughts you can pray about them to see if you can sense a peace or a confirmation that they are from God. A lot of times I will just step out by faith and share what I am sensing with the other person. Through being sensitive to the Holy Spirit and taking risks to share what you sense God is saying to you, you'll come to a greater understanding of when these "random thoughts" are actually God's thoughts within your own mind. Are you going to be correct and accurate all the time? No, but unless you step out on faith you can never truly grow in words of knowledge and hearing God's voice. So many times as I see images, God highlights someone or I get a sense about something going on with them. I will pray, listen and receive a series of flowing thoughts, a phrase or an inward knowing that will help me to better know what God is trying reveal and communicate to me. To be transparent, so many times what I get does not make logical sense to me and there is so often this tension between faith and self-doubt working within me. When I do choose faith and I share it with the person, then we both will often get a fuller understanding of what I am hearing, seeing and sensing from God. You will find so often that it's as you step out to share with the other person what your spiritually hearing, seeing and sensing then, asking them if it resonates with them, that you will actually get a fuller picture of what God is saying. It's like you both have a piece to a puzzle but until you open your mouth and step out on faith you won't really know if the two pieces fit together.

Kinetically, words of knowledge for healing can come with physical impressions such as senses of tingling, burning, slight pain, electricity, heat or pressure within your own body in relation to the body part God is showing you He wants you to pray over for healing. For example, one day when I walked into my local bank as I approached the teller my head began to tingle and I got a slight headache, personally I do not normally get headaches. As this happened I prayed and asked God, "Lord, what are You saying to me?" While I was listening I got a flowing thought that the bank teller I was walking towards had a headache and then I saw the word "migraine" in white block letters in my mind on a black background. So I was obedient to what I was getting from God, even though it was kind of awkward to share with her. As she waited on me I said, "This may sound strange but as I was walking up here I felt like God was showing me that you suffer from headaches and I saw the word "migraine" in my mind, does that make sense to you?" She looked very puzzled and said, "Well yes I do get headaches often, that's weird how could you know that?" This is a typical response of confusion and shock to words of knowledge. I said, "Well Jesus lives inside of me and He talks to me and I believe He wants to heal you." Then I asked her if she had a headache right now and she did. I said, "Can I pray for you real quick for Jesus to heal your headache? I know you're at work, but it will only take a couple of seconds." She agreed. I said, "Jesus I thank You that You're a healer and now migraine headache I command you in Jesus name to be removed from her and never bother her again. Amen." Then I asked her, "Please check to see if it is still there or if you have any pain." As she rolled around her neck and checked her pain level she looked at me in amazement and said, "It's gone! Who are you? How did you know that? How did you do that?". I explained to her, "I am a man who loves Jesus and believes that He speaks to us today and it was Jesus who told me about the headaches and it was Jesus who healed you." I also encouraged her she could do the same thing I am doing, which is taking God at His Word, listening to the Holy Spirit and being a doer of His Word.

Words of knowledge can also come through God bringing to your remembrance past memories that bring wisdom and enlightenment to what you are praying about. When I am praying for someone God will at times bring to my remembrance a memory of something that gives me an answer to, or guidance on, what I am asking Him about. For instance when I was speaking to a lady at a dinner party as she started talking about her grown kids I "randomly" saw a scene in my mind of my friend Doug. I began to think about him and I sensed through a flowing thought and an inner knowing it was one of her children's names. I took a huge risk and I said, "Pardon me for interrupting you. This may seem a little odd but I got this thought about my friend Doug and I get the sense God is showing me it is one of your son's names, is that true?" She nodded her head yes, then looked at me very puzzled and said, "Did I tell you that?" I responded, "No, Jesus gave me that name." I then shared with her the creative process of word association God used to give me that name. She began to cry at the sense of God knowing her heart for her son. I could sense and see God's Presence wrapping around her in a big Holy Ghost hug! It ended up being her son's middle name which was Douglas not the exact name but close enough that we both knew it God was speaking. It turns out she had been very concerned about both her sons, but the one God highlighted was especially heavy on her heart, because he was going through some very challenging things in his life. We both realized God was calling us to pray for both of her sons, and the one God gave me a word of knowledge about in particular. I asked her what she felt they needed prayer for and then I allowed the Holy Spirit to lead me in my prayer for them. I said things in my prayer for them that didn't make sense at the time I was praying but I have learned to default on the side of righteousness and pray out what I sense God is leading me to say even if it is uncomfortable. After the prayer was over I asked her about some of the things I prayed over her sons that I felt were from the Holy Spirit, but at the same time I had no logical leading on why I would pray those specific things for them. She smiled and said, "Yes, I was wondering how you knew some of the things you were praying over them." I again explained to her my process of being obedient to the Holy Spirit and trying to listen as I pray and speak out what He is putting on my heart. This is praying from a place of seeking out what God wants you to release and pray out over a person or a situation. When you aspire to get your will and your prayers in alignment with what God is saying and wants to do, your prayers become powerful, effective and bring breakthroughs! I also encouraged her that she could personally hear God speak as well and that the Holy Spirit wants to speak to and have a deep relationship with every Believer in Jesus. As followers of Christ we want be a people that God can flow through. However, in addition, we also want to equip others around us to have a deeper relationship with God by sharing our creative process in hearing God's voice and how He speaks to us personally.

When I meet someone I will often pray and ask God to give me a word of knowledge for them by asking God questions such as "Jesus I know You love them, show me something about them?" or "Jesus what is their purpose in life?". Then sometimes I see a vision in my mind or a mental picture that relates to them; like seeing them work with computers, singing, working at a business, dancing or working in a hospital. Then I will say to them "Hey, this may sound a little strange but when I was praying for you I saw a vision of you in my mind working with computers does that mean anything to you?" If they say, "Yes, I actually do want to work with computers I am going to school for that right now' or "That is actually what I do for a career." Then I often say, "That is so amazing that Jesus showed me that about your life! I want you to know that Jesus really loves you." Then I let the Holy Spirit move the conversation from there. If they say, "No, that does not mean anything to me" I will often respond by saying "Well I am learning how to hear God's voice and sense when He is speaking to me. I am still in process. Thank you for answering my question. I want you to know that Jesus loves you so much." Then if I have time I might ask them if they need prayer for anything. I have seen misses turn into amazing God moments where people felt loved and cared for by God because of me praying for them but at the same time I totally missed on the words of knowledge! I may even share with them times I have heard God's voice in similar situations and how cool it was for me and the person I got the word of knowledge for. I try to always at the very least encourage them in how much Jesus loves them, as well as in their own personal relationship with Jesus.

Just stepping out by faith can having amazing effects upon people's lives and when you do get it wrong at least you tried. There are plenty of times I still miss it, but the testimonies of the ones I do hear God correctly on far outweigh the misses!

One night I was in the grocery store with my wife and as the cashier was checking us out, as I often do, I prayed for him in my mind and said under my breathe "God is there anything you want to show me about this young man, or that You want me to tell Him for You?" Then I saw a vision of him working with computers and doing some kind of design work, but I was not really sure if what I was getting was from God. So I asked him, "Excuse me, do you by any chance want to work with computers or do some kind of computer design work?" He said, "Not really." At first I chalked it up to me mishearing God and those being my thoughts, which still happens sometimes. However, I felt the Holy Spirit just kind of nudge me to ask him what he meant by "not really" so I did. He said, "Well I use to go to school for computer design but I ran out of money for college so now I am not doing that anymore." My heart went out to him because he seemed like a young man who had lost his dream. I was planning to close out our conversation with something encouraging and letting him know that he is loved by Jesus. Then I got the flowing thought, "Ask him if he has applied for financial aid". I logically was taken back by what I sensed God was saying to me. So I began to argue with myself and with God in my mind right there in the checkout line in the grocery store, not one of my finer God moments for sure! I was saying to God, "There is no way Lord that he didn't apply for financial aid! That is the first logical step for anyone when they run out of money for college." Then I see the phrase in my mind "Just ask him" faintly written in white block letters on a black background which came with a flowing thought "Just ask him and see, you have nothing to lose". So not wanting to continue my futile argument with Jesus I was obedient and I just took a risk and asked him, "I know it is not really any of my business but I sense God is putting it on my heart to ask you if you have applied for financial aid?" It was as hard as cement to get out of my mouth but I said it. He looked at me and said, "No I never applied for financial aid." I was taken back by his answer. He said it with a sense of defeat but at the exact same time his demeanor seemed to shift to one of hope.

Then an inner faith and confidence rose up in me and I began to prophesy over him that God had a plan for his life in the computer field, that God was going to provide for him to go back to school and that his dream was still alive in God's heart! I almost looked around to see who was speaking those words but I knew it was God's love rising out of my heart for him compelling me to speak boldly. So right there I prayed a short prayer of blessing over him and his financial aid package. As I was leaving he said, "Thank you so much, I needed to hear that, you know what, I am going to file for financial aid!" Two weeks later I see him at the store and my first thought is to ask him about his financial aid package but then I got a negative thought from the enemy saying "don't ask him about that, what if he got denied, what if you were wrong about what you said to him" I immediately rejected that thought and did the opposite and asked him about everything we had spoken about. He told me that he had filed for his financial aid that same week and he said confidently "I am just waiting on my approval! Wow, what a turnaround in faith! God used a word of knowledge on a late night grocery store run to change the course of a young man's life, restore the dream he thought was lost and most importantly restored his faith and belief in Jesus and how much he is loved by Him! The Word of God describes clearly what the essence of living a prophetic lifestyle and moving in words of knowledge is all about. *"For the essence of prophecy is to give a clear witness for Jesus." Revelation 19:10 NLT* This Scripture came to life in this young man's life that night on his job at the grocery store in a very personal way where God used me to give him a clear witness about the love and power of Jesus Christ! The amazing thing is God wants to do the same thing through you and every person who is willing to care enough about what God cares about, which is people coming into a deeper relationship with Him. We do this through personally living in a close fellowship, friendship and communion with God. Out of this close relationship we become like Jesus taking on His very nature, then from that place of intimacy with Jesus we pray, listen and share what we sense God is saying to us about others. We treat others as Jesus would. This is the essence of prophecy, for our lives to be a clear witness and testimony of what God has done and is doing within our very nature and character by the way we live our lives everyday even when we think no one is watching or cares. The truth and reality of the Gospel is God does care and God is always near you and watching over you, because as a Believer in Christ God's Holy Spirit lives on the inside of you.

To be clear and candid with you, there are plenty of times I don't hear, see or sense anything supernaturally from God for the people I meet and people that I pray for. The Bible says you get words of knowledge as the Holy Spirit wills and gives to you. Even though it is as the Holy Spirit wills, we still need to be intentional about praying and seeking the Holy Spirit for words of knowledge and be expectant to hear and receive from Him. At the very least we can always manifest the Heavenly Father's Love by being encouraging, caring and generous towards others. I have come to realize that sometimes God just wants us to talk to people, listen to them, relate to them and enjoy their presence. Don't get into performance based faith, thinking you have to get a word of knowledge from God every time you meet someone or pray for a person and if you don't, "there is something wrong with you", "God does not love you" or "you're not being a good Christian". Remember your value and identity is always based off of what Jesus did for you. Who God says you are as His son or daughter and your personal relationship with God is the most important aspect of your life. That does not mean God does not want you to pray and seek words of knowledge from Him, because His Word says God does want you to continually seek after His heart for other people and the supernatural gifts of the Holy Spirit. So be empowered to be the love, power and voice of Jesus to others around you!

Another thing you can practice is that before you go into a store or before you go out for the day ask the Lord, "God is there someone You want to speak to or touch today?", then listen. Sometimes I will see a person in a certain color shirt, the face of someone in my family or on my job that God wants me to reach out to or pray for, or I may see a place God wants me to go that day and look for someone who He highlights. I may get a series of flowing thoughts from Him that give me some insight or guidance. It could be as simple as; "call your wife today and tell her how much you love her", "reach out to your parents they need to hear from you" or "just be My love to others". On other occasions all I get is a sense of peace and an inward knowing that God is going to direct my path and that I am to be watchful for His activity and guidance. What are you doing? You are putting yourself in position to hear from God about what is on His heart and who He wants to touch today.

Over the time of seeking God out for words of knowledge for others I have had countless mind blowing and amazing experiences in hearing God's voice. God is calling you to have the same kind of encounters and more! I have seen people's favorite cartoons as a child, favorite toys as a kid, the date of their birthday, parts of their bodies that needed healing, their first childhood pet, what they did or wanted to do for a career or job, information about their children and detailed knowledge about their lives that only they and God could know. God showed me these things not because I am some super spiritual set-apart person. The reality is I am just like you. I am a beloved child of God that wants to hear His voice. What I have experienced is only scratching the surface of what God wants to do in you and through you! As I have these encounters with others I often will explain my creative process of hearing God with them, by telling them what I spiritually hear, see and sense by engaging God in prayer by asking Him questions about them and then listening. I also enjoy asking them how they hear from God. I have learned so much by listening to other people about how God communicates with them. This activates and equips the people we encounter to hear God for themselves. A lot of the people I talk to begin to hear God for themselves as soon as they know what His active voice sounds like, how to listen and begin to engage the Holy Spirit by faith in prayer.

So many times as I am explaining to them about God's active voice many people realize that they have heard God's voice before, they just dismissed it as their own conscious talking. Some people share with me how they just realized while we were talking some ways God spoke to them in the past which they just chalked up as something weird, coincidence or luck. Through this awareness of God's activity their daily relationship with God is deepened and they begin to hear His voice. Because they have experienced words of knowledge personally and have been encouraged by you, their faith grows in that area and they are empowered to begin to seek God for words of knowledge and prophetic words for others around them. As you step out on faith in words of knowledge and share your creative process with others you are actually inviting people to encounter Jesus for themselves. You are also modeling for them how to connect with God's heart personally and for other people. They in-turn become part of the cycle of activating and equipping other people around them to hear from God. We can all live a lifestyle of actively equipping people to hear from God themselves which deepens their relationship with Him. This happens through the overflow of their relationship with God and encouraging them to share with other people what they sense God is saying. This is the supernaturally normal Christian lifestyle Jesus modeled and empowered us to live! The

Father's heart burns with love to tell you and show you comforting, uplifting and encouraging information about other people. Knowledge that you don't get by natural or logical means, but by information supernaturally communicated to you by God, filtered through His love and how He sees them. It is important to understand that you do not control the words of knowledge that you get; they are as the Holy Spirit wills. ***"All these things [the gifts, the achievements, the abilities, the empowering] are brought about by One and the same [Holy] Spirit, distributing to each one individually just as He chooses." 1 CORINTHIANS 12:11 AMP*** Even though we don't control the words of knowledge we receive from God we still all pray and engage the Holy Spirit for words of knowledge for other people through praying for them and asking God questions about them. We are essentially partnering with God by engaging Him through prayer to find out what He wants to show us about someone or something.

WORDS OF KNOWLEDGE PRACTICAL APPLICATION AND EXERCISES

Here are a few examples of open-ended questions that you can use to engage the Holy Spirit in prayer for words of knowledge. Ask God: "Father, is there anything about this person that You want to reveal to me?", "Jesus what is the gold and treasure that You see in them?", "Lord I know You love this person, what are You saying about them?", "Jesus reveal to me, what do You love about them?", "Holy Spirit is there anything You want to heal in their bodies or in their lives?" "Holy Spirit what images relate to their lives that You want to show me?" then, as you know by now, when we ask God a question we listen and wait expectantly for Him to respond to us. Depending on the time, circumstances and situation you may want to ask God one or several of these questions. Then you can share what you spiritually hear, see and sense God is saying to you about them.

I have found it helps if you write down the questions you are asking God on a piece of paper or in the notes section on your phone. Of course this depends on the time you have, along with the circumstances and situation your in; just be Holy Spirit led on what to do and how to do it. In other words follow what God is putting on your heart to do and how He wants you to partner with Him in each specific situation. Then ask God the questions and write down what you hear, see and sense God is saying to you. This will help your concentration and focus in hearing God's active voice. I have found I am much more accurate and I get a fuller download of revelation from God, especially in words of knowledge and prophetic words, for other people when I am intentional about writing down my questions, listening, and then journaling what I sense God is communicating to me.

During this time of prayer you want to focus in on how much God loves them and acknowledging He knows everything about them already. Take the time to focus on the person and surround them with God's love and compassion as you seek to hear God's heart for them. An example prayer is, "God You know everything about this person, Jesus, You love them so much. You have a burning compassion in Your heart for them, please talk to me about Your child." When you are going after words of knowledge for someone where you have the time to devote to hearing God's heart about them, I generally write down four categories of questions. Then I go after God's heart in regard to those questions. I also use a variation of the questions I have shared throughout this section on words of knowledge.

The four categories are purpose, gifts, gold and images. The questions which go with this section are very simple in nature and open ended in order to give God room to share with you how He sees them, what He loves about them as well as what God wants you to share with them specifically.

1. Purpose: God what purposes do they have in their life?
2. Gifts: God what gifts do they have?
3. Gold: God what gold do You see in them, what do You love about them that You want to share with me?
4. Images: God what images do You want to show me that relate to their life?

After you ask each question listen and journal what you spiritually hear, see and sense God is saying. If you happen to get stuck and don't sense God saying anything focus back in on how much God loves them. The truth is that God knows everything about them. Visualize God's love surrounding them and you. Then maybe go to another question. I often-times kind of bounce around following the flow of God's voice. Even if it does not make sense just write it down and share it with them. Because as I have shared in this section sometimes those can be the most profound words of knowledge. Those can also be times that you totally miss it, but you will never know unless you take a risk and share with them. I have had the most success and detailed words of knowledge when I use this focused prayer and journal method. I invite you to try it out and practice this method and then like everything else in this book I pray you take it, adjust it, then come up with your own creative process of hearing God's voice and sharing His love with others! As you make this a lifestyle you in essence live out what the Bible says which is to: **"Apply your heart to instruction and your ears to words of knowledge." Proverbs 23:12 NIV**

A fun exercise you can do is practice getting words of knowledge for your friends or even their friends that you don't know that well. Ask God these questions above or make up your own. Then write down what you sense God is saying and share it with the person you're practicing with to check your spiritual hearing, seeing and sensing. I learned the most by practicing, doing, experiencing and taking risks. When I began to operate in words of knowledge I started out practicing on and with my family, friends, coworkers, clients, my waiter or waitress at restaurants, my Church family and people I met in my daily life. You can also practice words of knowledge and hearing specific information from God by asking God to give you a page number in your Bible to read or listen to for the day or a specific page number in your daily devotional that God wants to speak to you through. My wife likes to practice hearing God's voice like this and it's amazing how blessed she has been by this relational process of hearing God in specific ways. Often the page God leads her to speaks directly to her circumstances or what's been going on in her life and heart. There are also those times where she goes to a page that's blank or not in her Bible at all and she senses she didn't hear God correctly and through that process she will tell you it has helped her to know what is the Holy Spirit's voice and what is the voice of her own soul and conscious. Remember this is a growth and learning process with plenty of grace and again it's not about getting the "right information" it's about turning your heart to hear from God, coming to know Him and growing closer to Him everyday.

I also want to suggest and encourage you to journal your successes and your misses. Journal how it felt to receive a correct word of knowledge. How did God communicate the information to you? What did you hear, how did you hear it, how did it feel when you heard it, what did you see, how did the images come to you, did you sense anything, did you have an inward knowing, what kind of sense came with what you experienced? Did you get goose bumps or have a feeling of peace? Did you have any negative thoughts and how did you overcome them? These are all questions you can use in journaling about how you're hearing from God. Also ask those same question when you get the word of knowledge incorrect and some differences you noticed from the times you heard God correctly. This practice of journaling will help you to recognize and cultivate your own personal creative processes with God. As you journal, your awareness of certain aspects of your creative process will grow and open up for you, becoming more clear and defined. I have learned a lot about how God personally communicates with me by journaling my experiences. As I described what I heard, saw and sensed I began to notice things about my interaction with God which I did not notice at the time I was praying or sharing with the person. Journaling will make you more aware of how you personally hear from God which will help you develop and grow in your spiritual senses and discernment.

To be candid with you there are still times I hear, see and sense things from the Holy Spirit even when I write them down and I feel as if I am hearing God clearly where I still have to come out of fear, doubt and nervousness before I can step out on faith and share with others what I sense God is saying to me about them. It is normal to have these kinds of thoughts, feelings and emotions, as well as the enemy trying to put doubts and fears into your mind. By now hopefully you understand what the enemy's voice sounds like and you know how to take those negative thoughts captive and step out against those types of things into faith! It is important to understand opposition is going to come when you're doing anything for the Kingdom of God. Especially anything with real supernatural power that people can experience which will radically change their lives by revealing their true value and identity in Christ. Power that demonstrates God's tangible love and through the gifts of the Holy Spirit, helps them develop a deeper relationship with God, thus becoming more like Jesus! So when you experience things like this, and the tension between faith and doubt we spoke about earlier, recognize you are not alone in this and make the choice to step out in the faith, love and power of Jesus! I want to encourage you not to take yourself too seriously, just have fun partnering with God in the process of learning how to hear His voice, getting words of knowledge and living a prophetic lifestyle do it with a childlike faith before your Heavenly Father, He loves it!

When I am seeking God for words of knowledge for someone and I don't sense anything I usually will ask God a different question about them. Sometimes it is as simple as getting the idea and impression "Tell them I love them deeply and I see them". Then I will in turn say to them, "Jesus told me to tell you He loves you very deeply and He sees you" or "I sense Jesus is putting on my heart to tell you, He loves you very deeply and He sees you". I have had occasions where those simple words seemed to rock the person's heart to the core, times they just smiled and thanked me, other times people have rolled their eyes at me or made some condescending comment to me about God not loving them and even God not being real at all. In all occasions regardless of their response you want to love them where they are, give them what you sense God is leading you to share with them and you don't allow yourself to get offended by their response no matter what it might be.

There are times when I pray for people and God seems to give me an information download from Heaven about them and in those times you have to be willing to take risks and step out and share what you hear, see and sense God is saying to you even if you don't understand logically what you are getting from God. Sometimes the process of getting words of knowledge feels more like a guessing game than it does a spiritual communication between you and God. To be honest there are times I still feel like I am playing a guessing game instead of hearing God's voice for words of knowledge but now I have so many amazing God experiences that I treasure in my heart to back up what Jesus modeled for us to walk in through the Holy Spirit. As you step out on faith in words of knowledge you will begin to know by experience and get a better gauge of sensing when God is speaking to you and what your own thoughts feel like and sound like. It is one of those things that you could read about for years but until you step out and begin to experience it firsthand for yourself, you just won't truly know what I am talking about. If you have been reading this book and engaging the Holy Spirit in prayer through the exercises and model prayers we have given you then most likely you are already hearing God's active voice and have become more aware of how He speaks through all kinds of ways in and around you. So congratulations you are already empowered to engage the Holy Spirit for words of knowledge!

I want to share a short God story with you about how even when what you share seems to not resonate with the person God can use it for His glory. One evening I was talking to this young man who had recently gone from being an atheist to a Believer in Jesus Christ and as he walked away to get something I began to pray for him. I was praying for him and asking God, "Lord, what gold do You see in him, what do You love about him Jesus?" In my mind I see him on a stage with a guitar leading youth worship in a Church. Then when I opened my eyes I saw what looked like a music note over his head like a faded hologram. I sensed God was confirming what I had seen. I shared with him what I saw and I said, "Does that make sense to you?" He said, "No, Sterling sorry but I don't even play the guitar." I said, "It's ok maybe I heard God wrong let me pray again." I did and I got the same thing. I shared what I sensed God was telling me again and I said to him, "Maybe I am not hearing God correctly on this, I am still learning how to hear God and it is never an exact science. It may also be a talent you don't know that you have but God knows about and wants to develop in you." We both smiled, shrugged our shoulders and left there wondering if what I had seen had any validity to it as far as it being from God. To be transparent I have misheard God plenty of times when trying to get words of knowledge and I have found when that happens I am usually assuming and thinking something based on what I see with my physical eyes and making judgments based on what I see, hear and sense with my natural senses instead of my spiritual ears, eyes and heart. Through experiential knowledge of stepping out and acting on words of knowledge I have come to a fuller understanding of when I am hearing God and when I am getting ahead of God and acting on my own natural senses and thoughts. The more you step out in faith, the more discernment you will have between your natural senses and your spiritual senses, but remember it's not an exact science and everyone misses it at times, it's about relationship with God not perfection or performance. Based off the conversation I had with this young man which, could have been looked at as me totally mishearing God, two months later he decided to pick up a guitar and try it out for the first time. He realized that he really liked it. Afterwards, he got one of his own and realized he had a natural ability to play the guitar! He learned how to play at a rapid rate and he could even play things by ear just by hearing music. He was a natural at it! I saw him later and even got to hear him play the guitar. We both talked about the prophetic word God had given me about him leading worship and a word of knowledge that he possessed within him an anointing and an ability from God to play the guitar. So even when what you're hearing, seeing and sensing does not resonate with the person or make sense to you, just be faithful to share it with the person and you never know how it will end up working out. I have given words of knowledge that I thought were going to be so powerful and they ended up landing flat, as a total miss. On the other spectrum I have gotten words of knowledge where I thought for sure I misheard God because logically to me what I was getting had no significance, but they ended up being accurate and amazingly powerful to the person receiving them. The key is to take the risk, step out on faith in what your hearing, seeing and sensing from God. As well as knowing that the spiritual gifts God demonstrates through you, will always flow the most effectively from hearing His voice within your daily personal love relationship with Him.

LOVING OTHERS TO TRANSFORMATION: LOVE NEVER GIVES UP, LOVE ALWAYS WINS

I want to share a God story with you of a wonderful yet challenging time in my life where I was newly out of federal prison and trying to rebuild my life, which from a lot of worldly aspects had been destroyed. I made the daily decision for over two years to live a prophetic lifestyle and love people into transformation, even when I felt disqualified, unmotivated and stressed at times. Testimonies and God stories are like big beautiful windows, that you can see spiritual concepts of faith and God's truth modeled through. Please allow this God story to be empowering and encouraging that you too can live a prophetic lifestyle of hearing God's heart and loving the people closest to you into transformation, if you will choose God's love, power and grace even when it is inconvenient and downright difficult to do! I worked for a season at an in-treatment drug rehab facility for young people ages 12-25 where the average age of the people we worked with was about 16 years old. We encountered all types of issues ranging from verbal abuse, physical abuse, sexual abuse, to lack of nurture, absentee parents, to kids who have been bullied and bullied others. You can imagine we see all kinds of bondage, hurts, habits, hang ups and strongholds there. However, even while working with people that had massive challenges I held onto God's truth that; valuing people and displaying the love of Jesus is a powerful and supernatural life changing force! By faith I would call out the seeds of greatness in these young people even when no one else saw it, including themselves. I would ask God: "Lord show me the gold and treasure in them." "Show me how You see them." "Let me see them with Your eyes God." I was intentional about listening to them, I talked with them and treated them based on who the Bible says they are in Christ and how much the Father loves them. Most importantly I backed these words up with my actions, especially when it was challenging to do so, because of their negative behavior. You can tell a lot about what is truly in your heart during challenges, adversity and times of stress, that's when it's most important to be intentional about walking in the love and power of Jesus. Even during times of great stress I walked in a persistent mindset and attitude of God's love and compassion, I always referred to them as "my blessings" not based on their behavior or my feelings, but on the Word of God that says in *Psalms 127:3 Children are a gift from the LORD; they are a real blessing. GNT*

I treated them as treasured possessions and righteous heirs of the Heavenly Father even when they were not acting like it. How could I do that under great stress and adversity? It was not because I am some super Christian, it was not the power of positive thinking or being in denial about their negative behavior. It was because before I went to work I spent intimate time with God in His presence and in His Word and I stayed in constant contact and communication with Him throughout the day. I continually experienced God's unconditional love, grace, joy, presence and mercy being deposited into my heart on a daily basis through knowing Him intimately. Knowing and experiencing companionship with God allows you to extend to other people what you have freely received from God in a real, personal and powerful way. A powerful and practical thing you can do is to look up a couple of scriptures that speak to what you want to pray over a particular person or over a situation. For instance if it's for your children find a couple of scriptures that pertain to them and that speak to your heart about what you want for them in their lives. The same can be done for your spouse, your boss and any life situation your facing as well as fear, worry or whatever it may be. I usually Google the topic I want Bible Scriptures for and go with what I feel speaks to my heart. Then begin to mediate on the Word of God concerning those things and speak them over your life, your situation and the lives of others!

Through using practical spiritual tools like this and by working the exercises on repentance, forgiveness and taking thoughts captive shared earlier in this book on a daily basis, I was able to walk in a constant and perpetual state of forgiveness for them. Because as you can probably imagine, loving on and working with a group comprised of 12 to 15 teenagers for 6 to 8 hours at a time that are coming off of covering up their heart hurts with years of abusing drugs and alcohol can be very challenging and stressful. However, I kept my focus on who they are in Christ and I knew from reading the Bible that is what Jesus did. When Jesus walked on the Earth He treated His disciples and other people He encountered as though they were forgiven, redeemed and righteous even when they were not acting like it. He valued them when no one else did and He looked beyond the dirt in their lives, dug through it, by seeing and calling out the gold within them, when others including themselves, did not see it, nor believe it. Thus Jesus demonstrated the Father's love in such a way it compelled people to change and turn from their prior sinful ways and follow Him. Jesus also spoke the truth in love which is an important part of transformation. We are called to be grounded in the truth of God's Word and to speak, deliver and share it in love. ***"Instead, we will speak the truth in love, growing in every way more and more like Christ." Ephesians 4:15 NLT*** This is a very simple concept but when you get upset or frustrated it is easy to let your feelings and emotions be your guide instead of God's Love, Word and Spirit. I often have to forgive myself, God and others and make sure I keep God in the middle of everything I think, say and do. If you put yourself in the center you can be easily offended and irritated by people, which will cause you to come from a place of frustration and not God's love. Having a God centered mindset says "I woke up today for Jesus, I live my life for Him, not for myself, not for my family, not for other people. I love myself and I love them all but I live my life because of Jesus and for Jesus and His Kingdom. No one owes me anything but I owe Jesus my everything." This type of mindset and attitude will keep you out of the center and when you do get irritated, frustrated, worried, offended or any other negative feeling, you immediately can locate yourself most often in the center, making your life about you or about others and not about Jesus. Make the decision to not take things so personal because you don't know what other people have going on behind the scenes of their lives. So often what you are experiencing with them is caused by something deeper, beneath the surface of their lives which is influencing the actions and behaviors you are seeing and experiencing. Instead, ask God for His perspective on them. Ask Him to give you His compassion for them and ask yourself what could they be going through currently or have been through in their past to cause them to act like this? The amazing thing is keeping your life God centered actually empowers you to live in freedom as a more authentic you, not being controlled by fear, worry, people pleasing, unforgiveness, irritation, pride and self-esteem issues!

Were there times I fell short of walking in God's love and forgiveness? Of course I did, that's part of being human, we are all going to miss it sometimes. And depending on the situation I would ask God and them for forgiveness and also forgive myself for getting irritated, frustrated and defensive. I would take accountability and let them know that what I said and did was not Jesus it was me acting out of my hurt, pain and frustration, that Jesus loves you no matter what and He wants a healthy intimate relationship with you! They would see the joy, patience and peace I had on my life and ask me, "Sterling how do you stay so patient and loving all the time with us even when we are being so bad?" First, I always reminded them when they called themselves "bad" of this truth, there are no bad people, only bad choices and actions. People are hurting, thirsty and hungry for God and don't know it or don't want to accept it. They may have made bad choices and done bad things but bad is not their identity, bad is not who they really are. Then I would encourage them with Bible truths about who they are in Christ and how a relationship with Jesus can transform anyone's life who is willing to choose Him. I would often explain to them this is Jesus living inside of me that you're experiencing and it is an intentional decision being Christlike on a daily basis. I share with them that being like Jesus comes from having a loving relationship with God, not a religious duty, not just going to Church, but having a spiritual relationship where you come to know God through experiential knowledge and through the Holy Spirit breathing on God's Word for you causing the Bible to have great power in your life! I was also very transparent with them that I, like anyone else, have challenging days, struggles and shortcomings. I am still in the glorious process of becoming like Jesus and I would encourage them to stay moldable in God's hands! They would make statements such as, "You treat us different than other Christians I have met." "I did not know Christians could be like you." "No one ever explained Christianity was having a real spiritual relationship with God I just thought it was about following rules, being good and going to Church." I heard those types of statements over and over again. Those statements have saddened my heart time and time again. I meet people all the time that have been hurt and condemned by Christianity and Christians instead of loved, cared for and valued by us as a people group.

So many people experience Christianity as a *works based religion* with their success determined by their behavior, Church attendance and just knowing about God. As well as condemnation and self-righteousness based on your own works, this is not Jesus and this is not true Christianity. That is man-made religion and there is no eternal life and intimate relationship with God abiding in *religion*. That does not mean I didn't give them the truth of the Bible about having a radical life transformation. I spoke about and modeled for them what it looks like living a life of righteousness, purity and holiness in Christ. They asked me a lot of hard questions about what God's Word says about sin, why having a relationship with Jesus is different than other religions and why such bad things have happened to them and their families. I spoke the truth of the Bible to them in God's love. It is important to always speak truth in love when you are speaking to people about their lives allowing the love and wisdom of God to be your filter. Through speaking and believing God's truth in love the Lord blessed me to model a prophetic lifestyle for the young people I worked with. I experienced people being healed by the supernatural power of God spiritually, emotionally and physically. God enabled me to prophesy over many of the young people that I had the honor of working with. God would regularly give me words of knowledge where He would show me details about their lives, desires of their hearts and purposes for their future that only He could know. I saw His radical love rock and transform the lives of so many young people during that season of my life, along with my own life being continually touched and marked by His presence and voice.

As I loved people and demonstrated the love and power of Jesus through my actions, reactions, prayer, godly wisdom, letting the Word of God and His Holy Spirit be my guide I saw their lives change and their walls come down. Then the freedom, peace and healing came! I pointed them toward an intimate love relationship with Jesus that is healthy, real, personal and powerful! Knowing it is being in a loving and devoted relationship with Jesus that actually compels and motivates us to be changed and transformed by His Holy Spirit (2 Corinthians 5:14)! I lived out and modeled what that looks like even when it was not easy, when they were acting out, when they were being hard to love, when I was having a rough day, when personal issues were trying to weigh me down I kept focusing on God's love and seeking His presence. I continually was praying and listening for His direction, guidance and praising and worshiping Him even when I didn't feel like it. I also stayed in God's Word and spoke it over them and myself. I made a commitment that no matter what, I am going to show forth to others the love, grace and power of Jesus! As you do that, especially when adversity and challenges come, because they will, when you continue to seek God anyway, you will see your life and heart change and the lives and hearts around you be rocked and transformed by God's love and light flowing out of you! This kind of mindset and heart position is not about perfection or trying not to make mistakes or performance. It's about persistently seeking God on a daily basis and when you miss it: humble yourself, take accountability, repent, apologize and forgive yourself, God and others. Then keep on seeking God with your whole heart! *"But first and most importantly seek (aim at, strive after) His kingdom and His righteousness [His way of doing and being right--the attitude and character of God], and all these things will be given to you also." Matthew 6:33 AMP*

Have the people I loved well and done my very best to encourage them in their faith in God still stumbled, sinned, fallen short, backslid and even fallen away from God? Yes, of course I have experienced that. It is a fact of life that those types of things will happen in the lives of the people that we love, no matter how well we love them and demonstrate Jesus to them. They are still in the process of becoming more like Jesus and everyone is in a different place in their own process of becoming Christlike. Will the people we choose to show God's love to still make mistakes? Sure they will, that is part of being human. Your responsibility is to not get discouraged and to manifest God's love to them in how you treat them and care for them, no matter what happens, all based on what God's Word says about their value, identity and future. The individual person still has daily freewill choices to make. They have the opportunity to choose to follow God in a daily relationship or not. They have the choice to renew their minds with the Word of God or to allow the world system and life to speak louder than the truth of God's Word. The aim and goal for our lives is that OUR RETALIATION and DEFENSE in every situation IS TO BE the LOVE of JESUS. No matter what it looks like in the natural, the Bible promises that God still loves them and He is still at work on them. It's our job to be the love of Jesus to them in the way we live our lives and in the way we treat them and encourage them in their relationship with Jesus, which is the most powerful change agent in existence!

Hebrews 12:2 says *"that for the joy set before Him Jesus endured the cross,"* we as Believers in Jesus are that joy! The joy that motivated Jesus to endure the cross was you being made His righteousness! Jesus longed to see us redeemed, set free from sin and connected to God in a loving spiritual relationship once again! Make it your goal to always keep your love and joy switched on like Jesus did. Sometimes your feelings and emotions are not switched on to God's love and joy where they need to be, that is part of life sometimes but make the decision to not allow your feelings and emotions to be your authority and guide. Try to keep your love on and open to God's heart for the people around you. The Bible says, *"God, Who through Jesus Christ reconciled us to Himself [received us into favor, brought us into harmony with Himself] and gave to us the Ministry of Reconciliation [that by word and*

deed we might aim to bring others into harmony with Him]."
2 Corinthians 5:18 AMPC

We are all in the full time "Ministry of Reconciliation" we are to try our best to keep a heart culture of valuing people as God values them, wanting to see their restoration to God's original intent for their lives, for them to live in the divine favor of God. Ministry is simply transferring the life force found in Jesus to others, His love, power and grace. We are all called to help and restore people to divine favor and harmony with God through the way we live and conduct our lives. To help people to know what it feels like to be loved by God and treat people like they are sons and daughters of God. Working and serving God is simply knowing Him intimately and making Him known throughout the world by the way you love and live your life through the supernatural empowerment of the Holy Spirit. I want to challenge you to love people and treat people so well that they want the JESUS You Have! That kind of love is not by feeling or emotion but by determined daily decisions of trusting and relying on God! *"For we are God's masterpiece. He has created us anew in Christ Jesus, so we can do the good things He planned for us long ago." Ephesians 2:10 NLT* If I can experience the transformative power of God's love working in the lives of young people who were facing very challenging situations, then you too can do the same within your own household, family, job, school and community!

I have experienced the love and power of Jesus lived out loud change, transform and cause breakthrough in every situation where the people made a commitment and decision to live in an intimate love relationship with Jesus that is rooted in the Father's love and your identity as a son or daughter of God and empowered by the Holy Spirit! The love and power of Jesus is to be demonstrated. Faith thinks, faith speaks and faith acts! Now go out and be the love and power of Jesus that you and this world so desperately need! The choice and the power are yours! Always remember Jesus *loves* you, the Father *knows* you and the Holy Spirit is *in* you! Now go out and *become* the *love* and *power* of God!

AS YOUR JOURNEY CONTINUES

We want to thank you for taking the time to spiritually engage and interact with this book that God has put so heavily on our hearts to share with you. Our prayer is that you utilize this book and that it will continually help you to cultivate and grow your intimate love relationship with God! We do not want this to be a book that you just read, but a book that you put it into action within your daily life. Allow the Holy Spirit to work through this book in order to bring about transformation within your spirit, soul and body!

We love you. We are so proud of you for taking this journey with us. We want to encourage you to make this a book that you go back through several times. Our prayer is that you are transformed and conformed into the image of Jesus and that your mind is totally renewed by the goodness, presence and power of God! We want to conclude this book with blessing you and your family right out of God's Word. Please read it aloud and declare it over yourself and loved ones!

THE PRIESTLY BLESSING

"And the Lord said to Moses, Say to Aaron and his sons, This is the way you shall bless the Israelites. Say to them,

The Lord bless you and watch, guard, and keep you;

The Lord make His face to shine upon and enlighten you and be gracious (kind, merciful, and giving favor) to you;

The Lord lift up His [approving] countenance upon you and give you peace (tranquility of heart and life continually).

And they shall put My name upon the Israelites, and I will bless them." Numbers 6:22-27 (AMPC)

Always Remember: THE FATHER LOVES YOU, JESUS DIED FOR YOU, AND THE HOLY SPIRIT LIVES IN YOU!

SPREADING GOD'S LOVE AND PARTNERSHIP

If this book has been a blessing to you we invite you to spread God's love by recommending it to your family, friends, Church, coworkers and loved ones. When God called me to write this book He said, ***"I want My people to hear My voice I want you to give this book away freely so that My people may know Me better."*** Keeping to the spirit of what God said to me, we have offered this book free of charge on various platforms. So if you or someone you know needs additional copies of this book please email us and we will send you the book at no charge to you. Our heart is to get this book into the hands, and more importantly into the hearts, of as many people as possible.

We also would like to encourage you to prayerfully consider partnering with us financially, so we can spread these books and the Gospel message of an intimate relationship with God all over the world! The truth that God is alive, He speaks, everyone can hear His voice and experience His presence! Just talk to God about what He might potentially like you to give into our ministry either for a monthly contribution or a one-time gift. Whatever God puts on your heart to give would be a blessing to us even if it's just $5 a month. No matter if God moves you to give into our ministry or not, we pray that this book and our ministry resources have been and will be a blessing to you and your family for years to come!

GIVING

Your generosity enables Sterling Harris as well as the Sterling Harris Ministries Team to effectively minister the Gospel worldwide. Every available resource that God provides for this ministry is through the generosity of our Partners and Friends. Together, we are able to minister the good news of the Gospel to the world. Your donations will be used to teach and equip people with the message of salvation, faith, healing, freedom, intimacy, prosperity, and a vibrant relationship with God worldwide.

STERLINGHARRIS.ORG/DONATIONS

CHECKS CAN BE MAILED TO:

Sterling Harris Ministries
PO BOX 28
Jarrell, Texas 76537

You can send donations via PayPal using our scan code below by simply opening up the camera on your smartphone like you are going to take a picture of the barcode and your phone will prompt you to open up PayPal and take you right to our Ministries PayPal Page.

Thank you for playing a vital role in this ministry of sharing Jesus with the world!

"Give, and it will be given to you. Good measure, pressed down, shaken together, running over, will be put into your lap. For with the measure you deal out [with the measure you use when you confer benefits on others, it will be measured back to you." Luke 6:38

AUTHOR BIO

Through the Word of God, Sterling's mission in life is to inspire people to reach higher; by starting and developing an intimate love relationship with Jesus Christ that is real, personal and powerful, led by the Holy Spirit. That powerful relationship will enable anyone who abides in the Word and lives in close communication with the Father to overcome any of life's circumstances and all adversity. His passion is helping fellow human beings experience God's love, power and presence.

Sterling's goal is to illustrate how through a love relationship with Jesus Christ and by putting the Word of God first place in our lives, we can all empower each other to achieve true success and prosperity. God promises in His Word that a prosperous life in Him will be whole, healed, free, and victorious! Sterling wants to inspire other people to reach their true potential and God's Best by teaching them how to operate their Faith at Christ Kingdom Levels. Thus, causing them to live out their intended purpose and calling; which is to model and demonstrate God's love and power to the whole world.

Sterling Harris was born in Dallas, TX and grew up in Terrell, TX. Sterling was a high school football standout with an array of awards including Super-Prep All-American, All-State, All-Area, and All-District, as well as a top four finalist for Class 4A Player of the Year in the State of Texas. He also excelled in the classroom as an honor roll student, and he graduated in the top 10% of his class from Terrell High School. Sterling was voted "Best All Around Boy" his senior year. During this time, he also owned and operated his own company specializing in acreage mowing and commercial cleanup.

During his years at SMU, Sterling worked for a variety of companies that include Morgan Stanley Dean Witter, State Farm Insurance, Sewell Motor Companies, and ORIX Real Estate Capital Markets where he refined his business skills. Sterling holds a Business Management degree from the Cox School of Business at Southern Methodist University. While attending SMU, he was a four-year football letterman at the right tackle position. After graduation, he signed an NFL contract with the Cleveland Browns. Sterling suffered a broken foot during his rookie season. After battling back from the injury, the Browns sent him to NFL Europe where he played and started at the offensive tackle position for the Frankfurt Galaxy. Sterling was forced into early retirement by a recurring foot injury he suffered in NFL Europe after his second year in the NFL.

Through this difficulty and other challenges Sterling learned how to overcome adversity by seeking God's Word, presence, Spirit and will for his life, even in the midst of great hardships. As he sought the Lord, he realized it is how you respond in faith to challenges that determine your true success in life. Through surrendering to God's will and eventually God's calling on his life into the Ministry, he has stayed God-motivated, and he has been able to live as an overcomer. Sterling has always had a giving spirit, and his spirit really bloomed as the Father began to teach him how to have a spiritual love relationship with Jesus Christ empowered by the Holy Spirit. Experiencing the heavenly Father's love has transformed Sterling into the free and giving man of God living in a love relationship with Jesus Christ and being led by the Holy Spirit, that he is today.

Sterling also spreads the Love of Christ through motivational speaking with his adopted brother Devonric Johnson.

Sterling is happily married to his wife Leah and they have a beautiful daughter named Gracie with more to follow if the Lord says the same. They also have two lovable dogs.

God Bless YOU! And remember this always, Jesus loves YOU!

#SpreadGodsLove

SOCIAL LINKS:

- facebook.com/sterlingharris.org
- twitter.com/shministries75
- instagram.com/sterlingharrisministries
- youtube.com/sterlingharrisministries

Made in the USA
Middletown, DE
13 September 2020